LEE STRASBERG:

THE IMPERFECT GENIUS OF THE ACTORS STUDIO

Also by Cindy Adams

SUKARNO: An Autobiography

MY FRIEND THE DICTATOR

JOLIE GABOR: An Autobiography

LEE STRASBERG:

THE IMPERFECT GENIUS
OF THE ACTORS STUDIO

Cindy Adams

1980
DOUBLEDAY & COMPANY, INC., GARDEN CITY, NEW YORK

ISBN: 0-385-12496-1
Library of Congress Catalog Card Number 79-7191

LEE STRASBERG:

THE IMPERFECT GENIUS
OF THE ACTORS STUDIO

OPENING

He's called rabbi by some, pope by others. Guru, God, or genius, fake, charlatan, or the Ultimate Shrink, Lee Strasberg has produced five generations of actors. The Method according to Strasberg developed John Garfield in the thirties, Marlon Brando in the forties, Steve McQueen in the fifties, Dustin Hoffman in the sixties, Robert De Niro in the seventies.

In public Al Pacino honored him. When he won the British Best Acting Award he gave it to Lee Strasberg. In death Marilyn Monroe honored him. When she died she willed all her personal effects to Lee Strasberg. In general Karl Malden knocks him. "He allows no room for imagination. His stuff ties you up. Lee Strasberg is constipating."

Academy Award winner Jane Fonda took basic training in Lee's private classes as well as in his Temple, the Actors Studio. She says of the famous acting teacher, "Without him I would be a quivering piece of amoeba." Academy Award winner Ellen Burstyn's *Alice Doesn't Live Here Anymore* featured seven members of the Actors Studio. Ellen says, "Everything I have today I owe Lee Strasberg. I wish him the glories of the universe." Alternately a dévotée and an enemy, Kim Stanley told actress Shirley Knight, "Sometimes I hate the son of a bitch but he knows more about acting than anybody else in the world."

The big question is, what is a Lee Strasberg? Short, white-haired, nearly eighty years old, weighing 138 without his glasses, it is he who refined the esoteric, dramaturgical ideas of Russia's Konstantin Stanislavsky and made them into the now internationally known phrase, the Method. What took Stanislavsky the best part of eighty years of life plus two thick volumes to get together, no civilian wandering into its midst can grasp quickly. Its practitioners simplistically explain it as the art of experiencing rather than imitating. Its murkiest facet is that to convey an experience convincingly, the actor needs to tap a similar experience from memory.

It took an unschooled immigrant boy to adapt it and thereby change the scenery of the American theatre. In the old days when Burgess Meredith was starting and the only place to learn was at the feet of Eva Le Gallienne, the theatrical royalty—Le Gallienne, Cornell, the Lunts—viewed "this little mystic from the Lower East Side like a salmon swimming upstream."

The going technique was not naturalness but imitativeness. Not reality but theatricality. The Delsarte System taught acting by precise directives for precise situations such as where to position the hands, feet, face for each theatrical response. It was the traditional "bird's wing" gesture and "pear-shaped tone" of the mannered theatre. Lee declared war on measured movements, conventional phrasings, drawing-room diction, and pompous, stentorian actors who twirled and postured and courted applause after a climax by bowing in the middle of the speech in the middle of the stage in the middle of the show. Before the Stanislavsky/Strasberg axis, this was the classic commercial theatre.

Although Lee Strasberg is a major influence in the theatre internationally, he inspires passions on both sides. Of the big three of acting teachers—direct descendants all—Herbert Berghof credits Marilyn Monroe's breakthrough as the reason for why Lee is where he is. Sanford Meisner has spoken out at the Neighborhood Playhouse against the Method in general and Strasberg in particular. Stella Adler considers "It's a kind of insanity that this personally ugly little man should have become the leader of the American theatre."

Even non-actors scratch at his doors, from the heroine of Washington's sex scandal, Elizabeth Ray ("She had possibilities. Actually, she wasn't bad. But she says I'm the only one who didn't try to lay her. I think that's insulting to me.") to the Shah of Iran's once-upon-a-time Empress, Soraya, who seemed best in the role of princess. ("It was ridiculous the way she was being pushed into a major role. Acting is an avenue of self-expression not exhibitionism.")

Even non-students solicit his opinion. In that twelve-room theatrical museum on Central Park West in which he lives, he has received such pilgrims as Ava Gardner who is scarcely your prototypic Method actress.

Even non-Americans praise what Ben Gazzara once labeled, "the finest mind in the American theatre." Sir Michael Redgrave and Britain's Academy Award winning director for *Tom Jones*, Tony Richardson, agree that he has done more for the American theatre than any other man in history.

An educated guess by peers puts the percentage of theatre people influenced by this High Priest of the Method at 50 per cent. Actors, directors, and playwrights who were his students plus actors who coach other actors, actors who model themselves after his actors and third-generation teachers who were pupils of pupils of those pupils of his who became teachers. "Two thirds of the top fifty actors give him a good deal of congratulations," figures friend Burgess Meredith. Yet there's a hard-core third to whom this living legend is an exploded myth.

The debacle of the 1963 London company of *The Three Sisters*, directed by Strasberg, starring George C. Scott, may be influential in Scott's colorful vivisections of "Lee-you-should-excuse-the-expression Strasberg." Scott resents Lee telling actors to look deeper and deeper into themselves. He loathes the raking up of one's own emotional experiences to condition one's sensitivities. He spits, "despicable" at any actor who "smears his own hangups over any role." This, despite his daughter's enrollment in Lee's classes and his wife's membership in the Studio.

The new kid on the block, Sylvester Stallone, also takes a potshot. "I work with the outside, from the wardrobe and makeup.

When I work from the inside it tightens me up. With the Method I was so tight that if I had cut my throat the audience still wouldn't have been with me."

"Lee believes he's Christ but I don't," jabs contemporary Luther Adler. "Shit, I don't even think he's a genius. My sister, Stella, can't stand him at all."

Morris Carnovsky knows Lee from the twenties. He and his wife, acting teacher Phoebe Brand, had a student who studied with Lee. "She was in knots from working so hard subjectively that inside she was all messed up. We finally straightened her out. She said to us, 'Oh, you're so marvelous. You make acting so easy.' Would you believe after all that she went back to Lee to study?"

To producer David Merrick, "Lee has set the theatre back a hundred years. You can always tell Lee's students. They're the ones you can't hear behind the third row."

Push the button marked "Strasberg" and actors light up. They start punching. The intensity of this litmus-test reaction is proof—good or bad—that he affects them. "Brilliant," rhapsodizes Shelley Winters. "Destructive," Julie Harris calls him.

Geraldine Page and her husband Rip Torn were worshipful supporters. Artistic differences ruptured the relationship nearly twenty years ago. Actors are good at remembering lines. The wounds have yet to heal. The Studio was a combination kindergarten-gymnasium for Anne Bancroft. Her first shot at singing was before Lee Strasberg. She bumbled her way through *My Fair Lady* in front of him. Today she avoids him.

Over 1,000 audition annually for the Actors Studio. About 10 make it. What happens to the remaining 990 who are rejected, as were Jack Nicholson, Barbra Streisand, George C. Scott, and, originally, Al Pacino, Sylvia Miles, and others who made it subsequently is that (A) some never go on, (B) some go on but amount to nothing, (C) some go on and make it small. A, B, and C never like the Studio or Strasberg.

In the case of a biography of this man who bears the title Artistic Director of the Actors Studio, the biographer's digging is not necessarily productive of bedrock. When one interviews actors the problem is finding bottom, because the peaks and valleys of an actor's ego are built on shifting sands. Today he's grateful. Tomorrow, like the ingrate whose mother-in-law financed him through medical school, he's ungrateful. Today his name is billed over the title and he doesn't need anyone. Tomorrow he can't land a walk-on in a cheapie B-movie and out goes the SOS for Big Daddy. The seeds of dishonesty are sown within an actor.

In some, maturation takes place sufficiently to realize, "I had that in me all the time but he had the key to unlock it." Such is Steve McQueen. "Nobody gives you talent. You either have it or you don't. But what Lee gave me was definition."

Card-carrying egotists, if they're good in a part it's, well, naturally, I'm a great actor. If they're bad in a part it's, well, naturally, my jerk agent gave me lousy advice. Another source of ingratitude is that people go to Lee as to a dentist. They're in pain. When the problem is healed they don't stick around. Who adores a dentist? You go away and the tooth works well for years. You forget the pain. More, you don't want to remember the pain.

One, eager to knife his mentor under the umbrella of guaranteed anonymity, puts it that, "When he's been betrayed by famous favorites, he rationalizes that *they* betrayed him. *They* defected. The negative things he does are unknown to him. His ego is his saving grace."

Strasberg can be insensitive to one's needs. He triggers anger and disappointment because one cannot reach the man as a person. He loves acting, not necessarily actors. "He's fascinated by us," Celeste Holm says. "We're things to study, to experiment with. But he can't make contact on a personal level as one human being to another."

Lee will not make you feel special. He's not loyal. He's deficient socially. No cuddly pussycat who'll snuggle up when you flop near him, he won't pat you on the back palsy-walsy style. He won't ring you on the phone to be friendly. If he doesn't see you for years, he's liable not even to notice it. An associate who found the priestly severity unappealing disappeared, not to speak to him for two and a half years. She agreed to come back "only if Lee called me." He didn't call. Somebody else called. She came back. He appeared unaware anything had happened.

He wouldn't have the dimensions professionally if it weren't that he is what he is personally. His very limitations form the reservoir on which he draws. Within the inability to give anything of himself lies the expertise in wrenching it all out of another. Emotionally incapable of releasing his own colors he, therefore, becomes a clear transparency. His greatness as an original theatrical mind is that within his reflection of you is mirrored your own inadequacies.

Worship his talent and you may be a winner. Crave his love, you'll be a loser. Viveca Lindfors came to him as a film star from Sweden. "I owe him everything. He taught me my craft. But I go after him professionally and accept him for what he is. I forget him as a human being." Then, along with everyone who rationalizes him away, "When he doesn't notice me or care how I am, it's not a posture. It's that he cares only for the work. He's very pure."

Not everyone slots the coldness and/or rudeness as "purity." Another rationale is to psych him as a poor immigrant who, when thrown into the heavy intellectual atmosphere of the Theatre Guild of the twenties, retreated even further into a natural shell. It is now part of him. Lee communes with his own consciousness in the middle of a busy world. The shell which has thickened into armor seals in his own private world and locks out the intrusive, aggressive one of students with ceaseless questions of how and what.

In the classic love-hate relationship, his students call him interchangeably "my salvation" and "my disappointment." His personality is prickly. When they need him, they overlook it. When they don't, they don't.

When one particular star appeared in a show, she needed and wanted her teacher's praise. She dispatched opening night tickets. He didn't come backstage. As the story is told, she humiliated herself by telephoning. "Weren't you there?" "Yes." Pause. "Well, how was I? . . . Was I OK?" "I suppose so." If those were not his exact words, they're close.

One theory suggests that only weak creatures stick with him because sooner or later anyone with backbone leaves. That theory proves unsupportable. As a man he may be tough to take. As a certified genius his talent is admirable. Nobody exists in this universe with the original thoughts of this theatrical philosopher. Who else could say, "A theatre experience exists only in the memory of man. It's written in snow, which melts." But not even an earnest biographer can codify what defies codification. Lee Strasberg is a bona fide, intellectual, theatrical, psychoanalytical genius who caught onto a golden thread. He is also a flawed, self-limiting, hurtful personality.

A hostility for which he isn't responsible is that of people who refuse to accept him without coming into contact with him. Ann-Margret asks, "What does he do, make you lie on the floor and do some kind of primal scream?" Tyrone Guthrie, who's never been to the Studio, wrote an article against "the humphs and grunts and inarticulate croaks" of Studio acting. Elizabeth Ashley, after seeing his film *Godfather II:* "I had my stiletto out. He's been telling pros what to do all these years. I figured, let's see if he knows what he's talking about. Now I say, 'Jesus, that son of a bitch is good. He knows.'"

Daughter Susan Strasberg says, "People who don't know my father resent his high standards as a tacit put-down of their lower standards. That's not fair. He has his dreams. They have theirs."

To quote Lee, "The Method, which seems even more confused than politics, is merely the sum total of the experience of the great actors throughout all ages and countries. The best things in it come from Stanislavsky. The rest come from me."

It sets no rules. It points a path that leads to control rather than hit-or-miss inspiration. It fosters fusion of the actor with the character. It is now represented in universities and with workshops, dramatic schools, and little theatre groups in every corner of every hamlet.

Eighteen years ago when Ellen Burstyn was Ellen McCrae and her major ambition was to be Debbie Reynolds, this most influential acting teacher in the world pronounced her work natural but not real. "I cried for two weeks. I didn't know what the hell he was talking about."

Worshipers call him a brilliant theoretician with powers of observation so great "he could tell Johnny Carson more than his analyst just by watching him." Unfortunately the examples they offer are esoteric. "It seems to me you either laugh or cry," he told Ellen. "Of course, if you laugh and you cry at the same time then you really have something."

Explains Ellen, "He always knows how to tell you what you need exactly. Your work progresses then needs another step. You don't know where you go from there and he'll say just the thing.

Then you say to yourself, 'Of course. Split the levels. Get a sur-face going with an undertone. Like a fugue. Two melody lines going together.'" In her next film, *The Last Picture Show*, she laughed and cried at the same time. "I was dying to say, 'You mean like that?!'"

Now, if that doesn't explain it, hang onto Shelley Winters, who requested the Master's assistance on a complex characterization. She was a callgirl. Gangsters were after her. She was scared, only she didn't quite know of what or whom. "But she had guts and was going to stand up to the bastards. Lee gave me a weird direc-tion. He told me to, 'Be afraid of the furniture. You have this nameless fear. Every once in a while, just look at the furniture like you're afraid of something.' It was almost a mystical direction but it was perfect. It worked. It broke the whole thing for me."

Now, if that doesn't clarify why he's this planet's greatest drama coach, have this from Sylvia Miles who flunked ten audi-tions before the Studio accepted her and who credits Lee with her Oscar nomination for *Midnight Cowboy*. "He taught me to make all things in life work for me so that I could play anybody. He told me to experience everybody. He lectured me to give up my kind of theatrics. Do away with the fail-safes. The safeguards. The escape hatches. Be extremely vulnerable. Become the person with-out performing, without indicating. Allow yourself the freedom of being totally stripped bare.

"Because of that I got the part in *Cowboy*. Listen, I pray he lives forever and not because he's so sweet and loving to me per-sonally. He's not."

It is said that Lee's laser-beam insight pulled Robert De Niro away from characterizations, from acting behind a mask. He makes his pupils rethink things. He transports them to another world. It's not to say he's always understood. Patrick O'Neal be-lieves "It's his crazy neurotically talented souls who grab onto his stuff. It's probably me, but all I can say I got out of him was confidence."

"Another like him won't show up for generations," volunteers Estelle Parsons. "Very seldom such an ability to teach shows up. He makes you discover yourself and your limitations. He has a deeper level of truth than anyone else."

And if you don't understand *that*, neither, always, does Al Pacino. "You have to *listen* to Lee. Listen hard. It's tough to listen. I only get some of what he says. It's easier to take advice when you've really got the part by the cojones, as they say. I've come to him when I'm hung up on a part. Then if he says a key thing it can help me. We talk for hours. I don't always understand him totally."

Nobody understands him totally. He's elusive. Evasive. He's somewhere else. Walk in and he's likely not to glance up from his book, albeit you're the only one there and you're expected. Wait for him to start a conversation and you'll grow old. He's cold, aloof, undemonstrative. Say hello and he might not even respond. Say good-bye and he might not even care.

He is aware he doesn't say hello or good-bye when he walks in someplace nor when he leaves. "In my upbringing we never said, 'hello.' Who said, 'hello'? My mother with her army of children and boarders and husband and God knows what else would take time from washing the floor to look up and say to me, 'hello'? Nor did anybody say, 'how are you?' Who ever said, 'How are you?' She would maybe ask, 'You want a glass of tea?'

"From my upbringing you didn't get that in your house. If you learned it in later years, then it's that you adjusted quickly to your new environment. In my childhood who even noticed if I walked in? And who said good-bye? What does that mean, good-bye? You walked out, called over your shoulder, 'Okay, I'm leaving' and slammed the door. What kind of nonsense is 'good-bye'? Sure I could have learned, but it wasn't easy for me. I wish it was different but it wasn't.

"So I have this natural reticence because I never had nor did I even know the social graces. I didn't even know who says hello first. Do you wait for a person to say hello to you or do you say hello to the person? Who do you introduce to whom? I never knew how to do it but at least I *knew* I didn't know how to do it."

Neither is he used to being kissed. In the old days when someone came near to hug him or reach out for him, he literally didn't know what to do. "That French style of grabbing and kissing one side of the cheek then the other, I didn't know how to do that. I didn't grow up with that in my family. I didn't know how to handle it, so I moved back from the whole thing."

There is a story about a playwright who visited by appointment. Mr. Strasberg sat in the living room reading. The man stood patiently. The man shifted impatiently. The man coughed. The man rustled. Mr. Strasberg turned a page. The man sat down. The man stared. Mr. Strasberg turned another page. For nearly an hour this nonchoreography continued and Mr. Strasberg remained reading. The man stalked out.

The explanation was Mr. Strasberg was too pathologically shy to speak first. Then, when too many embarrassing minutes passed and the bizarre situation continued, he absolutely did not know *how* to begin.

When Carroll Baker lived in his building, they caught the same bus the same time the same mornings to ride together to the same class. Twenty minutes later they disembarked at the same stop and never exchanged a "Hi." Carroll was afraid to break in on him and he, of course, didn't greet her. They'd ride the whole way down as though neither knew the other.

Another explains an early meeting. "Lee's eyes were kind of lidded. I put my hand out but got no response so I quickly pulled it back. He didn't utter one word. I felt I hadn't connected. Worse, I felt threatened. I'd listen intently, hoping to find the man underneath the façade. There has to be a human being there! But all I could find was a body with an intellect. Wheels. I could see wheels. It was macabre."

A while back the Studio featured sessions in fencing, dance, gymnastics, classical Chinese theatre, and speech training. Speech teacher Alice Hermes was there nearly two years. Lee never once greeted her. She wondered aloud something about nobody being *that* shy.

Actress Elaine Aiken, who repeatedly dated one man high up in Washington, D.C., circles, patiently reintroduced him each time. "I'd say, 'Lee, do you know Mark?' . . . 'Lee, you know Mark' . . . 'Lee—Mark' . . . *Ummm* was all I got. At a party at Shelley Winters', Lee was standing nearby eating and as usual I began, 'You two know each other' and Mark deadpanned, 'No, I don't think we ever met.' Stunned, totally disarmed, Lee said, 'Oh yes we have.' "

During Group Theatre days the gay, effusive actress Margaret Barker drove Lee into Danbury, Connecticut. They came onto the rise of a hill which afforded a lovely view with the valley and sunset and she exclaimed, "Oh, how beautiful . . . how perfectly lovely." For anyone to be so openly demonstrative made him uncomfortable. To him this was false. Margaret Barker was so jolted she'll never forget it. "He spat out the words, 'Why do you say that? Why don't you just look at it?' In 1931 he was a quite frightening person."

Harold Clurman, a cofounder with Lee of the Group Theatre of the thirties which spawned John Garfield, Franchot Tone, Karl Malden, Lee J. Cobb, Clifford Odets, J. Edward Bromberg, and Morris Carnovsky, overheard him remark, "When I was a young man I could have used an analyst to get over some of my inhibitions." Clurman and Strasberg visited a discothèque together. For individuals to jump around, swing around, let themselves go and exhibit such freedom was meaningful to Lee. He replied thoughtfully, "A person who can do these dances doesn't need an analyst."

About the complex individual he has known fifty-five years, Clurman says, "He holds his emotion under leash. It's hard for him to express except to animals, children, and the mortally sick. It isn't something that comes natural. His emotion flows easily only when it's punitive."

Two experiences with Franchot Tone appear illustrative of Clurman's view. Franchot wanted to quit the Group to strike out on his own. On their last colloquy with Franchot, Lee was strong and loud. His reaction was *too* sharp like telling your fiancée, who has announced she's walking out, "Okay, go to hell, who cares!!" Clurman admitted Franchot's defection was a blow. "Lee shouted, 'What do you mean a blow? We can get along without him. To hell with him. We don't need him.' It was as if he wanted to slap Franchot. He was full of venom."

Many years after both achieved success, Franchot fell ill. He visited his old friend near the end. The deeply troubled expression on Lee's face floored someone who was present. "There was such compassion not in his voice but in his eyes. As Franchot left, Lee put his arm on his and said, 'Take care of yourself' then turned and walked away. I saw tears in his eyes. Afterward he said to me, 'Oh, isn't it terrible . . . just terrible . . .' And he sat there and stroked the dog. That was as much emotion as ever I saw. That was as full an expression of grief as anybody ever saw. He held the dog on his lap and stroked it and stroked it and stroked it."

Clurman believes another reason his colleague stays behind the veil is to camouflage the insecurities. "He tries to hide because otherwise there might be something to point a finger at. He might show a fault. Lee has difficulty admitting he has faults."

He has less difficulty today. Protecting him today is the cloak of age. And security. He has two homes—a labyrinthine apartment in New York, a sprawling house in Bel Air—and a chauffeur, maid, and secretary in each. And success. At seventy-three The Hollywood Foreign Press Association nominated him the most promising new actor.

And beyond anything else, love. His beautiful, young, brunette wife, Anna, has changed him enormously. He now allows himself overt expressions of pleasure. He smiles when he sees a friend. He calls a favorite "darling." Anna has given him two young sons. She's given him a new life. She's put laughter in his house. Exuberant, volatile, outgoing, "she is very open in the expression of her feelings which is something I never had," praises her husband. "She's warm and giving. After I met Anna I became much more open." "Humane," is a better word, drawls one who is neither warm nor giving.

In those tense, eager, insecure days he had more of a temper. Of those early critiques Paul Newman says, grinning, "Lee prepared you for the New York *Times*." He was then totally committed to what he was doing. He has since mellowed. He no longer needs to compensate for lacks. He doesn't have to prove. Replacing that "little mystic from the lower East Side" is a highly recognized movie actor in black velvet 38-short Saint Laurent suits ("Just the sleeves have to be shortened"), Cardin jackets with gold buttons ("Anna selects them") and Saks Fifth Avenue suede and cashmere jobs ("They know my tastes. They bring out what I like.").

Recently, in discussing a particular star's unattractive attitudes, Lee commented, "People who have these unpleasant behavior patterns aren't just doing it to you or to others, but they're doing it to themselves as well. They're suffering from it, too."

Today, the once squirrely uncle can even laugh at certain of his handpicked faults. In May 1962, John Kennedy invited him to the

White House for a State Dinner honoring André Malraux. After
shaking hands with President and Mrs. Kennedy, he was supposed
to shake hands with Vice President Johnson. "Well, I have a
thing about that. I don't shake hands. It just isn't something I do.
   "Anyway, I didn't see him. There was this tall guy standing off
there in a doorway all alone with no guards, no Marine Corps ad-
jutants, no secretary, aides, nothing. I walked right by him. Go
know it was Johnson over there on the side by himself waiting
to get his hand shook. I literally stiffed the Vice President of the
United States!"
   Meet Lee Strasberg after seeing *Godfather II* with Al Pacino or
Cassandra Crossing with Sophia Loren and your reflex thought is
he's less imposing than one remembers on screen. In person you'd
pass this bantam in spectacles without a second look. Slight, unas-
suming, about five foot six, he looks more a clerk than the medicine man some believe "could work a miracle if only he would
speak to me."
   People eat the little man's flesh. Anytime his circle closes in on
him they want pieces of him. It's always give me . . . give me . . .
what do you think about that, Lee . . . what do you feel about
that, Lee . . . how do we work about that, Lee . . . They beard
him on streetcorners or in bookshops to learn the whole secret of
talent or how they can break into acting. He tries not to go backstage, but if he goes, it starts immediately. "Well, Lee, this is
what I had in mind. . . ." The telephone calls come in two,
three, four in the morning from all over the world. Student Jacqueline Bertrand "always phoned whenever I had an acting hangup
and he always gave me the answer to whatever ailed me."
   Summer, winter, East Coast, West Coast, Sunday is open
house. From afternoon through evening, critical cases drop by to
get his ear. Some for ten minutes. Some for an hour. Sometimes
there are half a dozen people. Sometimes two dozen. Those in
need of special conversation come as early as eleven. Anna disap-
pears, surfacing only to speak to whomever she wishes whenever
she chooses.
   Sometimes there's food from a nearby deli. Sometimes Anna
sets out roast and salad and it's every man for himself. Sometimes
Lee prepares sukiyaki. He loves Japanese food and doesn't love

going out, so he learned to make it. "Chopping up the vegetables is like an art."

At big parties he is often in the kitchen. Standing for hours over a stove, mixing, chopping and serving a hundred or more is hard work. To sit with his guests would seem easier. Maybe it's up-manship. Doing something nobody else can do. Maybe it's *his* way of showing love. Giving what he can give. Maybe it's hiding. In any case, the mundane things—do you want the window open, shall I show you where the telephone is, would you like a drink—he leaves to Anna.

Lee strips himself at work. When he's monitoring an actor he doesn't fidget, isn't impatient, has no need to go to the john. His entire being he gives to the talent. Any teacher constantly giving of his brain needs to revitalize. Lee is so drained at times that "I shudder if someone's going to ask me one more question. I can't even talk."

For self-preservation and to push his students out lest they cling forever, he has learned to click off. Director Marty Fried, an inti-mate, says, "He exhausts himself so much in class that he scares the shit out of whoever comes over afterward with, 'Lee, I have this little problem. . . .' He just stares at them, seeing nothing. He's blank. El funko. He just wants to watch TV Westerns and wash problems out of his brain."

His powers of concentration are so deep and he burrows so within that he literally switches off, neither hearing nor seeing. Harry Belafonte, a favorite, threw him a "Hi, Lee" on the street. Lee ignored him and ambled right by. Anna nudged him. "That was Harry Belafonte you just passed." "Where . . . where . . ." he asked.

The ability to be alone in a crowd is a quality he has honed to a fine degree. One average Sunday, O. J. Simpson chatted with Anna in the kitchen while Cheri, the Strasbergs' aged pedigreed Yorky, yipped after O.J.'s kids, who were running around with masks and candies with Lynn Redgrave and her two children and Marthe Keller and hers. Dick Cavett was munching a pastrami sandwich and Alejandro Rey was talking Spanish to some Argen-tinian hopeful and Mike Nichols was wandering and Lionel Stander was spouting to anybody who paused long enough to lis-ten and the phone was ringing. "This is Paul," came the voice.

"Paul who?" "Newman." From somewhere a shitzu, a cat, and something else fluffy that one very nearly stepped on raced out from deep within and all the while Lee, erect and attentive, stood in a corner speaking deeply and passionately to Elia Kazan, oblivious to all.

His days off, he pokes in bookshops. He buys records and books. At home he is reserved, withdrawn. He reads. Listens to music. "Office workers and factory workers want to communicate when they come home at night," he says. "I want a rest *from* communicating. So much of me goes out that I have to put something back. I need something for relaxation. Music relieves the tension."

In California there's the garden and the outdoors. He leaves for class at 10:15 A.M. and some days he works beyond 8 P.M. In New York it's one closed environment after another. "Even if it's polluted air, I should get some. The only outdoors I get is what I have moving from the house to the car and the car to my classes. I used to walk a little, but now that we have a chauffeur I feel like I'm wasting him if I don't let him drive me."

Rather than parties with the possibility of dull conversation and more questions, Lee prefers "dinner with Walter Cronkite" on a tray in the bedroom. Those who come by complain he's not paying attention to them and that he keeps his eyes riveted to the TV when they're speaking. "That's because they're not saying anything I have to address myself to," he says. "Anyhow, I can hear without looking. That in fact is what I teach—that you can do several things at a time and remain in touch with them all. I don't have to listen *hard* and talk into someone's eyes with *strength*.

"I don't make small talk. One reason is that eventually the talker will say, 'What do you think, Lee?' It always comes down to that 'What do you think, Lee?' thing. So that's why I don't engage in small talk, because it always comes down to me pontificating."

There are enemies, students, sycophants, and acquaintances. The real friendships are with people who aren't stopped by the barriers. People self-censor. They hang back. For those who aren't intimidated, he reserves that small, warm part of himself.

Lee quotes Diderot's phrase: "What makes the human being of supreme excellence is a kind of balance between calculation and

warmth." If love is genuine, he responds. Witnessing the phenomenon of old friend Juleen Compton freely planting a kiss, a famous
actress swooped down to follow suit. He pulled away. "When
Juleen does it, it's for her. With you it's for show. To see me
react."

Underneath the heavy is a gentle soul who personally pries open
the can of dogfood, squats to plop the concoction in a dish on the
floor then calls, "Superstar . . . hey, Soupy . . . Soup. . . ." A
mongrel resembling a blond hairpiece happily trots forth to lick
the fingers of the quintessential Superstar himself. The human
being I grew to know well enough to giggle with and gossip with
has his hair cut in his book-lined—Proust not Julia Childs—
kitchen. Anna's longtime hairdresser friend awaits Madame's instruction on how to bob the white laurel wreath while The Guru
Himself in Person sits patiently in a kitchen chair. That done, he
in turn shampoos the curly head of Adam Lee, aged eleven, and
the straighter hair of Number Two son, nine-year-old David.

I have hugged him. He hugs back. I have showed up uninvited
for lunch. He fixes me a plate. I have sat in on his private classes.
He escorts me home. I have house-guested and padded into their
bedroom looking for friendship when the host and hostess were
snuggled cozily into a double bed watching television. With head-
cold and rheumy eyes, the host sighed softly and wrenched himself from the Western to the pesty house guest without a groan of
complaint.

I bothered friends. I interrogated enemies. I was never asked
not to see someone or to lay off something. When unfavorable aspects were surfacing he said, "If there's a really bad thing then all
I ask is the opportunity to present my side of it."

He didn't definitely want his life story written. He didn't definitely *not* want it written either. Lee's preference for a memoir was
My Life in Art which deals primarily with Stanislavsky's artistic
points of view. "Stanislavsky as a human being takes second place
to what he was. He's a difficult man to write about. I'm also a
difficult man to write about. I'm a difficult man period. I am not
the type who likes to tell what I find wrong about myself. I prefer
not to talk about things like that. I'm more open now in expressing things, however. Previously I expressed only things involved in
my work. Other things I wouldn't even bother with. And I'm not

concerned with other people. I'm concerned only
doing. So I'm difficult.

"I'm a pessimistic optimist or an optimistic pe
ever way you put it. My habit is to give people e
hang themselves. I expect the worst and hope for
never judge in advance.

"All my life I've worked with others, therefore I accept that
sometimes—but not often—the other person may be right. So, if
it's my feeling that this biography is maybe not going to turn out
best for me, well, who knows it's not going to turn out? A lot of
things *do* turn out."

Discussing the critique that he's a destructive influence, that he
makes actors psychologically dependent, he replied wistfully, "I
wish it were true. Then that would mean they would be more
grateful." Discussing those who have spat on his gift and later denied him, he sighed, "I don't expect gratitude. When you're way
up people throw things at you. Other systems have come and
gone, but I've stayed. The proof is in the work."

He holds no grudges. At most he'll say, "I have more respect for George C. Scott than he has for himself. Scott has the
capacity to be great, but I have never seen greatness in anything
he's done. And if I really answered his slurs at me I would have to
be cruel and I don't want to be."

About Stella Adler, it's, "I don't like to call names. I haven't
wanted to call attention to reviews she got after she left me. She
was criticized for her hysteria. She thought, well, sure, on her own
she could go places. So, where did Miss Adler go? Is she still working as an actress? I don't like to do or say what I must just to answer Miss Adler. That's why I wouldn't like to write this book
myself because I don't want to throw stones."

Meanwhile his detractors heave boulders. You're told he's star
crazy. An unsuccessful actress swears only after she wrote for top
publications was Lee nice to her. "Before that he never recognized
me." A top star swears only after copping Best Actress Oscar was
she invited to a private dinner at his home. I believe that inside
the international savant lives the little kid from the Lower East
Side who is still impressionable. I also believe Joanna Miles.
Joanna was a waitress years back with no money and no prospects.

OPENING

When Lee realized she also had no presents at Christmas, he presented her personally with a silver key ring from Tiffany.

I also believe another who was invited to come over the night a cable was received announcing a death in his family. Lee never said a word. He just sensed the fellow didn't know what to do with himself. "If I hadn't had somewhere to go, I don't know what I would have done. Lee's very soft when you're in trouble."

Many reach out for Lee Strasberg in deep moments. There exists an irresistible fascination. An oddity is that at the end of their lives even those who have turned from him turn toward him. Having pulled away when Lee opposed certain of his plays, the fact remains Clifford Odets came back. His first wife, Luise Rainer, and his second wife divorced him. His mother was gone. He didn't like his father, and he was a negative parent. With a house in California and a New York apartment but without a sense of home, Clifford came to live with old friend Lee.

When Clifford died, Lee was the executor and guardian of his son and daughter. "Odets was a big collector. His art collection was like two hundred thousand dollars, but I had to sell the stuff because he had no ready cash. I went around to friends collecting money for the kids to go to school.

"Outside of a great, huge desk with marvelous drawers and a marble top, the furniture was nothing. We had to pay to cart it away. We put the desk in the Studio, but even though it was Odets' desk, they were throwing it out. What the hell can you do? So I took it."

The hostilities directed at Lee Strasberg seem never to be forgotten. Nurtured like prize possessions, they're taken out and examined from time to time. One lady hissed, "He's ungrateful. He never acknowledges anything." She sent flowers in 1966. She still ruminates about how he never acknowledged them.

You're told Lee's "navel picking" and "psychoanalytical approach" pulled a dark-haired, attractive, budding star's insides into a knot until she quit the profession. He "broke her down without building her up with his terrible insistence on getting to the truth . . . whose truth? . . . the playwright's? . . . hers? . . . his? . . . whose? . . ." Well-adjusted, happily married Rebecca Darke, now working again, blames herself, not him. "I wasn't strong enough to take his rejection of me. Lee became important and found big stars to play with, but he didn't twist my insides. I was going to a shrink before I ever met him."

Another reputedly hostile, denies it. Director Alan Schneider insists he "loves" Lee but can't go all the way with him. He complains Strasberg's students are too literal. He directed one who suddenly clambered onto a table onstage because "he felt impelled to do this and Lee said they were to honor every impulse." When Schneider directed another to move faster, the actor issued "a whole megilla about 'motivation' and how I had to give him a 'reason.' I figured, 'Hey, pal, that's your problem. Go find your own reason.' "

Despite elocution years back from one accredited to The American Academy of Dramatic Arts, Lee's manner of speech is convoluted, his diction home grown, and his grammar high school. His orations made one bitchy old-timer believe "he must be tone deaf." They're peppered with mop-up phrases such as the all-pervasive, all-purpose, catch-all extension hooks of "and so on," "as though to say," "point of view," and "the thing."

This might partially account for his acquiescent attitude toward an actor's inaudibility. "If the big problem, so to say, is in the speaking of the thing, then we should have great Shakespearean performances all over the place," says teacher Strasberg. "From that point of view if the emotions of the characters and their relationships to one another and so on is not made evident then all the elocution in the world won't help. And don't forget if Marlon had simply mumbled he wouldn't have won all those awards."

An artificial atmosphere surrounds any manipulator of lives and careers. There are sycophants who are secret haters. They wait until the safety of space protects them. They knock him but they want to come back, so they ventilate anonymously. "We're all worshipful in his presence," slices one. "He needs that asslicking." They loathe his personal qualities. They love his professional abilities. They need him. They won't be quoted. "He's living. I'm living. Don't use my name. . . ." ". . . Sure, go ahead, say this . . . but don't use my name. . . ."

Even those who deride are careful to praise. Karl Malden was deliberately careful and cryptic. "He was a big force in the American theatre and he deserves an awful lot of respect. But times change and people change and whether it's for better or worse only time can tell."

The deepest fissures go back to the twenties and thirties. Actor J. Edward Bromberg's widow, Goldie, wouldn't even be drawn into a telephone conversation. Firm. Cold. "I don't know anything about him and I don't want to know." Click. Set designer Boris Aronson thinks Lee "harmed" people but couldn't come up with anything positive. He wouldn't say bad and couldn't say good, so he said nothing. Director Robert Lewis wouldn't meet at all on any book about Lee Strasberg.

The most Machiavellian was Elia Kazan whose relationship snakes through half a century. In the thirties Lee was a theatrical leader, Kazan a struggling nobody. In the forties Kazan was a hotshot director and Lee a struggling teacher. In the seventies Lee is again running hot, at the helm of a whole new generation.

For two years Kazan insisted he was too busy to spare even an hour. Ultimately he was backed into an appointment at his tiny office. When I arrived midafternoon he was watching television. Feet up on the coffee table, his exact welcome was, "You can't get shit out of me."

I voiced the circulating rumors. "Listen, are you jealous of Lee's new success?"

"Shit no," snorted Kazan, rearranging his feet. "What the fuck would I be jealous of Lee for?"

"Is it all right with you if I use a tape recorder for the interview?"

"No. No tape recorder."

I took out pad and pencil and Kazan, whose feet were now settled, rearranged the smirk on his face. Arms folded, he sat without uttering one word. In that case, would it be correct to assume that he in fact loves his old pal?

"I love my wife. I love my kids. I can't say I love Lee. Love is a strong word. I like Lee. I like him even now. I like him a lot . . . yeah, I like Lee. . . ."

"So how come you sat in the corner and refused to get up in his behalf at the informal party at the Studio last week where everybody spoke about Lee?"

"Maybe that's just my peculiarity. I don't stand up for anybody." Interesting choice of words. Not that he doesn't "get u but he doesn't "stand up" for anybody.

I dredged up an old Kazan comment from *The Drama Review* which ran: "I wish to God people could be more candid, not less; more personal, not less; more direct and involved, not less."

"I don't remember saying that. You can throw it back in my teeth or not, quote it or don't, I don't give a shit."

This high-level conversation unfolded for another half hour broken only by the one phone call he received. When he hung up, he stared at me and laughed, "I told you, you'll get shit out of me."

Whatever I asked he couldn't remember. "I forgot . . . that slips my mind . . . who the hell knows . . . that's so long ago I have no way of recalling that. . . ." Nonetheless, Kazan has kept notes of everything he has lived through over the years beginning with his high school days. Sometimes he kept the diary religiously but even when it was sketchy he always kept it. He admits, "I have every single thing that ever happened noted down."

In the Strasberg house a visit from Kazan is meaningful. One is always informed Kazan was just there or just coming or just going. Why then was Kazan playing this game with a man who considers him a friend?

The gray-haired director, once considered one of the most powerful men in the business, leaned back in his chair and propped himself against the door. "I'm doing my own autobiography and I'm writing about all this myself."

"Oh well, in that case I guess I can understand your reticence. When will you finish your autobiography?"

"I haven't started it yet."

"When do you plan to start it?"

"I haven't thought about it yet."

Putting pad and pencil away, I snapped my bag shut. My interviewee and I locked eyes. He smiled coldly, enjoying the experience.

"Do you have any ideas about when you plan to think about it?"

"I haven't thought about that yet . . . either."

As his guest departed so he could again watch television, Mr. Kazan asked, "Why the fuck would you be doing a book on Lee

Strasberg? Why would anybody be doing a book on Lee Strasberg?"

Cheryl Crawford and Harold Clurman are others of those days
who take big bites. "Nothing much would have happened to Lee
if not for the Actors Studio, which came from my womb," says
Cheryl. "Today it's Lee's baby. Nobody's ever mentioned in connection with it but Lee." Then, discussing their differences, "I've
never sat and talked with him about them. He's too defensive.
You can't get close to him and he can't talk about anything where
he was wrong." But she adds, "He's still the greatest teacher of
acting in the world."

Clurman: "We're friendly except there's a little gap between
us which is as wide as a mile. I've learned many values from this
able and talented man of the theatre, but we get along because I
don't argue anymore. See, he's terribly rude. I asked him, 'Did
you read my book?' In front of a gathering of people he answered,
'Only the parts that interested me.' When he was going to see a
play of mine I said, 'Enjoy the show.' You know what he said?
'I hope so.'"

Stella Adler calls Lee's teaching, "a jolt into the world that
opened up a great many of our talents, therefore one of the most
important theatrical experiences of our lives in spite of the misery.
Nobody can say Lee is a pleasant fellow. His students have such
sickness that you can't deal with them. They're lost. Crippled."

Marlon Brando has commented that all actors are neurotic.
Apart from the visceral feelings directed at Lee personally, maybe
it just comes with the territory. Maybe it's that all actors are an
insecure, jealous lot. The truth is, in the Studio pigeons are coo-
ing, floors are creaking, seats are moving, doors are opening and
closing, people are walking in and out yet the loudest noise of all
is the undertone. Sylvia Miles about Estelle Parsons: "Let her
screw herself. I saw Estelle in an Israel Horowitz play. If not for
the Studio, Horowitz wouldn't have any fucking play to do and she
wouldn't have a goddamn job, yet she put the Studio down like it
was a piece of shit. I said, 'If I didn't like you, Estelle, I'd tell you
to go fuck off. I worked my ass off there five years. Where the hell
were you?' Well, she finally came back."

Estelle Parsons about Sylvia Miles: "Sylvia's not really trained.
Does she fancy herself a Method actress? She's just a personality. I

don't really call her an actress. She's Sylvia Miles. She's herself. Sylvia's always Sylvia."

Shelley Winters about everybody: "Those who've criticized Lee and left, their work has suffered. People who've stayed with him like me, our work has improved."

Sylvia Miles about what Shelley Winters said: "And if that goddamn Maureen Stapleton would come back to the Studio she'd be a good actress again. She's been away so long she can't act her way out of a paper bag."

Mention that Marilyn Monroe's once-upon-a-time husband Arthur Miller talks against him, and Lee says only, "I don't think that's true." Mention that Laurence Olivier excoriates his work, and he says, "I don't think so." Buttress it with Olivier's own statements, and Strasberg repeats only: "I don't think so."

Interviewing for this book gave birth to mind's-eye pictures as varied as those of *Rashomon*. In Lee's small office a group were reliving a party. Everyone carried a different memory of it. "I ought to know about that party because I gave it," volunteered actress Elaine Aiken. "It was Lee and Anna's engagement party."

"It was not. It was for our wedding," corrected Anna.

Lee summed it up for everybody with, "Party? What party? I don't seem to remember any party."

Lee's senses are more finely honed than anybody else's. He recalls sounds and sights and smells from seventy-five years ago. But he couldn't remember Elaine's party. Squinting into his crowded past, he muses, "I remember your Park Avenue apartment but I don't really remember any party. . . ."

Cheryl Crawford had herself hypnotized for two hundred dollars to remember details of her past. In any case the memories of them all are at variance. If each wrote a book each book would be different. The only sure footing was to go with the common thread. If everybody called Lee dogmatic ("which, of course, they confuse with dedication") it was to be understood he was dogmatic.

"The truth is," said Lee softly when I explained my problem, "there's a little bit of truth in everything."

Another truth is a biography can be written from a neutral, negative, or affirmative position. Although I have labored to present the subject fairly and honestly, warts and all, I personally have considerable affection for Lee Strasberg. The earnest biographer may never develop an ulcer but, sooner or later, he becomes a carrier. A biographer's life is fraught with danger. You teeter constantly on the edge. You enter a person's life. You become part of him. You're the repository of his past mistakes and future worries. You know his vulnerabilities. You become emotionally involved. You're caught between wanting to protect him and doing your job.

Clearly, one cannot please everyone. Lee will appreciate the effort but may have expected the blemishes to be airbrushed out. And whereas Lee's infra-red perception sees kaleidoscopic shades of gray, normal vision may only color events black or white. His wife, despite the brightness of her own light, is still the satellite revolving around the star. Anna won't countenance any tarnishing of the Golden Image. Anna's tendency is toward deification whether or not in every instance she actually believes it.

Example. While they were moving into their house, a sliver of mirror ripped her arm. She was rushed to the hospital in old jeans. "I told them who I was but they couldn't believe it. 'Oh, you couldn't be,' they said. 'I mean, Lee Strasberg is God and you couldn't be married to Lee Strasberg.' So I said, 'I'm Anna Strasberg. Mrs. Lee Strasberg. Call somebody. Take me to the Studio. I'll show you who I am.' And they said, 'Are you *really* married to *the* Lee Strasberg?' I said, 'Yes . . . yes . . . I'll prove it later but would you first, right now, right away, please sew up my arm?'"

The pro-Lee faction will fault the book for carping. The anti-Lee faction will fault the book for admiring. Since there is no attempt to parallel the hecatombs that have been written about Stanislavsky and the Method, those consumed with these theorems will complain it isn't a sufficiently dramaturgical work. Those eager to know him humanly insist the man's a cipher and I'll never be able to be real or personal enough. I say the man's a controversial character and even after publication he'll stay one. In 1970 the New York *Times*'s Murray Schumacher described Lee's eyes as "blue-gray." A British reporter reported them "dark." Even the color of his eyes engenders controversy.

His search for The Way goes back to the twenties. He was an actor in *Red Rust*. When he exited there was a laugh, although nothing was happening on stage. Unconsciously, as he left the set he finished his emotion by shaking his hand at the hero. It resulted in an unexpected laugh. But a laugh that was expected didn't come. Lee sensed a beat was missing in the phrasing. He added the word, "still," which served the purpose of making the line come out less bluntly. He said, "I *still* think so and so and this and this." With that handle he got his laugh. Again, at one point he got unexpected applause. In the scene two people were making love, and his showstopper line was, "Real American technique." It got the laugh but when he held the pose and the line and the look . . . it got unexpected applause. He couldn't explain it.

Lee Strasberg is undeniably the force directly responsible for the condition of the American actor, and the American actor is generally considered to be the best actor in the world today. Through the era of ugly people with pimples, a preponderance of the best actors in this country have come out of the Studio. A preponderance of the best actors in this country have studied with Lee. Behind him stands Yiddish Theatre, amateur theatre and professional theatre, drama clubs, dramatic schools and Stanislavsky workshops, the Theatre Guild and the Group Theatre, Broadway and Hollywood—and the Actors Studio.

But the Studio has lost excitement. Of five hundred members only a hundred are active. Rod Steiger plodded through half-a-dozen years ago, had coffee, sat through part of a session, ambled out, and nobody's seen him since. Marty Balsam ("It's great to hear it again, to get that booster shot. I genuflect when I see Lee") rarely re-enters the Studio unless he's pushed. Patricia Neal, who worked there years ago hasn't been around much since. Lee Grant, Carroll O'Connor, Ray Walston banded together to film birthday wishes for Lee a few seasons back but nobody sees them in the Studio. You might possibly see Sally Field who in her zeal to shake the image of *The Flying Nun* and *Gidget* has been studying. Last year she won the Best Actress Award at the Cannes Film Festival.

A theatrical workshop's health depends on the theatre's health. A teaching style complements what's happening in the theatre or it struggles for its identity. In the fifties Tennessee Williams, Paddy Chayefsky, Arthur Miller, and William Inge complemented the Studio's acting style. Paul Newman, who gives Lee the credit or blame for what he's doing as an actor—"If you don't like me, it's his fault. If you do he takes the credit"—says, "The Studio isn't flourishing because today the theatre has no idea what it's about."

Today that gymnasium is not Lee's whole, sole life. He almost no longer needs the Studio. Year in, year out, like building a pyramid, he has risen to overlook the others around him. He has had it all. He has done it all. For nearly thirty years he has sat week after week, year after year, instructing the latest crop of raw kids. When others nailed a movie and went away, Lee stayed at the Studio. When others had a show opening and went away, Lee stayed at the Studio. When others couldn't be devoted at the expense of their pocketbook and drifted away, Lee taught on forever. The man has paid his dues.

Still, he can't give up the Studio. It's his reputation. Over the decades he has been depressed, he has felt unappreciated, he has teetered on the verge of quitting. Still he comes. While Lee Strasberg is physically able he will not voluntarily leave the Studio.

The detachment of his heightened position walls him in from the encroachments of intimacy. One who can impersonalize the afflictions of mankind cannot personalize on a man-to-man basis. A philosopher for the masses doesn't throw an arm around a crony. The omnipotent, omniscient guru isn't a pal, a chum, a buddy, or even a father.

Lee's son, Johnny, tried drugs, vegetarianism, kung fu, and a shot at being a Buddhist monk "always searching for some kind of comfort. Anything so I didn't have to live day to day." Johnny's lived in Canada and California. He's had psychiatry and Reichian therapy. He's been divorced and remarried. He's gone the whole route, there and back. For a while his memory was affected, "but it's better now. I have a straight head. Nobody could do anything to me anymore that could make me lose my head again."

For a time Susan moved away from her father. For a time she resisted studying with her father. Today they're close. She, too, teaches acting but not at her father's school. "I told them no. I can't deal with that. I prefer to fail or succeed on my own."

While his immediate family were removed, others could never creep close enough. In the winter of 1971, ten years after Marilyn Monroe's death, a moving van unloaded a wall of boxes and crates. After years of settling the estate, what was delivered at Lee Strasberg's apartment was the remnants of Marilyn Monroe's life —in cartons. She had bequeathed to him all her personal effects.

Books on poetry with underlined passages. A Golden Globe statuette, cracked, with the lead filling visible. Bone-color stationery embossed with "Marilyn Monroe." Unmailed letters dated '59, such as one instructing Dior her dress was to be "the simplest, most tailored, and least busy in line."

A whole room in the apartment was crammed with Marilyn's ordinary furniture. A gooseneck reading lamp with the paint chipped off. A plain wooden desk which now graces an anteroom adjoining the bathroom in Lee's New York Institute. Plastic dishes.

Stuffed into grocery cartons were black fur outfits, leopard hats, white mink muffs, ermine coats, double-skin white fox boas with silk between and piles of heavily beaded professional gowns with thick chains sewn completely around the inside of the hem so the weight was considerable. Such stage wardrobe as was worn at the Circus opening or at President Kennedy's birthday party bore the theatrical labels: "Marilyn Monroe from *Gentlemen Prefer Blondes*." In one box of her personal clothing a moth flew out.

Monroe had two of everything. One set for *the* Marilyn Monroe, the other for when she was herself. The theatrical makeup in a black case initialed M.M. held bright greens and blues for her eyes, not the kind of makeup worn at the supermarket. Although Marilyn denied she wore bras, she had two sets. For Marilyn Moviestar she wore decolleté special no-bra bras that looked like nothing. Her personal brassieres were the simplest and plainest and poorest, like a secretary's.

The offstage dresses went to thrift shops anonymously. The stage gowns met with a tragedy. A burst pipe spewed raw sewage onto them. A freak ending in the mode of the Golden Girl herself.

Marilyn and others of the faithful labeled their teacher a genius. Genius being that which nobody else can do, Lee feels the word best anoints those whose talent is sufficiently amazing as to be without training or preparation. Example: An eleven-year-old who can do calculus is a genius. An adult who sweats out solutions to problems and finds they come as a result of 90 per cent hard work is not. "Einstein wasn't a genius. I'm no genius. I merely apply what I've learned."

A source of pride are his books. British publisher Sir George Weidenfeld pronounced the collection the world's finest on the subject of theatre. Dealer Anna Sosenko values it at roughly half a million dollars. Sniffs Harold Clurman, "As long as they tell him a book is on theatre he takes it. He never reads half the stuff. He has books in Chinese and Japanese which he can't possibly read. It's a demonstration of how intellectual he is." Call it. Tell Lee it's partially ego on his part and, depending on his mood, he may agree amiably.

When the IRS threatened to disallow the deductions claimed for the purchase of these books, Lee's business manager, David Cogan, invited the agent to his apartment. Seeing books in the kitchen, the toilet, the clothes closets, the agent said, "Listen, I don't think you take off enough!"

When it comes to the really proper way to make a chocolate soda or what baseball player rapped into a double play in 1926, the Olympian wisdom is pocketed and he's like a kid. Dane Clark invited him to share a friend's box when the Giants were at the Polo Grounds. The entrance was at first base. The seats were opposite third base. In the minutes it took to trot around to their section, Lee bought a baseball cap with the "New York Giants" logo, three hotdogs, and a pennant.

Those who cast about desperately for some connecting link find he'll talk easily on simplistic subjects. Because she couldn't think of anything else, author Rona Jaffe had a long conversation about aluminum foil. "We discussed intellectually why Saran Wrap clings."

At a high-toned cocktail party for *Equus*, guests queued up for their turn to pump the Great Guru. He stood locked in an intense discussion. The gathering wondered what glittering nuggets were being panned. Mr. Strasberg was discoursing on the price of tomatoes.

Squinting back from the twilight of his life, he concedes he never dreamt he'd become important. When he began teaching there was no thought of personal gain. "Who imagined I'd become a star or anything like that? For years I've worked hard to get people to do what I found out I also can do. Now I have no intention of foregoing it. It's too easy."

The "new face" takes pains with himself. Years back he "went on the cholesterol thing" and lost ten pounds. Now if he puts on two he takes off the two. In *Cassandra Crossing* he portrayed a beggar with a beard and a beret. When the movie was released he adopted the same beret and precise style beard. When it bombed he quickly dumped the beard and stashed the beret.

Besides acting and teaching and contributing to periodicals and giving global seminars, he's writing several books on theatre. He plans to rectify the misunderstandings of the Method and "give the public an idea of what the hell all the shouting is about." He also has an itch to direct a modern production of Clifford Odets' play about Noah, *The Flowering Peach*.

About the only avenue he won't be drawn into is committing the Studio to commercial productions. "Lee was a failure at that," says Burgess Meredith. "He won't get into that again." "You can't push the idea of a Studio Theatre anymore. The time has passed him by," says Shelley Winters. "His limitations have constricted the Studio from doing what it should be doing. He's just not able," says Alan Schneider.

A big earner today who earns over a quarter of a million dollars yearly, he spends it. There are ways to make him immensely wealthy. Although its practical side is a few years away, technology exists to televise the Lee Strasberg lessons from one to 100 and disseminate them via cassettes piped through closed-circuit receivers mounted atop TV sets. The fee of one dollar per lesson could be charged to a subscriber's monthly bill. The projection was one million dollars per month. The stumbling block is the star himself. He's off in a million directions. You can't pin him down to the time needed for the filming. Sighs an associate, "He's too imprudent, too impractical, and too busy with other things. He's always off getting awards!"

Lee has several fears. Fear of heights. Fear of getting hit on the head. Fear of getting drawn to a subway platform edge. Fear of the dark as a kid. Fear of swimming. The ocean stirs him. He loves the sound of water "but I'm pulled in by it so I never get too close. It's inviting but I don't want to get involved."

Lee, however, seems without fears of death or age. His doctor

OPENING

...t this point it would be beneficial to down one straight ...tch or brandy daily for medicinal purposes. He doesn't do it. The landing gear on a plane to Boston jammed and thoughts of getting killed filled the cabin. He wasn't frightened. At such moments your life supposedly flashes in front of you. Not his. "I only wished I'd said good-bye when I left. I'm not big with these things. I still don't say good-byes. Somehow I know the experience taught me something but I don't know too much what."

His worries are for the family. "I die three times when Anna's sick, not just once." The new career, the new family, God's goodness toward him, which he views as exchange for many things that were not so good "always gives me a shaky feeling. Suddenly I always feel concern. I never know what can happen."

Twice Lee has experienced the thrill of an overwhelming Power. Standing on a plateau overlooking a village in Nazareth he "experienced a sense of Christ." Another time in the American desert he became aware of its sparseness. "With no people to interrupt, you could really feel nature. I felt I was alone with God."

At moments of peace and tranquillity the little man stands still and, in wonderment, ponders what hath Strasberg wrought. The now famous word "Method" was coined by outsiders. It came into being when its work became known through the movies made by those who became stars through it. Its center was Stanislavsky. Its circumference was Strasberg. Its practitioners referred to it loosely as "Stanislavsky's idea." Its watchers captioned it with the word "The" to differentiate between just any method and THE Method as taught in the Actors Studio. Today what is known internationally is not Stanislavsky but The Method. When Peking took a potshot at Stanislavsky a while back, the headline out of the Far East read: "Chinese criticize The Method"!

Nonetheless, there is little enjoyment directly derived from the position he occupies. The top is "scary and shaky. My major contribution toward my own enjoyment now is what I can do to help other people to do. Unfortunately that activity has become tougher. I don't have the equanimity as in the past."

Actress Shirley Knight is one who worries that the sands of time have run out. She tortures herself that once he wanted something from her and she didn't give it. "I was selfish. I had an opportunity to put him first and pay him back for the security I owe him as an actress and I didn't do it." She wrote him. She begged his forgiveness. She received no reply. She expected none. "It's just that he's getting old and I don't want to suddenly discover he's dead and I haven't said, 'Thank you.'"

For a man who had so little Lee Strasberg has grown so big.

BOOK ONE

"CHAIA"

CHAPTER ONE

Budzanow

Israel Strassberg was the baby of the family. Bluma, the eldest, was the only girl, followed by Anshel, Zalmon, and another boy who didn't survive. Baby Srulke—the diminutive of the name Israel—was born November 17, 1901, in a clay house with a thatched roof and a dirt floor in the Jewish quarter of Budzanow, Poland.

When the midwife was tying a bellyband around Srulke and wrapping him from head to toe according to custom, Poland belonged to Austria and the province of Galicia was part of the Austro-Hungarian empire. Today that valley at the foot of the Carpathian Mountains lies somewhere in Russia. The tiny village can no longer be located on any map but a line straight down from Lvov along the Seret River to Romania should find it.

Because turn-of-the-century Budzanow teetered on the border of Russia, the Austrian army paraded their noblemen and cavalry once a year. Actual military maneuvers took place somewhere on the mountains and then, with the Carpathians rising straight up along the sides like fortresses, the uniformed horsemen galloped down the valley and full speed through the village. This exercise didn't end up doing anything for Austria or Poland but it did something for a small boy. He never forgot it.

He also never forgot his breakfast. "Uncle Feter Hersh lived next door and every morning I went in to him and he made me hot freshly brewed tea with milk on his little spirit stove. And Uncle Feter Hersh had a real cellar, a big cellar where he kept huge barrels of delicious sour pickles. Pickled apples that were green and mouth-watering he also had. They stood there in that cold cellar the whole winter. At the end of the day I would come by and get my pickle and bring it home. But . . . oh . . . those breakfasts. Hot freshly brewed tea from Uncle Hersh's spirit stove plus black bread and butter is something so delicious I can still smell it."

The spirit stove had given way to the hot-water spigot on the office watercooler and the freshly brewed essence was a teabag with a limp string dangling down the side, but he still had both hands wrapped around a glass of tea as he relived memories of three quarters of a century ago.

"Across the street from us was a garden and on the edge grew scallions. When they were ripe I simply went by and pulled them up. My brother used to tell me, 'Go to Uncle Hersh and ask him for the tea a piece of sugar.' This with the pickle with the scallion was my dinner. Oh, it was so good. Also rose-petal jam I had. In our village the main food was rose-petal jam. It cooked in huge copper kettles the size of caldrons. We would have meat maybe twice a week. Also we would have chicken sometimes. My mother spoiled me. Once when I was sick she got me *tybeloch*, and to taste that pigeon it was worth having a cold."

Mama and Papa Strassberg were hard-working, pious Jews. In an even smaller, more rural *shtetl* outside Budzanow, Baruch Meier Strassberg had an inn where travelers could enjoy a meal and stay overnight. A deeply religious man, he always found time despite long hours to walk to the synagogue daily and *daven*. As he thus prayed one morning, he looked out and spied this beautiful girl in the field. Baruch Meier Strassberg immediately informed the *shadchen* or marriage arranger that Chaia Diner—petite, five feet one, chestnut hair—was the girl he wanted.

When Baruch's father died, the couple inherited his simple house in Budzanow. In back of the house but within walking distance was the synagogue. In front of the house lay a ditch which caught the water during heavy rains or snows and ran through the whole town to the lake. In heavy rains Baruch and Chaia brought the garbage from their outhouse to the ditch. On the other side of this stood a tremendous courthouse extending half a block and featuring a stone bench in front and the garden with the scallions behind. With Russia crowding one border and Austria the other, the language of the courthouse was Polish, Lithuanian, and German, while most of its petitioners spoke Yiddish.

Along the side of the house ran an alley inhabited by a widower who was a distant relative. Across the alley the street continued with more little houses reaching to the square, a walk of about five minutes. Including the shops and marketplace in the square, this whole section constituted the Jewish quarter. Only the drugstore on the Strassbergs' corner was "Gentile." Others who shared that time and place recall "there was no Jewish drugstore" and this owner "was a tall man and when we entered there we somehow felt we were in a holy place."

Their little house was near the Seret River. On the opposite bank across the bridge lay Gentile Budzanow. The family had many relatives, because when you were born there you lived there and you died there. Rarely did anyone make a move to go anywhere else. With what? To what? Uncle Shloimy lived near the bridge and Lee retains a feeling that something happened in that river because as far back as he can remember he's always been afraid to swim.

The Strassberg house was the end of the Jewish ghetto in a row of identical houses straight down to the well at the end of the block. The well was sweet water and couldn't be used for cooking. Its wheel creaking is a sound he hears still.

They were the last of the poor houses. Abutting them with a wall for separation was a house of wealth. The back of their toilet was right up against it, directly on the other side. This magnificent estate with giant sunflowers which in season grew so tall they hung over the wall and with a street that was treelined and shaded belonged to the Pototzkys who owned much of Poland.

"The Pototzkys had a bright red car. This was about 1906. On a Friday night before the sabbath, Count Pototzky drove it straight into the square then up around our synagogue. It was the first car I ever saw."

One side of the street leading up from the square led to the mountain dominated by a fortresslike cloister. Budzanow's Christian community was powerful. On Gentile carnival nights little ones in the Jewish quarter lay awake listening to the Christians getting drunk and celebrating until morning. It was a trying time for the Jews. They never knew what to expect.

They were particularly fearful of the peasants. The main road leading down from the mountainside and in from the countryside ran in front of the Strassberg house. When the peasants massed in that neighborhood and marched into town behind the priests holding their icons aloft, it was frightening for a Jewish boy. He took his life in his hands if he was outdoors. "You couldn't stand and watch from outside. You'd get killed. They'd kick you off your own streets. I was not only off the street, my mother kept me deep in the house. I peeked out through the windows in the attic.

"Soldiers riding through on military maneuvers we were never concerned with, but the Christians we were. That's why it took me years before I ever entered a church. I was in my late forties before I stepped foot in one and then only to hear the Matthew Passion in the Cathedral of St. John The Divine. In my youth a church was what you spit at when you went by. Me, I didn't ever spit because I didn't have that in me . . . but fear, yes."

Little Israel Strassberg whom everyone called Srulke was nearly killed by a wild runaway horse when he was a year old. The streets were dark. Passersby walked with lanterns. Parked by Papa outside a store in the marketplace his perambulator was in the direct path. The horse kicked him in the head; he still carries a scar. An old lady pulled him out of the way before the horse stampeded him again. "My only real memory of this is a great fear of getting hit on the head." He was critically ill for months, and his life was saved by a doctor named Shteckel who, being Jewish, lived in their ghetto.

The Strassberg house was at street level. Dug deep into the ground and accessible from the vestibule was their storage hole, called a *kama*. In summer a block of ice was shoved in occasionally, but ice cost money, and they were poor, and anyway, the hole stayed cool. In preparation for winter, foods were stocked away and anyone needing stores pushed aside the cover and lowered himself by means of a ladder. Another pantry was the attic. In advance of Passover, the traditional Pesach matzos baked in oversize squares were suspended in the attic inside a hanging bedsheet. So that Bluma or Anshel or Zalmon or Srulke couldn't hit the matzos before Pesach began, the stepladder to the attic was taken away.

The vestibule opened onto the one large room. The children slept in two beds and against the opposite wall stood the stove and bake oven which reached from floor to ceiling. Part of the children's chores was to chop wood for that unit, which was the focal point of the house. In fact, it was the central point of all life. The fire which came from below greatly warmed the entire cement wall and the clay top of the oven itself, a ledge twice as wide as a piano, could house two small, huddled bodies. With the help of a stool, Srulke and his brothers Anshel or Zalmon scrambled to this top, because throughout the night, long after the oven was shut down, the embers of the dying fire warmed a little child's bones.

In Yiddish this sleeping area is called a *pekalik*. "Except for those nights when Mama closed the chimney to retain the heat and the bad air backed up and we got headaches," a mattress consisting of a sheet over a layer of straw on top of a pekalik and a fat quilt or *pookh* of fine goosefeathers such as immigrants carried into the new world from the old country, makes the best sleeping arrangements in the world for a five-year-old boy in Russian-Poland.

On the other side of the bake oven lived Uncle Feter Hersh, but the wall between was thicker than cement. Feter Hersh, who was addicted to long, curled-up Meerschaum pipes that grazed the floor when he sat, was not really an uncle. He wasn't even a close relative. Nobody knows how he came to be "uncle." Nonetheless, he and "Aunt" Mimi Scheindel lived in the same house, but the connecting door was in fact the only connection between the adjoining apartments. For reasons long buried in protagonists long gone, there was absolutely no communication. Baruch Meier and Chaia Diner didn't speak to Feter Hersh and Mimi Scheindel. The door which led to them was right next to the stove "and I alone went through it. I was the only one who spoke to them."

Uncle Hersh was a merchant and he had no children. Friday being Market Day, every Thursday "a *minyan* of kids" including Srulke helped pull the wagon, loaded with whatever Uncle Hersh had collected that week, into the marketplace. Uncle Hersh was also a *melamed*, a religious teacher. He taught around his kitchen table, around his *only* table, every morning. The classes were in Yiddish. The textbook was the Torah. The pupils were aged four and five. "The Gentiles had real teachers and real schools, but for us a melamed was the only kind of teacher we had there." Everyone got up very early. So, having finished his morning prayers, Srulke picked up a kerosene lamp and in the dark slipped through the door for his breakfast tea and his lessons.

Papa Strassberg was a deeply devoted member of the Jewish community. Come Friday night shabbas services and high holy days Papa performed the cantorial songs with so beautiful a voice that he moved the faithful to tears. Not only did Papa sing but he officiated. A *baltvilla*, a term of respect meaning the head of the community, and a *boltkorah*, signifying one who represents this community before God, Baruch Meier Strassberg was given the honor of beginning the prayers and ending the prayers and being designated an official reader of the Torah.

Papa Strassberg let himself go only at the time of Purim during which even religious people permitted themselves. This merrymaking festival joyously celebrated in societies where anti-Semitism prevails is characterized by feasting and hilarity. Relatives claim serious Papa Strassberg would play-act at these times. "Once he went to the bedroom to make believe he was delivering a baby. We heard infant gurgling sounds and everybody laughed. At Purim, Papa Strassberg showed he had the spark of an amateur actor."

If Purim was a high spot, the rest of the year was bleak. Life was hard. With his only brother, David Solomon, Papa Strassberg had inherited his father's stonecutting business. Every day Papa Strassberg walked three miles straight up the mountain to his quarry and back. Large stones were sold for sidewalks. Smaller slabs were chopped into twelve-inch oblongs, ground flat, then pointed at one end and sold for sharpening stones.

Stonecutting could barely support him let alone his brother's family. After much conversation and much praying, Papa consented to join his cousins who had made the decision to try their fortunes in the New World. His two eldest, Bluma and Anshel, followed. Mama and her babies, Zalmon and Srulke, settled down to wait.

Except for one friend who spoke only Polish, a language he didn't understand, and one little girl with whom he played in a barn, Israel Srulke Strassberg had only his brother, Zalmon, and the two were inseparable. Together they ogled the gypsies. The gypsies were always being arrested and hauled into the courthouse and we "would watch them do their toilet things in the ditch in front of us." Together they played at the river and gaped as the summer sky turned into a flaming ball of fire. Roofing for the poorer houses was compressed and compacted straw, and somebody must have lit a match someplace because they "watched the cinders fall from those flaming rooftops." Together they snuggled into the pookh on the pekalik on the bake oven and listened to the wedding music of the Jewish musicians who were imported from big cities for such events and marched through the Jewish area playing the *doyna*, the Romanian flute.

Meanwhile in the Golden Land, Papa and Bluma and Anshel lived with *landsleit*—friends and cousins—as boarders and Papa sent home to Mama half his earnings, eight dollars a week. To hasten the day that they, too, could join Papa in his fourth floor walkup in this Land of Opportunity, Mama chaperoned dances Saturday nights. After the sabbath service young boys and girls flocked to Mama's house and paid ten cents a person to dance Strauss waltzes "particularly with Zalmon because he was a good dancer" and sing Viennese songs. Socially this Junior Club was a success. Financially it was a necessity.

It took four years, but with the little Papa could send from the new world and the little Mama could earn in the old country, the day came for Mama and Zalmon and Srulke. From thousands of miles away Papa wrote to settle the differences with Uncle Feter Hersh who wanted the house and Mama who wanted him not to have the house. This was resolved, and Uncle Hersh fell heir to the ancestral real estate.

It was an exciting time for a little boy. On the eve of departure the baby was given a present, a black raincoat. "I put it on and I paraded up and down in front of the house. I was so excited. Mama and Zalmon and I had tickets from America! I wasn't concerned with missing my friends from the old country because I didn't have so many friends and I was going to join my family whom I almost couldn't even remember."

Saturday after the sabbath they left, traveling all night up over the mountainside by carriage. With the cold wind in his face, he fell asleep. In the morning there was the train to Hamburg where they were to catch the steamer. All immigrants were billeted in certain houses near the port. "We took a walk near the dock and never did we see such cleanliness. I couldn't get over the shock of seeing those clean German streets."

It was a bright August day when they steamed out of Hamburg. The German Lines ship was packed with immigrants. They, naturally, were in steerage. Zalmon and he didn't get out of their beds the whole eight days. "We didn't feel so well. We would lie in bed and call *metross* which means 'sailor,' and the one on duty would get us coffeecake."

It was another sunny day when the S.S. *Amerika* steamed into Ellis Island. However, clouds soon blackened the horizon. Authorities refused to admit the newest arrival, Israel Strassberg—despite his eager shining face and his new black raincoat. The doctors chalked a big yellow "X" on his new black raincoat. They pronounced him diseased. They diagnosed him as a case of trachoma. It was somehow explained that he didn't have this disease but that he'd always had one weak eye since birth and that he was otherwise perfectly healthy. Still, the authorities detained him.

Finally . . . finally . . . they allowed Israel Strassberg, aged seven, to step into his destiny.

CHAPTER TWO

Clinton Street

Home was 40 Clinton Street, two flights up over a millinery store. From nearby Stanton to Attorney Street a few blocks east, the Lower East Side of New York was predominantly Polish. Even in 1909 the Strassberg name evoked controversy. The newest émigrés were considered a little bit Russian, a little bit Hungarian but "more like Austrian." Papa and Mama used to say, "But we're not Austrian. We're from Galicia. We're Galicians." Yes, nodded the pure-bred Polish, you're Austrian.

It was a neighborhood of pious European Jews—women with babushkas, men with beards. The pleasantries were not "hello" or "good-bye" but on holidays "good yuntiff" and on Fridays "good shabbas." Yiddish bookstores flanked Number 40 Clinton—one alongside the stone stoop and another across the street. Close by on Delancey Street were the all-day, all-night pushcarts of fruits and vegetables. When the young boy with the strong taste for scallions and pickles ate his first tomato off a pushcart, he "spit it out right on the street. It had no taste. I also ate my first banana off a pushcart. The banana I also spit out."

The walkup was shared by Baruch Meier Strassberg, his wife

Chaia Diner, their children, Bluma, twenty-one, Anshel, eighteen, Zalmon, fourteen, and Israel, eight, plus two lady boarders and assorted cockroaches. "Mama was heroic when she saw cockroaches. She sprayed the corners to get rid of them and I shuddered when she'd stomp one to death with her foot. I was so squeamish about cockroaches."

After 10 P.M. the hall lights were turned off on alternate floors. Their floor was pitch black. As the youngest, whenever anybody wanted a piece of fruit or a slice of bread, Israel was the one delegated. "Going to the store at night I didn't mind, but I was fearful of that dark hall. Somebody would always have to walk me down.

"I had an intense fear also of Chinatown. I tried hard to walk *around* that area and avoid those streets totally, but if I had to go there my body was pulled tight, my teeth clenched and my eyes darted nervously, expecting something murky and mysterious to leap out of every corner."

Including the boarders, they numbered eight persons in two bedrooms with no bathroom. There was one toilet in the outside hall for each two families and four families to every floor. This was a step up, since most toilet facilities were down in the yard. For the Saturday night specials which in those days meant the once-a-week bath there was a public bathhouse on Allen and Rivington. "At home we only had the washtub in the kitchen. Next to the regular sink stood this washtub that was used for pots and pans and clothes—and us."

Papa was a pants presser. He rose at five to be in the shop by seven. He couldn't even read a newspaper at work. There was no time. He worked from seven until seven and rarely saw daylight. This was the quintessential sweatshop. Papa Strassberg worked in his underwear shirt.

Israel Strassberg enrolled in the public school which went up to 4B, on nearby Attorney Street. Mama took him personally by the hand on registration day. The problem was starting a year late. The kid from Budzanow was eight. His fellow pupils were seven. The first day of school can normally be traumatic, but this was the first day in a new school in a new country. He had neither friends nor guidelines. His brothers had learned to read and write Polish and a little German from tutors in the old country. Structured formal education was a first for them all. Add to that, the American school system functioned only in English. The new student communicated only in Yiddish. It was the language of his house.

An ardent youngster, he wanted to learn and he applied himself. Despite having to learn English concurrently with all the other subjects being taught to him in English, he experienced no difficulty. In fact, he soon excelled in English. In P.S. 160 on Rivington Street which ran from 4B to 8B he even won a prize, a set of Edgar Allan Poe's works done in imitation red leather with fancy gilt lettering. He won a second prize for penmanship.

Although he was far above average in several subjects such as history—colorful, dramatic events and their reasons for happening interested him—he was a good, bright student who maintained straight A's in everything. The authorities skipped the little boy two classes, which brought him to the proper age level of the others. In addition they made him a monitor.

One morning the snappy, straightforward principal called on his teacher. "May I have the books with everyone's names in it so that I might make a list of promotions of those in your class?"

Poor Mr. Barrett suffered severe myopia. He could not see well and he peered around wildly for his monitor, who was off just then collecting money for a Jewish charity for Flag Day. ("I'd walk around shaking the 'pushky' and everybody would drop coins in it.") Unable to focus on the one face for which he was searching, he apologized, "Our class books which list each pupil's marks are kept by our monitor, Israel Strassberg, and he seems not to be here at the moment."

"So," crackled the principal, "even if you can't locate Israel Strassberg, can you not locate the books?"

"No," squinted Mr. Barrett. "He's in charge of all that and unless we find him we can't find the books." The whole academic process—promotions, grades, report cards, everything—ground to a halt while another pupil was sent running for Master Strassberg.

So busy was he doing his monitoring chores and keeping the records that he had no time to study or concentrate on little things like homework. "If anybody had given me a written test at that time I doubt that I even could have passed it!"

He was never too busy, however, to be without a book. Books he gobbled up even at mealtimes. Frank Merriwell books on sports heroes, Horatio Alger stories and those Nick Carter mysteries he bought on pushcarts then exchanged when he finished them, he read while standing, while eating. There were always boarders and how large could a kitchen table be? "Since there was never any room for me, as a kid I would eat and read my books and at the same time walk around the living room. I grew up reading and standing up at mealtimes, a habit I have still."

Friday night was a typical Jewish dinner complete with the shabbas licht, the shabbas candles. Of course Mama didn't cook on the sabbath. Everything was prepared in advance. Like other Orthodox Jews from Europe, Mama prepared *cholent* the day before. This was the Saturday meal which all the women brought Friday to the neighborhood bakery to cook overnight, a good twelve hours. Saturday on the way home from shul they picked it up. An amalgam of meat, beans, potatoes, dumplings, gravy, and anything else available all thrown together, cholent is a one-pot meal which is delicious, filling, and fatty. Very fatty. And very heavy. Others who were weaned on it crack, "Just to be able to eat it is a test of strength!" Following the morning prayers, one o'clock was the big time for the big meal. The menu was unvarying: chopped egg with radish, cholent, and a glass of tea "with sugar to bite."

Shabbas or not there was still never any room at the table, so cholent or not, Israel Strassberg walked around—one hand holding the fork, the other the plate and the book—eating and reading.

The school was nearby and he never had pocket money, so he came home for lunch. He was always home on time. He was a good boy. After school hours he went to *cheder*, instruction in the Jewish religion. He doesn't remember a family tale about being lost in the subway but concedes, "I have a recurring dream about getting lost, so this fear must be from some long-buried experience." He does, however, remember passing a moviehouse on the way home from cheder one early evening. Admission was two people for a nickel. "We'd stand outside hawking, 'Who's got two cents? . . . Who's got three cents? . . .'"

So enthralled was this little boy with what was unfolding that all alone he sat through the biblical epic twice. It was 9 P.M. when he arrived home. One of their boarders, a "very special, highly intelligent lady," tore out of the bedroom she shared with Bluma and the other lady boarder. "Where were you?" she demanded.

"Where's Mama?" asked the culprit, peering around the empty apartment.

"Out looking for you," she retorted sharply. "Everybody's out looking for you. I'm the only one here."

Shortly afterward his mother ran in. She didn't hug her son in relief. She didn't kiss him. Mama wasn't that kind. "Everybody is searching all over for you," she panted in rapid Yiddish while untying her babushka. "They've gone to the police and everything." As long as he was alive and unharmed, Mama wasn't interested in explanations. "Get right into bed. Geh . . . geh . . . (go . . . go . . .)", she commanded pointing to his cot in the kitchen. Her son had plopped onto a bed in the "front room" and was stuffing bread into his mouth because he hadn't eaten. "*Yetzt!*" thundered Mama. "Now!"

"*Fa vuss*, Mama . . . Why, Mama?" he asked, getting up quickly.

"Because," said Mama, pulling off his sweater, "if you don't get into bed and act like you're asleep and like you've already been home for a long time, your father will hit you as soon as he sees you. Quick . . . into the bed."

Maybe Papa would like to have been a pal and would like to have been close with his children but he toiled long hours. His only outside activities were for the shul. He was still a baltkorah and a baltvilla and a part-time chazen or cantor. He wanted to know things about his children but there was no time and no strength for such matters after a long day. He felt completely exhausted. Whatever small reserve was left he poured into religious activities.

The fact is the baby of the family was not close to him. In Budzanow he never knew him. At a tender age they'd been separated and he hadn't seen his father in four years. He didn't remember him before America. "I practically didn't even know my father.

"My mother I was a little bit close to. I was my mother's boy in the sense that I was the youngest and the three of us—Zalmon, Mama, and I—grew up together. When we came here my connection and my communication was with my mother."

Chaia Diner Strassberg was a good woman, a deeply religious

woman. She was not, however, a demonstrative one. Mama Strassberg did not adore her husband. He was widely read in terms of Yiddishkeit if not in English, but she made reference to him as a fool. She never showed affection to her husband and, in fact, thwarted whatever warmth he may have had.

Mama was strong and Mama was cold. None of her children basked in any close relationship with her. There was never touching or cuddling by Mama to any of them.

Nobody in the family was demonstrative. Certainly neither parent showed overt love. Papa didn't have the time. Mama didn't have the nature. "My father least of all where I was concerned," says Lee, "and my mother only a very little bit but even then not."

Those formative, growing-up years were characterized by a lack of visible affection. There was no hugging or loving or touching flowing from or to any of them, not from parent to parent nor parent to child nor child to parent. Not much even from child to child.

Bluma, the eldest and one of the earliest to arrive in America, was dug into her world. While baby Srulke was still communicating only in Yiddish, her name had already been anglicized to Becky. When he was discovering the world of books, she, who never opened a book, was dating. Their worlds were apart and before either could build a bridge to the other Becky moved out. Short, plump, with chestnut hair and a pretty face, Becky was married in 1912 when she was twenty-four and the baby brother was eleven. After being separated from her mother for those early years, Becky, who was in the needle trade, left Mama's house a couple of years after Mama arrived. There was never to be any closeness between Mama and Becky.

Anshel, whose name had been anglicized to Arthur, was putting himself through college by laboring in an alligator handbag factory whose standards were so elevated that the boss earned only eighteen dollars a week. "The skins were so thick that you couldn't work the needle through until you soaked them in hot water."

The baby's closeness was to Zalmon, who was nearest him in age and had been together with him in Budzanow. He had always turned for companionship to Zalmon since each was all the other had in those years. The relationship continued. Sensitive, emotionally and spiritually the closest to the little boy, Zalmon was possibly the most intellectual of them all. Bookish and slight of build, he was gearing up to be a writer.

Zalmon was interested in Yiddish culture. He attended the first Jewish seminar organized in New York. It was held on East Broadway with Zalmon one of its earliest and most brilliant students. The younger brother followed his older brother's deep interest in Yiddish literature. At ten, Israel Strassberg was enrolled in a Yiddish school. This, the first secular Jewish school in America, was the Jewish National Radical School on the Lower East Side. The curriculum was in Yiddish. Its second language was Hebrew. Organized by Pola Zion, the Workers of Zion (which later became Israel's ruling Labor Party), two-hour classes were held Saturdays and Sundays. Orthodox Papa came down to satisfy himself that they didn't write on shabbas. Tuition was ten cents per session. Israel Strassberg at age fourteen was in the second graduating class.

"Unfortunately, one of my teachers, Chaim Leiberman, was unhappy with me because I always came in sweaty. I loved playing stickball, but since balls cost money we played with a ball made of stockings. He resented my presence because my appearance was definitely not intellectual-looking enough for him."

He played in all kinds of weather. There was the summer day his friend, Malamud, fetched him at home for a practice session in the park nearby. Absorbed in their stocking ball, they didn't notice the park was absolutely empty. Not one other soul was there. When they dragged home hours later drenched in perspiration, they were deposited hastily in the kitchen washtub. It was then they learned this had been an all-time scorcher—the hottest day on record.

The stickball expert's position was behind the batter not because he wanted it but because nobody else wanted it. "I also didn't want it, but I did it. I just put my mitt out." One time he put his stick out as well and succeeded in smashing a glass on a streetcar. "I ran around the block and hid for hours for fear they'd find out I did it."

Another area of expertise was dice. He could palm them and shake them without actually moving or displacing the dice. His talent was such that he could regularly deliver the number he wanted. But came the day he lost a few pennies and Mama wrenched the dice away from him and threw them out. "My mother interrupted a terrific career I could have had as a gambler."

Lee's senses appear more heightened than the average person's. The sharpness of a memory which dredges up vivid colorful details of a lifetime ago, he shrugs off with, "It's nothing special." Recently he was in a record shop. A 1904 cantorial by the famed cantor Sirota was put on the turntable. At the opening bars of this old Hebrew chant Lee exclaimed, "My God, that's the very first thing I ever heard on a phonograph in Budzanow! A lawyer near us had a machine and I heard this from outside his window in 1908! From memory I can sing the whole chant." In this record shop in Manhattan the man from Budzanow sang the passages of the ancient Hebrew cantorial he had heard seventy years ago.

Similarly this supersensory memory has a large vault someplace where it stores pain. Unpleasant events of days long gone wound as much today as when they originally happened. He remembers them in searing detail. The pain is such that he tries not to discuss these incidents—even six or seven decades later.

When queried about one happening which occurred when he was thirteen and running an errand for his adored Zalmon, he replied in a barely audible voice, "I don't like to discuss it. I hate even now to think about it. It was the worst experience I ever had.

"It was," as he related it hurriedly and emotionally, "Passover eve. Zalmon wanted a suit cleaned so he gave it to me to bring to the cleaner. The cleaner was a half a block away on the opposite side of the street. I went there and they were too busy. I didn't know what to do. A heavy, roly-poly man standing there on the street saw my consternation. He said to me, 'You looking for a cleaner?' I said, 'Yes, I am. I want to get this cleaned and pressed.' He said, 'I know the place. I can have this done for you.'

"He took me around the back to Stanton Street. He explained the key to the store was upstairs on the third floor and told me where to find it and said that since I was a young boy and he was an older man he'd wait downstairs for me and I should go up for the key. I gave him Zalmon's suit rather than *shlep* it.

"It seems silly that I could do something like that but I was eager to do this for my brother and I thought I was doing something good. So I deposited the suit with him and I started up the steps. I didn't even get to the third floor. When I reached the second landing it came into my head what I was doing. I ran downstairs and the man was gone.

"This was a loss of something so terrible that I can't even think of it now sixty-five years later. Years and years after that I bought a cashmere coat and I lost it in the library. I didn't like to lose it but so what? I got home and I bought myself another coat. But this was different. Who could afford to lose something so valuable in those days? Oh, it was a terrible experience."

As he recounted this Lee stared vacantly into space and beads of sweat formed on his forehead. He passed his hand over his forehead repeatedly as though to erase the pain. Then he dropped the subject abruptly.

CHAPTER THREE

Townsend Harris

Max Lippa was a steady visitor to the Strassbergs during the years he courted their daughter Becky. By day Max traveled around buying and peddling old gold. Nights and weekends he indulged his passion for the theatre. His hobby was theatrical makeup. A member of the Verband, a Jewish organization which put on one show—usually a historical tableau—annually as part of a fund-raising activity, Max's contribution was to transform the members into European characters such as "Hassidim", religious scholars, characterized by beards and "payess" or sideburns.

In addition, Max, his brother, and his brother's wife were active in the Progressive Dramatic Club. This nonprofessional group was part of a modernistic, avant-garde theatre movement taking place throughout the world. Their standards were high. They performed fine works from the classic European repertoire and it was this Progressive Dramatic Club which ultimately led to the Jewish Art Theatre.

In a clubhouse off Second Avenue the group met evenings. One dinnertime—which is when Max usually planned his visits—he announced to Becky, "The club's next production is *Glicken Vinckle.*"

"'Happiness in a Corner,'" translated Becky. "So where are you going to hold it?"

"We already have a place on Orchard Street where we're going to hold it every weekend for six weekends."

"Is it all cast so far?"

"Except for the part of a little boy who can handle himself and who can speak a good Yiddish."

"You mean you can't find a kid in this neighborhood who can speak a good Yiddish?" asked Becky.

"No," sighed Max helping himself to a second spoonful of *tzimmis,* a carrot and prune concoction sweetened with honey.

A skinny arm brushed past Max headed toward the same bowl. Max looked up. Becky looked up. When the hand with the spoon with the tzimmis retracted and its silent owner walked away eating and reading, two pairs of eyes stared at him. After a beat, both pairs of eyes turned back and locked on each other. "Nu? . . . well . . . ?" queried Max quietly. "What do you think?"

"I don't know," shrugged Becky.

"Listen, that kid's always got his head in the books. Maybe this is what he needs. Maybe he should get away a little bit from the books."

"So, okay, give it a try. I mean, why not?"

Max prevailed upon his about-to-be kid brother-in-law to sit down. "My club is doing a play. In it there's a part for a boy like around fourteen. You're a little small but I think that's OK. Look, one of the boy's lines goes, 'What Fritz can do I can do anytime.' Say this to me in Yiddish."

Israel Strassberg repeated in perfect Yiddish, "*Vuss Fritz ken tun ich ken tun allamul.*"

"Come with me," said Max, grabbing the kid by the hand and slamming the door.

Mama's son the actor had a pleasant debut. He enjoyed the reaction. Playing with a professional and the professional's two brothers, it was little Israel who got the laughs.

Three years later at the Neighborhood Playhouse which was beginning to achieve a heightened status in terms of modern theatre, Jacob Ben-Ami, a young, upcoming actor, did a special perform-

ance of three one-act plays by the Yiddish artist and playwright
I. L. Peretz. Again, the little boy was asked to play a part.

When the Jewish National Radical School planned to immor-
talize the festival of Purim, it was a bantam weight with a white
face and weak eye who was selected for the role of Queen Esther's
heroic foster father, Mordecai. Beyond helping the school partici-
pate in a religious play, to honor student Strassberg the experience
meant nothing. It wasn't leading to anything and he had no great
interest in it. Nonetheless, the performance stirred a mini contretemps. His teacher praised him and told him how good his acting
was. Another teacher berated the first one cautioning, "That's bad
for the boy. He mustn't be told how good he is."

The argument amused the little boy. He was not a theatrical
type and couldn't understand the concern. To him the whole
event was nothing meaningful and didn't matter much one way or
another.

The next occasion was for Max's Progressive Dramatic Club
which had now flowered to where its yearly performance was held
in a regular theatre, the Liptzin. In a play by Hermann Suder-
mann, he was to play the brother of a woman who had an affair
with a man outside her class. The action called for him to light a
lamp and set the mood for a romantic moment. They rehearsed in
a room without props.

The Sunday night of the actual performance, he walked center
stage to the table but never had he seen such an old-fashioned
hurricane lantern with a chimney open at the top. He lit the
match and stuck his hand deep into the opening. The chimney
created a vacuum and the fire flared. The whole thing blew up
and his hand was scorched.

Frozen in shock, the little boy blacked out. There's no memory
of what transpired afterward. He was not motivated toward a theatrical career, but had things gone well, and had it continued, who
knows . . . he might have remained to become a star in the Yiddish Theatre. As it happened he became nervous and gun shy
about stepping onto a stage again. Whatever pleasurable aspects
he'd associated with the theatre were killed that very night at the
Liptzin on the Bowery.

The Lower East Side was in foment. Culturally, socially, and politically the district was churning. Yiddish dominated the area.

There were forty bookstores devoted to the language and six cultural clubs including the Yiddish Cultural Alliance of which big brother Arthur was the prime mover.

Arthur's organization was special because they had a library. Actually they had a bookcase. Actually they had a few shelves. The father of one of the members owned a restaurant and donated space off to a side. The people came and browsed and borrowed from the little stock as though it were a bona fide library. "Even Papa was serious for knowledge. He would come and pick out heavy subjects in Yiddish. We were all searchers," explains Arthur.

To some, Yiddish was the language of the Jews. To others, Hebrew. Into this arena charged philosopher Chaim Chitlowsky, one of the outstanding theoreticians of the Jewish national movement. Dr. Chitlowsky's thrust was the primacy of Yiddish as the language of the Chosen People. Chitlowsky came from outside Jewish environs. In the forefront of the revolutionary movement, he was a leader of the dominant revolutionary party in Russia, the party of the peasants. Designated official speaker of the Russian Social Revolutionary Party, it was he who debated the Bolsheviks in Zurich with Lenin in 1904 in that famous discussion on polemics. Chitlowsky was not a Marxist. He was not a Communist. He was a Socialist.

Early on in Russia, Chitlowsky, believing that each group within the state deserved what is called cultural autonomy, had become imbued with Yiddish as a primal language and with the theory that world Jewry must speak, read, and write Yiddish literature. Arriving in America to collect money for the revolution, he discovered this seething mass of Yiddishkeit on the Lower East Side. In tandem with the political revolution he remained to propagandize his cultural revolution.

In 1909 Dr. Chitlowsky settled in the Jewish community to publish a monthly magazine. His dedication to the history of the Jews, his concepts on their cultural and social future, and his ideas on the secular movement of Yiddishkeit brought him into the auditorium of the Jewish National Radical School in which Israel Strassberg was already registered.

The organizer of the Yiddish secular section of the East Side had decided his little brother should receive this exposure and personally escorted the brand new pupil to Chitlowsky's lectures. Arthur had become involved with Chitlowsky and was deeply influenced by him. They knew each other as intimates. They visited each other's home.

Israel Strassberg also drank at the fountain of guest lecturer Chitlowsky. He read his articles, discussed his stratagems, and took his first halting footsteps into the world of Lenin and Marx. With both his brothers intellectuals, he, too, was socially aware. In his early days he was influenced by philosophical ideas. He grew up in the Socialist environment, in a district that was the hotbed of the movement. Even the youngsters electioneered. Says he of this period, "I was busy doing what everybody else was doing which was following Jacob Pankin from place to place trying to get him elected judge."

His district also elected the first Socialist to Congress, Meyer London. "When our new congressman attended my public school graduation it was a big thing for us and everybody asked for autographs. He signed a few. Maybe a half dozen got his real autograph. The rest got my forgery. See, I was very good at forging. I signed all the graduation autograph books and distributed them later. Most people who saved Congressman London's autograph as a historic memory of that graduation have *my* signature!"

In high school the teen-age boy learned he needed glasses. Upon enrollment he was examined and the bad eye from birth tested. Told he couldn't return to school until he had glasses, he purchased his first pair on East Broadway for one dollar cash.

This complete physical examination with nurses in attendance was the first he ever had. "They made me get undressed. How should I know the nurse would still be there after I took my clothes off? That was a great shock to me standing there naked!"

In class he sat next to a big toughie with a mug face who beat everybody up. Lee helped the toughie with his homework and in turn he called his pal, "Brains." They were "Bully" and "Brains." "Bully" became very protective of his seatmate. When Mr. Robowski, the teacher, sent "Brains" out for hotdogs, "Bully" went right along with him. From then on nobody could touch the small-sized Strassberg.

In high school he developed a taste for Egyptology. He read *The Empires of the East* on Egypt and Babylonia. Since his earliest friends were books, he spent hours soaking up works on archaeology. "In our neighborhood they had a hurdy-gurdy and it continually played selections from *Il Trovatore*. I was always reading about Egypt and I was always hearing the hurdy-gurdy and to this day whenever I hear *Il Trovatore* I smell Egyptian tombs."

In first term he wrote a play about an Egyptian king. He also wrote essays on Jack London for which he was singled out. But not even he could win 'em all. "There was this red-haired mathematics teacher with a florid, typically Irish complexion and eyes so blue you could see all of Ireland in them. I was good at whatever had to be worked out, but dull, dry facts I couldn't remember. Those don't move me because those I can look up. So he flunked me. The truth is he was a brilliant mathematician but such a lousy teacher that most of the class also flunked, so I didn't feel too badly."

He enjoyed high school. Mama fixed him his favorite salami sandwich lunch every day and with the money she gave him for a drink he bought a chocolate ice cream soda. "Oh, my God, that combination is so delicious you can't believe it."

Townsend Harris in the Bronx was the three-year high school of City College of New York. Admission was by test and only those with the highest IQ gained entrance to this free city high school for precocious children. Here the specially gifted could make four years in three and graduation automatically guaranteed entrance to CCNY. When Israel Strassberg graduated from public school he was awarded a prize as the outstanding student in English composition. In Townsend Harris his electives were French and German. Chances were after college he would teach in a Yiddish secular school.

In 1918, his final year in high school, the flu epidemic ravaged the city. Every member of the household was felled by the disease. One took sick then all the rest followed. Zalmon's fever was high and it was either you passed the certain moment and recovered or you became worse and then it didn't last long until the end.

Zalmon could not survive the crisis. The physician came early one morning and after examining the patient he turned to Papa, closed that ominous black bag, and in grave, hushed tones said, "*Er iz zehr kronk* (He is very sick)." The physician then picked up his black bag from the kitchen table and said again to Papa, "Er iz zehr kronk."

Mama was beside herself. She kept repeating, "It's because he ate only vegetables. Who ever heard of a person eating only vegetables?"

"Please," soothed Papa, who was calm in his grief. "*Zy shtill* . . . [Be still]."

Mama was distraught. "Always for years already I would have to go to special places for special foods for him. How is it I could have had a son who didn't eat meat? That's why he can't get well because he never ate meat."

"Please . . . please . . ." soothed Papa.

"He can't fight this because he had no strong meat in him."

Zalmon hadn't been sickly. He simply contracted the flu when everybody else had it. There were so many deaths that collections were en masse. Multiple bodies were hauled away in trucks. One gray evening the truckman who was collecting other bodies in the same house on Clinton Street came by for Zalmon and brought him to Mount Hebron cemetery. He was twenty-four.

Zalmon was his younger brother's world. There was no intimacy with anyone else. "My connection and my closeness was with Zalmon." His death was a terrific blow. When the adored brother died he could not recover from it. "His death did something to me. Maybe it was because it was my first experience with death. I only know his passing made a lasting impression on me."

As a result Israel Strassberg didn't graduate. He had been out of school two months during the epidemic. A year was two terms. This was the first term of his last year. He could have made up the missed classes as many others did, but with less than a year to graduation, he had no heart for it. The appetite had been taken away. He somehow could not go back to school.

"With Zalmon's death, part of my life was over. I left school and I grew up."

CHAPTER FOUR

Bond Street

Israel Strassberg didn't know what to do with his life. He was lost. He was loose. He didn't know what he wanted to do or be. The thought was, "possibly something in the cultural line like I might settle for teaching Yiddish" since to teach anything else would require a college education. He had no career direction. He had not even work direction.

He was perfectly willing to work but he wasn't prepared for anything. At this moment Zalmon had died and whatever money Zalmon had brought in was gone. He himself wasn't old enough to bring in real money, although he knew he had to, and yet he couldn't turn up a single offer.

There was an intense desire to educate himself, to make something of himself. He had an insatiable appetite for learning. His hunger was such that he was never without a book. Since he couldn't satisfy himself with a job, the soaking up of knowledge became his prime food.

This sense of search led to the library. The library became his life. Back and back he went to the main branch at Forty-second Street and Fifth Avenue. There at least he could feed himself. He became interested in oriental and biblical history. He became engrossed in the reality behind the symbolic events. He thought maybe he'd write a history of the Jewish people. He spent two years formulating a chronicle of the Jewish people and compiling pages of research in his neat Jewish hand. "I still have calluses on my fingers from taking notes."

He still needed to work. He landed a clerical job at *Die Tzeit* and doubled as a messenger "taking down engravings to an address near City Hall." When the Yiddish newspaper closed a year or so later he went to work as a stockroom boy on Seventh Avenue, pushing handtrucks through the streets of the garment center.

Arthur, who had married in 1914, had a brother-in-law named Abraham Kalm. Abe was "in the feather business" in quarters he shared with an equally small wig business. Each was half of a divided loft on Bond Street.

One morning Levitt, the owner of the Human Hair Novelty Company, which had the rear of the loft, shuffled wearily into his friend's feather place in the front half, sighing, "Listen, Abe, I can't do so much anymore and I could use somebody to take a little load off."

"So what kind of person you looking for?" asked Kalm. "I mean, if it's a specialist with the wig business, then this I couldn't help you."

"No," said Levitt, fiddling with a "rat" which is what ladies stuffed inside pompadours and buns in the hairstyles of the day. "A shipping clerk I need. You know a kid who's available?"

"Oh, do I know someone who's available!" nodded Kalm.

"Also maybe he could keep the books for me. This I could also use."

"Well, the kid I got in mind isn't exactly an accountant, but he's intelligent and for the kind of books that you keep in the kind of place that you got, he's good enough."

"Okay, so let's say maybe close to the neighborhood of fifteen dollars a week."

"And you'll like this boy," assured Kalm. "He's a nice, quiet boy."

"Good," said Levitt. "Also since the workers are foreign girls like from Poland and Russia, if he could speak Yiddish it would also be not bad."

The new employee began with taking care of the packages. Unlike Seventh Avenue, where they delivered the merchandise, here they shipped it. That meant walking all the way to the post office handcarrying cumbersome, heavy boxes with rope that cut into the fingers. As Israel Strassberg began to assume more duties, Mr. Levitt did less. Soon the hired hand supervised the manufacturing of the wigs, the importing of the hair from China, and the financial transactions. He couldn't sign checks, however. He wasn't yet twenty-one. Slowly this one-man business was passing to another man. Levitt, a World War veteran, was suffering not only from shellshock but also from lovesickness.

Levitt's adored didn't return his love. She didn't consider him sufficiently brainy. In hopes his resident intellectual would give him a little reflected glory, Levitt dispatched the employee on a subway ride to his beloved in Brooklyn under the guise of delivering a parcel. It didn't help.

Eight months later, Levitt experienced a breakdown and was found wandering dazedly in the streets. He died shortly thereafter. A spokesman for the family said to the new boy, "Mr. Levitt was the sole owner, but although there is nobody to take over his business we don't necessarily have to close it. Since you already know a little something, maybe you could remain here."

"And do what?" asked Abe Kalm, who had been sitting in on the negotiations.

"And run it," they suggested. "Maybe we could make some sort of an arrangement."

"Actually he's already running it now," put in Abe, buttressing the position of his noncommunicative relative.

The young man himself was silent. Mentally and emotionally he was far removed from manufacturing braids and wiglets, but financially and practically this was all he had going for him. "So maybe you'll give him more money to actually take over the complete responsibility for the whole operation?" suggested Kalm.

"Well, maybe we'd make some sort of an arrangement," they hedged.

Since the Levitts were not disposed toward any salary adjustment, Mr. Kalm, a supersalesman, stepped in. He announced to the family, "I'll take over the whole loft and buy you out, and this boy I'll make my partner. I'll be the outside man. He'll do the inside things."

In 1923 the partners moved their business to new quarters at 20 Bond Street. The "inside" man was to open in the morning, but he'd always be late so the 8 A.M. opening would be 8:30. He'd keep the books, order the raw materials, pack the goods, and ship the stuff to their nationwide outlets.

Another duty was to unbraid the "fall" (as the long, loose hair was called) when it arrived and card it across wire spokes riveted to the table. In the process of grabbing the end of the hair and running it through the spokes, one wire bristle lodged in the middle finger of his right hand and tore it straight up from the nail to the knuckle. Hair clotted in the cut and the finger became infected from the dye.

Arthur, who was studying dentistry and knew something about medicine, incised the infection with a scalpel, cleaned the cut, and stuck the finger in a solution to soak. Whatever the acid, it actually ate away the inside of the infected area. He dressed it and bandaged it tightly. The healing was slow. "Still today I have a scar, but if not for Arthur's quick work, who knows what would have happened to that finger."

A couple of steps up was the factory where fifteen girls built the hairpieces on netting. Off to a side was the packing and shipping department where the Inside Boss did the packing and shipping himself. The office area, a front room with large windows on Bond Street, included the work space of a pretty girl. For working until 6 P.M., six days a week, Sally's weekly wage was six dollars.

Fifty-five years later in her neat little house in Long Beach, Long Island, this petite, handsome woman with brown hair and porcelain skin spoke shyly of her feelings for her ex-boss. "He was not the type you'd bang on the back but he would smile at us. I liked him very much. I crocheted him a black tie which was in fashion then and he wore it to the office. He was neat, clean, always nicely dressed.

"Shirley, our forelady, thought I was a chatterbox but he never told me the bad things she said about me. He was gentlemanly. Shirley was sweet on him and she hated me because he defended me. He said I was a good worker. There was another American girl there who liked him but he paid no attention to any of us. He didn't fool around. He didn't run around with girls.

"We were subjects of fascination for him not necessarily to get close to but just to examine. He was fascinated with people's faces and expressions."

Then, blushingly and shyly, her faintly rouged cheeks reddening, Sally said, "He wasn't my boy friend, but once he made a date with me to go on a Fifth Avenue bus ride on one of those double-decker buses. He promised to come by on Sunday afternoon—'if he could,' he said. Well, I dressed up in a beautiful black satin suit. And I waited. And I waited. He never came."

Israel Strassberg was neither light nor gay. The serious young man didn't bother much in terms of social life. He was different from anybody in his family. He was different from anybody anywhere. The period following Zalmon's death was a low point. Some of those with whom he'd been studying at the Jewish school, his fount of culture, belonged to the SADs, Students of Arts and Drama, a club in the Chrystie Street Settlement which was near his house. Shy and reserved, he had no interest in the theatre but he had an interest in surviving.

"I needed something. I needed someone." Settlement Houses such as the Henry Street Settlement and the Grand Street Settlement were social centers. Some featured sports activities, some political activities, some artistic or social or theatrical activities. For some the object was to Americanize the Jewish people. Settlements were a strong factor, a great stimulus, on the life of the Lower East Side.

They drew people out of their environment. In neighborhoods where gangsters comprised a percentage of the alumni, it was needful to pull out of what you were. In neighborhoods that were Yiddish-oriented, it was a touch of working with Americans in English. The wife of financier Paul Mazer was chairman of the board. Mabel A. Talmadge, another who gave of her time, was associated with the Little Theatre movement. "They helped us who lived in that area to make our way out of the environment we were in. And that was something I needed badly."

CHAPTER FIVE

Chrystie Street

The Chrystie Street Settlement's activities for young people included a dramatic group. The Students of Arts and Drama did two free productions a year. The stage was a marked-off floor of the gymnasium. Backstage meant walking behind a curtain. The SADs were a limited group of a dozen but they had special things going for them—zeal and determination.

Art student Hyman Shapiro, the set designer, remembers, "We ourselves painted flats and built sets of blocks on blocks. Our actors walked up right from the floor. We had no money so for a biblical play we sculptured costumes from pieces of shiny yellow and blue oilcloth."

An employee in a factory which manufactured electrical quartz fixtures was the lighting expert. This translation into another world made Benny Slutzky's life as a mundane electrical worker bearable. On the magic carpet of oilcloth, woodblocks, and lightbulbs he was transported into a universe of literature and art and for this Benny eagerly paid the price of toiling late at night every night in the gymnasium at Chrystie.

Ann Slutzky, who married Benny's brother, Yudel, was a bookkeeper cum thespian. "Friday nights when the Settlement was usually closed, we were there working. We even came Sundays to build scenery."

The newest SAD left his wig business after six, then worked at the Settlement sometimes until two in the morning, then waited interminably at the subway because at that hour trains didn't run often and he'd have to be up before seven.

America was entering the era of Little Theatre groups. A vast movement on a national scale, operations such as Theatre Pasadena, Theatre Chicago, the Vieux Carré in New Orleans were all part of the modern movement in the theatre before it hit the professional bigtime of Broadway. The drama clubs within settlement houses were offshoots of this Little Theatre movement.

The settlements held yearly contests for the outstanding single performance. Each presented its best production and someone of importance in the theatre selected the winner. In his first competition which was to be judged by a Mr. Stuart Walker, head of the Portmanteau Theatre, Strassberg was to play a middle-aged Jewish father in a one-act drama translated from the Yiddish.

The day of performance he lay in bed with the grippe. His brother Arthur and Benny Slutzky came to visit in the afternoon. Mama left off pickling the beets for home-made borscht and let them in. This being Friday, Mama pointed to the freshly washed floor. Carefully stepping on the Yiddish newspapers spread across it, they made their way to the patient. "Please," begged Benny, staring at him. "Don't do the show tonight."

"You have temperature. It isn't necessary to go expose yourself to the night air. Stay home," commanded Arthur.

The star of the show lay back, his pale face flushed with fever, his hazel eyes half closed. "*Er geht nisht . . . er geht nisht,*" repeated Mama, assuring everybody while shaking her purple-stained forefinger that he won't go, he won't go. Since Mama was too pious to view any performance, to her this nonsense was definitely not necessary. Bearded Papa, a member of the culturally oriented Amalgamated Clothing Workers Union, which supported the Yiddish Theatre, entertained a little curiosity about his son's acting, but he never went to see either.

Mama looked at her baby Srulkele, little Srulke, perspiring on the pillow and repeated firmly, "Er geht nisht."

"We're going to go down tonight and see the show and we'll let you know what happens," promised Benny.

"Who'll take my place?" asked the star.

"We don't know yet," shrugged Arthur, "but don't you dare go with your temperature."

"No, whatever you do, don't get out of bed," cautioned Benny.

Mama escorted them to the door and picked up her apron to turn the doorknob. "Er geht nisht," she said and slammed the door.

That night when the curtains parted, the audience beheld a stranger. A stooped old man with a beard was mouthing the words of the young man at home. The voice was unlike any they'd ever heard. The walk, the movements, belonged to no one they knew. The face devoid of makeup was an aged face. The friends in Chrystie murmured. But surely this was no actor. This was really a little old man. But who? Who was he?

Only backstage when they were face to face with the young man whom they had left in bed could they believe he had played the part. "But he was wonderful," exclaimed Benny to Arthur. "Where did he get such imagination from? I never noticed he had this before."

"I also didn't see this before," replied Arthur. "I don't ever remember him fancying or daydreaming."

"Such characterization to play an old man so believable, this I can't believe," said Benny.

"Such determination to force yourself because a show must go on, this I also can't believe," said Arthur.

That year Chrystie won the competition and Israel Strassberg took the prize as the outstanding Settlement actor of the year.

It was in the settlement that he changed his name. It had always been cause for confusion. The double "s" lent itself toward the Germanic-sounding "Strashbourg" whereas a single "s" forced the correct pronunciation and his first name invariably took a Yiddish twist or was picked up mistakenly as Isadore. Nobody ever addressed him correctly. "Lea," the last letters of "Israel," he shifted sideways and the first time his name appeared in a program it read, "I. Lee Strasberg." Eventually he dropped the initial "I."

Following the opening of the fall production of 1922, the

brand-new Lee Strasberg was unbuttoning the uniform of the young blind soldier he played when Louis Noskin, another of the SADs, ambled backstage. He was accompanied by a man who was the prototype of a Jewish lawyer. "This is my friend who goes to the same voice teacher, Lemuel Jacobs, as I go to," began Noskin, "and he came here tonight to see me."

The Jewish lawyer type stood quietly, saying nothing. He gazed at Lee steadily.

"And he wanted to meet you," finished Noskin lamely.

The fellow continued to appraise Lee coldly. Finally he extended himself. "My name is Philip Loeb. I'm the casting director of the Theatre Guild."

Lee waited. Nobody spoke. Five beats later, Loeb asked, "You interested in acting professionally?"

"No," said Lee.

There was no reaction. Loeb didn't argue. He didn't pursue it. He said only, "If you ever are, look me up."

Lee's research into Zoroastrianism and Buddhism and other primitive religions and their origins and developments and the study of what caused their rise was unknowingly preparing him for his theatrical career. The effects archaeological discoveries had in creating a new concept of Babylonia led him to Egyptian civilization, then to the Bible. Fascinated with the social view of history, he was led to a work by Heinrich Ewald, a biblical scholar of the 1850s. Translated from German, it was an interpretation of biblical stories, historical material, tribal traditions, the relation to pagan ritual, and what was back of it all.

"And that's when I got in the habit of interpreting scripts. When I read a script I became used to seeing the life behind the written word. That was the beginning of my going inside for motivation."

In Chrystie they were doing period plays and classics and Jacob Ben-Ami had gifted him with three volumes of Peretz plays. Possessed of an intense, searching nature and consciously trying to develop an awareness, Lee Strasberg widened his reading to include books on theatre. His first was Hiram Motherwell's *The Theatre of Today*, which inflamed his imagination. He read Edward Gordon Craig's *On the Art of Theatre* and the works of Kenneth McGowan. He learned about the Moscow Art Theatre.

He was assisted in this by the New York subway system. The hour ride downtown was productive of some of his best reading. Becky and her husband lived in the Bronx, and since Max Lippa was on the road weeks at a time and really couldn't afford the six-room apartment on his own, he had invited the old folks and Lee to live with them.

The three-story building at 790 East 181 Street on the corner of Mapes Avenue was a curious building. Over the stoop in the rear lived the Lippas and their children, Ruthie and Cy. On the first floor were Arthur's in-laws, Mr. and Mrs. Huberman. Across from them directly over the Lippas were the Kalmanowitzes from whose loins came Lee's partner, Abe Kalm. Abe Kalm's wife, Rose Huberman, and Arthur's wife were sisters. Above the Hubermans lived Abe Kalm and above the Kalmanowitzes lived other relatives.

When Ruthie Lippa came home from school on Fridays "it was something you can't believe. Everybody baked in the morning and by the afternoon the whole place had that smell of *gefilte* fish and *challa* bread. It permeated the hallways because the Kalmanowitzes made and the Hubermans made and the Kalms made and the Strassbergs made and the Lippas made and everybody made and we all went from apartment to apartment."

The Lippas' apartment was entered by a hallway which opened to two bedrooms. The first was shared by Lee and the male boarder, a cousin named Joe Diener. The other by Ruthie and her brother Cy. Next to that was a large kitchen dominated by a table which constituted the major social center in the apartment. The kitchen had a stove against one wall and windows on another. At this ground-floor window Mama Strassberg invariably positioned herself. A self-appointed monitor, her lifework was to chase the boys who were playing ball. "*Geh avek* (Go away)," she hollered at them thwacking the panes of glass with her hand. When they didn't budge, white-haired Mama hurled the lone English word she had almost learned to pronounce. "Ya bastya! . . . Geh avek, ya bastya . . . !"

The bathroom abutted the kitchen. Plumbing for both sinks decorated either side of the same wall. That bathroom was interesting. From a nail fluttered cutouts of newspaper in approximately twelve-inch-long strips. This doubled as toilet tissue for orthodox Mama and Papa, who couldn't tear paper on the sabbath.

At the far end of the hall, beyond the master bedroom, stood the Front Room which held the black leather lounge chair with the built-in pillow. This was referred to strictly as "the lunch." Papa, who was slight of build, used to snooze on the lunch Saturday afternoons. Back of this lay the commodious sleeping area for Mama and Papa—one single bed at one end, another at the opposite end. Mama was always repainting these beds personally. At the slightest provocation, Mama took up a paintbrush.

The Front Room had a mystique. Its French doors were shut four weeks in advance of Passover. Everything was covered with white sheets, the table was made kosher and the room sealed off. In the words of Ruthie Lippa, "With a bomb we couldn't get in there." In honor of the holiday Mama stacked up home-made strudel which she locked away in the kitchen closet with a key. Once Becky pleaded for a taste, and despite Papa's support of Becky's petition, matriarchal Mama wouldn't budge.

The Passover holiday enveloped everyone. Papa brewed his own home-made sweet raisin wine for the children. The winery was strictly the bathroom. With the children to help stem the Concord grapes, Papa sat on a stool, Lee on the edge of the tub, Cy on the toilet, and Ruthie on the tile floor. A barrel a foot and a half high was set in the bathtub and months in advance Papa stirred, fermented, and sampled.

Lee burrowed deeper into Chrystie. The apartment in the Bronx was not really where he felt at home. His elderly parents embraced a different world. Papa assigned seats at the seder and Lee sat near him, but Papa's chemistry prevented him going as far as a hug or gesture of overt affection. What each might have felt inside neither could express openly.

Gray-haired Becky was the practical sort. Her husband's gut was in his avocation, the art of theatrical makeup. Hers was in shoes for the children. Stout Becky was a nibbler whose nibbles were larger than her meals and her feet were ofttimes too swollen to wear shoes. Becky's was a frustrated life. She didn't care for Mama, whom she considered selfish, nor was Mama partial to her. As for the baby brother, his was another spirit she couldn't reconcile.

Neither was there to be any rapport with his roommate, the

boarder Joe Diener, who was a simple soul. Lee spent his home
hours reading. Through the books on theatre a whole new world
opened for him.

At Chrystie he flowered. Says Ann Slutzky, "We were a vitally
interested group of nothings who wanted to be in the theatre and
didn't have anybody to be in it with. Even at the extreme beginning of Lee's profound interest, he was the pedantic teacher and
we the ready-made audience. His avid reading which he then
poured out to us was made to order for us—and him."

Says Hyman Shapiro, "He read theatrical biographies and early
issues of theatrical magazines and he had a concentration that ex-
cluded everything else that could happen to a person—family, outside interests, even facial expressions."

Lee's tunnel vision, manifested in a complete absorption in his
subject and total rejection of everything and everybody else, resulted in a revolution. It became apparent he could contribute
more than the entire teaching system of the lady in charge of the
drama club. The SADs rebelled against her limitations and a vote
was taken. They demanded their boy take over. Lee Strasberg became the director of the Students of Arts and Drama of the
Chrystie Street Settlement.

The new director began to give lectures. He magnetized his listeners. He was so informed that although everybody shared the
same age and background, nobody challenged him with, "Who
the hell are you to tell us when all you've ever done is read
books?" They *believed* him.

His strongest believer was a handsome, dark-haired man who
was uneducated but a good human being. Benny Slutzky and Lee
Strasberg grew up side by side. Benny and his brothers, Yudel and
Yankel, and their sisters lived across from the Strassbergs on Clin-
ton Street. The Slutzkys had a candy stand at Clinton and Stan-
ton. Nobody remembers a buddy in Lee's school years other than
Ben Slutzky, and when Zalmon left a hole in Lee's heart it was
Benny who moved to fill it.

Benny yearned to do for Lee. Despite their mutual compat-
ibility, it was a one-way love affair. Lee became Benny's whole
life.

The new director's newfound sophistication led him into
wicked ways of smoke and drink. One night Benny and he saun-

tered out of a little restaurant on Rivington Street right into a fight in progress. Lee somehow ended up in the middle and the ringleader smacked him with the flat of his hand. Down went Lee on the sidewalk. He had just come from a heavy meal and from dragging heavily on his Pall Mall. "With that plus the shock of being hit, I retched. I suffered such nausea and became so physically ill that never again could I stand the smell or the taste of cigarettes."

The short-lived drinking habit began and ended when a daughter of the Slutzkys was getting married. "At the wedding at Benny's father's place in the country I tried a little wine. With the excitement of the singing and the dancing I got so sick that I threw up. After that I couldn't take a drink without my throat literally closing, so that was the finish of my drinking spree."

Together they attended the theatre. Lee's earliest memory is Walter Hampden in a Thanksgiving matinee of *Hamlet*. Benny and he came in late and, as their custom was, they asked for the cheapest seats. But, as the theatre's custom was, they were seated down front in the orchestra because the seats were empty.

Shirley, the forelady at the wig factory, furnished his next experience. She had a ticket to the Metropolitan Opera for a Saturday matinee of *Boris* starring Chaliapin. The seat was the topmost balcony way over to the side. He couldn't see. He had to crane his neck down and to the side even to glimpse just a little bit.

"Still, it was so awesome that later I paid seven dollars and bought my very own first ticket to the Met for the very same opera so I could see him as well as hear him."

Shortly after he was walking to the library when he spied tall, imposing Chaliapin in person. As Lee worshiped from a few feet away, his God hawked and expectorated with such power that his mouthful of spit not only cleared the sidewalk but landed well into the street. "And here I was so naïve and such a hero worshiper!"

In the autumn of 1923 the Moscow Art Theatre came to New York.

CHAPTER SIX

Moscow Art Theatre

The world's most celebrated acting ensemble had been separated during the war years. The freshly reunited Moscow Art Theatre enjoyed a newfound intimacy on its American tour. For the month the Russian company performed on Fifty-ninth Street, the director of the Students of Arts and Drama of the Chrystie Street Settlement House did not miss a performance.

Viewed from the perspective of the modern movement of the American theatre, the Moscow Art Theatre was scenically old-fashioned. Having been through the war with no opportunity to develop, their scenery was worn and tawdry, their sets were painted, the makeup overdone. Still, for the director of the SADs, the experience was the living culmination of not only what he had read but what he'd dreamed. His eyes widened at what unfolded on that stage.

America had experienced Eugene O'Neill, the Provincetown Playhouse, the Theatre Guild. America had witnessed real acting and stellar performances—Jacob Ben-Ami's *Samson and Delilah,* John Barrymore's *Hamlet,* "the greatest actress in the world"—Duse—but what it had seen exemplified in wonderful individual performances on the American stage, Lee Strasberg suddenly saw totalized. What moved him, what he found exciting in the Russian company was that *everybody* on that stage was great!

Each single practitioner was interchangeably as good as the star. In fact, the "star" was the over-all ensemble. Beyond anyone's imagination, the Moscow Art Theatre represented the most unified ensemble that ever existed in the world. The extras as well as those who held center stage possessed identical degrees of reality.

America did not have this concept of the unified production as an art form. America had pick-up companies that played well with outstanding hand-picked actors, but an ensemble which took years to create, all working together in harmony and not just for one single production was truly a work of art. To see a Stanislavsky and a Kachalov rotate in the same part was a theatre America didn't have. To see six top names playing small parts—stars one day, bit players the next—was a sense of ensemble never before realized. Every heart on that stage, regardless of how small the role or how large the reputation of the actor, shared the same conviction.

Back and back Lee went. He saw Chekhov's *The Cherry Orchard*, Gorki's *The Lower Depths*, Dostoyevski's *The Brothers Karamazov*, Tolstoy's *Tsar Fyodor*. Night after night he discussed with Benny what he saw. "Even a walk-on with no lines makes an impact. At the Moscow Art Theatre he becomes a living, real person instead of just a silly extra running around with a spear for no reason."

"Okay, but so do you know how they do it?" asked Benny.

"I only know they get results. Not even the least of them depends on manners or customs. This whole natural style of ensemble acting is such that even the smallest player goes with emotions and dispositions and works from the inside. I can't tell you the impression this has made upon me. Why isn't this something we could do?"

"But their sets are dull and their lighting is dim," countered Benny.

"But their performance is of the greatest standard in the world and they have a whole ensemble that's great not just one star. Remember the other night how the action was to bring in a

chair the master was supposed to sit on and how just the ...
way the extra *carried* that chair he already conveyed the impression it was for some lordly personage? Well, that's the point. The
whole group is great. Each and every one on that stage is as good
as the other."

"But did you notice their costumes were shabby and their
makeup wasn't good?"

"I only know in terms of acting they can't be equaled. In every
detail every one of them is wonderful. It's a totality of greatness."

This presence of greatness within the Moscow Art Theatre
stoked the fires of inspiration within the young man. The Moscow
Art Theatre made him realize that to be an actor you didn't have
to be a Barrymore or a Chaliapin. He had never thought of himself
as an actor. He wasn't a theatrical type. His involvement in
theatre had been little more than an interest. It hadn't been personal. He had taken it up because it made a bond between himself and others.

Now there was the thought that a person could be in the profession even if he wasn't a star, that he could be a small actor in
the company as great as the greatest actor in the company. The
unformed idea that the theatre could somehow be built by and involve equal talent on the part of everyone in a production began
coalescing into an "I think I can act, too" sort of thing. Sitting inside a darkened theatre, his eyes riveted on a group of sincere artists, Lee Strasberg's hopes for the future were kindled. He would
become a professional actor.

He would also quit the wig business. Having seen him poring
over a technical book detailing the layout of a theatre with pictures of rows of orchestra seats, his coworker, Sally, knew he
didn't belong there. Even Abe Kalm could divine that hairpieces
were not exactly his partner's life. A deal was negotiated and Abe
bought him out at the rate of twenty-five dollars a week for a year.

Lee enrolled in the Clare Tree Major School of the Theatre,
which was an all-day affair. "I was ignorant enough to join a conventional school. I enjoyed it. Particularly I loved the ballet class.
I was pretty good at it, even though I wasn't strong enough to
leap or lift any partners."

Classes were on West Thirty-ninth Street at the Princess
Theatre, which came complete with lofts and wings and flies. It

was a beautiful old building falling into ruin and its directresses were of the same genre. The school was run by two handsome English sisters, ex-actresses, both of whom sported hennaed hair and velvet gowns.

On the top floor they taught costume design, on the bottom they taught scenic design. In between they gave you Shakespeare and Delsarte and put on playlets. Says actress Phoebe Brand, a classmate, "Lee looked then as he does today, only younger, and I wondered why his very unactory sort would go into the theatre. He was distinctly withdrawn. You did not get friendly with him or link your arm through his or anything. He was a strange one."

He was strange in many ways. He startled his teachers with an excellence in Restoration plays and classics despite an accent that was wall-to-wall Lower East Side. He studied from a little book called *Elizabethan Punctuation* by Percy Syms and with Shakespeare he cut out all punctuation marks in order to give the meaning as he thought it should be. The directresses were flabbergasted. "You're very good," they said to him.

"Of course. You're quite right. I am very good," he replied.

"How is it possible you can do such a perfect Cassius?" asked the elder Miss Mercer.

"Because punctuation was different in Shakespeare's day than today when we do it grammatically. So you must punctuate in terms of rhythm otherwise the verbal patterns will unconsciously block you and limit your expression."

"Ohhh, yes . . . yes, of course," nodded Miss Mercer still as flabbergasted as before.

"I didn't want to have to lower my energy because someone stuck a period someplace and then have to build up force again and then stop it again just because a comma was forced on me. I put in my own punctuation as it suited me."

"Ohhh, yes . . . yes, of course," muttered Miss Mercer.

Says Phoebe Brand, "Those ladies would do a thing and then you'd copy them. They didn't know how to teach you to do it. They weren't really imparting any technique."

Although his classmates deemed this the best training ground of its kind, Lee was dissatisfied and shopped around for another school. A fellow student from Boston told him one late afternoon, "I heard of a place yesterday that I think you would like."

"What place?"

"It's called the American Laboratory Theatre. It's way down-town around Greenwich Village and it's only in existence a short while."

"So what's so different about it?"

"It's run by two Russians named Richard Boleslavsky and Maria Ouspenskaya and. . . ."

". . . but they were members of the Moscow Art Theatre," he finished excitedly. "I myself saw Boleslavsky onstage."

"Yes, and as I understand it they stayed behind to open a school that would teach the same techniques. I just figured it might be a place that would appeal to you."

Along with other events that directed and protected the life of Lee Strasberg specifically, this, too, came about accidentally. This unknown young man, whose name and face Lee doesn't recall, was the pivotal point that changed his life.

January 1924 the eager applicant found his way to the door of the American Laboratory Theatre on Macdougal Street off Washington Square. In the audition he was made to flex his sensory memory by picking up imaginary items from the floor such as pearls and papers that had blown away and become stuck with glue. To test his creativity and spontaneity, they gave him an improvisation. He was to wheedle another fellow—who was an older, more experienced actor—into loaning him money. His third test was a speech from Shakespeare. Naturally, he tackled Cassius. Last, the scene they set was for him to beat his way to a hidden treasure which lay on the other side of such terrors and obstacles as voracious animals and poisonous snakes. His imagination proved so facile that the admitting teacher terminated the audition before its conclusion. Lee actually *saw* those snakes and tigers and lions.

Ouspenskaya, who answered strictly to "Madam," had a didactic personality. Strong, imperious, aloof, Madam was a believer in discipline. Nobody came late. Nobody wasted time. Nobody took liberties. There was no smoking, no joking. The funny-looking little lady was the sort who could have brought a ruler down on a student's knuckles.

Madam treated each human being coldly. In place of praise Madam utilized dissatisfaction. She looked down on everyone. If a production was in rehearsal, students were expected to work all night long. Nothing was ever enough. No one worked hard enough. The theatre was a sanctuary and less than total dedication was not tolerated.

In classrooms over the theatre, Boleslavsky contributed to the austerity of the antiseptic, loveless instruction. He ripped away all superficialities, permitted no clichés, plunged into the psychology of emotion. Teaching students not to display more than they felt, Boleslavsky discussed the emotion of killing. "We complained we couldn't re-create that feeling because we never had it," recalls Lee, "and Boleslavsky replied, 'It cannot be that you don't ever remember wanting to kill. Everybody has wanted to kill a mosquito at some time and the energy and the emotion needed to swat out at that mosquito is all that is required to kill!'"

The famous and brilliant Madam Ouspenskaya had an intensity and drive which she willed into her pupils. Professor Tilley's Method of Speech, a phonetic system promotive of unaccented pronunciation, was espoused in the school, but Madam herself was limited in English. She therefore spoke little, relying heavily on an assistant. She would watch everything icily, then point with her finger and tear it apart.

Madam's efforts lay primarily in the exercise work. In Konstantin Stanislavsky's total immersion system there were exercises, called etudes, to develop concentration so that the actor learns to be private in public and exercises to develop relaxation because with the audience a constant threat physical and mental release is essential. There were exercises to sharpen the imagination and exercises to stimulate the observation.

Students were taught the how-to approach. How to approach a play, grasp its motives, understand the kernel of a character, analyze the action of a scene, find the motivation behind everything. Students were taught the use of improvisation. Contriving extemporaneous situations was considered vital to the fluidity required to create afresh each performance, to develop the art of listening and to force the actor to respond with truth rather than to recite skillfully and mechanically from memory, and to break unconscious adherence to conventional theatrical patterns. Students were taught to revolt against theatricality, bathos, declamation, overacting, and all customary manners of performance.

Boleslavsky taught that the actor actually experiences on stage. Boleslavsky specialized in the memory work teaching that in a person's own experience certain thoughts excite certain memories which in turn detonate certain emotions and reactions. The art of great acting, as theorized by Stanislavsky, was attainable via the reliving of past analogous experiences. The actor recalls an event from his past. The recollection stirs those feelings involved in the original experience. In this framework he is geared to do the scene calling for the particular mood this exercise, called "affective memory," has evoked.

An example is the British tragedian Edmund Kean who summoned genuine tears whenever he commenced the "Alas poor Yorick" speech. Kean, for some reason, thought of his uncle when he gazed at Yorick's skull and this unfailingly caused him to cry.

An early example was the actor Polus who, playing "Electra" in ancient Greece, was to carry an urn ostensibly containing a brother's ashes. Polus' own son had recently died. Polus substituted the ashes of his own son. His lamentation was thus unfeigned.

Konstantin Stanislavsky, a cultured, rich amateur who evolved into a passionately serious actor, teacher, writer, and director of the Moscow Art Theatre, had labored to comprehend the technique of great acting. He had long pondered how those resources could be harnessed into basics. After analyzing the bedrock principles, Stanislavsky formulated a program of training and preparation. He did not invent anything new. He merely channeled what actors have always done unconsciously. He isolated the creative magic, chemicalized it into an exact science, and reduced it to a practical scale.

Boleslavsky and Ouspenskaya noticed Lee's special abilities. After about six months, someone informed him surreptitiously that they were entertaining the notion of incorporating him into the organization. "They had good people there but, theoretically, I felt I had learned all I needed to know.

"What I had gotten was extraordinary. It changed my entire perspective. I had read Freud and already knew the things that go on in a human being without consciousness, but they showed me what it meant. They gave me the key to things I'd seen, heard, and known but had no means of understanding. So, from that point of view it was cataclysmic, but, in an odd way, I didn't feel their theatre as such would work anymore. It didn't have a sufficiently American base."

What he'd assimilated had stirred his personal initiative. To, "Well, what am I going to do?" the answer came to take Phil Loeb up on his offer. Although the Yiddish theatre was highly lauded, with its world-renowned Rudolph Schildkraut and its Emanuel Reicher from Germany and its Reinhardt actors, having been led out of the East Side environment Lee knew that what he wanted was to be in the American theatre.

Late in 1924, after about nine months as an apprentice, Lee realized the time had come to strike out as a professional.

CHAPTER SEVEN

Broadway

Having heard Stuart Walker, who had judged the settlement-house acting contest, was doing some plays, Lee called on him. "What can I do for you?" asked Walker.

"I would like a part in one of your productions."

Walker peered at him. "You're an actor?"

"Of course. You even saw me act," Lee reminded him.

Walker peered at him more intently. "But who are you? I don't remember seeing you before."

Lee cleared his throat. "But you gave me an award."

"An award? I did? For what? What kind of award did I give you?"

It was Lee's turn to peer at Walker. "Don't you remember? I was the old Jewish father in the Chrystie Street production."

"Oh my God," exclaimed Walker. "But you look so totally different. That was really a special characterization."

"No," said Lee softly. "Nothing special. At least for me nothing special."

Lee didn't fit anything Walker had available so he wrote Phil Loeb, the casting director, that he was now ready to be an actor.

He received a return card to come see him. Loeb's office was on the top floor of the Garrick Theatre on Thirty-fifth Street. Lee trudged all the way up the stairs to what looked like a warehouse. The office was dusty and cluttered with props.

Past the desk of Theresa Helburn, executive director of the Theatre Guild, past piles of stacked scenery, deep in the room with his back to the desk sat Loeb. Without turning around, Loeb grunted, "Sit down." Still without looking at his caller, he took a card and wrote on it. Lee figured, "What the hell did I have to come all the way over here for him to see me when he isn't even seeing me."

A month later Lee received Loeb's card to report for rehearsals at the armory on Thirty-fourth Street for the Theatre Guild production of *Processional*. The opening was January 1925. He played a Ku Klux Klan member, a union organizer, and an assortment of other diverse dramatic parts, all silent walk-ons. He also played a drunk. Filling in behind the premier dancers was a bunch of peasants, three of whom did a Mexican number under a sombrero. He was one of them. He even did a couple of comic leaps. His main role, the lone speaking part for which he was listed in the program, was that of a young soldier. "When I had my few lines, my God! did my voice ring out in that theatre!"

Rehearsal was four weeks for no money. "That was to show you were artistic." After that he earned fifteen dollars a week plus his right to be part of the Guild. His next rung of success was as assistant stage manager for *The Guardsman* starring Lunt and Fontanne. He was upped to twenty-five dollars.

A whole series of back-to-back *Garrick Gaieties* followed. In the 1925 version he sang and danced. Those present the day he auditioned say that, suddenly, from behind a closed door came a high-pitched Irish tenor voice warbling, "Did you ever hear the story of where Ireland got its name?" "See, when I went in, Richard Rodgers asked me, 'Can you sing?', I said, 'Yeah, not particularly, but I guess I can.' So he asked, 'You have a favorite song?' Well, 'Little Bit of Heaven' was a famous song which I'd heard on records so I said, 'Of course.' And I did it in dialect, yet."

However, a Caruso he wasn't. In the show there was a takeoff on a modernistic opera and the brand-new singer had to come out and hit the key note. Never did he get anywhere near the correct sound. Even the orchestra tried to help round out the clinker, but no matter how hard they tried and how hard he tried, he couldn't get that note right.

He stage-managed the 1926 version. He ran the whole operation with one assistant. One performance the harassed stage manager was standing in the wings when someone hit a crescendo and he thought they were at a later point in the number, the blackout point. Naturally, being superefficient, he turned and gave the signal to the electrician. The dancers were dancing, the singers were singing, the hoopla was unfolding, and the big number was still going strong, but "what the hell did the electrician care? I signaled, so he blacked out the whole damn stage. Everybody was stunned."

And there was that number on "American Beauty Rose" where the orchestra started up and somewhere the cast came on too late or stage manager Strasberg gave the cue too early. In any case, on his signal the stagehands brought the curtain up and nobody on the stage was ready. In full view of the audience the actors raced around to find their places. "I must say that I did occasionally get mixed up. Very few times, though."

All the girls liked him. He was good to them. In the hot summer months he bought them ice cream. The truth is, he went out for it himself because he loved ice cream and wanted some. And he was a big shot. He paid for it himself. One of the girls was Rosalind Russell. Roz had a quick change to make. He'd pop in and out of her cell-like dressing room to check how she was coming, how far she'd gotten in her change. Since he was busy stage-managing and she was busy changing, neither of them paid attention to the fact that she was naked most of the time.

Whatever spirit Lee Strasberg had within him in those days he left inside the theatre. Introverted, vastly different from other young men of his years, Lee admits, "I was even more solemn than I am now."

A loner, his companions were his books. Says Ann Slutzky, "He was unbelievably reticent. His shyness bordered on the inferiority complex. You could sit in the same room alone with him for hours and he would not utter one word."

In the years Hyman Shapiro worked at Chrystie, he can't remember a single conversation Lee initiated. "If you didn't begin he wouldn't talk. Then if the conversation was on theatre he'd hold forth and not give an inch. Otherwise he wouldn't speak at all. He had a consuming interest in the theatre—but none in people."

Becky Lippa was of the opinion that her brother was "a little bit of a bum . . . an actor! What is that for a job for a nice Jewish boy?!" Becky plainly didn't understand this odd creature who could sit alone in his room impervious to the family's criticism. "He's *meshugga* . . . crazy," she'd say to her kids. "Better he should go back to the wigs and make a living."

Nobody in the family figured he'd amount to much. Sickly Mama, whose face was now drawn, needed to see her baby settled. "*Vie lang tsu parnussah?*" she'd cry. "How long until he makes a living?" Semiretired Papa was nearly seventy. If not exactly thrilled with his son, Papa was at least tolerant. Papa would like to have tasted Lee's world. He once sighed, "If I had known I would have lived this long I would have learned English."

Little Srulke was now mingling with professionals. He was now in the Theatre Guild. The chasm had grown wide.

BOOK TWO

"NORA"

CHAPTER ONE

Marriage

The Lenox Hill Players, a semiprofessional group a cut above
Chrystie, offered the actor-singer-dancer-stage manager an opportunity to direct *The Vegetable*, F. Scott Fitzgerald's dreary depic-
tion of American life. The Lenox Hill Players had a reputation,
some degree of theatrical standard, and their work was reviewed
by critics. It was a step up.

The tyro director worked hard, and opening night he felt he'd
succeeded in showing exactly the stupidity and drunkenness of
Fitzgerald's image of Americana. In his mind he went to bed a
hero. Then the reviews came out. "I don't know what the hell
went on last night at the Cherry Lane Theatre," read the more favorable of them.

"Actors always remember their worst notices," he grins, "and
mine were *The Vegetable*."

Since its Students of Arts and Drama director had several
Broadway productions to his acting credit, the Chrystie Street Settlement House decided he was now professional enough to be
paid. Lee nurtured no thoughts of widening his professional vista.
He wasn't interested in becoming a director. He was interested

only in experimenting with himself as an actor. Through the al-
chemy of the SADs he could probe actors other than himself and
expand the experiments begun at the Laboratory Theatre. The
salary was twenty-four dollars a week.

A natural evolution was to explore innovative ideas about
directing, and in this Chrystie Street lab the actor cum director
mixed the whole bag of concepts. In one play he borrowed an idea
from Meyerhold, the young actor-director who left the Moscow
Art Theatre to explore more vivid theatrical forms than Stanislavsky allowed. In another he applied a "Vakhtangov variation."
Whereas Stanislavsky posed the question, "What would I do in
this situation?" his gifted pupil, Yevgeny Vakhtangov, altered it
to, "If I want the actor to do something, what must I do to make
him accomplish it?" He adapted an idea from the German theatre
of Max Reinhardt.

He went through the whole repertoire of theatre styles. He
staged Andreyev's *Anathema*; an Irish play, J. M. Synge's *Riders
to the Sea*; Anatole France's *He Married a Dumb Wife*; S.
Ansky's *The Dybbuk*; the works of Oscar Wilde.

An early production was *Esther*, a stylized three-act play dealing
with kings and queens. The problem was how to infuse a simple
Jewish peasant with the consciousness and majesty of a sovereign.
The answer came from Lee's intellectualizing.

Even if she couldn't fathom a queen, a Lower East Side factory
worker could comprehend a nun. She'd seen a nun. She knew how
a nun walked, how a nun behaved. Spoonfeeding the milk of
Stanislavsky, he bade his actors act out extemporaneous situations
paralleling the scenes of the queen in the play but based on the
behavioral patterns of a nun. Within this psychological framework the bearing, carriage, dignity and regal quality he wanted
could be achieved. "This adjustment that I made was correct for
the role of the queen. It worked. *Esther* was almost the best
thing I ever did."

Lee's eager youthful amateurs harbored no preconceived no-
tions. They were excited at being part of his growth. Ann Slutzky's
family owned summer resorts and they willingly trooped up to
Pine Lake Park to try out his newest innovative refinements. Lee
was the unquestioned authority. Whatever he ordered they did.

All but a certain young Turk, that is. Prior to one performance

1. Lee (lower left) and his childhood friend, now Dr. Malamud (lower right) and faculty of the Jewish National Radical School, about 1910.

2. Lee's father with grandchildren Ruth and Murray; Lee's nephew. (Courtesy of Ruth Lippa)

3. Group Theatre, 1930s. Top row Lee (far right), with Harold Clurman next to him. Second row from top (right to left), Paula Miller, Stella Adler, Luther Adler, Elia Kazan. Fourth row from top, Clifford Odets (far right) with Cheryl Crawford next to him. Fifth row from top, J. Edward Bromberg (far left). Sitting on ground is Sanford Meisner (second from right), with Morris Carnovsky next to him. (Courtesy of Tony Kraber)

4. Paula Miller at time she met
Lee, 1930. (DeMirjian Studio)

5. *Men in White*, 1934. (Right to left) Luther Adler, Sanford Meisner, J.
Edward Bromberg, Clifford Odets, Tony Kraber, Russell Collins, and Lou
Leverett. (Photo by Alfred Valente, Courtesy of Tony Kraber)

6. Lee (on right) with his brother, Arthur, 1936.

7. Lee's mother with granddaughter Ruth. (Courtesy of Ruth Lippa)

8. Johnny and Susan about 1941.

this fellow dared question the authority of The Unquestioned Authority. An argument ensued and the rebel stormed out. There was no understudy for his part of a blind prophet. Without being up in the lines, Lee had to step into the role. Came the cue the "blind" prophet walked through the play reading from a manuscript in his hand.

Harold Clurman, a playreader at the Theatre Guild who also tripled as a fellow actor and stage manager at *Garrick Gaieties*, was introduced to Lee by Phil Loeb. In *The Fervent Years*, Clurman describes his first sight of actor Strasberg: ". . . a palefaced man of intellectual demeanor. He was very short, intense-looking, with skin drawn tightly over a wide brow. He spoke with a faint foreign accent, had a large head of rather curly hair and a face that expressed keen intelligence, suffering, ascetic control . . . he did not seem like an actor."

Clurman, in turn, introduced Lee to the famous French director Jacques Copeau, whom the Theatre Guild had imported from France. To honor this great leader of the theatre, Chrystie staged the Copeau production, *The House into Which We Are Born*, a simple play about a family and a grandfather and French home life.

Monklike Copeau sat in the back of the gymnasium alone. There was no audience. The cast was highly nervous about such a VIP in their midst. Strasberg was not. "I'm never nervous. But I was excited." Copeau was intrigued. He hadn't seen his play performed except in his own productions and with professionals and here it was being performed in English and with amateurs. At the end he said, "Very nice . . . very nice . . ." Then, in a flourish of understatement, "We did it differently."

Harold Clurman stood ready to translate, but "Lee didn't say anything. Upon meeting Copeau, Lee was absolutely rigid. It was as though, 'I'm just as good as you. I know just as much as you. I'm not going to let you impose on me.' He was geared to maintain the prestige with his actors in case Copeau said something disparaging." Clurman's first glimpse into the gut of Lee Strasberg showed a man of enormous control, "a man terrified by his own fears and insecurities."

Lee's version differs. "I didn't have a dialogue with Copeau because he was the author of this play about his own family and, anyway, he was the great Copeau, which was enough even if this wasn't a double excitement for me. Besides, he didn't speak English, but . . . even so . . . I didn't because in those days I wasn't too easy to have a dialogue with no matter who it was."

The man who wasn't family-oriented, who didn't date or socialize except with his warm friend, Benny, had "enormous difficulties in making commitments and friends. At that time new contacts and new environments were difficult for me."

One of the SADs was a slim, fair-skinned girl in her early twenties. Her brown hair was combed simply. She was pretty but not ravishing. Nora Z. Krecaun had no pretensions—not even about her future as an actress. Nora came from a Yiddish theatrical family. Her aunt was an actress of note in the Yiddish theatre. Her mother was a wardrobe woman, a dresser to actresses on the Jewish stage.

Nora's father, whom she resembled and toward whom she leaned, was dead. Mrs. Rosenzweig, her mother, had remarried and the relationship was strained. Mother and daughter were both strong. The mother made demands. The daughter parried them.

"Nora was quiet, but it's true she was a powerful individual," says Lee. "She had a lot of energy. She had good social adjustments, the kind I didn't have and couldn't have."

Nora Krecaun had great respect for the director of the Students of Arts and Drama. She shared his interests and supported his efforts. The togetherness unfolded in the Settlement House, and Nora became Lee's girl. Nobody had money to take anybody out so the high point was to drop into a local place for coffee. After a while he broke it off "but Nora did not lose her feeling for me so I went back to her. She loved me very much. She must have, otherwise we would not have gotten together."

It took three years for Lee to marry Nora. Instead of being ecstatic, his mother was upset. She didn't want it. She hollered at him, "So now you'll have a wife. So what will you do with her? You'll be off on your own with what? You have no money. You have no nothing."

Nora inherited some money from relatives on her father's side and invested in a red dress. There was a civil ceremony at the city clerk followed by a Jewish ceremony in the rabbi's study on Norfolk Street which was not far from that fourth floor walkup where

Papa had been in residence with Becky, Arthur, a family of five and four boarders when he first arrived in the Golden Land.

Mrs. Rosenzweig gave the reception at the Romanian restaurant a few blocks from the rabbi's study. Despite her little boy insisting he was now a big boy, Mama Strassberg cried the whole way over.

CHAPTER TWO

Career

The newlyweds' tiny, newly built studio apartment on Minetta Lane in the Village was entered through a balcony. It had an L-shaped dining area and a bedroom so small that to get past the bed you had to walk on top of it. The kitchen had no sink. The sink was in the bathroom. The walls were unpainted plaster. The furniture was upended boxes. The knives and forks were from the Lippas.

Marriage did not transform the groom socially. He still did not involve himself on a personal level or indulge in the everydayness of things. Nor did he, to anyone's memory, demonstrate visible affection. It nonetheless seemed a superb union. Housewifely Nora was mad for her husband. Attracted to his intellect, she made few demands on his ardor, appeared not to be put off by its lack and concerned herself with making him comfortable.

Evenings they might fall into the Russian Bear near the settlement for coffee or play bridge or troop out to Coney Island. The big enjoyment was the theatre. The big problem was the money. He borrowed $250 from Ann Slutzky, which to her was a fortune, all she had in the world. "I was out of work and desperate and he owed it to me so long that I had to go after him to get it back. I very persistently asked him many times. I actually had to beg for it."

Their hand-to-mouth life troubled Becky who came to visit and found her unemployed brother with a sword in his hand. He had no prospects for a job and no money and he was taking fencing lessons. "Parasite!" spat Becky. "Crazy . . . meshugga!"

Although the bankroll was flat, Lee saw Duse in Ibsen's *The Lady from the Sea*, and Laurette Taylor. Despite language barriers he went to the Bowery's Chinese Theatre to see actor Mei Lan-Fong and, with fifty dollars borrowed from Harold Clurman, to the Thalia to see Italian theatre. Repeatedly he went to watch the stocky, asthmatic Sicilian Giovanni Grasso playing a lover. Bald and with a hoarse, guttural voice, Grasso exuded such sexuality that Lee shivered in his seat.

"In one scene Grasso swallowed pills. He just didn't throw his head back, pop them into his mouth and gulp down the water. It was as if the taste was left on his tongue. He stuck it out and made an appropriately distasteful grimace like the pill had dissolved and he felt its residue. I had never before seen such technique."

He invited Stella Adler who had studied at the Laboratory Theatre and fellow Guild actor Morris Carnovsky to see Grasso providing they paid their own way. They came when Grasso had an off night. Lee sank lower and lower into his seat pondering the mystique of acting—why some performances were good, others not. In the second act he sank even lower. But in the third act he —and Grasso—redeemed themselves. "Grasso caressed a woman with a gesture of genuine love. Just the way he touched her created an electrical impulse. He wasn't acting. The blood burst into his face. He *really* was *loving*."

Leaving Chrystie behind forever, Lee's involvement in the professional theatre increased. In Franz Werfel's *Goat Song* he understudied Eddie Robinson later known in Hollywood as Edward G.

Suffused with the techniques of characterization, Lee downgraded Robinson's portrayal of the Wandering Eternal Jew. "Eddie plays ordinary values. This character should represent a historical quality, some sense of confrontation with what is involved with the history of the Jews." At the understudy rehearsal Lee's interpretation conveyed his sense that the character's mistreatment was not against him as an individual but because he was a Jew. Phil Loeb concurred this reading gave the play an added dimension.

Lee's hardest dialogue was in a Philip Barber play about America's miners in the 1860s. He couldn't get by his first line, "Hi, partnerrrrr." Whenever he said it he cringed. "My God," he thought to himself, "it sounds so wrong." It bothered him sufficiently that he put in notice to quit. "But you're very good," he was told. So he stayed and the line stayed—"stuck right in my throat."

Muni Weisenfreund worked with Lee under his brand-new name of Paul Muni. Only once did the aloof Muni, who ordinarily displayed no warmth whatsoever, show a glimmer of friendship. The company had gone to the beach and Lee had lain on his stomach and suffered a severe sunburn. When he came on stage that night Muni added a gesture that wasn't in the script. He banged Lee on the back. Lee didn't flinch. He carried on exactly as he was supposed to in the scene. "An actor must have this kind of control."

In 1929 Lee stopped the show in what he regarded then as a triumph of acting. *Red Rust* was the first play imported from Russia after the revolution. The setting was Red Square and "The Internationale" was played as part of the production. Director Herbert Biberman, later named as one of the Hollywood Ten, had gone to Moscow and returned infused with their ideas.

Franchot Tone, Luther Adler, and Lionel Stander were cast, and an appointment was arranged for Lee to meet the director. Biberman, swarthy, well built, imposing, was not too thrilled with this unimpressive figure. Biberman surveyed him as though to say, "What the hell did they send me this guy for?" and announced, "I have nothing for you."

The solemn figure said only, "Okay."

Biberman then peered at him more closely. "There are only two parts left. One is a peasant type. The other is a comedy thing. Which would you like to read for?"

Humorless, Lee looked him straight in the face. "I'd like to read for the comedy part."

In a take unlikely to be equaled, Biberman's eyes nearly crossed. "It takes all kinds," he thought. Aloud he said, "You're supposed to be funny, you know."

"Yes. I know."

His name in the play was "Pimples" because the character had bad skin. He had determined not to paint on blemishes nor to wear makeup. He played what he calls "inner characterization. My feeling was that he was like a running sore. I had worked out the part and my idea was to play him with a perpetual cold. I built the entire character around that. It was a fanatical kind of thing, the inner feelings I built up about this character."

He took a brownish Ace bandage, stepped on it, crumpled it, and wrapped it around his neck. From the moment rehearsals began, he never took it off. He wore it to sleep. Its filthiness provided the color and the characterization. For the rest he patted on a little talcum to make his face pale and that was it.

Somehow the audience believed they saw pimples on his face. After his laudatory notices, Benny's sister, Clara, announced she was going and would bring her friends backstage. She never came backstage. Weeks later he met Clara on the street. "Why didn't you come back? Didn't you like the show?"

"We loved it. We didn't come back because you looked so terrible in your makeup we thought we'd leave you alone to take the stuff off."

It was his greatest compliment.

CHAPTER THREE

Destiny

Nora and Lee had moved to a larger three-room walkup in Crystal Gardens, a housing project in Astoria, Queens. An occasional visitor was Harold Clurman.

It is necessary to note that the passage of years plays tricks on the memory. The mind tends to becloud some issues, heighten others. When the elapsed time has been half a century, what stands out is usually only that mountain peak of excitement or that valley of unhappiness, those moments of extreme pain or pleasure that are so permanently graven on the memory that one can recall them brilliantly—or, rather, can somehow never forget.

The earliest beginnings of what came to be known as the Group Theatre were not ushered in to the accompaniment of seismic rumblings nor drums banging nor cymbals clanging. There was no sonorous deific pronouncement from On High signifying that Thou, Clurman, or Thou, Strasberg, shalt create a temple. Like so many fortuitous events in Strasberg's life, this had no conscious origin. There was no hard decision to go forth and make a dream a reality. It was just something that happened.

Born in idle conversation, a formless project of the spirit and soul of two idealists, it had a slow synthesis that took place over a couple of years. Neither knew theatrical history was unfolding in those first minutes nor that there would be in generations to come a zeal to record the precise word-by-word progression of this incipient stage of creation. Thus, although many recollections of Lee Strasberg and Harold Clurman blend in later unfoldings, the precise genesis of the Group Theatre is subject to whatever version appeals.

According to Lee, "Whatever ideas Harold had, whatever ideas I had never materialized or became defined in terms of a theatre. I didn't speak of that and he didn't speak of that. He spoke along the lines of what he considered was wrong with the theatre and of his dissatisfaction. I remember the occasion quite well because it is after all an important occasion."

A reconstruction of the scene goes substantially along these lines: Sitting in Nora and Lee's kitchen-dinette, a downcast Clurman mused, "I was happy in those days when I was a student in Paris and you know what I think I'm going to do? I'm going to go back to France."

Lee, who had learned to cook certain homey foods that his mama used to make, was throwing together a pan of salami and eggs which for him was a true Lucullan delight—at least the way he made it. He looked up from his frying. "Why?" he asked.

"Well," sighed Harold, "nothing much is happening here so I think I'll go back there."

"Do you have work there?"

"No, but I don't seem to find any place for myself here," replied Clurman.

"Okay, so you'll stay there for a while, but you won't stay there the rest of your life, right?"

"Yes . . . so?"

"So," said Lee, poking the salami, which was sticking to the pan, "you'll do there whatever it was you did there before and then you'll come back here and then you'll be exactly where you are now. Therefore I don't see what is gained by your going."

"Well, if there was some reason . . . something to stay for. . . ."

"I have no ideas for you so I can't suggest anything. All I know is, if you want something to happen you have to make it happen."

"Like what should happen?"

"Like you always talk about what you consider is wrong with the theatre, so why not try out some of those ideas on production you always talk about."

"I don't know of a production I could do."

"So what else would you like to do? Think."

Over the salami and eggs and tea with lemon, they shared their idealism. Lee envisioned theatre geared to the acting point of view. Harold pushed theatre based on artistic, not commercial, values. Lee's ideas were theatrical. Harold's ideas were literary. After supper they moved the conversation into the little enclosed porch.

Lee discussed how the Moscow Art Theatre's sincere artists were created by the art itself, bolstered by reassurance of its importance and duration and perfected by intensively working together for years in a dedicated organization. He marveled anew at how, although different in looks and traits, the actors were the same in emotional truthfulness and character embodiment and how each interrelated competently in each part so that small roles were acted by big talents all meshing with teamwork rather than all supporting one star. If, subliminally, Lee would have or could have ever entertained any far-off someday utopian achievement, it might have been to experiment within an ensemble. A sort of Moscow Art Theatre American style.

Harold thought not in terms of technique but of content. In place of European plays or little romantic dramas or empty melodramas, he wanted American plays with contemporary social themes that spoke to the times. To Harold a play was more than a story, entertainment, or abstract piece. It communicated something the author was trying to say, and he believed a company could not realistically convey an idea unless they related to the idea. Therefore, he leaned toward an entire unit—the playwright to be part of the actors and each to be part of the whole.

For Harold, what was important was the sense of the play and what was behind it. For Lee, what was important was the reality of the play and what could be done with it.

The preceding fragment was the beginning of the Group Theatre according to the Gospel of Lee Strasberg. The succeeding fragment was the beginning of the Group Theatre according to the Gospel of Harold Clurman.

"I don't remember anything about Lee saving me from going back to Paris one night at his apartment. I only know we used to walk and talk. My education was literary. My theatre was based on intellectual and critical aspects. His was purely theatrical. When we exchanged thoughts and contributed to one another, I learned a good deal in terms of developing my theatrical feeling and he learned that plays had a meaning in relation to the world and society which went beyond the theatrical."

Clurman's need was to see everything in the theatre as expressing a part of the whole of life. Lee's need was to see the connection of all stage elements—the set, the costumes, the dialogue— all working together with the actor's movements and moods and rhythm. It was Lee's technical processes versus Harold's interpretive aspects.

"Then," says Clurman, "all of a sudden my eyes opened. We were walking along Fifth Avenue and we stopped at a street light in front of a men's clothing store on Forty-third Street. I was stunned. I heard Lee say, 'We'll form our theatre on this basis.' *Our* theatre? *What* theatre? We were just talking. We weren't weighing realities. I had been expounding on what this country required culturally. These were *my* ideas and suddenly we were forming *our* theatre. My ears came to attention.

"I mean, *our* theatre was only an unformed extension of our inspired realism and now, suddenly, just by talking we were forming this? He didn't say, 'Let's see what we can do about this' or 'How do we get this going?' None of these things."

The memory on which both concur is that these amorphous discussions with no materialized concepts in view took place over a period of time—at Lee's, at Harold's, walking on the street, sitting in a restaurant. Sanford Meisner, an actor friend who had worked at Chrystie, joined the discussions. Morris Carnovsky, a working actor under contract to the Theatre Guild, lent an ear. Franchot Tone, a handsome, stiff-looking leading man in a play called *International*, sat in on the talks. They spent their spare hours probing and interpreting a Waldo Frank play, *New Year's Eve*, in a studio over an apartment building at 138 Riverside Drive. The building's owner was Sidney Ross, a junk and salvage dealer whose interest in redecorating his image fostered a willing-ness to indulge in cultural pursuits. His willingness, however, did not extend to backing *New Year's Eve* for Broadway.

Pursuing their novel concepts, the small group turned their tal-ents to Padraic Colum's *Balloon* and the workshop theories ad-vanced. Stanislavsky's system was emphasized. Affective memory exercises were tried. The play was worked improvisational style without scenery or props. Despite the excellence of the work, the project was short-lived.

The master plan had been to go away to a summer place in the country and work on plays in a quiet, dedicated atmosphere far from the Sturm und Drang of the city. It was predicated on the agreement that Sidney Ross would subsidize the operation. When it came time to put up the necessary capital, "he didn't say, 'no', he just sort of dropped out," recalls Lee.

The promise to stake the fledgling enterprise on an ongoing basis never progressed beyond the promissory stage. Thus uprooted in the springtime of their hopes, the tender seedlings of the Group Theatre withered on the ground. It was 1928. The time was not yet ripe.

Death

Nora brought great happiness into Lee's life. Perhaps those memories have pinkened with the passage of time because it was his first love and so long ago and for so short a time, but it was truly a season of great love.

Within two years Nora became ill. Following an examination by a neighborhood doctor in Queens, they made an appointment with one of the first women internists in the city. A peculiar woman with a set face etched in lines like a mummy, she recommended another opinion. The elderly surgeon, who prior to retirement had been the top of his profession, corroborated her findings and recommended a radiologist.

White-haired, immaculately dressed, with a cool, distinguished quality which set him apart, I. Seth Hirsch, head of the infant department of radiology at Beth Israel Hospital on Fourteenth Street, then consulted with Dr. Ewing. When Lee delivered a specimen to the laboratory Ewing, one of the early authorities on cancer, looked at him with sympathy. "Too bad," he sighed.

Lee didn't know how high the fees were. He only knew what he had. After the biopsy he asked, "How much is it?"

"How much do you have?"

"Well, I have fifteen dollars." And that, paid in full, is what the grieving husband gave the leading analyst from Cornell.

Nobody could anticipate that a girl Nora's age could become so ill. The knowledge produced a rare emotional experience. It never lessened the way they felt but, inexplicably, made the love deeper and more special, although it was no longer physical. "You invariably hear only about a couple's sexual relations and all the rest that goes with it, but at this moment the physical expression of the relationship could not be the primary satisfaction yet we were more in love than before."

This experience conditioned his future behavior. It taught him the fragility of life. . . . Grab today because you never know what can happen tomorrow. It also conditioned his attitude toward medical institutions. He had difficulty after that going into a hospital.

Following the operation, the doctors could do nothing more for their young patient, so she was sent home for the final period. Lee took his wife to his sister. There was no place else to go and she needed assistance. The family was speechless at the care Lee tendered his bride. He alone administered the injections of morphine. Nora's suffering was such that the pressure of footsteps on the wood floor jarred her. Heavily sedated, she lay in bed resting her arm on a pillow. She whispered to Papa in Yiddish, "I would like very much to escape the hands of death."

On an afternoon in the Thanksgiving season of 1929 Nora passed away. The consummate professional, aware of his responsibilities and in command of his emotions, Lee would not indulge his grief at the expense of others. Comments from those then associated with him range from revulsion at the fact that he played the following performance to respect for his show-must-go-on professionalism to "she had been out of it for so long already that it really didn't matter."

The blanket of self-control slipped only at the funeral, and Lee wept. At the grave site he clapped his hand over his mouth. Trained to stifle the inner screaming and to be strong, he commands the nerves and emotions and they obey. Such rigid restraint creates an insuperable barrier to human relations. There are those who self-censor and don't reach out for fear of rebuff.

There are those who reach out awkwardly and, indeed, meet the anticipated rebuff. Aaron Copland's memory is that he was about to offer condolences when Lee shucked him off and the moment for human warmth was gone. Harold Clurman insists Lee "thought I was a no-good, heartless bastard because I never expressed my personal sympathy. But how? He never talked about it. He never invited it. He resented it when we didn't introduce the subject but he rejected all attempts."

A first love is free of any element of repetition. It forms a part of that period when a human being comes into his own. It is a major event in a life. "The first love always has some sort of special value," agrees Lee.

In the first weeks after Nora's death, the sad-faced man had a strange experience. It was nighttime. He was coming to the Second Avenue and Tenth Street apartment of Mrs. Rosenzweig, Nora's mother. In the doorway of this small house of three floors stood a quiet, simple blonde pickup, reasonably good-looking, shivering in a camel's hair coat. When he opened the door, she solicited him. "Would you like to go with me?"

He couldn't go with her. He wasn't that kind. But it was cold. He could see she was chilled. At that moment she needed somebody as much as he needed somebody. She was in need in the same way he was in need. He felt sorry for her, almost protective of her. "She was doing her job like all of us were. My whole attitude toward whores has been fixed by that. I have a very sympathetic attitude toward them."

Franchot Tone offered to share his apartment on Eleventh Street, and Lee moved in with him. His place represented a whole different way of life. Franchot was wealthy, social, educated. Franchot's incidental music was Stokowsky's rendition of the Beethoven Seventh. Franchot had a manservant, a Filipino valet.

It discomfited the house guest who didn't know how to conduct himself in such circumstances. "I had none of the social graces. I avoided shaking hands because I was never sure who put out whose hand first and I was afraid I'd do it wrong or clumsily, so I didn't do it at all. Franchot's tastes and manners were impeccable and I envied him that. I admired that easy ability. I left his apartment after a few days. It made me too uncomfortable."

CHAPTER FIVE

Survival

Lee moved in permanently with his only friend, Benny, who lived in London Terrace, a large housing development on West Twenty-third Street between Ninth and Tenth Avenues. Benny's wife, Mascha, was reticent and withdrawn. Benny was dominant. Mascha adored her husband and honored his wishes. Despite the difficulties of an extra person living in her apartment, Mascha never complained. She did not, however, share her husband's adoration of this strange spirit who shared their home.

Lee was complicated. His was a continual search to learn more, to grow intellectually. He was an endless ocean of specialized knowledge. If you stuck him with a pin knowledge poured out.

After a college student majoring in religion expounded on the Bible, Lee commented quietly that many ethical qualities predated the Bible and stemmed from Mithraism. "From what?" asked the college man. "Mithraism. That's a religion from Persia which opposed Christianity in the third century." "No kiddin'," marveled the theologian, "hey, you come up with stuff that even our professors haven't talked about."

Ever the consummate scholar, anything—such as the science of philosophy or the study of the theatre or oriental religion—in which Lee had an interest he had a *deep* interest. He not only consumed everything, he retained everything. He not only studied the authorities but those books the authorities studied. While others accepted what they obtained from secondary material, he probed deeper, researched further, and was never satisfied until he'd tapped the root, the original primary source.

What did not interest him was idle conversation. Lee's spare hours were spent burrowing inward. The cast of characters to whom he was newly exposed came from a different environment. Harold spoke French. Franchot had all the cultured graces. The Theatre Guild's Lawrence Langner, a lawyer, was highly sophisticated. His totally alien background was not promotive of lolling about making charming small talk. "I didn't grow up with that in my house. Small talk I don't make."

Lee's avenue of communication early came through the route of the teacher. The young man soaking up knowledge was even then dissolving into the teacher. Immediately he assimilated information he was committed to transmit it. In his twenties, Lee's forcefed communication was on a professional and theatrical level. When it came to the personal, he had not the patience, the strength nor the know-how.

When one is transplanted into the unfamiliar, suffering can be a concomitant to growth. The unsure and insecure tend to cover vulnerability by walling themselves in. This conscious or unconscious defensive armor insulates from hurts. It's not that Lee deliberately opted to build a wall. It's that certain situations trigger certain reactions. Some of Lee's nonoutgoing personality was the result of adjustments. He was adjusting to those qualities he discovered lacking and those social circumstances in which he found himself a foreigner. "It was hard for me. I didn't know things. Also, I was single-minded, intense. I was fighting for something."

Mascha had a separate little piece of the apartment so "I don't think she minded my living with them, but in any case my relationship was with Ben." In their years together, Mascha could not recall his addressing anything personal to her. He did, however, supply theatre tickets. The Jewish stenographer who took dictation in Yiddish thus gained a little glamour in her friends' eyes, but those who remember insist it was hard for Mascha.

What Lee saw in Benny other than devotion is not certain. Lee's zenith of affection is recorded in these words: "I liked Ben. Everybody who came into contact with him responded to his soft quality." Lee never showed emotion, so nobody can swear for a fact Lee loved Benny. They supposed it. They imagined it. They didn't see it.

Ben's persistence in this one-way relationship supports the position that he derived something from it. Benny's total immersion in Lee's life allowed him to feed from Lee's artistic storehouse. Lee put the milk and honey into Benny's life. In return for this certain depth and certain intellectuality and uncertain passport out of a mundane world, Benny gave a great deal. Benny gave his money. He gave his home. He gave his heart to somebody who overtly didn't give it back. For Benny his wife was secondary. His son was secondary. His sister-in-law put it this way, "Ben actually sacrificed his whole life for Lee."

Lee could do no wrong with Benny. He went up to Benny's summer place carrying the first album he ever bought, an imported RCA label with eight recordings costing an astronomical $2.50 apiece. Following a Saturday evening performance he took the hour train ride to Croton-on-Hudson, then a taxi. Benny waited up for him. Although it was two in the morning, Benny didn't mind that Lee went right to the record player with his armful of Schubert songs. The first recording the guest put on was "Der Leiermann" ("The Hurdy Gurdy Man") with Elena Gerhardt, a lieder singer known for her loud, operatic voice.

Laughs Lee gaily at the memory, "The cottage was set back in a forest of trees and such crystal-clear silence in that countryside at that hour you can't believe . . . and then like a shot came that German voice shattering that stillness . . . !"

Neither Ben nor his wife ever spoke about how much they gave. Lee paid no rent. In fact, good-hearted, generous Benny carried his friend financially. Said Yudel Slutzky, "My brother adored Lee, but I tell you the truth, I couldn't see why. That man's behavior I didn't care for."

Still, Yudel's wife, Ann, insists she caught a flash of that other person who lives inside the man. "True, he gave little but I must admit once he was extraordinarily kind to me. I'd been having some unhappy love affair and he sat near me in Mascha and Ben's living room and wanted to know why I was so unhappy. That was the only time I ever saw him make an overture or be friendly or exhibit concern. He saw I was unbearably miserable and he reached out. So, he has that ability. There's just something that holds him back. Maybe it's extreme self-consciousness."

There was no self-consciousness in terms of expressing his professional views, however. About acting he was, to quote Harold Clurman, "as concentrated as a jeweler over the inner mechanism of a watch." Asked why Russian theatre was so advanced, Lee launched into how Chekhov probes people, not things, and how in lieu of theatrics and artificial heroics the Russians learned to sustain within themselves a vivid inner life in order to live the part completely. Asked how American theatre could receive the respect accorded the other arts, out poured a lengthy treatment on how it demanded the coherence expected of such trained ensembles as the great orchestras and ballet companies and how instead of a succession of separate productions each should be a link in the creative continuity that characterizes the activity of any artist.

Lee's ability to discourse on his subject knew no parallel unless you count Clurman. Clurman never spoke if he could exhort, never discussed if he could lecture. Where Strasberg was an ascetic, Clurman was a romantic. Where Strasberg was always controlled, Clurman was invariably impulsive. Strasberg was precise. Clurman extravagant. Clurman, who understood great art even if he couldn't afford it, was theatrical—the type who sported a black coat and matching homburg.

Clurman and Strasberg, both graduates of the Lower East Side, both Jewish, both the same vintage, both from the Laboratory Theatre and the Theatre Guild, were dissimilar in many respects. In their passion for the theatre, however, they were as one. Harold philosophized about a permanent theatre where plays could be produced for their artistic value. He argued American theatre should relate to American life and be founded on contemporary values with emphasis on American plays, American companies, and American playwrights committed to works with a social purpose that would mirror American lives and suggest the possible amelioration of American problems. "Our interest in the life of our times must lead us to discovery of those methods that would most truly convey this life through the theatre."

Lee was interested in exploring techniques on the stage. An actor who was going to earn his living as an actor, he was motivated from the acting point of view. The possibilities of a maybe someday ongoing organization wherein he could work on a continuing basis within a professional company in overcoming clichés and theatrical gimmicks and in perfecting his craft were attractive to him.

Lee and Harold's pursuit of their individual ideals led to Cheryl Crawford. Gentile, midwestern, and nonverbal, the then casting director for the Theatre Guild refers to her joining these two on their glorious quest in these words: "We were a bizarre trio, two Old Testament prophets and a WASP *shiksa.*"

On the threshold of an important career, Cheryl was being groomed to assume Theresa Helburn's position as head of the Theatre Guild. Lee still marvels that she turned her back on the major American theatrical organization of the day. "She gave all that up for two schnooks like us."

Cheryl, too, was an idealist. Harold and Lee's ideas inflamed her imagination and their ceaseless, boundless rhetoric eventually "seduced my mind." Sensitive, literate, a reader of poetry, this portion of Cheryl's spirit somehow never surfaced visibly and even her active idealism came all covered up in pragmatics. . . . So what are you going to do with this great idea? . . . What's your plan to get out of fantasy into reality? . . . What about money to create this permanent theatre?

Cheryl's participation led to serious discussions with fellow professionals at Cheryl's place, Harold's place, anybody's place. Lee shrugs, "I didn't really see any future in this at this point, but it certainly didn't hurt."

Morris Carnovsky had read "with envy" how the Russian theatre functioned under Stanislavsky and he had heard "with excitement" how this group was committed to that. He was agitated with the hope of extending himself. "I'd always had a nagging sense that I wasn't altogether the craftsman I wanted to be. I knew acting was more than just walking on, being inspired. Listening to Lee, I was eager to reduce all this to a science of acting of the highest degree. This new thing was exciting."

Carnovsky was then in *Elizabeth the Queen* with the Lunts. Also in the play were Mab Anthony, who dated the author, Maxwell Anderson, and Phoebe Brand from the Clare Tree Major School. Phrases such as "The group will be at my place tomorrow . . ." infiltrated the dressing rooms. Understudy Tony Kraber, walk-on Ruth Nelson, youngster Dorothy Patten, and fellow cast member Bill Challee who worked in *Red Rust* sat in on the talks. Discussed exhaustively was Broadway's hit-and-flop system whereby you finally get lucky and land a play which then quickly closes and you're back doing the agents again and back waiting an hour for somebody to show up to audition you, only to be told you're too tall or too fat or too something. The idea of steady employment, and of working together with a unified technique through the product of not one production or two but continually, had an appeal.

Every Friday after showtime throughout that whole winter of '30–'31, dozens sat on the floor in someone's crowded living room hearing how this group "is going to challenge the professional theatre." Among them were Sanford Meisner, character actor J. Edward Bromberg, who came from Eva Le Gallienne's repertory company, Franchot Tone and his friend Margaret Barker, who came because Franchot rhapsodized over Lee's "wonderful new way of working," Russell Collins who came from the Cleveland Playhouse, Robert Lewis from the Civic Repertory Company, Mary Morris from the Eugene O'Neill organization, and Clifford Odets, who came from secondary roles at the Guild.

The daughter of the Yiddish theatre's Jacob Adler, Stella Adler, came from "already being successful as a leading lady." Stella's interest was piqued because "this had a high-mindedness. I thought this fashionable new idea embodied a revolutionary literary concept. Besides, Clurman was a forceful speaker. He had a kind of mysticism about him, saying 'We are building the great American theatre.'"

Eunice Stoddard, an ingenue with white-blond hair and pink and white translucent skin, brought Katharine Hepburn, who was understudying her in A *Month in the Country*. Hepburn and she had traveled to Europe together, steerage, and were close friends. Nonetheless, Katharine Hepburn did not share her enthusiasm for this undertaking.

When the numbers reached over fifty, somebody managed to get a hall to accommodate the standees. Ruth Nelson had a secondhand, broken-down, black Ford roadster with a rumble seat in which she clanked around fetching the actors from their various theatres and transporting them to meetings. There was that icy night when Ruth, Eunice, Hepburn, Margaret "Beanie" Barker, and another actress, Virginia Farmer, returned to Eunice's wealthy parents' brownstone on East Sixty-fifth Street between Park and Lexington following a session at Steinway Hall. Eunice piled in alongside Ruth. Virginia and Beanie crouched way down for warmth inside the rumble seat, and Hepburn, wrapped in the car rug leaving only that shiny, bright face exposed, balanced herself atop the rumble-seat ledge.

It was one in the morning. The servants were no longer about. Eunice heated some milk in the enormous kitchen in the rear and they all carted that plus a supply of cookies to Eunice's third-floor bedroom. Ruth poked up the fireplace and the girls made themselves comfortable. This was the generation that came into the profession on the wings of a dream. The talk was about this theatre that was to come. The tone was philosophical. They would elevate the social climate.

"The theatre of the twenties came out of the war and so it was veddy social," began Ruth. "It was all elegant and gay and partying and pretty and pink cotton candy and fluff. I'm intolerant of this today when people are lined up for soup handouts. Shouldn't theatre be meaningful?"

"Yes, it should," put in Beanie. "That whole gay glamour of the twenties is gone along with high heels and bubbling champagne. We all need some sort of reality. That's why this project is meaningful. It's born in the Depression. It will talk to our times. It will make positive statements while the other plays we are seeing do not. After all, the Lunts are doing Molnar and the Guild is staging Andreyev!"

Ruth nodded agreement. "It's true we really should do something for the American theatre instead of importing all these foreign successes."

Hepburn, stretched out full on the floor, flat on her stomach, raised up on an elbow. "You know, the actors who are pushing these meetings are being laughed at by everybody else who is secure and successful in the commercial theatre."

"Then we should look down on them and laugh back," came

Ruth's answer. "We're like a little band out in the middle of the ocean and we have to cling to one another."

"A bunch of young idiots is the way outsiders are referring to all of you," commented Hepburn, sipping her milk slowly.

Virginia Farmer inched closer to the crackling logs. "Well, Eunice and Ruth both have been to the American Laboratory Theatre, so they particularly appreciate this kind of acting technique that Lee Strasberg was telling us about and, frankly, it fascinates me."

"Maybe we're all idealistic but the thought of a permanent company where people work together all the time is a thrill," added Beanie, who was up for the ingenue lead in *The Barretts of Wimpole Street*. "I'm caught in this idea where there won't be stars and where everybody will play in all plays. I'm willing to give up my great role which promises to be the hit of this season to be part of this."

"Yes, I'm sure it's an interesting idea," drawled Hepburn, "but it's not for me. I've got to go it alone."

Eunice's parents, who were active in cultural and artistic pursuits, had helped finance the Boleslavsky school. "To me from my background," explained Eunice, "this is what theatre should be. Ensemble. Moscow Art Theatre stuff. The Stanislavsky kind of thing."

Hepburn saw the handwriting on the wall. "I'll have none of it. I cannot understand why this is something you'd want to do."

Beanie fished out a cigarette and warmed to her subject. "Harold's talks are inspired and persuasive and this is his brainchild and he's the inspirational leader. So, okay. Maybe it's just that he's so compelling a speaker, but it seems to me he's passionate about this being a theatre, not a producing organization. That means you have a permanent life, not just that you're there only to do a play for as long as it runs. There are benefits to working all the time. At least you always know where you are, right? And you have to be willing to earn less in order to earn always."

"Look, I'm doing the lead now but it's all hit and miss, as you well know," cut in Eunice. "You could play a week and then it could close. You go on tour and then it folds out of town and you can wait another year for another plum role. It's all this sort of gamble. Or there's that Hollywood thing." She looked around. "Do you want to do Hollywood?"

"I certainly do!" boomed Hepburn.

"Well, not me. I'm terribly against a movie career. It just seems to me it's the bottom. I hate to get into that kind of stuff where your life is ruled by managers and when the result finally comes out your best things have been cut. I mean, that's not acting. It's not any of the things I believe in. So it's very natural for me to gravitate toward this hope. It's a place to really live to act."

Katharine Hepburn stared at her friend. "Eunice, I can't go along with that Stanislavsky nonsense that 'there are no small parts only small actors.' This bunch is advocating a nonstar system."

"It's a collective, Kate. It's young actors and actresses in their twenties who all want to do not just front-line theatre but more interesting theatre and are willing to assemble into a group to achieve it."

Virginia Farmer poked up the fire. "We've all had disappointments and maybe this is a way to avoid them in the future. Maybe this is a new wave. It's the beginning of an important development in our business."

When Virginia took her place back on the floor, Katharine Hepburn made it plain that "this is just going to have to develop without me. I want no part of the idea because I am simply not willing to set myself up to not being a star. It's that pure and simple. There's no ensemble non-star kind of theatre for me."

The dedicated nucleus who was prepared to shed the shibboleths of success and share in this extraordinary experiment searched for an appropriate name. ". . . so what shall we call the group . . . who knows, I don't know . . . we're just a group. . . ." When nobody surfaced with anything better, they christened themselves the Group Theatre. The self-appointed directors were Harold, Lee, and Cheryl.

Actors invited to join the Group Theatre were either known to the directors or had submitted to personal interviews. Each needed sufficient flexibility to adapt to major and minor roles in whatever vehicle might be chosen and to work not for individuality but within the group as a whole. Despite theatrical ability, an exhibitionist or overly seasoned "name" might militate against

the homogeneity. Choices were on the basis of talent, affinity for
the Group's aims, plus a capacity to develop.

The final selection was made by the triumvirate. Meanwhile,
the still casting director Cheryl Crawford had cast the still actor
Lee Strasberg as the peddler in *Green Grow the Lilacs*. From the
road where he was on tour, he sent letters pages long listing his
candidates.

By the spring of 1931 Lee had returned to New York, Harold
had dispatched acceptances to twenty-eight actors, Cheryl had
located a country site for the period of basic training. Everyone
was enthusiastic. There were no expressions of apprehension. A
person only worries when there's something to lose. These young
people had nothing to lose because they had nothing. As for Lee,
"I was building a career. I didn't even yet have a career to lose!"

June 8, 1931, the caravan set forth for Brookfield, Connecticut.

BOOK THREE

"PAULA"

CHAPTER ONE

Brookfield Center

An hour's drive from New York, right off the main road then up a hill lay this once-upon-a-time spartan adult camp. There were bungalows of assorted shapes and sizes and a main house with the community dining room and kitchen plus four bedrooms and one bathroom. Cheryl, who found it through a newspaper ad, appointed the rooms personally. "What I did was, I gave myself a nice one and the rest depended on who lived with who and needed extra beds."

Flashes of memory illumine Franchot banging on the john door for someone to hurry up; Lee in a cell crammed with books; Carnovsky playing music loudly on the steps of his cottage which was right off the road; and lovers Harold Clurman and Stella Adler arguing repeatedly in their ground-floor quarters.

In the bar, which had a sweet-smelling loft at one end, someone produced a canvas director's chair. Lee—with his shined shoes and white ducks—sat in it and unfolded the tenets of Stanislavsky. Since volumes of technique fill libraries, this book makes no attempt to detail such theorems. Substantially it was that Group members would not handle stage emotions mechanically, would not pretend, would not just deliver lines as excellently as possible but would substitute authenticity of feeling for tricks of stagecraft and true emotion for theatrical performance.

They were taught the use of "affective memory" which was parsed as the reliving of an experience minus its literal presence. An example is breaking up a love affair, then months later meeting a friend who says, "Hey, I just saw so and so. . . ." The heart pumps, the blood flows, although the actual lover is not present. Since this memory bank affects all of life, it is the matrix from which a subjective actor can pull what he needs.

Affective memory encompasses sensory memory. Example: the dog hears the bell, he receives food, his saliva starts. Eventually he becomes so conditioned that his saliva starts with the bell. This sensory memory is conditioning by connection. In the case of an actor who is resurrecting a remembrance, he concentrates only on the sensory objects: what he originally saw, heard, smelled, touched, tasted. Was he seated? What did the chair feel like? How did the room smell? Was it dark or light? Natural light or electric? The technique probes further into other kinetic sensations. What was he wearing? Short sleeves or long? Wool or silk? Warm or cool? Recollecting such details creates an associative chain which unlocks the experiential fear or happiness or sadness.

While pecking at the shell of this new way of working, each inched through every object in his experience to determine its conditioning factor. This lengthy plunge into the abyss of one's mind was ultimately to be reserved for the classroom, the bathroom, the dressing room—anyplace but the stage. As one became adept at bringing these memories and their subsequent emotions into play, the process quickened. Lee equated it to getting dressed in the morning. It could take an hour, but you can do it in five minutes.

The Group Theatre phrase, "Take a minute," began to be likened by outsiders to some magical incantation. It actually meant you were one minute away from performance, so you were to click into your preparatory work. It was not to be done earlier nor last longer. It was to be done the minute prior to the cue so that no actor would be sapped before his big moment.

It was a rainy morning in those early days. Franchot Tone was laboring to respond naturally on stage while concentrating on his special remembrance. Franchot would speak, then pull back in his memory, then return, then throw another line. Lee hung up his Captain Ahab outfit, a long yellow slicker which ill became him, and hovered over lost Phoebe. "Why don't you work more like Franchot?"

"I really don't know what he's doing."

"What do you mean you don't know what he's doing? He's thinking. He's going back. He's thinking what the line means. Why don't you do that?"

"I can't. I'm trying because I know everything you're giving us is right and we all believe in it but I just don't get all this subjective stuff. I mean, we're all learning a tremendous amount and we know that a lot of things are starting right here and that it's all your contribution . . . and, well, I want to please you but . . ." She looked at him and finished off lamely, "What you want stops everything. It stops the action."

"Do it anyhow."

"I'll try." What came out was forced emotion.

"No good. No good." He had grabbed her tightly by the arm. At the same time he was stroking her with his free hand.

When Phoebe tensed up, Lee growled, "Rrrrrreeeelaaaaaxxxxxx, darrrrlinggggg, rrrrreeeelaaaaxxxxxx!"

Offers Phoebe, "Lee was a God to us. We truly admired him. We wanted to do what he wanted even if we didn't always understand it."

They worked like dogs and considered the labor sacred. Comments set designer Boris Aronson: "I always felt everybody there took a goddamn oath of holiness." Nobody smoked during rehearsal. No cigarette butts littered the stage. Nobody read a magazine or newspaper not connected with the work. Lee demanded strict devotion to the work. Since Stanislavsky was a disciplinarian, it was conceded Lee's conduct stemmed from good reasoning. There was total commitment. You enter the sanctum sanctorum, you shed the outside world, you concentrate on your craft.

Rehearsals for Paul Green's *The House of Connelly* commenced immediately. Morris Carnovsky's character was a drunken southern colonel whose action was to clamber onto a chair and lift his glass in the air. They did it repeatedly. Lee was searching for a certain effect. He was not to be rushed. His face was fanatical. Again and again Morris hoisted himself up and again and again lifted his glass. Each time Lee was dissatisfied. Each time he explained what he wanted. Each time it was "do it again." Each time Morris was stopped as he lifted his glass. Morris grew "goddamn weary of this. After all, I was already an established name while Lee was a nobody."

The fifteenth time Morris raised his glass he permitted himself the gesture of dropping it on the table as though to say, "Oh, Christ, when the hell are we going to get this god-damn thing right!"

"Lee's face went white. I mean, he was passionately . . . no, I'd say . . . sinisterly . . . devoted to acting . . . and there was a dead silence from the others assembled."

Morris knew he'd done wrong. The crashing down of that glass broke the law of the Group which was that they must be *unified*. Each to be willingly submerged to the common need.

Quietly Lee said, "Okay, let's go on." Morris clambered back onto the chair so there was a bit of movement while he got in place and by then he was told, "That's all right . . . enough for now on that one piece of business." He attempted to go forward with the next speech, but Lee had gathered his strength.

As Morris tells it, "He tore me apart for my behavior. 'You . . . ,' he sputtered. 'you . . . you are committing a central crime against the whole spirit of the Group. We are aiming to form a collective theatre here. For anyone to transgress is a crime.' He kept ranting that there was a principle which he was going to lay out for me again and that is that there was to be no big star but only the whole—only the Group.

"He was suffused. He was about to break a blood vessel. I finally calmed him. 'All right, Lee,' I said, '. . . all right . . .' He was our lofty center. I had to save him for us. He was literally vivisecting me and I was being careful about saving him! And we weren't alone. This was in front of everyone. A Broadway director would have called you aside, but not Lee. This lesson he had to convey to the whole assemblage.

"Well, I knew the principle but I also knew the practice. The principle of equality was there but the ass-kissing of Strasberg was also there. The principle applied to everyone else but not him. He was the omniscient, the all-power. He alone held the tablets. He was not only Moses but God also. There was no higher power to punish him so he could break the rules but only *he* could!"

That the very examination of their capabilities as actors in the Group was an act of love, that each one's sense of self was expanding in the atmosphere of this holy society, that there was a zeal of commitment to a purpose over and above yourself, that the body was consumed with this religiosity and willingly and worshipfully accepted Lee's divinity was made manifest when member Art Smith attacked Morris. The law of the Group like the law of the jungle had sunk into his bones. 'When you dropped that glass on the table, I hated you. I HATED YOU!"

The incident which was indelibly etched on Morris' memory nearly fifty years ago didn't scratch Lee's. He doesn't even recall it, dismissing the whole conversation with, "Actors are like children. This kind of temperament goes on in all creative processes. You can't take such an incident of excitement seriously."

That first summer Bobby Lewis brought his cello. Franchot, Morris, the youngest member, Herbie Ratner, and others grew beards because of the lack of hot water. Herbie shaved his off the day his girl was due and succeeded in stuffing up the sink in the common bathroom. A few found some rods tucked away, some worms wriggling away, and fished for trout. There were picturesque riding trails, so Alix Walker, who came from the wealth of upstate New York's Tuxedo Park brought up horses which were stabled under the barn with Tony Kraber doubling as stablemaster. The horses came to know Tony so well that "when I'd be upstairs rehearsing and I'd say a line and they'd hear my voice they'd go whinnying—and right in the middle of my big scene."

Eunice Stoddard's dark-haired, handsome mother and tall, stately, bespectacled father had a summer place in nearby Washington, Connecticut, and she invited the whole crew one Sunday afternoon. The long white house set amid rolling lawns was staffed with servants in starched uniforms. The dining-room table, which sat fourteen was stocked with food. Outside they were toasting marshmallows and everywhere they were consuming applejack. The Groupies had located a nearby farmer who supplied limitless quantities at four dollars a gallon.

It was hot. Everybody came in shorts or slacks. Everybody was drinking, playing party games on the lawn, and having fun. There was, however, a rehearsal that night, so at eight o'clock the world's greatest ensemble-to-be lumbered back to their "cathedral" stoned and noisy and dopey and all played out.

The lone member who had not attended the picnic was waiting —clean, cool, shaven, sober, composed—to begin work. Lee angrily surveyed what was left of his actors. His compressed lips were bloodless. When he ultimately parted them it was "to scream and shout at us," recalled Beanie Barker. "He was hysterical." Whatever spirit was left in the men was wild. They were tight and by way of answer they ripped off their clothes and dove into the pond. The rest stripped their things off, too, and everybody swam naked. Later a select group vomited in a bathtub. The sanctum sanctorum was totally destroyed.

Lee was "insane with rage." It was precisely this hysteria that made everything go mad. Everybody broke. It wasn't just against Strasberg. It was just a terrible need to break.

The boys pulled the pillows apart and had pillow fights with the feathers flying all over. Beanie thought Lee was going to die. "It was awful. He had like a seizure. He screamed then something happened in the back of his throat and he was tongue-tied. I was terrified for Lee."

This episode Lee remembers well. He cites the fact that in the Moscow Art Theatre the stage was clean as a hospital and the students rose when the master entered. No, the Group didn't have that kind of rigidity but, yes, he wishes they could have. He asks the rhetorical question, can you see Toscanini leading a sodden orchestra or directing the string section while the percussion section is reading newspapers or, worse, laid out flat?

They were assembled for a high level of creativity in which he believed strongly. It demanded total concentration. Whether his rages contributed to the achievement is not certain. What is certain is that there was achievement.

In *Connelly* Morris' character had killed himself and the people rushed onto the stage crying and carrying this dead body. To achieve an effect Lee stationed extras on the stairs at the highest and farthest point from the stage and at successive landings. The sound started from way up and far off and at the cue the farthest people ran down into the next group screaming and hollering, then that knot of humanity ran down into another bunch whom they collected, and the commotion and the army of bodies built, with everyone literally running into one another huffing and puffing and out of breath. At the last station they took up Morris and carried him onto the stage.

The effect was so real that the caretaker seated outside did not believe it was make-believe. Hearing the gunshot and the ensuing panic and seeing everyone running, he ran too. He looked around wildly in the knot of people when another bunch plowed right by him carrying the inert Morris. So caught was he that he called out, "For God's sake . . . why doesn't somebody do something . . . a man is dying!"

The actors were so passionate and the scene so allegro that the dialogue was sometimes incomprehensible—even to Lee. "We were forcing ourselves to our own conceits, as Shakespeare says, to create those results which we did in fact actually create and I didn't mind being blamed for an actor's occasional incoherence. I alone knew what I was building for."

Inside, he wasn't all that secure. And when he wavered he covered. He would just grow together tight. His legendary anger stemmed in part from fear and uncertainty. He was scared.

The first Friday after the company returned to the city, Lee invited his brother to rehearsal. He appeared tired, almost physically ill. For months he'd been at nerve's end, forcing himself beyond the point. He looked cadaverous. It was the noon lunch break with everybody heading out by twos and threes. Lee stood alone. "Arthur, you want to take a little walk?"

"Sure . . . of course . . . so, tell me," began Arthur as they started slowly around the block, "how you making out?"

"You know, the production is all my responsibility and it's a great strain. In a week we have the opening and it's really working on me."

Arthur's blue eyes searched his younger brother's face. "I understand what a major step this is for you and I hope it proves successful because everybody says you have been very strong in your opinions."

"So what's wrong with that? When I know something is right,

it's right. I can't help it if what I know, I *know*. Maybe nobody else knows it but I know it."

They walked and talked and Lee, fighting to get his ideas over, seemed so little, so in need of someone to throw an arm around him. "Let's go someplace and get a sandwich and something sweet," suggested Lee. "I feel like something sweet."

The "rigid and sometimes terrifying man" downed a large-size chocolate drink. Having permitted himself to pleasure himself he headed back to work.

House of Connelly garnered twenty-two curtain calls. The opening-night party was in the tiny, top-floor walkup of member Walter Coy in the West Forties between Fifth and Sixth Avenues a few doors from Cheryl's, where, all alone, she waited out the reviews. At 2 A.M. she phoned with the raves, then walked over. It was after five when Broadway's newest stars floated out the door.

Reviewers pronounced Lee's direction "exciting." They wrote personal letters of praise. The Group was "flabbergasted." Never could they imagine such instant fame and acceptance. Newspapers wrote that not since the Moscow Art Theatre had New York seen anything like this unusual ensemble.

And this ensemble really was unusual. There was handsome, egotistical, self-centered Franchot Tone, who'd been christened "Pampered Tone" at Cornell. An Easterner from two aristocratic families reaching back to the Revolution, Franchot was to the manner born. Then there was the lanky midwestern farmer with the yellowish complexion and trusting eyes. "Friendly Ford" as he was called eventually resigned with, "Ah come to realize that the thing ah love mos' is the smell of cow manure."

Eunice Stoddard, Virginia Farmer, and convent-educated Ruth Nelson contrasted sharply with the sharp aroma of European East Side Jewry as exuded by Lee, Harold and Stella, and Luther Adler. Of her pipe-smoking, admiralty-lawyer father from New England, Eunice commented, "This was a breed the Jewish segment didn't know. Nor did they understand Yankee habits or collegiate ways or typically Americana customs. They'd never seen people like us."

There was Art Smith, a solid drinker, and Beanie Barker, now reformed but then, admittedly, "a drunk." There was Alix

Walker, who had a need to get away from her mother, and there was Clifford Odets who loved his delicate, sad mother but had a need to get away from his father who came complete with cigar and pride of financial success, a type he later satirized in his writing.

There was sweet, "sort of pathetic" Herbert Ratner and "tight, morose" Lee and "good for a laugh" Luther Adler who came up later. There was handsome Sanford Meisner and bald Morris Carnovsky, tall, taciturn Cheryl and short, garrulous J. Edward Bromberg. There was Dorothy Patten with her allowance and mink coat and rich father in Chattanooga, and Paula Miller, who was too poor to get herself up so she borrowed clothes which she belatedly returned after wearing and tearing. There was heavy-set, unpretty Alix with the serious emotional problems and inability to have a meaningful relationship with a man and blond Phoebe, who was so cute that, recalls Luther, "We had a 'Fuck Phoebe' club, which doesn't mean we ever got near her, but, oh boy, did we all have a lech for her."

There was Stella Adler who was handsome with dark blond hair and lovely skin, and there was Stella's clique, consisting of Bobby Lewis, Sandy Meisner, and later Paul Morrison, who broke into theatre by carrying a spear in a Guild production. While the clique sprawled about in wilted shorts and sweaty faces, glamorous Stella sashayed about in peau de soie and long gloves.

And there were the tensions. Unapproachable Harold was consumed by his love affair with Stella. It was a disease. Theatrical to the marrow, Stella staged a huge show all the time and Harold was obsessed, alternately fighting and making up.

There was the Franchot-Morris schism. Loner Franchot didn't spend free time with his confreres. Franchot was a rising star. He was charming but unhappy, lost and emotionally torn. His problems made him testy, and he preserved his individuality by being as apart but as noticed as possible. With a hunting knife he'd hack at the barn and carve its walls or floor to bits. Nobody reprimanded this small-boy indulgence and so he persistently whacked out whole divots of wood during rehearsals. Franchot didn't have anybody. He palled with nobody. At intervals he'd jump into his car, disappear, then surface days later.

Morris was a talker. He fed on causes. He sat up nights with

Bromberg, Lou Leverett, or his other pals, debating, exchanging opinions, righting wrongs, and healing the ills of the world. It was the Fourth of July, and while Morris lounged on his back porch struggling to enjoy Mozart, Franchot was setting off giant firecrackers in the yard. After several nerve-shattering explosions Morris began to self-destruct.

He shouted, "For Chrissake, Franchot, will you cut out that idiotic noise!" Franchot growled, "I am celebrating. It is my right as an American citizen to celebrate the birth of my country." "So celebrate a little quieter." Gesturing toward Morris' portable phonograph, Franchot shouted, "Besides, I don't like *your* noise." He fired off another, then disappeared to return two days later—still upset.

There were others with their own private demons, such as the actress who became so tense that she slapped an actor's face in rehearsal, and the frustrated Clifford Odets who, striving to find his place as a writer, yearned for what seemed out of his grasp and spent solitary hours practicing chords on a piano. There were agitators and wastrels, those who couldn't integrate and those who needed people, the haves who hung together and the have-nots, the ones weaned on Yiddish theatre and the ones addicted to bobbing for apples. There were temperaments and crises of living in close proximity. They were new people with new surroundings and a new system of working. Despite their common center, it seems in retrospect a task of herculean proportions for a Strasberg or any other mortal to have composed these variants into one harmonious theatrical relationship.

Living collectively being a natural concomitant to living together, this revolutionary group began breaking ground in its love relationships. Decades before unmarried brides and grooms freely roomed together there were Morris and Phoebe, Stella and Harold, Ruth Nelson and Bill Challee, and, shortly, Lee and a plumpish strawberry blonde named Paula Miller. Then there were, as several have described it, "Franchot and anybody, Clifford and anybody, and Luther and anybody. Luther was a grabber."

Franchot kept his sex life apart. He stashed his women outside the complex and drove off for frequent visits but he never imported them. Clifford, who would make you if he could, was wildhaired, wild-eyed, bespectacled and had a crush on platinum-haired, waspish Eunice, who was devoted to her architect fiancé, Julian Whittlesey. Clifford's cottage was two hundred yards from Eunice's, yet daily he went to the post office and mailed her a love letter. It always went unanswered.

On the one side this eclectic body had its homosexual relationships and on the other there were marriages including that of pretty Molly Thacher to an earthy, unattractive latecomer named Elia Kazan.

Come evenings, some would take a walk. Odets prowled burlesque shows. Lee occasionally went for an ice cream soda with Beanie, who characterizes herself as "a gentle soul except I had an alcoholic problem and as soon as something went wrong it was wow! down-the-hatch and I'd scream my head off." Beanie remembers "the softness of Lee's tiny, almost feminine hands" when he'd relax her shoulders in her hairy moments. "I think, perhaps, Lee loved me a little bit although he certainly never said anything."

Lee was attracted to Beanie. "If I'd had more gumption I probably would have made an approach, except I could never make an approach to anybody." And so Lee's unvoiced affection for Beanie remained just that. Paula Miller had meanwhile wormed her way into Lee's bones in the same way Paula did everything—deliberately and aggressively.

Paula was earthy and physical and warm. She remained good-humored despite jibes poked at her rough manners and language and total openness. One ninety-degree day Paula, outfitted in the barest clothing, tripped on the lawn. Her sundress flew up, and Odets, who swooped down like a predatory bird, cracked, "Oh, God, a real blonde!" Paula laughed the loudest. Paula plopped her full weight onto a fragile make-believe prop which was doing service as a table. It came crashing down. Lee lashed out indignantly. "Actors must have respect for their tools. Our people must know better than to plant themselves on props. . . ." Paula was not offended. Paula was jolly. Paula was pleasant. Paula was smart. Paula knew what she wanted and Lee was it.

Ambitious Paula was determined to get ahead. Relates one of her peers in sentiments echoed by others, "For Paula, Lee's position was an important one and she decided she was going to nail him. But it was so blatantly open. You couldn't really accuse her of anything because she was not hiding anything. She just went right ahead and got what she wanted, and you've got to hand it to her."

The Group, to whom life itself was a group proposition, was eager to pursue serious works which were connected with their own struggles and meaningful to the society in which they lived; *1931*, Claire and Paul Sifton's episodic drama, dealt with unemployment. Its thrust was that the endemic turmoil of modern society prevents the attainment of even the basic desires of the average man to live and marry and, thus, he will be forced to revolt.

Franchot and Phoebe were featured in *1931*, with the rest tripling in smaller roles. At the climax Morris, Stella, Joe Bromberg, and the other "unemployed" massed together and like a phalanx charged to the footlights thundering "Revolt." Underneath Max Gorelik's set (two warehouse doors which worked up and down like an elevator) was a basement the size of the stage directly overhead. There the offstage people made whirring sounds of a factory and noises of the city such as elevated trains. At their cue they'd rush upstairs, speak their lines, then rush downstairs to do their sound effects. Lee had painstakingly worked out these sounds and set everyone's behavior complete with gestures to afford maximum reality, although none of it was viewable by the audience. Embarrassment was neutralized by everyone doing it in deadly seriousness.

Lee's passion for perfection, his fanatic insistence on each actor being a transparency for reality even if he was the lowliest extra in the farthest corner of a tumultuous crowd scene was keenly displayed one raw, wintry night shortly before the opening. Friendly Ford, soon to shuck the culture of the East for the manure of the West, seemed not to be demonstrating sufficiently real emotion. The master of introverted feeling left his seat in the darkened theatre, climbed onto the apron, and began coaching Friendly right in the midst of the final rehearsal with the entire company assembled. After thirty minutes of theory of how he, Friendly Ford, was not just a warm body within a crowd scene but was, instead, experiencing for himself individually the trauma of the moment, he then launched into the rhetorical questions.

"Friendly, why do you want to become an actor . . . ?" After whatever Friendly burbled, the exercise shifted to more artistic probes. "Okay, now, Friendly, you are not just an actor making sincere noises. You are an instrument for truth. This experience must be real to you. Remember, you are playing a man without any prospects for getting a job. You have obligations, pressures, responsibilities. Think, Friendly . . . in this scene where do you come from . . . what are you doing here . . . what is your motivation . . . what are you looking at . . . who are you talking to . . . what is your action . . . what are you trying to accomplish. . . ." and on and on with a demonstration of introspection usually reserved for the classroom.

The authors fidgeted in the rear of the house, wondering what happened to their runthrough. From the back an irritated male voice rang out, "We don't give a goddamn at this moment about teaching acting. We want to see the play for God's sake. We open tomorrow."

The compact figure of Lee Strasberg, clad in a bright blue sweater, barely turned. In his iciest manner, Lee replied, "There are some things even more important than your play. We are a Group Theatre and this is a moment of teaching and I shall pursue it until I am finished. You do not understand what is happening here, so you will please not interfere. As for opening this play on time, I am responsible for that, not you." The author shut up. The lesson continued.

That Lee was brilliant was an established fact. That his direction was inspirational and innovative was acknowledged. That he could talk and talk and never reach a point was becoming rapidly apparent. The Yiddish-speaking members referred to him as a melamed . . . a Yeshiva *bucher* . . . a Talmudist . . . all words symbolizing a learned holy man. His religion was art. Deeply analytical, he would invariably plunge beyond the necessary to mine yet another vein of advanced theory and counterfact. He'd run far afield. He turned every point into a lecture.

His listeners waited and waited and he would spin and spin and finally, finally wind down, and they'd heave a collective sigh. Said Maxwell Anderson, "We used to wait for Lee to come to the end of a sentence. Now we wait for him to come to the end of a paragraph."

Detractors theorized it took so many words to say something because it was an unconscious desire to inflate himself, to disseminate his scholarship because, after all, who had studied as much as he? Devotees rationalized he was an intellectual fountainhead who knew so much that it simply all gushed forth like waters in the lowlands when the dyke opened.

The critics decimated 1931, branding it leftist and political and more depressing than the actual year. "What the hell is the Group Theatre doing?" inquired one reviewer.

One thing it was doing was struggling financially. All together the Troika—Harold, Lee, and Cheryl—couldn't scrape up one bona fide patron to provide backing on a permanent basis. A friend of Harold's knew millionaire Otto H. Kahn and from a second row center seat the financial genius saw 1931. As the theme unfolded, he grew progressively more ashen. You could almost hear him thinking, "Jesus, what's going on here? They looking to overthrow the capitalist system or something?"

To convince this iffy angel, Harold and Cheryl and Lee traipsed down to Wall Street. Dapper Kahn wore a blue serge striped suit and high collar. A small man, he also had a short attention span. They had to get the pitch in fast. Harold threw in everything he had. Following Cheryl's opening billboard, Lee outlined their principles. Harold, his gaze riveted on this sphinxlike audience of one, interrupted, "And there's one thing that cannot be overlooked—our passion. We have a passion about acting, life, politics, everything. Even about our refusal to be beaten down by commercialism and materialism."

Nothing from Kahn. He sat mute. The only noises emanating from him were the sounds of his legs crossing and uncrossing. Lee took another shot. "See, Mr. Kahn, everybody said you can't hold people together, but we're doing it and not by signing our actors up and giving them money because we don't have money. We're holding our people only with our enthusiasm."

These were not precisely words that could be translated into collateral and when the two nonfinancial minds eventually ground to a halt, Kahn gripped the arms of his dark leather chair and said tersely, "I'm not in a position to help you."

"But Mr. Waldo Frank, the critic who is all in favor of what we're doing, said that you were disposed toward us," countered Harold.

The highly nervous Croesus fidgeted in his great chair. With his chauffeured Rolls and his townhouse on the Upper East Side, he knew that unemployment, resentment toward the establishment and other leftish oriented themes were not for Otto H. Kahn's money. He also knew that a depression was in full flower even if the perspiring trio in front of him were too poor to feel it themselves. "You'll succeed," he nodded. "You have a lot of energy."

It was Harold's turn again. "Perhaps it seems we have conceit, but we believe in ourselves and when you're sure you're right you fight no matter what. Maybe we're fanatics because we're flaming, we carry torches but we believe that. . . ."

"I have been severely affected by the crash," interrupted Kahn as the supplicants tried desperately to align with his problem. "And much as I empathize with your efforts I am not in a position to do anything for you."

"We appreciate your difficulties," dived in Cheryl, "but we also feel that as a new artistic and cultural entity we are deserving of your support."

Picking at an invisible piece of lint on his hospital-clean suit while concluding nobody who's sane would try to establish a theatre in the depression even if their ideas meant money in the bank, he stood up. "Well, I'm afraid I have to go. I have an appointment."

Bookends flanked him as he walked out. Wall Street being narrow, it was impossible for all to walk abreast. That meant one of them trailed behind while the others continued importuning. Not easily intimidated, Harold or Cheryl stayed alongside, while Lee kept dropping back and running to keep up. Kahn walked into an imposing building. He bypassed the regular elevator and headed for the special one on the opposite side. Seeing their quarry disappearing, Lee launched into an impassive pitch ending with, "We've always known Otto H. Kahn would support the theatre regardless of its ideas."

The archcapitalist peered at his threadbare idealists and sighed, "I appreciate your ideals but your ideas are somewhat revolutionary." Then he turned to the starter and said, "John D."

The backbone of the organization, Cheryl performed the administrative labors of which Lee and Harold were not able.

"Harold eliminates Cheryl like she was a minor thing," complains Lee. Harold thunders, "I'm the one who insisted she had values for us. Lee's the one who wanted to kick her out." Aghast at Harold's "convenient lack of memory," Lee reaffirms, "I told Harold he couldn't propagate money because the theatrical fraternity had no respect for his ability in that area nor for mine either but that for Cheryl they had a great deal."

Cheryl brought in backing from Eugene O'Neill, Maxwell Anderson, Edna Ferber, Herman Shumlin. She supervised a subscription series. She instigated a symposium to raise funds. She accepted contributions from Franchot, from Dorothy Patten's father, from the office of play publisher Samuel French, and from whatever friendly spirits she could wheedle out of whatever dribs and drabs.

The Group's next try was Maxwell Anderson's political drama about the Spanish grandees of early New Mexico and their struggles against the invading Americanos. As *Night Over Taos* was constructed, nothing took place save discussion. Lee's special-effects ideas, which he believed would have extended the script, were "licked" by the heavyweight status of scenic designer Robert Edmond Jones. "Jones did not support my thinking and I couldn't yet afford to have such strong ideas about scenery, so I didn't push it."

There was yet another disability. Inevitably parts arise for which there are better choices outside. Being bound to a permanent company, a director cannot cast as freely as on the open market. This lack would, hopefully, be compensated for by the training and creative process by which Lee could elicit from his lesser performer the same degree of believability and flair he would have from his optimum dream choice with the exception of the personality of the superior person, that lone ingredient you cannot get elsewhere.

J. Edward Bromberg played the lead, a war-weary Mexican general. Theatre magnate Lee Shubert, whom Cheryl had cast in the role of possible backer came fresh from Florida to see. When the parts had originally been handed out, Bobby Lewis had received a one-page script on which appeared the single line: "You are an old Indian. When the curtain rises you are seen leaving the stage." That creative old Indian scurried around corners, peered in windows and padded his part before he ultimately exited.

Deeply tanned Shubert watched this Indian impassively. When Bromberg entered, he watched interestedly. After Bromberg's big scene, he nudged Lee. "For this part you should have had Lionel Barrymore."

Lee flared. "Why? You think he would have been better?"

Instead of retorting sharply, "Sure, he's a much better actor . . . he's a star," Shubert replied equably and with great wisdom, "No, but the audience would have thought he was better."

The cast also featured newcomer Burgess Meredith, who did not sign on permanently because Clurman had turned him down as a member. That, however, was not the Group's only mistake. Another was producing this four-star flop. It opened at the Forty-eighth Street Theatre on a blustery night in March. The weather proved warmer than the critics and it closed immediately.

9. Family gathering, 1954. Clockwise—Susan sitting on Lee's best friend's lap, Benny Slutzky, Mascha Slutzky, Arthur Strasberg (standing), Lee, Paula, Ruth Lippa, and Johnny. (Courtesy of Cy Lippa)

10. Paul Newman at the Studio, early 1950s. (Magnum/Eve Arnold)

11. James Dean at the Studio. He's third from left in the front row.
(Magnum/Dennis Stock)

12. Johnny and Susan, 1955. (Courtesy of Ruth Lippa)

13. (Left to right) Richard Burton, Paula, Susan, and and Lee. (Magnum/
Dennis Stock)

CHAPTER TWO

Dover Furnace

Barking dogs, wheezing cars, scratchy Victrolas, portable radios, squawling children, and even Franchot's temporary nearest and dearest, a good-looking blonde, made the pilgrimage the second summer to Route 22 upstate through Brewster, New York, to Dover Furnace. Benny Slutzky, whose family was in the summer hotel business, ran the place, engaged the help, and managed the laundry and the dining room with the not-so-great food.

Up a long, hot road, past a dead valley lay the hotel. Some of the five-thousand-dollar rent was defrayed by apprentices who paid twenty-eight dollars a week. The spacious grounds boasted a few unwanted mice and one central house with a large drawing room. Another ramshackle building with assorted bedrooms featured cracked ceilings and tiles falling through which Alan Baxter and Beanie Barker spent hours repairing.

Dover Furnace was sweltering. They swam in a creek a half-mile down and worked in T-shirts and shorts. Franchot's daytime costume was a jockstrap. At night when he was applejack-logged and running around heaving billiard balls against doors, he'd be a symphony in pajamas. He and Odets were good at whanging those billiard balls. The doors didn't break, but next morning there were giant dents in them and Alan and Beanie were back at work.

It was an exciting summer. The conversation was erudite, the atmosphere heady, the climate productive. The air was filled with inspiration and creativity. The previous season a kitchen worker had translated Russian theatre books aloud. At Dover Furnace Lee personally translated Yiddish theatrical works aloud.

Evening festivities were experimental games: in fifteen minutes fashion a costume for the role of Ariel in *The Tempest* out of whatever can be found. Sanford Meisner created musical personalities on the piano. One actress was sharps, flats, off key and all discombobulated. Beanie was immortalized as "The Unfinished Symphony." These were not games for the faint-hearted.

Others recited sonnets while walking about swaying their arms. Elia Kazan, a fidgety arrival who answered to the nickname "Gadget," sloughed through a poem in French. Another lumbered about as though toting a fifty-pound weight. Mentally they willed themselves tall, small, fat. They'd be an animal, a tree. A specific tree. They'd convey bareness or droopiness or majesty. Such experimental work loosened the mind and body. None questioned the exercises. They were to explore means of projecting beyond the literal.

It was a university of theatre. Classes began after breakfast. Discussions continued into the night. Each was majoring in flexibility. Other parlor games were selecting a dramatic moment and acting opposite to the obvious, playing counter to the scene. Or researching a period, then discussing it in minute detail. Or zeroing in on one vehicle and recreating its style by inventing a way of movement or a rhythm of speech.

They played pantomime and charades. They developed gibberish. Conversing in nonwords, each had to glean from the intent, mood, and tone the other's meaning. Since words bound an actor, this made for a fluidity and ability to communicate. Feelings of silliness or inadequacy were overcome because interchangeably each was the other's audience.

Morris Carnovsky and J. Edward Bromberg were superb in their Russian-Yiddish-French-doubletalk gibberish. In their bums-on-a-parkbench improvisation, Joe Bromberg was down, pessimistic, great hate at the world. In gibberish Joe indicated he wanted to do away with it all. Optimistic Morris "replied": "Come on, the sun is shining. Look how interesting life is." Joe rumbled again whereupon Morris laid an imaginary table with wines. To clarify the gibberish they'd inset accessible words like "champagnsky." Joe pantomimed popping the cork and then went, "Aaaaah . . . boobly . . . boobly . . ." Joe developed hiccups. Morris kicked Joe. Joe stopped. Both sat back on the bench. Morris started to hic. Blackout.

Another experiment concerned a study of the characters in George Grosz's paintings. "Take that woman leaning on her arm at a table. Discover where the weight of the hand is. See what she's holding. Which finger is this way and which that way." They were to reproduce the identical pose to the enth degree, to the arch of the brow. They were to *feel* her dress. This created "heightened significance." Lee then selected arbitrary Bible passages which these upper bourgeois German characters, as live beings that had stepped from the canvas, were to recite.

There was a masquerade. Participants were to be identifiable at a glance. Alix Walker was tops as a Toulouse-Lautrec washerwoman. Ground rules allowed only personal articles found in yours or another's trunk. An old poncho, a belt, borrowed skullcap, some buckram, and *voilà!* Japanese kabuki. A bathtowel as a toga, and presto! a Roman emperor.

Lee and Harold assigned one-word improvisations. Odets did "America" by rushing his breakfast, running to the subway, racing to his office, then propping his feet up to do nothing. There were musical improvs. Virginia Farmer did a Ravel Waltz as a bored and sated soul. Tony Kraber did the triumphal "Toreador" aria as one undergoing deep, personal tragedy.

They juxtaposed ideas. "Gadget" Kazan was Sir Andrew from *Twelfth Night* with a thick Irish accent and a soupçon of commedia dell'arte, leapfrogging and somersaulting. Tony coupled an affective memory of climbing the mast during a storm at sea and miming a miser counting his money, utilizing a sense memory of the feel of the gold coins as the slow movement of Beethoven's Seventh played heavily in the background.

They sharpened the sense memory by threading a needle without needle or thread, combing their hair without the comb, brushing their teeth without the brush. They forced themselves to "concretize": is the brush heavy, cold, how does it feel? They had a voice coach, and Luther Adler taught a course in makeup.

They analyzed the Vakhtangov Theatre, the Meyerhold Theatre, the Chekhovian Theatre and the Moscow Art Theatre. Over coffee and midnight snacks they dissected America's Yiddish Theatre, Provincetown Theatre, and Theatre Guild. They were riveted to their Group. Not one wished to be elsewhere. To many that period remains the most exciting in their lives.

They analyzed Lunt and Fontanne. They laughed when one related how Alfred Lunt had announced, "The Group is not different from how Lynn and I work. We do exactly the same thing." Lee gift-wrapped Katharine Cornell as having "taken up the Belasco form of acting. In other words, she acts like she's a great actress."

In his expansive moments, Lee drew on his store of Jewish folklore. A favorite was about the elder who trudged from a small shtetl in Russia to see the Great Rabbi in Minsk and the Great Rabbi posed this riddle: "My son's father is my father's son. Who is he?" Came the revelation and the elder raced back to his village and repeated, "My son's father is my father's son. Who is he?" When they gave up, he answered, "It's the Rabbi from Minsk."

It was a large family of intellectuals. At intervals the visiting avant-garde—photographers Paul Strand and Ralph Steiner and composer Aaron Copland—sat in. This was a revolutionary group. It wanted to change the world. Discussions went deep. Political feelings flew high. A script was read and voices rose about why not do another with more message. The Group was a microcosm of the entire country. Actors' unions were being organized. Unemployed councils were being organized. The Group was very aware. The majority of them, too, existed on pennies. Inevitably talk about the Moscow Art Theatre led to talk about Russia. Russia was in the vanguard artistically. Russia had a flowering of theatres and artists. Russia also had a Communist revolt. It was in the air. It was discussed.

Arthur Strasberg read pages of *Das Kapital* aloud and they sat on the floor examining Marxism and political economy. Clurman loaned them the volumes of Vernon Parrington, a leftist university professor who was the first to assimilate intercultural studies of modern society. The main currents of American thought were being channeled that summer. From Lee's library members borrowed Trotsky's history of the Russian revolution. It was a beginning of a political awareness that had not heretofore polluted the atmosphere.

Pretty Sylvia Fenningston spoke her piece. Benny Slutzky, who felt similarly, aired his views. Stella, the quintessential grande dame in long, flowing diaphanous gown with picture hat and high heels, indicated her "involvement in Marxian philosophy" and her "ideological sympathy with the Communists." Others of their playwrights were sympathizers but, defends Luther Adler, "Everybody was sort of left then. If you weren't, you belonged to some other world."

Meanwhile life went on. In Budzanov Lee had seen people on that next-door estate "playing something which I don't know what and using words I also didn't know. They used the word 'love' a lot. I learned later they were speaking English and playing tennis." Lee was adept on a tennis court. Franchot, whose expertise stretched from billiards to horse racing could be heard hollering over the net, "Good volley, Strassy!" Beanie was another partner before she broke her toe on the cement court. At the nearest hospital, which happened to be an insane asylum, Beanie recited, "What a rogue and peasant slave am I" while they set the break without anesthetic.

One overcast afternoon, Paula Miller's estranged husband showed up. Lee learned his girl friend was married when he found a man waiting to speak to her on the street. Paula went off with him and there was a scene because he didn't want to let her go. When the gray-haired visitor came to Dover Furnace, Lee corralled Luther. "Stick around." "That was if there was trouble, like if the husband got wild, Lee should have someone to give it to him," explained Luther. The two men spoke intently. Lee told him, "You better divorce your wife because I want to marry her," whereupon Luther took a half step forward; but the confrontation stopped at hot words.

Lee did not have friends. The nearest was Maxwell Anderson. Anderson's girl friend, Mab Maynard, who was in the Group, and Paula had been roommates, so the four spent time together. "My first pompano amandine I had with Max. My first bouillabaisse I had at Max's house. It was served in individual earthenware dishes."

The relationship with Paula wasn't sudden. It developed. When they took a trip with Max and Mab and stayed overnight, Paula and Lee shared a bedroom. "That was our first night together and so we started living together after that." At this, Lee's mother heaved a shuddering sigh, then issued the practical comment, "Thank God at least she's a Jewish girl."

Paula inspired divided opinions. From "good-looking" to "dumpy-looking." Stella called her "an uncultured innocent who didn't know from anything." Phoebe called her "a tough lady." To another she was "loving and fun." To another "lost, with no connection to anybody." Outgoing Paula was good for her shy, strange man. While others considered him "uncomfortable" and "uncompanionable," Paula was all over him. Nobody felt close to Lee. With Paula he didn't have to worry. She did the getting close.

"Lee was maimed," confided a member. "Nobody linked an arm through his or engaged him in personal conversation. He was grim. When my father died he unexpectedly reached out to touch me as though to comfort me. I was so taken aback that I involuntarily flinched. I repaid his only gesture of human kindness by shuddering."

Paula didn't suffer from these sensibilities. Paula made the moves and countermoves. Kazan hissed, "She probably does the climbing on top of him, too." Lee was incapable of pursuing and with Paula he didn't have to. "Paula," he concedes, "made all the advances."

He needed a Paula. Wanting to be wooed means wanting to be sustained, supported, helped. It means standing still while the spirits dance around you. It means knowing you have a defect and must be advanced beyond it. From a respectable, economically poor Jewish family, Paula had a plainness of speech and diction but, nonetheless, a richness of heart. She was kind and giving. Paula had the ability to build him up. Lee's antenna told him what he needed and Paula Miller was it.

"A lot of times I was lonely but nobody knew it," sighs Lee, recollecting those years. "In personal things it was never easy for me. I never had that ability to make intimate connections and I didn't have the monetary means to ease my lonely existence. I wasn't like Franchot, who had his own place and could do his own thing. I worked under the same conditions as the other people, but I had no friends and no outlet. That's why Paula came into the picture so strongly."

Lee never spoke of women or of sex. Odets and Franchot thought him naïve. He asked Clurman "simple questions about condoms that a twelve-year-old boy would have known about. He seemed terrified." If true, his inabilities to give would make it natural for him to shy from intimacy. To be able to let yourself go, to be capable of rejection, to risk a mistake, one must first permit oneself to be vulnerable. Lee was too afraid.

Paula confessed to a friend, "I'll take a famous, important and intelligent leader over a great lover any day." Kazan gossiped about how this powerful ambitious drive first seduced Lee. "I can imagine how she did it. She must have said, 'Come here you . . . !'" Kazan painted a picture of Paula grabbing Lee savagely by the back of the neck and physically thrusting him into bed "so she could do the whole job."

Those lacking Paula Miller's intestines found it rough to penetrate. Lee permitted penetration only when he wanted it. Luther says, "Everybody pissed in their pants when this scary character came toward them." For his initial meeting Luther arrived to find Lee standing in the middle of the room. Lee didn't greet his guest. He kept reading. Luther stood there while Lee continued in silence. Luther figured he'd finish whatever engrossed him then they'd talk. Lee put the book down but he picked up another.

Ultimately Luther said, "Look at you . . . look at your face . . . you've got that kisser that looks so terrible. God forbid you should freeze that way."

Warmed up from zero to two, Lee said only, "Be quiet. Don't talk so much."

"To bulldoze the Old Stoneface you had to give him his own stuff," says Luther. "He was a bitter guy, bitter politically, bitter socially. Whatever made for this bitterness made for his general expression. He's a Chekhovian character. All Chekhov's characters are peculiar. They're strange ducks. Lee also."

While Lee sat taciturn, Luther said, "I come from the streets and I'm not afraid of you. I'm coming into the Group. Do you

want to ask me anything? Do you have any curiosity about me?"
"No."

"I want you to know I have no loyalties. I want to stand on the best stage with the best actors doing the best plays, and my condition is if I find anything better anywhere I dump the Group."

"That's all right with me."

"Nothing you want to say to me?"

"You have a big mouth."

As with all the plays, *Success Story*, starring Luther, was first read aloud. The characters' relations to the play and to each other were discussed generally. Roles were assigned. Seated around a table the cast read their individual sides. As soon as possible they were on their feet and scripts were laid aside.

The message was that money and power, the American goals, are valueless when obtained by a violation of one's sense of truth. Central character Sol Ginsberg, a tool of capitalism, was caught between his secretary who loved him and his femme fatale wife whom he hated yet couldn't let go. Stella Adler was spectacular in the powerful role of the secretary. The femme fatale was played by miscast Dorothy Patten, who lacked the necessary allure. They didn't have a Rita Hayworth–Lana Turner–Ava Gardner type and, since casting outside would negate the Group's principles, therein lay the flaw. "Even Franchot's girl at the time who looked like a girl everybody wanted to go to bed with we could have used," sighed Harold, "but we were fanatics and fanatics always make mistakes."

Seated in front of a brightly lit room on a huge, thronelike chair, Lee Shubert watched a drama about a man from the Lower East Side who came up in the world much as he did himself. He backed the play although he didn't think it was great. The play didn't ring true. The femme fatale would say, "You don't care about me. Let me go." And the hero replied, "Never. I'll never let you go." Says Lee, "The audience wondered 'so why the hell doesn't he let her go?' For it to work we needed a vulgar kind of beauty so the audience could understand the pull of that type of man to a Gentile golden possession who looked like money as well as sex."

Vain, egotistical Stella was another headache. Tense, high-strung, always involved in some enormous up or down, Stella threw tantrums. Stella didn't like the Group, but Harold was there so Stella was there.

Stella hated "being surrounded with nothing people who had no style. The Group was a disaster for me and they didn't like me either. I didn't fit. I loathed that rawness of life, that community eating and living and shlepping about. I was too conditioned to stardom, to this absolute leading-lady quality I'd inherited from a family which produced stars."

It is suggested Lee did not fare well with ladies. He wasn't comfortable with them. To the types who married him he was fascinating. With those who found him nonfascinating or asexual, he lacked security. Whatever the factor, Lee and the imperious, brilliant Miss Adler were not designed to get along. Stella adored theatricality and "Lee was plain. Absolutely plain. Two cents plain."

She made no attempt to cultivate or nourish him. "Oh, I was glad when I could be rid of him. I was sick of him. He was not nice."

While it is easy to speak of Lee's personality problems, never does the Group mention their own idiosyncrasies. They were all temperamental. Stella's emotional hangups made her impossible to handle. You had to approach gingerly. You could not be critical. Lee "had to work my ass off with Stella. Her emotional output was heavy, schmaltzy, Yiddish theatre style. She'd say, 'You want it this way or that way' but it was all the same way."

For *Success Story* he wanted from Stella an element of reserve, an inner quality whereby one behaves with full reality yet with a sentiment that never exceeds a limited point. He pondered the proverbial shipboard romance. A person's aboard ship. There's a moon. An attractive passenger of the opposite sex wanders on deck. You'll never see the person again, yet you confess things you wouldn't ordinarily. It struck him here was his "adjustment."

Whereas Stanislavsky stayed with the literal, Strasberg had begun to explore. He discovered he could manufacture an effect the actor couldn't achieve ordinarily by inventing an optimum kind of situation in which the actor could handle the problem. Strasberg began to develop a process of substitution. This "adjustment," the word he coined, was pure Strasberg. It was a move away from what heretofore had been strictly Stanislavsky.

Fearful that if he implied what he wanted she would again click into something prearranged and conventional, he led Stella through a series of shipboard improvisations without her understanding what or why. "Stella doesn't know to this day how her effect was achieved. She may remember only that when she was at the door doing an emotional memory which led to crying, I said, 'If you cry I'll kill you. I don't want you to cry.' I wanted it all pent up. If she cried she'd be Stella again. Stella cries the contents of several buckets, then she creates the bucket, too. Her problem's defining and containing the emotion. If I'd let Stella act like flamboyant Stella acts then she'd play only one part over and over.

"So Stella had to act a scene physically with an improvisational adjustment going mentally. That's not easy. So, maybe they're right that working with me was hard. I only know *Success Story* was Miss Adler's greatest performance." Stella's energetic mama, the wife of famed Jacob Adler, had a stiletto out for everyone. About Phoebe: she was "a chaser. She chases the public away." About Alexander Kirkland, who joined subsequently, she didn't think he had any warmth; "Ehr's a kalta tookhiss" which she freely translated for all into, "He's a cold ass." Bromberg, whom she disliked, was "a butcher." Paula "should push a carriage." With her own, Mama rhapsodized, "Not because it's my son and daughter but when you see Luther and Stella on the stage you see a personality." Adds Lee, "Too *much* personality. They're *too* theatrical."

After *Success Story* opened at the Maxine Elliott, Franchot Tone broke from his mother bonds. Franchot's heart was in the theatre, but his dreams were in the movies. His defection was a blow. Individually and collectively the Group implored him to stay. "I would never quit," flung Beanie at him tearfully. "Jane Wyatt's mother says Jane is not happy in Hollywood," exclaimed Eunice passionately. "She says Jane says that what the Group's doing is what's *really* interesting."

In the leading-man category Franchot was the best. His departure would be a serious loss. He was torn but dogged. "I want to go to Hollywood. And I want to marry the biggest star out there."

This handsome playboy had a wild streak. He fell for girls who were bad for him. He drove recklessly to Tony's, a night spot on

West 52nd Street and plowed into fights and got beaten up. He
had few friends. Ruth Nelson was in the dressing room sitting in a
wrapper at her makeup table when he walked in to say good-bye.
Their eyes met through the mirror. Neither said anything for a
minute, then Ruth turned squarely around, propped her elbows
on the back of her chair, and looked straight at him. "Why are
you doing this? Why are you leaving?" asked Ruth.

He sat down heavily in the empty chair next to her. There were
tears in his eyes. "Oh, Ruthie, I just have to. I just guess I have to
find out what it's all about."

"But we all know . . . that is, I know at least . . . that you really love the Group passionately."

"And I always shall," he replied softly. "It's just that I have to
go. What else can I tell you? I guess I just have to, that's all."

Neither could think of anything else to say. For want of something to do, Ruth dug her hand deeply into the Albolene jar and
liberally greased her forehead. Franchot stood up, and with Ruth's
right hand and forehead still larded with grease, he swooped her
up in his arms and hugged and kissed her. "Good-bye, Ruthie," he
said and walked out.

Franchot's decision was tantamount to a betrayal. Lee was "terribly angry." It was not a fertile period. *Success Story* proved to be
not so. The actors went on reduced pay and the directors lost even
their fifty-dollar-a-week salaries. Idealists all, somehow they still
gathered nightly in somebody's dingy room and spun their philosophical webs. However, in this "Brother, can you spare a dime"
era it became apparent one day that not only didn't they have
much money they didn't have *any* money.

In a herd they removed to a ten-room cold-water flat on Fifty-
Seventh Street in a block of attached houses. Tenth Avenue was
not a choice part of town, but it was cheap. Their decaying walkup
was an old four-story brownstone with a stone stoop. Other
families lived on the lower landings, leaving the Group the whole
top floor. A chilly, floor-through railroad flat with one room after
another off a long, rambly hall, it had high ceilings, a low seventy-
five dollar a month rent and one pay phone in the hall. Signs out
front advertised: "Apartments for rent. No steam heat." That
whole winter sacks of cannel coal, a soft substance that can be
laid with wood, were dragged up three flights. It left white, pow-

dery dust over everything. Scrounging for furniture produced a dining-room table and chairs enough to sit on. Their theatrical wardrobe trunks doubled as chests of drawers and, it was asserted pridefully, "at least we managed to get a bed for each of us."

That appeared to be a major piece of furniture in their lives. The large open front room dormed three busy bachelors—Tony Kraber, Alan Baxter, and Phil Robinson. With scant privacy for lovemaking, Tony "had to creep next door to the little hall bedroom to visit my fiancée, Wilhelmina Barton, because for sure she couldn't visit me. I didn't always bother going back and forth. Sometimes I just stayed there. Let's face it, there was plenty of sex going on."

Next was Morris Carnovsky's room sometimes shared by Philip Barber, "a very nice playwright who never amounted to much," and occasionally by Phoebe, whom he could not yet marry because he was not yet divorced. On the far side was Lee's tiny room, shared with Paula. There was a bathroom down the hall, a dining room and kitchen across from that, and, way in the back, an infinitesimal bunk where Odets slept on a cot. This restricted the normally frisky Odets who, insists Clurman, "would have had to put a girl up against the wall if he wanted to have an affair because his room was so small all he could have gotten in there was a midget."

Functioning on a permanent basis, cemented together beyond the hours of a performance or the run of a show, they summered in the country for weeks, worked closely on a project for months, associated with each other for years. As the Group turned inward, propinquity propelled affinity, relationships developed, attachments formed and they fell into pairs.

The apartment was christened "Groupstroy"—*stroy* being a Russian word meaning "unit." Society viewed this communal housing project of freethinkers as a hotbed of free love. Rumors abounded that orgies took place. Outsiders considered them oddballs. Those on the inside did not consider themselves a Russian commune or a community of beatniks ahead of their time but pitifully poor people obliged by circumstances to live in a collective.

Contributions to the collective were made by anybody who had anything. Theresa Helburn helped. Beanie, who fell heir to checks from her father in Baltimore signed them over. Dorothy Patten, whose daddy provided a townhouse on East Fifty-first Street carted over packages of cooked foods. Franchot sent money from California. Arthur's Brooklyn dental office didn't produce a large cash flow, but every weekend he brought an offering from the butcher. One Friday, as he trudged up the stairs, Art Smith came bounding down. "I have to go to the Guild," Art gasped, out of breath. "You got carfare?" "Sure," said Arthur shifting the side of beef while he dredged his pockets. "How about the trip back?" "Oh, sure," and down Arthur went for a second nickel.

Each made his own bed. Sweeping and cleaning was divvied up. Cooking was done by turn. The most economical was Grover Burgess, who was big on thin soups. On special nights when Grover had KP, he'd throw in a little bread. Clifford was good at Jewish specialties such as stuffed cabbage or potato pancakes, which were cheap. When Elia Kazan drew the duty his signature was rice casseroles.

A chart was installed in the kitchen. If it was your turn to cook it was another's turn to market, and somebody else's to do the serving. Everyone prepared his own breakfast and tidied up after himself. There was no lunch, since it was off to work or to look for work or to do your chores. The marketing crew made for the pushcarts on Ninth Avenue, others set off around the corner for the weekend specials. Exercising extreme care without concern for favorite foods, they sniffed out bargains, tracking down cuts of beef for twenty-seven cents a pound and hamburger for twenty cents. "Stroy" ran on seven dollars per person per week. All the money went into a central pot with food bought for everyone equally. The lone exception was Alan Baxter, who always bought one special extra dessert for himself and ate it by himself. "The rest of us stared as though to say we hope you choke on this," said Lee. "We hope you go to hell with this dessert. Never would he offer it."

Lee's relaxation was mystery stories, but he couldn't take the tension, so he'd flip to the end, devour the denouement, then calmly return to where he left off. One evening Groupstroy threw together a dirty show. Invited to this wall-to-wall letting down of the hair, shocked Theresa Helburn snapped to Cheryl, "If that's the way your young geniuses occupy their minds, then I'm not interested in their genius!" Many evenings were spent listening to

Odets, who was in a chrysalis state. That winter the actor disappeared into a cocoon and emerged as a playwright.

It was a snowy night. Lee was walking and reading in the kitchen. Lou Leverett was stirring a pot of soup on the stove. Cheryl, the "ax lady," had dropped by from another fight with the Shuberts when Clifford shuffled out, brandishing a sheaf of pages. "I've written a play."

"What's it about?" asked Phil Robinson, ironing a shirt's collar and cuffs because that was all that showed so that was all he washed.

"It's about Beethoven." Odets removed his glasses to rub his lids. For the first time those assembled noticed how weak-looking his eyes were.

"So read it," ordered Lee, never removing his gaze from his murder mystery.

Previously Odets had written a play about a house in Philadelphia. After reading that aloud the opinions he had received were "Jangled . . . all mixed up . . . not focused . . ."

Odets' was an inflammable nature, which expressed itself unpredictably. On a routine stroll he'd suddenly exclaim, "Oh, look . . . look at the sky. . . ." He had just then discovered the beauty of buildings and at that instant an ordinary event became extraordinary. Mindful of this, Harold had commented, "This play about Philadelphia is like you, Clifford. It's a little disorganized."

Having surfaced again, this time with a work about Beethoven, Odets announced proudly, "It's set in modern dress." Paula ran to get a cigarette to fortify herself.

"Why Beethoven?" asked Lee reasonably enough.

"Because I'm crazy about Beethoven. I've read everything about him. I know his life. I love his music."

"But you can't play," taunted Grover Burgess. "At the piano you only hammer out thunderous, melancholy chords."

"Still, I'm like Beethoven's piano. I have so many things inside me that are just waiting to be played."

This modest statement lay there a moment, then Harold suggested, "Why don't you write about someone in your family? Why this kind of stuff? Why not write about people you know?"

The typewriter clacked ceaselessly. Balancing it on his lap on his cot for months, Clifford wrote in his cramped, chilly quarters all day, all night. He took to clipping newspaper photographs of disparate men and women—a bus driver, an actress, a professor—and pasting three together on his wall to assimilate their common denominator. He'd inspire himself to the kind of talk this composite human being would have. He took to following crowds and marking down what he overheard.

A campaign had been launched to save *Success Story*. There was the payday Cheryl divided the take and each actor received ten dollars. After that it slipped a little, prompting Luther to comment, "I'm the only actor who ever starred on Broadway and got seven dollars a week." Between them they couldn't scare up subway fare to get to the theatre. On just such a depressing night, Clifford decided to read his newest scenes.

"I have just been way the hell out in some goddamn forsaken suburban wilderness of Bay Ridge talking to some goddamn ladies in some goddamn flowered hats," commiserated Tony Kraber, warming his hands over the pot of soup on the stove.

"Why?" asked Odets, rearranging the pages on his lap.

"Why? Because Cheryl organized some of us to speak to theatre clubs and try to crank up theatre parties and try to scratch up humans to buy tickets, that's why."

"Hey, Tony," gasped Kazan, panting after running up the last flight. "Your girl friend, Willie, was pretty good with her speech tonight. She came out in front of the curtain at the break right after the first act."

"Were the houselights up?"

"No. And the people hadn't filed out yet. She urged them to subscribe to the Friends of the Group Theatre thing, whatever that is, and to sign up at the table in the rear so they'd get tickets at reduced prices and get invited to future dress rehearsals and all that stuff."

"Yeah," grinned Willie as she came out of her bedroom, pulling on a second sweater. "Some guy complimented me about how good my speech was. I told the audience I wouldn't hold them long, that they could have their smokes in a minute, but that there were a few things I had to say about the meaning of the Group and then I. . . ."

"Listen, we've heard all this crap before," interrupted Odets irritatedly. "You want to hear my script or you don't?"

Everybody settled down and Odets acted out the scenes he'd written. "Hey, as an actor you're not too good," cracked Grover Burgess, "but as a playwright you're beautiful. Some of those words sing to us."

"It's not bad," offered Art Smith. "I tell you the truth, you can actually close your eyes and hear somebody saying some of those lines. I mean, the dialogue really sounds natural, y'know what I mean?"

Lee, who recognized some of the lines from Odets' note pad, nodded silently. They talked about his characters until dawn and as the morning light crept through the window the first faint beams of *Awake and Sing* came to birth.

The Group office was a floating little dark hole wherever a free little dark hole could be begged. Once it was in the Forty-eighth Street Theatre, one hundred steps up, and now it was a niche in the Maxine Elliott. Came the morning a communication arrived into Command Headquarters from a Mrs. Motty Eitingon. The wealthy benefactress was requesting an audience with Mr. Strasberg. It wasn't difficult to see Mr. Strasberg. All you had to do was climb three flights.

Motty Eitingon was the world's foremost international fur dealer. Bess Eitingon was a do-gooder and a theatre buff. With her brown hair simply but perfectly coiffed, her petite figure in an elegant but understated designer suit, a jeweled brooch on the lapel and clutching an alligator handbag, Mrs. Eitingon left her penthouse for her limousine. Her chauffeur rolled to the garbage cans stacked in the gutter on West Fifty-seventh Street and, following the aroma of cabbage, Mrs. Eitingon began the ascent.

"It was like an attic. I thought I'd never get up there. It was clear up to the skylight and as I approached the smell of cabbage grew stronger." At the head of the stairs stood an attractive blonde, on the plump side, in a light blue smock with her hair in a coronet of braids. She sang sweetly as she opened the door.

"I have an appointment with Mr. Strasberg," announced Bess as she stood hesitantly in the middle of the large, empty front room. Following Bess's gaze as it swept the room, Paula apologized, "Please excuse the place but we haven't yet had a moment to fix it up. We're expecting the furniture very soon."

"Oh yes, of course," said Bess, blinking at the beds.

Both women stood tentatively in the center of the room. Paula made no attempt to introduce herself or to entertain the visitor. Moments later she disappeared inside, calling, "Lee . . . Lee . . ."

There was considerable noise in the background. Doors opened and slammed, the toilet flushed, voices conversed, pots rattled. Nobody entered with any offer of even a cup of tea. After some minutes Lee appeared. Thin, drawn, dry. He initiated no conversation. He did not extend his hand. "Mr. Strasberg," began Bess. "Allow me to introduce myself. My name is Bess Eitingon and I wrote you."

Lee nodded. He did not sit down.

"Mr. Strasberg," bustled Bess, gathering full steam, "I have with me a certified check for forty thousand dollars. I hope it might be of some use to you. My husband and I are deeply interested in this kind of theatre. You see, my husband, Motty, is Russian and he knows the Russian theatre and your concepts of Stanislavsky."

No response. Lee seemed not to be giving her his attention. He walked about picking his nose. She tried again. Aware she was doing a monologue with nothing coming back, she grew limper. "You see, Mr. Strasberg, we—that is, my husband and I—we're very interested in this kind of theatre." Motty wasn't at all interested but she leaned on "we" to draw strength. Lee's nonperformance made her "I" seem weak.

Figuring this man wasn't hearing, she dived into her bag and proffered the check. There was neither acceptance nor rejection nor notice of it. The moment passed. She couldn't believe what was happening.

"There are no strings to this money, Mr. Strasberg." Beads of perspiration formed on her forehead and the words tumbled into each other. "I ask nothing in return. You can do with this as you wish. It doesn't include my being a member or a producer or anything. You see, my husband, Motty and I, we've been to the Russian theatre and we know what kind of theatre that is and we've seen the Reinhardt Theatre and we've entertained Reinhardt in our home so. . . ."

"We are not in production at this time," intoned Lee, cutting off her generosity in a statement that bordered on insanity.

"But surely you can find some use for forty thousand dollars . . . I mean, we are offering it . . . surely you would accept. . . ."

"But we don't have any plays right now."

Lee's quest for truth blocked the pathway of compromise. Equivocation and its gray companions were strangers to him. They were starving, true. But that money, as he saw it, could not be used for food. It was for production. They weren't then in production so how could he take it?

Rejected, embarrassed, unable to fathom what she'd done to merit this rebuff, a teary Bess Eitingon turned and fled. She raced down the stairs. At the pay phone she poured her heart out to a friend: "I can't barely tell you how I feel . . . the experience has been a terrible blow," she sobbed. Down the stone steps and into the limousine she ran, weeping all the way.

CHAPTER THREE

Green Mansions

Nineteen thirty-three. The Depression. The coming in of Roosevelt. The country was in an unhealthy state. As this miasma thickened in the world outside so it deepened within. The Group was becoming radicalized. You're a kind-hearted person? You want people starving? You want people hurt? You want Jews in Germany beaten? The pressures of near starvation having considerably to do with influencing thought, the natural progression was for the theatre to mirror its times. Two years into the Group Theatre the Communist Party already had roots in the operation.

Art cannot lie. It reveals the spirit that gave it birth. Within the Group the organized left began as a loose feeling. The sociopolitical messages from across the footlights were reflective of the nation's thinking. They were not parroting a party line but were aesthetic dramas essayed in viable theatrical terms.

With the heightening of the Depression there evolved a more definite turn left. There developed a more outspoken attitude. The thinking was if we can do anything about these terrible conditions in these terrible times, let's do it. While many went to mass Sundays, many more applied their religious fervor to politics.

Russell Collins was a devout Catholic. Nobody tried to talk him out of it. J. Edward Bromberg's intellectual foment inclined him toward Communism. Nobody tried to argue him out of that either.

Russia was an ideal. Russian theatre was an ideal. Russian thinking was an ideal. Russia was the first country to provide its artists with new shoes. Russia fed its poor and put a roof over their heads. That spirit of banding together for the common good was compelling. Communism was a noble cause. It stoked within the fires of each breast the suspicion that anyone who wasn't a Red should be ashamed. To those members searching for an ideological base, the Communist thought interpreted their own desires.

A play's passport into the Group was not that it guaranteed to be a hit but that it had a message. This sense of mission only worked providing there were suitable craftsmanlike vehicles. The Group Theatre was a theatre. It had to do plays. Lee's point was, "If we find great plays that are expressive of the ideas everybody stands for, great. But if not, what is important is that we continue to do plays."

A green, scared, young playwright submitted a medical drama. When Sidney Kingsley's *Men in White* was read aloud, the verdict was "crap!" "Second-rate script," snorted Morris.

"The figures are rubber stamps," complained Lou Leverett.

"Nobody likes it. Anyway, it's not a play for us to do now," put in Art Smith. "We must speak through our productions."

"Agreed it's not good material and hasn't deep Group significance," sighed Harold, "but it's the only play available and it has germs of exposing and criticizing society, and those aspects can be stressed."

"It's cheesy," opined Phoebe.

The scene was the large theatre with the revolving stage on the grounds of Green Mansions, an adult summer camp in the Adirondacks where, in exchange for entertaining the guests three nights a week, the Group was again in residence. Lee rose. "A play is not in the text. It's on the stage. This is a sound work about idealism. It can do well. With this we can make our statement."

"But why waste ourselves on such sob-sister stuff," threw out Ruth Nelson.

"Agreed it has serious faults," began Harold, "but . . ."

"It stinks," interrupted a shouting voice.

Still on his feet, Lee continued. "We have refused to do classics and repertory and especially fine plays because we have committed ourselves to what is pertinent to our lives today. Okay, good, but there are just not enough great plays to go around that are contemporary American social drama."

Reluctantly Harold buttressed his position. "The stunted growth of America's artists has been laid to the lack of cultural unity. This is the output of a new playwright and such talents should be developed."

Anarchic, romantic, poetic Odets, who did not cotton to bourgeois Sidney Kingsley, grumbled, "Many phases of America need fundamental change and improvement. We've set ourselves to correct society's ills. This script lacks that clear message."

"The collective way is the only way forward," pursued Bromberg. "Supposedly our basis is to point up life's problems then point out a road for their solution. It's not in this script."

"It's very simple," summed up Tony Kraber. "None of us like this play and we don't want to do it."

"Everyone's thinking in terms of ideas," said Lee. "Assuming this doesn't read so great, think of it as a script for production. Its proof is what we do with it on a stage. I favor it because I see what can be done theatrically."

Morale was not high. A series of flops including *Big Night*, which closed after nine performances had created rumblings about the Group's obituary. Lee's early flush of success and divinity had paled. His audience was restive. This mood was enhanced by the negative personality of Sidney Kingsley. He was not hail-fellow-well-met. He was not warm. The Group did not take to him. Still, Lee pressed his point. "We court trouble when we confine ourselves to personal beliefs. A theatre must address itself to theatrical ideas. Ideologically this drama isn't opposed to what we believe in. It's progressive and idealistic and that should be enough for us."

"It stinks," said Alan Baxter.

"It's shoddy," said Bobby Lewis.

"It's shit," said Elia Kazan.

Lee was not one to argue much. "You can't change a preconceived opinion. It's useless to try and force someone to see something he can't see." However, Harold belatedly sided with Lee and
Cheryl and rehearsals began.

There were complications. The Group was not isolated. The
paying guests sometimes sat in on the al fresco workshops. Rehearsals sometimes dissipated into working on sketches with
which to entertain the guests on scheduled nights. The big night,
Saturday, they'd stage a scene from Chekhov or O'Neill or Odets'
still-in-progress, *Awake and Sing*. One Saturday Bromberg hung
from a tree croaking on cue because he was the sound effects of
frogs. Midweek ex-opera singer Tony Kraber did his folksinging
and guitar-twanging or Bobby Lewis did a comic turn or Bromberg and Carnovsky ground out a gibberish improv or a few threw
together hey-nonny-nonny madrigals or a routine from *Garrick
Gaieties* or Alexander Kirkland knocked off the balcony scene
from *Romeo and Juliet* or the dance teacher whipped a bunch—
none of whom were exactly high kickers—into a jazzy, forty-five-
minute revue.

It was a hard summer. The food was excellent, the physical
beauty such that nature had created a natural amphitheatre and
the actors worked outdoors on a carpet of green grass. Nonetheless, there was rebellion. Having been undersubsidized, the
members had been seeking new directions. Several had taken secondary jobs. Lee himself had directed *Hilda Cassidy*, an undistin-
guished outside play. The Theatre Union, The Theatre Collective, Orson Welles's Mercury Theatre, and other organizations,
some left wing, were surfacing, as were the unemployed Group
members who were lecturing and performing on these platforms.
Green Mansions, where they staged their own entertainments,
provided an extension of this individuality. For these extra-
curricular mini-productions, the actors rarely consulted the three
directors, relying, instead, on their own judgment. A pressure
began to be felt that membership wanted a voice in running their
collective if, in fact, they were to devote their lives and spirits for
the privilege of remaining hungry and poor.

As for *Men in White*, Lee observed the technical details in a
hospital but his direction was creative, not imitative. The work

was exemplary. Morris Carnovsky, who played a small role: "When an actor washed up in the operating room it was a kind of poetry." Eunice Stoddard, who played the head nurse: "It was an orchestrated performance, almost a ballet." Since a life-and-death struggle took place there, Lee's concept was to establish a priestly atmosphere. "Wash as if this were some great achievement. Don't wash your hands one, two, three. Wash slowly, methodically, carefully. Nurses get ready . . . they hold the gown . . . you step into it . . . the whole thing moves as in a sense of ritual."

With torrential rains pelting on the tin roof and with Kingsley still reworking the last act and with only half the sets in place, a run-through was held for the backers. They filed out in a grim line. Something was wrong, but what?

Lee's *modus operandi* was to retain a first impression of a play, since that's all an audience gets. He trudged back to his bungalow, reread the script, and retained his original impression. He liked it. It moved well. There had to be something wrong with the production, but what?

It was technically perfect. All details were absolutely exact. No doctor could take exception. "Because everything was correct—how you put on the gown, what you do with the glove—everyone said it was exactly as it is in a hospital," said Lee, "but it wasn't. No real doctors behaved like that. It's how they'd like to *think* they behaved. Real surgeons yawn and scrub up while cracking to the next guy, 'So how was that dame you were with last night?' Very casual, very ordinary."

He realized in an operating room there's a professional attitude. Impersonal. They don't take time for emotions. If someone asks something, they answer, but nobody takes *time* to answer or they'd be expected to say important words. "We didn't have those special thought-out words. Our words just kept going, so everything we were doing was actually right but the delivery was too heavy. If the words were simple but the acting was heavy, then it appeared the play wasn't coming over. We only needed to infuse that impersonal attitude. We'd missed what I call the professional adjustment."

Men in White presented headaches. There were temperamental problems. The Group remained dead against the play and treated Kingsley like a leper. Lee had to force them to rehearsals. During one of the many weary moments when nerves were strained, Beanie became hysterical. Lee slapped her. Again, when Lee couldn't communicate what he wanted, in frustration and rage Beanie threw a handbag at him.

There were talent problems. Comedian Bromberg was cast in the Einstein-like role of Dr. Hochman. To effect this radical transition, Lee invented another "adjustment." Bromberg was an FBI agent called upon to investigate something without revealing he was an FBI man. Within this mask of having power without flaunting it, there developed the precise quality of authority director Strasberg sought.

There were technical problems. Sitting in the darkened theatre Lee shouted at the electrician, "I want sharp lights. Sharp. Really sharp lights."

Eddie Kook, the head of Century Lighting, snaked through the rows to sit near him. "Lee, trust me. I'm an expert. If you get them any sharper you'll see the beam."

"It's okay. So don't worry. I don't mind. That's what I want."

"You want to see the beam?"

"I want a sharp, sharp light."

Eddie stared at him. "You're going to see the light beam, I tell you."

"And I tell you I don't care. I want a black-and-white effect in the lighting. I want the faces sharp."

"And so what if you see the beam?"

"That's your job. You don't want them to see your lights then you fix it up. That's up to you. I don't care what you do. But I want that light. I need that sense of art and if they see it so I don't care. It's not just a regular scene. It's an operating theatre."

"Okay, fine."

Eddie clambered back to his light board. From the rear of the house Lee directed what he wanted. "A little more . . . no, no, too much . . . no, not quite . . . a little less . . . a little more to the left . . ." Crews worked then until the small hours of the morning and he had kept them straight through the night. It was 3 A.M. The guys were dragging, so Eddie dismissed them.

He flopped down heavily next to Lee. Numb from weariness they sat there alone staring at the lights. Suddenly Lee yelled, "That's it . . . that's it . . . !"

Nothing had changed. His eyes had simply become adjusted to the flood of light.

There were scenery problems. They needed a winch for scene changes. "How much will it cost?" Lee asked Cheryl.

"Like five hundred dollars."

"I'd like to say what the hell do we need this extra expense for, but we need it. What'll we do? Can you work out some deal?"

Cheryl shrugged. "Let's wait. Lee Shubert's coming to the rehearsal tonight. We'll ask him for it."

At the curtain they walked over, and Shubert clucked and wagged his head from side to side. "Too bad . . . too bad . . . it's a nice production."

Lee licked his lips. Cheryl swallowed deeply. Finally she summoned the nerve to say, "Oh, I'm sorry, because we were going to ask you for something."

"Like what?"

"Like money."

Shubert peered at them closely. "Like what for?"

"For the changes. We need a winch to make the changes."

There was the space of a heartbeat, then Shubert asked, "How much you need?"

Lee found his tongue. "Five hundred dollars."

"Okay," Shubert nodded.

"How much do you want for that?" asked Cheryl quickly.

The theatre magnate just waved his hand and sauntered away.

"He doesn't want the extra he's entitled to for helping us?" Cheryl asked Lee in shock. "He could easily have asked us for 5 per cent. He could have held us up for a percentage because we needed this money."

"Yeah . . . and this is the tough Lee Shubert!"

Men in White made theatrical history. Its "peculiarly tense, internal" staging won the Pulitzer Prize. It re-established the Group. It established Sidney Kingsley. This was the first medical drama ever produced. It created a trend to be followed ad nauseam by the future Kildares of the world. It ran for a year. It won raves for everyone. Lee says, "Instead of the old, schmaltzy, vulgar earthiness, Bromberg came through as an actor. It got him the movie jobs. If not for this he'd have played nothing parts all his life."

Men in White was sold to the movies and starred Clark Gable.

Not even Lee could comprehend this stunning success. His direction had won the Pulitzer "with a play that was maybe not worth it." *Men in White* gave him a special dignity and distinction. It was hailed as a masterpiece.

Meanwhile, the newly dusted-off God of the theatrical world was marrying. When *Men in White* solidified the life of the Group, it allowed them to look further into the future than their next production. Some wondered why loving, giving Paula wanted Lee. Others rationalized she'd never be more than a middling actress without special gift or speech and that he was her salvation. Others wondered why he settled on Paula, who seemed removed from intellectual pursuits and lacked the manners and deportment he'd grown to notice in others.

They underestimated Paula Miller. Paula was street smart. Paula observed. Instead of being intimidated by a cultured Stella, Paula learned from her. And somewhere inside Paula a bell went off that signaled, "I can do it better." Paula was a trouper. If she couldn't make it on a stage she'd make life her stage.

There being almost no responsibility on his part in any of his relationships, Lee's requirement was someone to serve him—a young, attractive mother figure to do the whole job, all the things he didn't want to do so that he might remain the aesthetic scholar, the omniscient Talmudist. Inside the prize-winning director who had tasted bouillabaisse and pompano amandine dwelt a Hassidic Jew, that species of learned, holy man whom the communities in the old country supported and who, liberated of material and social encumbrances, could continue to digest the mysteries of the universe and dispense wisdom.

Paula knew her lines. She knew how to handle Lee. She'd badger him, bother him, even run him domestically in ways that pleased him, but she didn't and couldn't control him. When all else failed she wasn't above squeezing out a few tears. While crying didn't grab her those parts she wanted in Group productions, she did land the coveted role. March 16, 1934, Lee Strasberg married Paula Miller.

It was a civil ceremony in New Jersey with her girl friend, Molla Archer, as the witness. There was neither big reception nor big announcement. Considering they were only going to continue doing what they'd already been doing, the groom was so casual that he neglected to bring a ring and Paula had to supply her own.

A couple of weeks later the newly married Lee Strasberg took a honeymoon. Only it wasn't with Paula. He sailed to Europe as the guest of the grateful Sidney Kingsley. *Men in White* was opening in Budapest and the idea bubbled up so quickly there was no time for the issuance of their Russian visa. Russia, where Lee could visit the theatres and meet those personalities who had shaped his career, was the thrust of the trip. Both were assured the papers would be cabled to the Grand Hotel, their address in Paris. Sidney headed for Budapest, leaving his sophisticated, urbane, world-traveler chum to handle Operation Russian Visa.

Lee is a type eternally convinced he will be hounded and caught and sent to the guillotine for committing as evil and pernicious a foul deed as maybe filling out a document incorrectly. Years earlier super-law-abiding Lee found himself in the theatre district at the moment of intermission of a Jacob Ben-Ami show. It was closing night. The box office was already shuttered. The theatregoers milled about in the street. Dying to wriggle inside with them and catch the last act but ever-fearful "they" would seize him and manacle him and forcibly stop him, he hung back. This, therefore, was the mentality that was reporting to the Russian Embassy daily in Paris for a visa that had not come through.

Meanwhile, his French transit permit, a ten-day job, was running out. Not knowing what to do, he tried to extend his stay in France. A round of the proper authorities sent him to another set of authorities. He found himself in front of a lady. Paris was somber. Her citizens resented looking to the Americans. Through a translator he asked could he get his transit visa extended? "Non." Did she know where he could get this done? "Non." Had she any suggestions about what he could do? "Non." Did she know if this had ever happened to anybody else before? "Non."

The ten days were up. With Lee's paranoia, visions of the Bastille danced in his head. On the corner of his hotel stood the office of American Express. Panicky and desperate, he shuffled in. It was a slow day. Not one other prospect was present save this intense, skinny, small, white-faced, quivering criminal. He faced the lone bored employee, who was leaning on a table with nothing to do. On jellied legs Lee propelled himself toward this towering symbol of authority, prepared to pour out his whole heartbroken saga. "I laid before him my fear, my desperation, my hopelessness, my helplessness."

The man was distinctly not interested. "Yeah, so?"

"So," trembled Lee, "you see, sir, the problem is that I can't get into Russia and I can't remain in France."

The more Lee burbled the more disinterested the man became. He had previously bestirred himself to uttering two words. He now chopped it down to one. "So?"

"So as I have been telling you I cannot stay and I cannot leave. I don't know what to do. I need help."

The man was heavy-lidded. In utter disgust he leaned on his elbow at a ninety-degree angle as he half-focused on this perspiring creature.

Lee glanced around in hopes someone else could befriend him. Finding they were alone, he turned back to his sole salvation. "I mean, I'm in trouble and I need someone to advise me."

Never has man seen such a disparaging look. The employee peered down as though to say, "Oh, God, you stupid Americans" and roused himself only to inquire, "Are they bothering you?"

"No."

"So what are you bothering them for?"

Lee dispatched a cable to New York. The answer came back that visas were processed by number and his had been issued long back. Again he went to the Russian consulate. He flashed his cable and the official started thumbing back in the files and back . . . and back . . . It had arrived that first day, exactly ten days previous.

At five in the morning his train crossed the border of Hitler's Germany. There was a knock at his door. Everyone was wakened for Customs. Streaks of daylight filtered through the window and in the distance he could make out civilians being herded at gunpoint. He opened the door and in came the conductor, accompanied by a handsome German colonel in snappy uniform. In English the officer inquired, "Anything to declare?"

"No."

He pointed to the luggage. Lee obediently pulled the suitcase down. "Open please."

"Certainly." For some reason Sidney Kingsley figured just what the Russians needed was Vat 69 so he had bought two bottles. One he personally was carrying, the second he'd stuffed among his friend's things.

Crackled the officer, "You will have to pay duty for that."

It wasn't clear in his mind whether he'd smash the bottle or throw it out but Srulke Strassberg knew that under no circumstances would he pay one penny to Nazi Germany. "Why?" asked the suddenly brave traveler.

"Because the bottle is not yet opened."

A human being has only so many stylish moments in a lifetime. This one it seemed was to be Lee's. In even tones he inquired, "How much of it has to be opened?"

The colonel smiled in anticipation. Again Lee inquired, "How much of it would have to be consumed for it to be not taxable?"

A little sign with the thumb and forefinger indicated only the smallest amount. It was barely six in the morning, just after being shaken from sleep and before having breakfast. Teetotaler Strasberg broke the seal, uncapped the bottle, and took a swig. He then closed the bottle and stowed it away. The German was stunned. With an icy expression he spun on his heel and left.

Filled to capacity, the train pulled into Poland. At the station an army of passengers bore down on the only restaurant. They served wienerschnitzel. Lee consumed the huge platter. Suddenly "All aboard" blared over the loudspeaker and a hundred passengers dashed for the moving train. Forty-five years later, honest Strasberg asks, "Was this the train's obligation as part of the cost of feeding us or were we supposed to pay? I still don't know."

The day before May 1, Lee Strasberg arrived in Moscow. He was billeted in a respectable old hotel, and the next morning was ushered to Red Square, where a reserved place had been cordoned off for visitors. Sidney Kingsley arrived on the first of May but couldn't get through because of the parade. He stood hemmed in on the sidelines until a band of nurses marched by. Joining the women comrades as the only male delegate in their ranks, this brand-new capitalist marched with them across the square to rendezvous with his friend.

Lee's immediate plan was to see the man who had inspired his life. A decade earlier, when the Moscow Art Theatre electrified New York, Lee had spied Konstantin Stanislavsky walking on the street. Not daring to approach, he followed the Master for half a block. Now, again, on the other side of the world, a meeting was not destined.

Daily for six days he visited the Moscow Art Theatre. "It was so bad I couldn't believe what I saw. I kept returning to be sure." Among other lapses the leading man peered into the audience. Lee wanted to "climb up on the stage and kill him." For this reason he couldn't face Stanislavsky. So upset yet so respectful was he that he sacrificed the experience rather than risk the criticism. "What could I do? Tell him what I think of his theatre? Say there is nothing more I can learn from him? How could a young schnook say to the Master, 'What do I see on your stage?'"

Married life settled down in a small, fourth-floor walkup over a bakery in Greenwich Village. The aroma from Sutter's Bake Shop floated up those stairs. Every night around eleven Lee would traipse down and buy leftover bagels for half price. A feature of this Eleventh Street apartment was a steady supply of day-old bagels. Another feature was that the two rooms invariably overflowed with assorted souls. Odets and his typewriter were fixtures. Sometimes he typed in his corner, sometimes in the kitchen. Another was assistant stage manager Paul Morrison, who was reduced to pawning periodically for $2.50 the graduation watch his family gave him. Paul was so rarely in funds that he had no place to sleep. Lee suggested the living-room couch. Says Paul Morrison, "And God knows I appreciated it."

Had he had a full meal in him Lee might have reached 125 pounds. As it was he was constantly laid low with colds. Thin bowls of soup do not exactly stick to the ribs. While in Baltimore doing *Men in White*, the Group had stayed with Beanie Barker's family. They were fed home-made lemon meringue pie, stuffed veal birds, and fresh vegetables with thick Hollandaise sauce. Groupstroy and Paula set a slightly different table.

Beanie's father was Professor Emeritus of medicine at Johns Hopkins Medical School. Dr. Lewellys F. Barker trudged up the four flights. In his early seventies, stringlike, vibrant, he sat down and clasped his delicate hands together as he stared at the patient. "I hear you always have a cold, and so I have come to see you."

Lee, lying in bed, honored this statement with a loud sneeze.

The tall, white-haired gentleman said quietly, "I think you should gain weight and I will give you this advice free. I don't charge for it at all."

"Thank you," smiled the patient wanly, "but I have no money anyhow."

Dr. Barker's handsome face crinkled into a smile, and he continued, "Eat whatever you eat. Don't change what you eat. But at the end of what you've eaten take a glass of milk."

"Take it after, not instead of?"

"No, not instead of. A lot of people take it instead of. Don't do this, because it has no food value."

The patient wasn't used to milk. He gagged and so he decided to give it up. Not long after Dr. Barker was again in New York for a lecture. Again, Lee was flat out. Up came Dr. Barker. "What have you been doing about the weight gain?"

"I started as you told me and it seemed to work but the only thing is that I must be one of the few people for whom milk doesn't agree."

"Why?"

"It makes me feel nauseous so I guess it's better for me not to do it. What do you think I should do?"

Dr. Barker smiled at his friend. Reaching over to pat his hand comfortingly he said, "Continue taking the milk."

Although his friends could negotiate his four flights, Lee's bookcases couldn't. The cases were tall, the staircase was narrow and the movingmen couldn't maneuver the stairwell. A new recruit, Jules Garfield, directed the guys to back halfway down then turn the cases sideways to get in position to haul them up. This was the future John Garfield's first foray into the ensemble work of the Group Theatre.

Paula was a good woman with a strong sense of belonging. It was she who re-established the contact with the family. Before the advent of Paula, Ruthie Lippa, the daughter of Lee's sister Becky, was walking up Broadway and saw her uncle. They had not seen one another in the years since Nora had died and the Group had come into being. Ruthie called out excitedly from afar, "Hello . . ." As Lee neared, he replied, "Hello," and continued along his way.

Teen-aged Cy Lippa wanted desperately to see *Men in White*.

He rehearsed his request because he was fearful of rejection. Summoning his courage he said in a rush, "Uncle Lee, it would mean so much for me to go, and what do you think, could I come see it because I really hate to bother you but I would love to have tickets, would that be all right?"

"Sure," was all Uncle Lee said.

Chaia Diner Strassberg had known a long illness, many bouts with doctors, and years of suffering. In later years, her baby had not been close. His energies went in establishing himself. When Mama was rushed to the hospital it was Arthur who was in the ambulance. A week later, Mama was gone. For the longest time Arthur walked around "thinking I was going to vomit." Her death affected Arthur profoundly.

Not Lee. With Zalmon and Nora he had crossed the emotional Rubicon. "The sudden deaths of these young people whom I loved conditioned my future behavior."

Baruch Meier Strassberg earned a few dollars doing cantorial work. He was assistant to the rabbi and on holy days he chanted the prayers. Papa Strassberg read about his famous son in the Yiddish papers, and it was Paula who reached out. She saw to it the family was together at the seder table. She invited him for holidays. He'd peer at their fancy friends. "Er's a Chrisht?" Told yes, they were Christian, Papa was tolerant and understanding. He didn't push his Orthodox traditions. When his daughter-in-law cooked on shabbas, he ate dairy and eggs and drank out of her non-kosher cups. Considering it the greater sin to offend a loving heart, Papa Strassberg sighed, "With God I'll make my peace."

CHAPTER FOUR

Ellenville

Sam's Point in Ellenville was dank and damp. This abandoned summer camp with a dorm and a decaying Gothic house lay halfway up a mountain where fog and mist hovered over the great trees until the sun hit its zenith. Slime lay on the ground and the wetness never dried out. To the rhythm of a drumbeat, the dance classes would run and leap and slip and fall. One of the dogs went mad. Others developed ringworm. Alexander Kirkland developed ringworm. Few went into the pool because it was cold. Those who did developed an infection. There were bugs in the air, poison oak on the ground. Everybody was peeling. Everybody sported white salve.

Nobody was happy. In Ellenville the Communists tried to unionize Benny Slutzky's part-time season help. The Group was not a private organization. There was no product being manufactured. They'd had one hit in four years and the whole complement had to be sustained week in and year out. There were no surplus profits. The directors were, in fact, the lowest earners in the collective. Lee tried to speak to the issue one emotion-charged afternoon and his distress welled up in his throat. Words like "workers," "organize," "demands," "bosses," and "exploiters" bounced off everyone. The few were determined to stir the many. There were meetings scheduled, discussions pro and con. One "sweet, good-hearted soul" who married the daughter of a general wasn't a hardened Communist, he was a hardened idealist. A "darling sweetheart of a guy" who had three babies and a working wife and hadn't seen any decent money in years was a ringleader.

International events heightened political feelings. You believed in loyalist Spain? You were suspect. If you followed Stanislavsky you were a Bolshevik. If you didn't join benefits against Hitler you were a Fascist. Political sketches highlighted all leftwing causes. For one trade union benefit Kazan and Kraber did their *Men in White* improv. They were doctors operating on Hitler. They opened him . . . found he had no heart . . . blackout.

Alongside the naïve do-gooders fired with social protest were the influential professionals dispatched by the party to steer dissension and division. Repeatedly up that narrow, unpaved dirt road with the sheer drop off the side if you didn't hug the mountain and then over that foot-high bump with that sharp left up the hill came Mother Bloor, a grandmother-of-the-revolution type, "cultural leader" V. J. Jerome, a "Sidney Somebody" Cheryl remembers "whose teeth were knocked out somewhere down South and was always around with Kazan" and trade union organizer Andy Overgaard, Odets' friend, who set the political table and laid out the knives and forks. Under this tutelage the Group organized its own Actors Committee to agitate within the Group, to demand changes within its own union and to press for more radicalization.

There was Odets, the poet, and Kazan, who was programmed to hate the poverty of his life, and J. Edward Bromberg, who believed in a better world. Some were romantics. Paula was one. Garfield became another. Some were admittedly hot socialists who called Clurman "the Mussolini of Culture" and the directors in general "capitalist bastards." Luther Adler couldn't believe his confreres were real revolutionaries. "Those guys wouldn't give up a part in a play let alone their lives. Nevertheless, because of them we were getting the reputation of being a bunch of Jew Commies!"

Lee pronounced the Communist thinking "very fine." He

aligned with its basic economic interpretations but remained "separate and outside" in terms of its organization. Lee's genius and limitation stem from the immutable fact that his sole interest is acting. Possibly he doesn't care sufficiently about anything or anybody. Perhaps he cannot expand his island of concern beyond his world of theatre. In any case he remains no joiner of anything unless it be an artistic enterprise. He claims he pointed out that his colleagues did not understand they were getting involved with a professional revolutionary army which demanded blind acceptance, but he, characteristically, did not undertake to dissuade a single heart. "If a person believes his directives you cannot tell him not to. No reason why he shouldn't fight for what he believes. If he believes the world must be changed, so okay. After all, this was the Roosevelt era and the Communists weren't particularly against Roosevelt."

Lee's stand, typically, came only when the Communists insinuated themselves artistically. He didn't care if a play was communistic or fascistic as long as it was good. "The theatre is an artistic thing, and you cannot manipulate politically what must be handled artistically." The radicalized members tried to politicize the Group. Their next production, the tense, fervent *Gentlewoman*, coincided with their ideologies. It ran nine days.

There were pamphlets and slogans everywhere. There were commitments to join marches and sign petitions. There were coworkers handing out leaflets. Paula was involved in the cell. Paula was no intellectual but she *thought* she was, because this is what thinking people were. Her husband rationalized away her behavior. "She thought this was child's play. She did not understand the nature of the professional revolutionary movement in which rules are given and which you must obey." Since Paula was subservient to her husband, reason concludes he sanctioned her Party membership. This foot in both worlds presents Morris Carnovsky with "difficulty in coming up with any residue of feeling for this man whose behavior is so shoddy. This shit that he was an idealist, not a Communist, is something we all could have said!"

As time ticked away the nonpolitical voices also raised in dissent. The difficulties of satisfying a creative collective are seen in Beanie's dissatisfaction—"I was always being passed over for the good roles"—and Eunice's dissatisfaction—"I should have gotten the *Men in White* lead, but as usual they picked Beanie."

When *Men in White* opened, the banks closed. Since the actors were needed for the following production, they hadn't the luxury of profiting from a road company. Wary of an unprecedented medical movie, Hollywood bought their one hit for only thirty-odd thousand dollars. The actors repeatedly complained they wanted more money. So did the directors.

Cliques were forming. It was a bad summer. Lee hurt his back on the tennis court and an added fillip was the flu. He had hot poultices, cold drinks, doctor's visits, medications, and "every damn thing anybody could find, but nothing worked." Various committees traipsed to his bedside, demanding what he couldn't fulfill. The problems were interrelated economically, theatrically, humanly, and politically. They could not be appealed to individually. Lee was "so frustrated I almost wept. I could see the break coming but no way to stop it."

Ellenville was the first summer for Julie Garfield. Robbie, Garfield's seventeen-year-old girl friend, who worked at Macy's and wore home-made clothes, weekended nearby in a boardinghouse. They found ways to be together. Sometimes his lowly apprentice roommate, David Kortchmer "got lost and I spent the night," says Robbie. Gifted Garfield was a natural actor. Unaffected, relaxed and easy, he had no complications. Garfield's limitations were in the areas of culture and polish. He had none. Ambitious, raw, the kid from the streets would trip from lack of knowledge. The future John Garfield would announce, "with me from now on the study of Shakespeare is tantamount!"

Garfield had a lust for life and humor to match. Many remember him tight, riding a bicycle and brandishing a stick with a roll of toilet paper while reciting *Henry V*. He'd rig pans of water over the entrance to the john and, when someone needed the necessary, down on their heads came the pans, water and all. There was the day he and Morris smelled up the dressing room. They cheerily laid little pieces of fish skin from the hide of a salmon atop burning light bulbs. It fostered an aroma which immediately drove in Bobby Lewis. "Hey, you guys smell anything?" "Jeez, you're right," sniffed Garfield. "Yeah, what is that?" said Morris, inhaling. Finally it became insupportable. The building smelled like a fish market. In came Luther. "Come on, guys, you had something to do with this." "Naaaah, you're nuts . . . can't understand it . . ." swore Garfield and Morris. The stench had about reached the Rockies when Stella arrived, wearing a theatrical corselet, with, "Listen, I've worn this goddamn thing so long I figured maybe this was me but I know it isn't. Who is it?" "Hell, how should we know," grumbled Morris. "Yeah, it ain't us," whined Julie.

It was always Lee about whom Garfield talked with reverence. Lee was to be worshiped. The coming movie star forever badgered this small figure brandishing the riding crop. ". . . teach me to do this . . . show me how to do that . . ." Nothing would stop Garfield. In an improv session he was so completely absorbed that he crashed through a plate-glass door, cut his left hand, and was rushed, bloodied, to the hospital, where he emerged hours later with his arm in a sling and his face in a smile.

Gold Eagle Guy was Garfield's first alliance with the Group. In the dressing room in the cellar on opening night he sparkled, "I figure this here play with Lee's terrific direction and all these terrific actors in it and being the Group Theatre and all I figure it should run maybe a good at least two years."

Luther, the archsophisticate, blinked affectionately at this sweet innocent and yawned, "Personally, I think we're working on a stiff."

Midwinter, stranded, with zero prospects, *Gold Eagle Guy* rumbled to an end after 68 performances.

Lee's nerves were strung tight. He experienced one rage so absolute that he became unintelligible. Witnesses use the words "berserk . . . incoherent . . . so choked he could hardly articulate." He'd been caught in a mistake which pinpointed his fundamental lack of awareness. He'd staged a scene so that a society hostess was sitting while her guests remained standing. When the incorrectness was pointed out, it revealed he was unknowing in the area of societal behavior. His vulnerability wide open, those fears and insecurities which lay never far below the surface welled up. He lost control and had to walk out until he could recover.

There developed a resistance to his "impossible tyranny" which allowed for no contradiction. Lee operated on a frequency of unswerving loyalty. Clurman insists, "He required constant praise. If he couldn't piss on people and make them think it was Guerlain, he couldn't take it."

Others fault the Group. The Group forced certain levels onto one who wasn't all that omniscient and omnipotent and when their humanly created deity proved mortal, they trod on his clay feet. The Group giveth, the Group taketh away. Too easily threatened to thrash out issues on a one-to-one, Lee sank into a shell.

The Strasberg way is to probe himself solemnly and silently and alone. Deeply introspective, Lee never extroverts his introspection. At most he sighs, "The one person they pick out and pick on is Lee Strasberg. How come they don't pick on each other? They were all opinionated and temperamental."

The Moscow Art Theatre took twenty-five years to achieve greatness and years to perfect one production. For an American with a sense of dedication to weld a similar unity in a short time was not to be achieved by stroking. Stanislavsky has been labeled "tirelessly solemn, vain, and selfconscious" but he came from a wealthy environment and could therefore be a more confident, more romantic individual. By comparison he comes off as the more lovable of the two.

About his temper, Lee agrees, "It was something to behold. True, I was harsh, cold, and dogmatic. But how about my difficulty working with them? When they threw temper it was nothing? It was only temper when I threw it?"

A show of colorful Group temperament was staged impromptu when Franchot Tone surfaced in New York and hosted a lavish buffet supper. He presented his beloved Groupies to his celebrated bride. An artificiality underscored the party. From Joan Crawford's heights she could have looked down on her freeloaders, but these were the biggies devoted to the real art of acting, the fourteen-karat intellectuals of the theatre and so she went heavy on the gracious hostess role. She'd call, "Lee, you missing a napkin . . . ?" then zoom down to his end of the room. An elaborate service was laid in the labyrinthine Waldorf suite. Waiters, bartenders, flowers, and champagne were abundant.

The guests repaid her performance by deliberately misbehaving. They weren't going to be impressed by a Joan Crawford and all that she laid on. Neither were they about to be grateful for Franchot's support during his years in Hollywood. This load of thick glamour and fanciness fired them to assert their own quality in life. Bill Challee opened the festivities by tossing silverware, napkins, and tablecloths in remote areas far from the buffet. It was the weakness of poor people. The envy was such that others were inspired to swipe champagne, sandwiches, even a radio—whatever goodies were at hand.

"Anybody want to see my gift to Joan?" asked Franchot, overlooking these college pranks of his chums.

"Sure," enthused Harold.

"Okay," murmured Lee.

They obediently trooped into another room. "Here," beamed Franchot carrying his usual glow. "This is a reproduction of our actual dinner set at home in Hollywood."

There spread on a dresser twinkled an exquisitely engraved, golden service in miniature complete with every spoon and cruet and tray and tiny fork. Hundreds of pieces. Harold gaped in astonishment. "But that's a toy."

Franchot's eyes sparkled. "Yes, but what else can you give a woman who has everything?"

"Must have cost a fortune," mumbled Morris in the background.

"Oh, darling . . ." repeated Crawford to Franchot, ". . . oh, you shouldn't have . . . oh, darling . . ."

Bill Challee then did the only thing he could think of under the circumstances. He slid down the gleaming brass banister in the stately lobby and led an assortment of his pals in scattering the hotel's knives, forks, and soup spoons along the streets of Park Avenue.

Cheryl had "constantly to introduce Lee and Harold to each other all over again." Harold was incapacitated with emotional miseries and his mad love for Stella. Lee's personality had deteriorated. "He had become dictatorial and Hitlerian." He no longer wanted to be one of the three directors of the Group. He just wanted to direct his plays and let others do the nitty-gritty. During one quarrel, Lee exploded, "You agreed to make the decisions with your mind not your behind."

Harold replied angrily, "When you holler I can't understand what you're saying. Talk quietly. Say in normal tones, 'Harold, when you do this it offends me.' Just reveal yourself quietly."

"I can't. I can't do that," Lee said, according to Harold's memory.

Realizing his partner was telling the truth and that he, in fact, could not, many arguments later Harold suggested, "You put your grievances about me in a letter then I'll do the same to you."

"No. I can't take it. Don't do a letter to me." Lee, however, sent his letter to Harold.

And then there was Stella. To Stella, digging into oneself, and uprooting emotional reactions from the past was unpleasant. Stella opposed the affective memory aspect, believing one's storehouse of subconscious memories was not to be used and that the practice stripped sensitive insides, twisted the actor and "created a sick theatre." Lee's methodology provoked emotional submergence in an "abject destructive thing." The result, she called, "pathological."

No fan of Lee's, Stella admittedly told Stanislavsky, who received her in Paris that she disliked his Method because Strasberg made it "heavyhanded and unhappy. He never smiled, never brought cheerfulness into the theatre, never said good morning. His lack of cordiality infected everything." She told Stanislavsky that Strasberg "siphoned the joy out of acting. Because of him the theatre has become a horror for me. Acting is now rigid like Lee, and I hate it."

In August Stella returned to Ellenville armed with buckshot. It was a warm afternoon. A haze hung over everything. Following lunch, everybody gathered on the white wooden porch to assimilate Stella's report. Some sat on rockers. Some perched on the steps. A few sprawled on the lawn. Morris looked like Lenin, his face and forehead set in thought. Holding court, *Stella announced Stanislavsky* said they were working all wrong, that they were "misinterpreting" his ideas and that he "de-emphasized" the affective memory concept as emphasized by Lee.

With everyone staring open-mouthed, Stella stood in front of a blackboard and a chart, the original of which was in Russian and was posited to be a presentation of the "correct" ideas of Stanislavsky. Using a pointer, Stella tapped #17 and reported the Master said he used this affective memory originally but doesn't anymore, preferring, now, to utilize imagination. In other words, synthesized Stella, Stanislavsky said they must now pull out of remaining narrowly internal and subjective and take the path of action, of physical objectives.

What the empirical Stanislavsky also told Stella Adler was, "If the System does not help you, forget it . . . but, perhaps, you do not use it properly."

Lee sat strong-faced, all tucked in, salvaging whatever he could of his plucked plumage. The scene was played heavily in Stella's favor. Taking center stage, the leading lady dominated the action. Short on underplay and humility, Stella, looking glamorous in her fresh-from-Paris wardrobe, stood tall, towering over even those who were standing. Lee had no weapons. Annoyed, frustrated, with no voice to second his in this charged atmosphere, he did not say Stanislavsky's theatre had become the poorest in Moscow and that Russian theatre was becoming the poorest in the world to such a point that the Moscow Art Theatre brought in a man from the outside to try to steer it back to its former glory. He did not pose the rhetorical question about how could his work be "not good" and "all wrong" when his theatre had won a Pulitzer and Stanislavsky's theatre had gone downhill. "I couldn't speak. I just had a great feeling of being insulted."

Stanislavsky died four years later. In this last period, according to Lee, he experimented with new ways of handling problems which he, not the Group, encountered and which he could not solve. "It didn't work and this phase didn't pay off. Action we have always used but the emphasis on action as the main thrust, no. If you are unable to bring in emotion, then what is the point of action? Stanislavsky says clearly, 'If your senses are working and if you're in good adjustment with your partner *then all you need is the action.*' If everything works perfectly then you don't even need the action! However, if you have only action and the other things not, then nothing's working.

"Stanislavsky never told Miss Adler, 'I didn't do what you do.' He told Miss Adler, 'I don't do that anymore now.' He was experimenting with something new. It wasn't a correction. It was an experimentation. Unfortunately because he didn't do it anymore is not proof that his experimentation was beneficial. That new phase which he told her about didn't work. In fact, years later I learned Stanislavsky was, himself, so disheartened that he resigned about that time.

"I didn't change. *He* changed. He was wrong. Anyway I didn't care too much about his system as he was then teaching it because we were already better than his theatre."

Stella's position found support within the Group. A tough lady, Stella admits, "I inspired a little fear. People always said don't tangle with her." Those who found Lee's method too demanding and those who resisted his personality now found a legitimate channel for resistance.

That schism which began in Ellenville and has since riven the theatre world has run through all succeeding generations. It exists still today.

Within the Group the Stella-Stanislavsky confrontation was a widening wedge. Says Stella, "Lee was lost after that."

CHAPTER FIVE

Finale

Nothing happened in a moment. It happened by continuous happening. The fabric of the first American company to weave the elements of craftsmanship with the stuff of their own spiritual and emotional selves was unraveling. The Group teetered on disbandment. Its limited successes, its lack of stars, its left-leaning reputation contributed to a dearth of plays. At hand only was Odets' *Awake and Sing*, which had political and literary value but not, Lee insisted, theatrical value. Its prime value being availability, *Awake and Sing* was produced over Lee's objections with Harold Clurman directing. Unhappily, *Awake and Sing* did not. Within the membership the experience of this short-lived play tripped those confused emotions which masked other passions. Lee "stayed very unhappy. I backed off a little bit. I came back a little bit. But for the most part I stayed very unhappy."

The political judgments made by the unit thinking of the dissident block were crippling their theatrical judgments. Cut off from the mainstream of the play supply, no theatre can live. To deviate into a political theatre requires a sufficiency of radical works brilliant enough to transcend propaganda. "The whole thing wouldn't work," sighs Lee.

Maxwell Anderson, a financial contributor to the Group, offered his new play in verse. By then decisions were voted by the membership, some of whom were into the strong left. When *Winterset* was read to the company, they hated it. "Fraudulent . . . lousy . . . sentimental . . . no message . . ."

"I don't like it," chimed in Harold.

"Bad play . . . poor poetry," shouted the Group.

Lee believed it had "distinction." He attributes his passivity to theatrical limitations. He had no one to play the part. Kazan was "not yet ripe." Luther "not quite right," and he'd forgotten Burgess Meredith, who yearned to be in the Group. A more valid reason might be that the opposition was too overwhelming. *Winterset* was produced outside and was a success. Lauded as one of the best American plays of its time, it ran for a year.

Lee suggested romancing other playwrights. "We had a half-assed play by Samuel Behrman. Okay, so it wasn't great. So let's rewrite it." Nothing happened. Behrman, whom the Group lost, and Anderson "who figured the hell with us, he can always get his stuff done elsewhere" started the Playwrights Theatre. As with other facets in the tumultuous years of the Group Theatre, a vocal faction hotly negates whatever is asserted by any other faction. The leftists at whom the finger is pointed deny lack of material was contributory to their demise. They deny they turned down plays. Expostulates Lee, "Okay, so they didn't turn them down. The point is, because of them we didn't have any to turn down!"

There were tough goings-on in attempts to split the Group. To steer policies, influence happenings, and wield tighter control, the radical elements exerted veto powers and instigated pressures. Lee states, "Directives issued by the Party to its members, who at that time were dyed-in-the-wool Commies affected what we were doing creatively. It is clear their attitudes were direct results of decisions issued at meetings where people like me were never present."

One considered a card-carrying Communist at that time makes this comment: "Horseshit."

Others concur that the conflict came in separation of church and state artistically and politically. The party could not manipulate except through those who believed as the party believed and thus would lean to a radical ideology professionally because that's how they leaned personally. It was difficult to exist under this imposed regimen, for the half of a different mind who were not subject to that diet politically and thus could not swallow it artistically.

Meanwhile, Srulke Strassberg of Budzanow took a subway to the courthouse downtown near the Washington Market and was sworn in as a citizen of the United States of America. This momentous day had been delayed because he'd mistakenly gone to City Hall to collect his first papers. He was supposed to go to the Bronx, since he'd been domiciled in the Bronx. This feat he could not seem to manage, since he now lived in Manhattan. The one day he made it up there the office was closed. It took him another five years to stop off in the Bronx.

If lack of plays was a primary problem, a secondary issue was lack of money. The difficulty of attempting contemporary works without funding contributed to the miasma. The seminal theatre organization of the Depression had no foundation. Each new production meant a new financial undertaking. Any lone play had to support all the members and the sweat of an entire season often dried up in one quickie disaster rendering the members again insolvent.

One by one the great ones were leaving. Franchot, Bromberg, Garfield, Odets. Economics lured them to Hollywood. Relatives from the Bronx had given Robbie and Julie Garfield their wedding. When Robbie had trekked from the country to the doctor, friends donated the round-trip fare. With two bedrooms and a community kitchen, they had shared digs with member Walter Coy and his girl friend. Someone remembers lending Robbie thirty-five cents for the movies.

Then Hollywood beckoned. When a man sees a thousand dollars a week and he's broke and his life is on the line, the question of allegiance becomes academic. A hearing was called and guilty Garfield pledged his devotion to the Group but explained he owes this one, he's in hock to that one and it looks as if he can grab a few thousand for a couple of weeks work. His peers regarded him through slitted eyes. Carnovsky was bitterly angry. New member Lee J. Cobb harangued him. Garfield tortured himself. To one:

"They say the Group will collapse if I leave. . . ." To another: "But I have to know what's it like out there . . . what's it like with the big money and the glamour and the riches. . . ."

A lingering problem was the disposition of those who weren't summoned to stardom. There existed strong feelings of jealousy and antagonism. Why should he go and not me? Twenty-one of them left en masse to test Hollywood's waters, swearing to send money back. Some never got work. None sent money. Cheryl and Lee were left to cull scripts.

When they ultimately returned, so did the basic problems. The afternoon of what is called "The White Paper," a committee gathered in a member's apartment and read the list of grievances. They cited the defects and shortcomings of the three directors. Their particulars against Lee were primarily emotional. They dealt with his personality. There was terrible tension. There were many ways of pulling.

Benefactress Bess Eitingon was contacted by mutineer Elia Kazan whose plan was to take over and throw Lee out. At Kazan's request he and his seconds took Bess to lunch. Says Bess, "They told me their idea was to split from Lee and they wanted me to back them. I refused. I told them, 'No, gentlemen, there is no Group without Lee.'"

Echoes Tony Kraber, "Kazan was my close friend and I know for a fact that he wanted to make a move and get rid of Lee. Kazan thought Lee had nothing, and I said, 'You're out of your mind. Strasberg is absolutely loaded with talent.' Kazan was very ambitious."

About his alleged attempted takeover the Yale-educated Elia Kazan made this precise comment: "Bullshit. I never tried to take the Group over and I don't give a shit what anybody says."

What seems apparent is that the Communist-inspired roiling was a move to negate the power of the directors. Exhausted after years of struggle, Lee had no fight left. He was tired. He wanted no more of arguing with people behind a cloak. Since his presence interfered with their purpose, his only course was to let them go their way because they wouldn't let him go his way.

There seemed no ongoing role he could assume. In 1937, troubled and under a cloud, Lee Strasberg resigned.

CHAPTER SIX

Hollywood

The first baby was a very long labor. When Susan came into the world after thirty-six hours, her father "almost hated her. I said to myself, 'What did I need this for?'"

He could not bring himself to gaze at his first-born. He was in the hospital room the fifth day when the nurse bustled in carrying the child all wrapped up. "Here's your beautiful daughter, Mr. Strasberg," she chirped brightly. "Want to take a peek?"

The brand-new daddy recoiled. Cheerily the nurse opened the blanket. "Look . . . look at those eyes . . . so wide open . . . so blue."

Steeling himself for this "terrifying experience," Lee inched a step closer and peered into the clear face of his baby. "Oh . . . the skin . . . so white," he murmured.

The nurse stretched out the bundle. "Here. Want to hold her?"

Involuntarily he stepped back. "No. No, thank you."

"Afraid she'll fall?" she chuckled.

"Uh-huh." The truth is he couldn't gear himself to touch her. The actual contact would be too difficult.

The Henry Street Settlement was the pilot social agency to

develop pediatric nurses and disseminate them to the poor. Their duties were to stay in the homes of the newborn for two weeks and train the mothers. Jonesy was the first of the Henry Street nurses. This black lady fell in love with her beautiful charge and wanted to stay with the family. "But we can't pay you," apologized the nervous father.

"But I want to come with you. I want to live with you," insisted Jonesy. Since home was over a theatre on Fifty-ninth Street and Seventh Avenue, Lee explained, "We have only two rooms. Of course, the front room is large but . . . still . . ."

One evening found Jonesy cuddled into a soft chair, cradling Susie in her arms and crooning softly, "I'll take you home and paint you all black and you'll be my baby." In a household accustomed to sheltering strays, Jonesy found love and a sense of family. The Strasbergs kept the bedroom which overlooked the theatre and gave Jonesy twenty-five dollars a week and the front room. Jonesy was a member of the family for years.

Lee first touched his baby, who was named for the biblical Rose of Sharon when she was two weeks old. Paula was lying on the couch, still worn from the ordeal when Susie started throwing up. It being Jonesy's day off, with Paula not up to handling emergencies, it was incumbent upon the father of the house to do something. He picked her up, marched inside, cleaned her up, washed her all over "and after that I collapsed."

The Strasbergs were not obsessed with having children. The second wasn't planned either, but May 20, 1941, three years later, on the fifth floor of Lenox Hill Hospital "a Taurean on the cusp of Gemini," Paula said, arrived at 11:31 P.M. His parents liked the sound of the name John.

The family managed to exist. Paula theorized, "There are people who love us and if we need it we can always borrow until the time comes when we can pay it back." And borrow they did from Bess Eitingon, Sidney Kingsley, Franchot Tone and Dorothy Willard, a lady who backed some of Lee's plays, and Billy Rose, among others. Rose was hanging a masterpiece which he intended to give his wife when Lee arrived. Mrs. Rose's entire comment regarding this priceless Rembrandt was, "Don't make holes in my wall." It made a stunning impression on a fellow who had come to beg eating money.

14. Paula, Lee, Johnny, and Susan. (Courtesy of Ruth Lippa)

15. Some of Lee's alumni at rehearsal of *Strange Interlude*. (Left to right) Ben Gazzara, Jane Fonda, Franchot Tone, Geraldine Page, Pat Hingle, 1963. (Joseph Abeles Studio)

16. (Left to right) actress Barbara Baxley, Paula, Lee, and Carl Schaeffer. (Alan Grossman)

17. Lee and Paula with Marilyn Monroe, 1962. (MND Collection)

18. Two Actors Studio stalwarts winning Oscars together—Shelley Winters and Martin Balsam. (Globe Photos, Inc.)

A while later multimillionaire Rose telephoned. "I have a tenor in a show I'm doing. How much will you charge me to coach him?"

"Seven hundred fifty dollars," said Lee.

"Okay, but you owe me so I'll take off the five hundred dollars." By this simple expedient Lee paid off the debt.

Some years later Hollywood's famous producer David Selznick offered this nugget to the struggling acting coach: "Never borrow small money. If you call a bank to borrow twenty-five thousand dollars, they'll say, 'What's your name? Where do you work? Have you collateral? Who are your cosigners?' and you'll wait hat in hand at the man's desk. But if you say you want to borrow twenty-five million, they'll say, 'Could you please tell us what time it would be convenient to send a man to your house to discuss this?'"

The post-Group years were lean. Lee drifted. He taught at various places for indefinite periods and began his formal teaching with classes at home but there weren't many pupils. It was Paula, working as a secretary to Tallulah Bankhead, who kept them afloat.

Occasionally Lee landed a job. One was directing Tallulah in *Clash by Night*. For Tallulah, who kept a pet tiger cub at home, oddities were the norm. Lee knocked on her dressing-room door. "Come in, dahling." In walked dahling to find the lady stark naked and offering no excuses. "I acted as if nothing was happening just like a nice Jewish boy would," grins Lee. "She looked very good, by the way."

Temperamental Tallulah ("I'm a son of a bitch") and temperamental Strasberg did well. When he uncorked one of his Class A juicy outbreaks and let her have it, she not only took it silently but bought him a present and consulted with Paula on the best means to have it accepted.

Lee's ongoing career did not balloon any visions of theatre art. His *Summer Night,* starring Louis Calhern lasted one night. The first play about mental illness, *All the Living,* proved interesting albeit unsuccessful. Ernest Hemingway's *The Fifth Column* with Franchot and Lee J. Cobb under Theatre Guild auspices was not a redhot hit. He directed Luise Rainer in *A Kiss for Cinderella.* The European movie star found him like a closed shop. "When he gives you the key you find a great deal inside." This was a difficult time in Luise Rainer's life. Her father was ill and she had just divorced Odets. "Ours was a great love but after three years Clifford couldn't take my success. Lee knew I was suffering. Sweet Lee was most kind and tender. Seeing me minister to my father all night and rehearse all day, he put his arm around me. He felt my needs and he responded." The audience, however, was not similarly touched.

Another life he touched at this period is colored with memories at the opposite end of the emotional spectrum. A job-hunting actor who knew Lee well traipsed up to his tiny office, which was a corner of Cheryl's narrow office, to find him hiding behind a newspaper. The secretary typed away. The minutes ticked away. Strasberg read away. Will Lee announced he'd like to speak to Mr. Strasberg. Mr. Strasberg eventually finished reading "then folded his newspaper in halves, quarters, and eighths. I sat on the couch next to him. It took him forever before he looked at me. I said, 'Hello.' He said, 'Hello.' I said, 'I heard you're casting something, so I thought maybe there's something in it for me.' And Lee said, 'No' and that's all. That was it."

During these hungry days a delegation petitioned his return to the Group. He refused. Again, a member of the Party offered a large sum with, "If you need money for any shows, we'll back you." The man was told politely, "I don't have any plans for any future productions right now but if I ever do . . ."

In 1941 a meeting with Louis B. Mayer at the MGM office in New York culminated in a discussion about going to the Coast to learn film direction. It fell through, but a similar negotiation crystallized with Fox. The deal was a stock contract for a year, meaning you were paid as you learned and if you landed a picture the contract was sweetened. The family said good-bye to the East Side brownstone in which they lived, which, had they had the money, could have been bought in its entirety for ten thousand dollars. With Lee's first steady salary they settled into upper-class Brentwood with a car with a rumble seat which Paula drove and a house with trees and a garden and kids down the block whom Johnny "didn't like and who were bigger and older than I was and who peed on Susan one day."

Lee hung around studying the work of the top people. He

soaked up technique and became more and more knowledgeable. He was assigned to screen tests. A crackerjack script girl who knew the business showed him filmcutting and camera angles. She clued him to open close then dolly back for maximum effect so that his direction appeared highly skilled. Contrasting with the high-pitched voices the medium then adopted, Lee kept his actors natural. He was told Zanuck liked the voices up. He replied, "I'll take the responsibility." An early test was of Franchot's new wife. Lee picked Jean Wallace's scene and coached her. The results were excellent; 95 per cent of those he tested were sold. His work became known because his people were sold to the movies but never *made* any movies. When a heavy percentage zoomed into oblivion, their excellence proved to have been in Lee's coaching, not in their talents.

A young producer at Fox brought him a script written by a nobody. It was a simple play with simple behavior, set in an office, but things kept happening simultaneously so it seemed a lively, fresh idea. "I like this script. I think it has values. Does it appeal to you?" asked the young producer.

"Yes. Because it's the kind of thing I could do on a stage very easily and I assume it will translate itself onto the screen."

"Yes, well, some others didn't know how to handle this and that's why I approached you. I figure you'd know how to handle it."

"I must say this is right down my alley," Lee agreed. "I even have some ideas about shooting, like, for instance, one shot from outside the window shooting in."

"Ahh, good idea," murmured the impressed producer.

"The only thing is I will need the technical help of some film experts."

"No sweat. We'll supply that. My thinking is that this should all be done in closeups."

Lee blinked at the uncreased face across the desk and said politely, "Well, but, I don't really know how you can do this in closeups when you're traveling around in an office."

The help he was counting on was definitely not this kid producer who didn't know how you did it either. The neophyte film director commenced work on the script. About five days in he met with a scenario writer. She said, "The script is not properly written."

Irritably, he replied, "Every script has to be written in the old-fashioned way? The fact that it's almost in the form of a play is the thing I thought I could do something with."

Puffing her cigarette, the lady pro explained, "But it is not written from a movie point of view."

"What the hell are you talking about? I like this way it's written." Into the cloud of blue smoke he threw, "You people who go along always in the same way are cockeyed."

The shooting did not go well. On the stage, to establish people entering an office is easy. They arrive, shuck their coats, look around, sit down, all of which the audience sees. On the screen you must go with the person talking. To leave the talker and follow something else momentarily requires a new camera point of view. He learned fast that the script was incorrectly written without relation to: Who are you going to be on? Where's your camera going to be at that moment that this woman is talking? Who is talking? What are you going to see with the other girl? She's taking her coat off? The other person sees this? Then through whose eyes do you show this?

For one with stage orientation this whole movie concept of perspective, interrelation to characters, and interaction was a shattering albeit educational experience. Lee shot for three days. They saw the rushes. And that was it. Work was stopped immediately. Some while later a top director spied Lee on the Fox lot. "Hey, I saw your stuff that you made the other day and it was pretty good."

"So how come you saw it?" asked Lee as they strolled toward the commissary.

"Because they approached me to take it over, but even though Zanuck himself wants me to do it, I won't."

"Why?"

"Because I'd read the script and so I told them quite honestly, 'You know what you're paying me for? It's not that I'm better than Strasberg. It's that I already made that mistake and I won't make it again.'"

"What mistake?" asked Lee, standing still.

The director also stopped walking. "Look, there's nothing

wrong with what you did. It's just that the thing isn't right. The script is lousy, so I can't do it any better either."

Later George Cukor took up the same subject. "Why did you take that lousy picture?" asked the famous director. "Why didn't you come and talk to me first?"

"How did you know about it?" asked Lee as they commandeered a table in the commissary.

"How? Because they approached me first and almost everybody else in town!"

"Oh. They inferred it had been turned down previously but I didn't know by how many."

"We all felt the same way about that lousy script." George put an arm around his friend. "Everybody had taken a shot at it. That young kid decided he wanted to do it, that's all. The fact that nobody could do it is something else."

Armed with the lesson that failure can be a schoolteacher, a stimulus to more considered craftsmanship, the newcomer smiled ruefully. "Those three days taught me more about moviemaking than most people learn in a lifetime."

There were several trips cross-country. On the second haul to the Coast to join their parents, Johnny and Susie traveled with Danny Archer, whose wife, Molla, had been Paula's matron of honor. Danny wanted to play cards in the club car, so he tipped the porter five dollars to watch his charges. Johnny wandered around singing songs in his piping tenor voice and the soldiers who filled the train would call, "Who are you with?" and he'd say, "Nobody" and was rewarded with free meals and lots of attention. So beautiful was Johnny with his curly white-blond hair that one passenger gushed to Susie, "My, what an adorable little sister you've got!" Mommy and Daddy had carefully coached Johnny to say he was four, since at age five you pay full fare. The problem was that his fifth birthday happened on the train and at his precise moment of nativity this little person with the curls scampered to all the cars, announcing, "It's my birthday. I'm five years old."

Home this time was a smaller one off Sunset. The children slept on a screened-in porch with swinging saloon-type doors which Johnny well remembers because "that's where I swallowed a penny and my mother sprayed something in my mouth and I vomited green."

The Strasbergs enjoyed Hollywood. They visited John Garfield, who now spent big money gambling and now had great fame and great pressures. They saw Franchot and they saw Joan Crawford. With his quota of graces, Franchot had worked to raise Crawford's cultural level, and she rose while Franchot's frustrations at secondary stardom fed his excesses and he sank. They swam in Franchot's pool and screened movies in Crawford's projection room. They re-established a friendship with Paul Muni. Muni asked about his current show. "You could do more with it," came Lee's reply. "But why should I?" Muni countered. "You see, they love it the way it is."

Odets introduced them to Charlie Chaplin. Chaplin communicated with the totality of his being. His hello was a swift Pierrot movement. While his wife, Oona, who'd experienced it all before dozed in a corner, Chaplin taught Susan ballet, danced for Paula, spoke lengthily with Lee, and executed his whole bag of tricks for Johnny.

An acquaintance eager to be a producer had a script which required a transfusion. Lee sat in on the rewrite. The treatment was eventually accepted by Joe Mankiewicz, who agreed to direct it. Mankiewicz's first move, another enormous lesson to the fledgling director, was to check the chronology of each scene. Eight o'clock in the morning . . . twelve noon . . . three in the afternoon . . . afternoon of the next day. To note the continuity page by page, so if you've established late afternoon you don't suddenly spring broad daylight in the next scene had never occurred to Lee. A stage play's program simply states: Next day, 12 o'clock. "All things I'd never thought of," he marvels.

Mankiewicz revised the script, gave Lee screen credit as scriptwriter, and upgraded it from a middling B movie, where it would have squeaked through, to an A, whose qualities it didn't have. They shot it, they shelved it, and Lee came back to New York.

The children were parked in West Los Angeles for six months with Paula's sister, Bea Glass, while their father tried to make a living. Back where he was before, without knowing what to do or where to go, he couldn't get set. Money wasn't coming in. The surest way to a living was to make teaching his career. Paula was not shy. What had to be done she did.

Paula asked Bess Eitingon if they might live on her grounds, and for a year they dwelt rent-free in Hillcrest, the Eitingons' forty-six-acre fenced-in estate with the rolling woods, private tennis court, and private lake in Greenwich, Connecticut. Home for them was the handsome carriage house, a barn adjacent to the stables, consisting of a huge, lovely area the size of a ballroom with a massive, wood-burning fireplace in which they barbecued hamburgers and franks. There was a little kitchen, two bedrooms, bathroom, and balcony. Paula wasn't much for decorating. The barn quickly filled with things and books. Poverty-stricken Lee, whose records had been broken in storage during their California sojourn, borrowed to replace them. "I had to pay double for my Elena Gerhardt German lieder songs."

The Eitingons lived in a mansion with a spiral staircase, stone walls, and horses and cows with fresh milk daily. They skied on their own hills surrounding their private forests inside their private road, and they had assorted gardens. A large black snake from their "cutting" garden wriggled past six-year-old Johnny, who jumped three feet, then ran the length of that private road. Besides the caretaker in his own cottage on the grounds, there were three gardeners, a groom, cook, butler, laundress, chambermaid, and waitress. There were Motty's car, Bess's car, the station wagon, and a fourth car which somehow managed to get assigned to Paula which somehow managed to get smashed. Bess replaced it.

Many evenings the Strasbergs went to the "big house." Dinner was a formal affair with a series of silver forks and crystal goblets, a bit heavy for a struggling teacher from Eastern Europe. Often the Eitingons brought food and dropped in on them, although Lee was not fond of Motty Eitingon. He tolerated him, maintaining only the barest minimal contact. Paula made everything come to pass. Paula made an effort to entertain her benefactor, engaging him in conversation, flattering him, being affectionate, presenting subjects of interest. She worked at it. Lee never entered in. He poked about and snooped at his books. Charming Motty had an outgoing nature. It was foreign to his guest. It made him uncomfortable.

The permanent guest didn't see eye-to-eye with Motty on many things. "Even Motty's records were the popular Victor albums. He didn't have any of the special things that I appreciated." The Eitingons had one of the earliest Capeharts. Lee watched, stupefied, when the machine's arm, which flipped over the records, jammed. You couldn't stop or reverse the mechanism or interrupt it in the middle once the process began. That Capehart systematically chewed up a favorite record as Lee stood hypnotized, powerless to stop it.

One could add up five hundred negative things about Paula and they'd all be true. Bess didn't totally approve of her, but she did admire her. Her goal was to bring out Lee. To the simplest query, Paula replied, "I really don't know. I'll have to ask Lee about that." Lee was kneaded into a Supremacy. Despite his considerable endowments, on his own he might have decimated what he had. One friend estimates, "Lee absolutely wouldn't be alive if it weren't for Paula." Paula wound him up, mounted him in his form, made it all possible, focused everything on him.

"Paula's sheer animal guts and dedication gave him what it takes to stick," cites Bess Eitingon. "Paula's cement kept it all together inside of Lee. He didn't have that fire. He was insecure, without a sufficient sense of himself. But not Paula. Paula acted as though he were already a huge success."

If he wasn't, Paula was damn well going to make it happen or at least make you think it would. Interviewees describe Paula as "a pathological liar." Says one, "She almost couldn't tell the truth." Another: "She was a frightening liar." A third, "She'd build a story for whatever the occasion required. She'd say, 'So and so was here and he just absolutely fell in love with Susan. It literally made me ill how crazy he became. Said she was the most beautiful child he ever ever saw in his whole entire life.'" Paula fantasized. Paula was heavy-handed.

Cheryl says, "Paula was a kindhearted dame who desperately wanted to be more than she was. She wasn't unlikable, but you got tired hearing her children were the best ever and Lee the most talented ever. Lee's life afforded her opportunities for pretensions. All her desires to be important funneled through him."

Paula's machinations were not malicious. Paul Morrison says, "She knew she'd never become anything from her acting and her alliance with Lee is all that gave her status, so she determined to make the most of it."

Phoebe Brand recalls Paula telling a friend, "Phoebe just called. She's fine. She's wonderful. She just called to talk forever about everything." Snorts Phoebe, "Well, I hadn't called. But she had to be in the know. She couldn't be left out of anything. If someone asked about me and she didn't have the answer she'd lose status. But nobody challenged her on it. We kind of looked at her crosseyed and let it go. What the hell . . ."

There's the story of her flashing a bottle of perfume. "Look what sweet Joanie Crawford gave me." Her hearers knew it wasn't so but accepted that she had no way of knowing whether Joan had given anything to them and she had to have been there first. Daughter Susan prefers it this way: "Let's just say Mother was theatrical."

Paula monitored every inch of her husband. If he wasn't coming off in a dinner party, she put him into the conversation by tossing a question with a built-in answer. "Am I right, Lee, in that I seem to remember you said something to the effect when you were in that play?" Possibly he hadn't said it, probably he didn't remember it, but he had been in a little corner at the moment and she provided the way out. Those subtle machinations were not unnoticed. Luther recalls, "She held the promptbook on Lee. Paula staged one conversation with, 'Lee, now tell us, really what *is* theatre?' To his credit he said, 'Oh, come on, Paula, not now.'"

Cheryl had a hit in *Brigadoon*. A progressive producer who provided hospitalization and benefits, she also offered free acting lessons. Lee had taught at the American Theatre Wing, the Labor Stage, the Dramatic Workshop of Bertolt Brecht's one-time associate Erwin Piscator, and lectured at Yale. Now Cheryl proposed he coach the company on the Ziegfeld stage once a week. "My finding a way to help him when he was poor and helpless and couldn't get it together was not reason for him to be grateful, though," smiles Cheryl. "Lee's never grateful. It isn't his personality. I hired him for a hundred bucks a week not because I needed him but to throw him eating money."

Lee's view is "this was a smart thing in lieu of Cheryl giving them a raise. They wanted more money and instead of another five dollars she did this. True, it helped me. I was helping her, too. It was a very good deal for Cheryl."

Despite disenchantment personally, Cheryl maintained admiration for him professionally. Her suggestion to work together resulted in his return to Broadway in '48. He directed *Skipper Next to God* in which John Garfield played a captain with a shipload of Jewish refugees whom he could not bring ashore. In '49 Lee staged Odets' *The Big Knife*, again with Garfield, costarring Nancy Kelly.

Paula commissioned Garfield's wife to accompany her husband to a Feuermann, Huberman, and Piatigorski concert. To experience these world's great musicians with Lee Strasberg filled Robbie Garfield with apprehension. "What if I say something stupid?" she fretted. "I don't know how to speak to that man. I mean, he never talks. Should I go?" Reasoned her husband, "What's to be afraid of? If these guys are really great string players then you'd be a dope not to."

Robbie strained to cry, "Bravo" and stomp her feet but her escort stared straight ahead, deadpan, nary a word of appreciation or pleasure. In a burst of excitement she threw her arms around him. Did he return it? "No . . . but I'm sure he appreciated it."

Cheryl's *The Closing Door* with Richard Boone and Jo Van Fleet was a great claptrap murder mystery by Alexander Knox. The setting was a loft. The major prop was the elevator. Only by means of that shaft could anyone gain access. Examining each sketch, Strasberg interrogated the scenic designer. "Where does that pipe go? What is that cable connected to?" He pondered each detail until it was architecturally precise and each piece had "motivation." Even Paula began to develop motivation. At the New Haven opening she staged her husband's wardrobe. His cape and cashmere scarf did not help with the critics, however.

In 1951 Lee directed *Peer Gynt* with Garfield, Mildred Dunnock, and Group alumnus Karl Malden. Lee and Garfield always had had a relationship. Sharing a love of Chinese food, they sat over chow mein for hours. Garfield was tense. "I don't know if I can do this part. I just don't feel sure," he said at their favorite Cantonese restaurant during the rehearsal break.

"You'll do it, Julie. You will do it," repeated Lee, shoring him up.

Garfield downed a second scotch. "I just have no confidence in myself when it comes to doing this."

"It's just that this is a classic part which you're not used to."

"Yeah. Maybe. But I'm nervous as a son of a bitch."

Outside it was a soft rain and neither had an umbrella. "I like to walk in the rain," said Garfield.

"Okay," shrugged Lee turning up his coat collar.

Garfield was at a loss. At the stage door he pleaded, "Promise you'll stick right by me at the opening. It's the only way I'll feel secure." Lee appeared unsympathetic to his nervousness so he pressed the point. "Promise."

"Okay."

Sighs Lee now, "I should have been more sympathetic with his concern. I'm sorry now that I wasn't."

Karl Malden's memories are bitter. "Lee got special permission from Equity for an extra week of rehearsal. Going into the fourth week I hadn't even been rehearsed once and he announces we're having a full run-through. Onstage afterward he criticized us in full view of fifty guests. I gave it right back to him. Straight out I said I needed work, that I couldn't believe he had rehearsed all the big scenes but not the little scenes and not me once nor Millie Dunnock once. I really gave it to him. I was so embarrassed at his giving notes publicly when he hadn't rehearsed the whole goddamn play yet. Next day he rehearsed just me, only me, all alone, all day."

The Moscow Art Theatre took a year to rehearse a production. The Group Theatre took a summer. The Broadway theatre held a clock on creativity. Paula wrapped up her husband's tendency to turn every direction into a class with, "Lee can talk for three hours in one sentence." The wisdom which poured forth had to be dammed up and the constraint disrupted and distorted his natural flow. The exigencies of the commercial theatre created limitations for director Lee Strasberg.

CHAPTER SEVEN

Actors Studio

With the housing shortage eased and the delayed construction of apartment buildings underway, the Strasbergs moved into a new high rise on Seventy-sixth Street and Riverside Drive. Paula landed a bit in Gertrude Berg's *Me and Molly*, which also became Susie's debut. One night in a busy neighborhood scene Paula brought her onstage. Lee was still not settled into a work program. Paula opted for a grander view than teaching but nothing crystallized and at times her husband burrowed into near reclusivity.

Meanwhile Elia Kazan was running hot. Eight years his junior, Lee's former pupil ("I was like Lee's servant, his kiddo") won several plaudits including an Oscar for *Gentleman's Agreement*. In October 1947, simultaneously with staging *A Streetcar Named Desire*, he launched the Actors Studio with cofounders Cheryl Crawford and Robert Lewis. The character of the American theatre had been defined—a straight line from the Moscow Art Theatre to the American Laboratory Theatre to the Group Theatre to the American theatre. From Stanislavsky to Boleslavsky to Strasberg.

An extension of the Group environment which nurtured Bobby

Lewis, Cheryl, and Kazan, the Actors Studio was for actors to meet and explore their parameters. To prevent atrophying in the wasteland of unemployment or in the stultifying repetition of long runs and type casting, talent needed a place to stretch its capacity, to test untried concepts and to do those things people cannot do when they're not working and have no time to do when they are. Not a school but a workshop where professionals with stage craftsmanship could experiment and work together to continue their development, this artistic home would provide a constant theatrical stimulus in a climate ripe for creativity.

Post World War II saw a flowering of American classics equaled only by the efflorescence of the age of Shakespeare. Gadge Kazan was becoming a one-man national theatre. He directed America's outstanding playwrights—Thornton Wilder, Tennessee Williams, William Inge, Arthur Miller. He was not interested in teaching. He was interested in promoting himself commercially. Plainly, Kazan's pragmatic thinking was to supply—for himself—a pool of trained, flexible, adventurous technicians. To be free for his own career yet to keep this "farm" working, cultivating a new crop to feed his hungry needs, forced him belatedly to turn to Lee Strasberg.

"I'm against it," said Paula.

"You're annoyed at Gadge to begin with," answered Lee.

"Because he's using you. He's a user. Gadge is self-motivated and opportunistic. He needs you now plain and simple. If you're so great and he wants you so much, like he says, why didn't he ask you a year ago when he began the Studio?"

Lee sat on the edge of the bed and looked at his wife through the dressing-table mirror. "Gadge never considered me as being necessary to any endeavor of his. I don't think he fully understands my work. He came into the Group after we started and most of that early training had already been done, so he didn't really see what I did."

Paula wheeled around to face her husband. "He uses your work in his own work so he must know what you do."

"He knows the general direction but not the real processes involved. He never had a sufficient appreciation or awareness of my basic values. I've always known it."

"So you're going to teach at that Studio to help him? What

will you get out of it? It's a small little nothing operation too modest to get any money out of." Coiling up her long, red-gold hair, she spoke with tortoiseshell pins in her mouth. "And it's the brainchild of other people, so you won't even get any credit for it. Gadge will go on and direct big plays and movies and become more famous and make big money and you'll be slaving for no money and no recognition turning out the actors that he makes famous. Why the hell should you push your talents into a crappy place which has no possibility of ever becoming anything to grab onto?"

In the ensuing silence Paula reached across her cyclonic dressing table and from underneath a paper fan, a pile of recipes, a dish of dried fruit and the dark pink pencil with which she signed her name with a heartshaped flourish to the bottom of her notes, she grabbed another pin and stabbed it into her bun. "He's turning to you now only because he can't run the thing by himself."

Kazan romanced Lee over a period of time. It wasn't some big meeting where it was all finalized nor did Lee definitely decide yes or no at one big denouement. Says Kazan about the man of deep silences, "He had to be gentled into it. I didn't lie to him nor necessarily feed his ego because nobody means that much to me one way or another. I act, I write, I direct. To do all that you've got to be tough and independent."

At a visit to the Strasbergs Kazan said, "You're by nature a teacher, Lee. You've always been tacitly a teacher. You have that ability to adjust fully to each individual. I don't. That bores the shit out of me. To say the same things over and over is a fucking bore. But that doesn't mean I respect you any the less. It's just that you can do it and I can't."

Lee's first step into immortality—a crowded room with folding chairs at 1697 Broadway—was as a guest lecturer. He offered a series on the history of acting. To Paula he promised, "I'm going to wait and see. I've told them I don't want any official position at the moment."

"But they're going to involve you. They want you to be more definitely in command."

"I told Gadge no. I said I didn't feel like taking over. Maybe my ideas won't be theirs and who knows whether they'd be involved in my decisions and I'm going to feel my way around first."

Says Kazan of that period, "Lee didn't have too many places to go but, still, he didn't give reasons for his hesitancy. He's like an artist. He's half understood because he's half underground."

Cheryl proposed three who had worked for her: Eli Wallach, Anne Jackson, and Julie Harris. From his *Streetcar* company Kazan suggested Marlon Brando, Karl Malden, Kim Hunter. Interviews, auditions, and recommendations for Kazan's class for beginners drew such as Cloris Leachman, Nehemiah Persoff, Joan Copeland, Jocelyn Brando, Betsy Drake, James Whitmore. Director Bobby Lewis' advanced classes included Sidney Lumet, Patricia Neal, Maureen Stapleton, Kevin McCarthy, Herbert Berghof, Montgomery Clift, Mildred Dunnock, John Forsythe, E. G. Marshall, who dropped out claiming this wasn't for him, Jerome Robbins, David Wayne.

When Lewis and Kazan had a falling out and Bobby Lewis left, the teaching was parceled out. Sandy Meisner, Josh Logan, Martin Ritt, Daniel Mann, among others, sat in. Their primary outside interests permitted limited devotion to this nonremunerative labor. The consequent lack of adhesion, cohesion and continuity created an urgency to consolidate all units under one single instructor. In '51 Gadge pressed Lee to take over.

Lee's dreams were carryovers from the Group. Foreseeing this as a foundation for a someday theatre, Lee Strasberg became the Artistic Director of the Actors Studio. President Kazan, who was consumed with the over-all view was the longshot; Vice-President Cheryl, the liaison to finances and administration, was the medium shot; and Artistic Director Lee Strasberg, settled into the moment-to-moment reality, was the closeup.

The art of thinking for oneself was the Studio's imprint. Julie Harris' earliest improvisation was of a woman entering a pawnshop. Mentally she charted her plotline and characterization. She'd be a stranger about to pawn something. When she entered, however, the "manager," who was James Whitmore and was also improvising, called, "Hi, Julie." Completely thrown, the young actress dissolved into a tangle of confusion. Today, thirty years worth of stagecraft later, seasoned Julie Harris handles the unexpected.

An early assignment was building a scene around a song. Karl Malden became a janitor cleaning an empty theatre with a pail and mop. Entranced by the sound of his own voice on that huge stage, he burst into "Some Enchanted Evening." June Havoc, already "a goddamn star before I came to that unswept hole," shucked her silver mink, sequin hat, and reptile shoes to be a slovenly hag so beaten from life with a no-good husband that she brewed him a cup of poisoned coffee while singing "Tea For Two."

They widened their heretofore circumscribed resources. Tom Ewell whose forte was the lighter role did the lumbering character Lennie in a slice of *Of Mice and Men*. It brought tears to those present and "nobody ever cried at anything I'd ever done before." Maureen Stapleton, whose talent borders on heavy equipment saw her problems as always overcrying, overemoting. She "had to learn to play a woman not a gland." Willing to take her lumps and "if I screwed up at least maybe I'd find out why," Maureen credibly tackled drawing-room comedy.

Uncanny Strasberg manufactured situations which forced major efforts. Eva Marie Saint was self-conscious and unable to display emotion without feeling shame. She was assigned to be a weeping willow. "That liberated me because it roused me from fear of looking ridiculous in front of an audience." The kindergarten class also witnessed Cloris Leachman wriggling around a dirty floor in a light-colored dress. Miss Leachman was creatively engaged in being a snake.

They were taught to immerse themselves in a character's pre-play life, to understand those cross-currents which brought him to his onstage life, to fathom what might have happened in his childhood days, to recognize that the playwright's product merely climaxed the character's experience.

The earnest, eager Yale Drama School graduate Paul Newman stretched himself in speech and character by experimentally working on a monologue from *Taming of the Shrew*. "My major growth was in the Studio. Basically a sponge, I learned just by sitting and watching." The day dawned, however, when he had to learn by standing up and doing. The Studio was where you went to try and it was time for him to try. Lee suggested several improvements. He instructed Paul to return and give the monologue again in two weeks. Paul returned to give the monologue again in two weeks "whereupon Lee glared at me and said, 'You've improved this into a failure.'"

Lee stressed the difference between acting that is imitative and acting that is alive. Striving to live his character not imitate it, Kevin McCarthy was to look out the window at night for an on-coming car. Kevin creatively looked out the window. Lee's critique? "I didn't see the lights of the automobiles in your eyes." Unnerved Kevin mumbled, "Shit, that goddamn automobile has to do its own part." "I did not see you react to the offstage circumstances," pressed Lee. "You didn't blink, narrow your lids, shield your eyes to block the light or flinch at the beam." "Jesus, I can't work for this son of a bitch," thought Kevin.

Membership is forever and completely free. The only requirement is talent and eighteen years of life. "Before that what is there to train?" asks Lee. "A person must develop his own personality first." Since the Studio takes unknowns but not beginners, admission is via preliminary and final auditions. From the thousand applicants annually about a half dozen gain entrance to the Secret Place of the Most High.

"I was already a movie star with three Oscar nominations plus one Academy Award for Best Actress when I decided to become a member," related Celeste Holm. "When I told Joe Mankiewicz I planned to join the Studio he said, 'As a teacher I hope.' When I told Lee he said, 'You'll have to audition.' Like everybody I got five minutes and a guy held a stopwatch. I needed maybe another minute to finish when the bastard called, 'Time's up.' I mean, talk of coitus interruptus!"

Another accustomed to idolators was Sweden's Viveca Lindfors. "I expected some excitement over myself. I looked gorgeous and I felt superior because I was an established film star . . . right? Wrong. It was suggested I audition. Audition?? I should audition?? What is that audition?? Me???" Viveca later read with John Garfield who "being very Method" massaged her neck during the reading. The experience was unsettling to Viveca.

Reportedly Paul Newman had an aura. With Newman everyone felt it was Superstar Time. Already on Broadway in *Picnic*, Paul "shook with terror" when he did his audition. "Supposedly I was demonstrating anger but I was so nervous that my emotion was mistaken for anger. They figured I'd worked myself into such a state that I literally had the shakes so I sure must be one hell of an actor. I think I got into the Studio fraudulently."

The Studio was tumultuous then. A West Point of acting and with a waiting list, even "a green hick lady magician from Pennsylvania out of vaudeville" had heard of it. Having done a few TV commercials and walkons, Carroll Baker overheard a pair of British thespians deploring Strasberg's opposition to the classic method. Carroll "didn't know what the hell the classic method was but I was impressed that Strasberg was important enough to knock, so although I'd never read a play in my life I tried to audition." They dismissed her fast.

Considering that Hollywood pro June Havoc threw up before auditioning, it is understandable that Al Pacino, aged nineteen, was "terrified frightened." He was rejected. He auditioned a second time. He was rejected. "It meant so much that I lied. I pretended I was a member. I wanted it so badly." The third time he was twenty-six and newly out of his janitor's job. Too shy to work with anyone, he picked two monologues. In cut-off jeans he did Hickey from *The Iceman Cometh* then a soliloquy from *Hamlet*. All Lee said was, "As you see, we take all kinds in here."

Being rebuffed by this snobby group was not unusual. Geraldine Page, subsequently considered one of the finest stage actresses of our day, was accepted after nine tries. Afflicted with what Lee termed "the Hesitation Walk," Geraldine fluttered and flailed her arms. For *Mourning Becomes Electra* Lee ordered her to wrap herself around a pillar and not move no matter what. "I had to cure the mannerisms and differentiate between genuine talent and the banalities of personal habit, otherwise those arms would have lost their effectiveness when she really needed to use them."

Economy of style was a rule. "We learned we don't belong to AFMA, Associated Facemakers of America," relates Marty Balsam. "We learned to say, 'I'm very upset' without jutting the jaw out or baring the teeth. We can do chagrin or disappointment or holy-smokes-what's-happening from inside without screwing a face up. We do it every day."

A terror in getting up at the Studio was never knowing who was present. It had become the greatest casting center in New York. Joanne Woodward and Paul Newman watched a session in the late fifties. Shortly thereafter Patrick O'Neal had a part in their film, *From the Terrace*. Cheryl monitored a Kevin McCarthy workout. The result was that Kevin landed in *Death of a Sales-*

man. Kazan was there casting mentally. It was from the Studio that Geraldine Page nailed *Sweet Bird of Youth.* Eli Wallach's experimental work won him *The Rose Tattoo.*

As "Shannon" before Richard Burton played him, Patrick O'Neal was breaking in Tennessee Williams' *Night of the Iguana* at the Studio long before it hit Broadway. "Somebody kept laughing at all the wrong times. I snapped, 'There's a fucking fool out there gone bonkers. It's throwing me off. Who the hell is that laughing his head off at the wrong spots?' And director Frank Corsaro said, 'It's Tennessee.' I used to hate to know who was in that audience!"

The Studio evolved into the world's most exclusive club. Stars piled into it, stars emerged from it, stars were made in it. O'Neal sizes up how ultimate was this club. "To make extra bucks I was modeling. Female models always treated male models like total shit. We were that back of the shoulder or that piece of tuxedoed furniture in the background. I did a layout with Nancy Berg who was naturally ignoring me. Suddenly I dropped I was from the Studio. Nancy promptly wheeled around and focused every pound of her attention on me. Eventually I took her in and she became a member, too."

By the law of association Lee's omnipotence grew. You couldn't be around without knowing who the main man was. For a Broadway stage actor Lee was the main man in town and what other town was there? And who else was there? Operating under some theoretical abstract viewpoint of perfection, Lee's modus operandi was to expose every imperfection. If you could survive Lee you could mine untold riches. Working for him, shuddered one actor, "took more nerve than to perform live on TV to seventy million people."

There were never compliments. Praise would lessen the Godhead. The anointing emanated from the head of Zeus. It could not be transferred to a person. It took Patrick O'Neal fifteen years to receive his first positive reaction from Lee "and it was only when I was taking a leak." Having rehearsed for weeks in a basement, on a rooftop, in one guy's living room, in another's bedroom, Kevin McCarthy was Hamlet, Gerald Hiken was Guildenstern and two days before performance a nervous O'Neal was pulled in for Rosenkrantz. "Even afterward I was still shaking. I went down to the can and there at the twin urinal I found God. Himself. There we were the two of us with our things in our hands. Not even Lee could just stand there. He had to say something and it was the most he's ever said to me. He said, 'That's the best Rosenkrantz I've seen.' I was so excited I peed down my leg!"

The aroma of Strasberg permeated the audience. Nobody exulted, "Oh, you were sensational, darling." Anyone trying out always knew his neck could go. The Studio was anarchistic; the roughest, toughest, meanest, most hostile peer group in the world. An actor was tackling Norman Mailer's novel, *The Deer Park* in a tryout. It didn't come off. From the rear Mailer hollered, "If I had Olivier acting it would have worked" to which the actor stabbed back, "And if I had Tennessee writing it would have worked."

In such atmosphere Eli Wallach turned in a brilliant Odets monologue. Instead of offering approbation, Lee ticked off each bad habit into which Eli had nearly again fallen. His intellectual analysis was stunning. It was brain surgery. Eli labels him "a superb diagnostician who can detect your weaknesses. 'So you achieved a result quickly? So that means you should settle for that? It's not enough. You glide superficially over the character. You don't dig.' Subliminally his incisive comments eat on you until they take hold. The man never lets go."

Lee taught about subtext, that underneath the words lies the character's thinking. He taught his people to consider what the character was doing before he entered the scene. What are the other rooms surrounding the set? What's happening in the rest of the house? Outside? Nobody ever contemplated such before.

Marty Balsam sat there in shock wondering what was going on. "And he was impossible to please. His words were rough. 'How dare you use this place to try and impress us. . . .' This was our Stillman's gym and if we tried to show off he had no patience. 'What was all that about? This is a workshop. We work here; we don't demonstrate.' I caught it, too. He asked me specifically what I had worked for in my scene. 'Well,' I began, 'you see, I felt . . .' and he busted me apart with, 'Never mind what you felt. What were you *doing?*' We were all eager to please and our egos were so fragile. It was murder."

Able to stir up what Stella Adler calls "a kind of mystic emotionalism which is very deep down like he is," he picked at Geraldine Page in order to fire some elusive quality and when she began to cry he, stonily unmoved, said, "Fine, darling, now do this over again." Through her tears he made her do what he wanted. She was crying but giving.

Lee didn't attempt to soften. He didn't know how. Some fled. Some burrowed underground temporarily. Some dealt with it by putting the man and the work in proper perspective. Some parade wounds to this day.

There was to be no diminution of his autocracy. Ofttimes the tension was painful. At a session with standing room only, a young actor worked on the bare stage with no props. Lee reviewed him slashingly. "This didn't have the smell of reality. You parroted words. You did all external work. You weren't really in a garden. You were on a stage." The actor muttered the script lacked direction. "You want to be spoon-fed?" asked Strasberg. "This thing is a lot better as a script than you are as an actor." "The problem is. . . ." "Your problems I heard before. It's your solutions I'm looking for. And how come you knew specifically where to swoop down for that lost piece of paper? You didn't have to hunt for the thing? God whispered in your ear where it was? You're so nervous you can't take your time?" "It's *you* who makes me nervous," gulped the young man. "So if someone watches an operation and faints, that's the doctor's fault? I'm sorry. Here we're performing operations." "But I really assumed the part," parried the actor. "Another misconception," lashed out Lee. "In that case the actor playing King Lear has to become insane and whoever's Othello has to kill Desdemona. Stage reality is a fictitious reality." "Well, if you just could give me the secret of the Method." Impatient. "Oh, you just want everything in five minutes that it has taken me a lifetime to learn!" Exasperated.

Many hurt for the verbal assault yet none dared speak a word in season. Unwilling to grow if it meant swallowing what this sovereign authority was handing out, the resentful actor hurled, "Fuck you. I'm a member and you can't put me out!"

Ellen Burstyn "never saw Lee mean or attacking anybody. People are so defensive and intent on keeping their armor that just because he tries to disarm them they turn on him."

Any pioneer who breaks ground in a competitive atmosphere generates animosity, jealousy, even oblique attempts to downgrade. If Lee's security was threatened in class and he was moving fast, the challenger had to be prepared. While starring in *Rhinoceros*, Anne Jackson had a contretemps with him. Lee's karate chop to her was, in substance, "You have no right to say anything considering the performance you're giving on Broadway." The membership froze. Eli Wallach, Anne's husband, used a friend as a conduit. Said Eli to the friend, "You tell that man that Annie's very upset." "*You* tell the man," chickened out the contact. "You guys always tap somebody else to do the dirty work. You tell him yourself." "No, *you* tell him," reiterated Eli. "No, *you* tell him." The reportage varies but the point that finds agreement is the cowardice of the majority. They were resentful but obsequious. Behind his back they grumbled. To his face they begged advice. They wanted others to put him down while they pumped him up. In effect it is they who did the injustice.

One foreigner couldn't comprehend "how this skinny, short unprepossessing person with the bad grammar could be this giant of the theatre. Then for one hour I saw him show an extra how he, too, was contributing, how the scene couldn't have taken place without him. He gave the boy a reason for being on that stage. This unlocked my fear of what if I do not become a star. It taught me I might still be part of the profession as an in-between capable actor. Lee saved my life in the theatre and for this he suffers because our gratitude built him into a God. Who is he to pee? This creature whom we have ballooned larger than life is not a mortal who pees."

This creature's magic includes perception. He X-rays a man's soul. This zooming in on emotions extracted from one's selfhood permits scrutiny of the gut for the purposes of transforming the possessed spirit into some fuel from which an emanation of one's cloistered being peeks forth. Opponents declare it makes the student surrender his soul so the teacher becomes his control. Proponents declare it makes you conscious and aware and you cannot longer hide or lie.

An actor has a need for self-expression. An actor's quirky nature is the genesis of his talent and his problems. To free his expression and unblock his capacities, Lee perceived the value of harnessing the psyche and the self-taught psychiatrist became the ultimate shrink. The resultant chemicalization sometimes assisted the professional analyst.

In preparing for a scene James Dean was using an affective memory. He had a knife and, deep into reliving something, he nicked himself. Lee never moved, but Shelley Winters jumped up. "Stop the scene," she cried. "I can't stand this." Lee wanted to kill her. "Shelley," he said, "he's an unstable boy. He was just now working something through and you may well have stopped the one thing that could have helped him forever."

Called "a merchant of insecurities," Strasberg uncovers them all but, avers one veteran, "Afterward premieres and critics hold no terror. Once you've worked for Lee nothing else can make you fearful. It is in the Studio that you die and if you learn to survive that nothing can kill you." This is the school that believes you work off of that terror at a deep level, that those insecurities catalyze into a wellspring for the abilities and extra juices that begin to flow.

Embedded in each personality pattern are shameful or negative qualities the person is brought up not to show. Lee's teaching is to use them otherwise you close up. Explains Estelle Parsons, "He creates an atmosphere that forces you to open and draw the terrors out. This then creates a safety for you and you're comfortable with him. I've been terrified to work for Lee but afterward I felt like a great artist—highly exalted."

Lee delved into the subconscious and flushed out the mysteries. Purified in this white heat of creation, Julie Newmar, whom he "uncorked," took to flight distraught. Moments later she snuck back. "Despite the pain it can be an orgiastic experience to see your talent burst forth." Indulgence in the pain is not sanctioned. Another who broke was dismissed summarily. "Don't enjoy your ability to weep."

The need to help oneself is the deepest truth in life. To understand this complex man who moves into people's psyches and rearranges their furniture, it has been suggested he wanted to study actors only to study himself. All people of extravagant gifts have a nose for what they need. His was to understand himself. The outreach was a natural extension of the process whereby an analyst first analyzes himself. Greater than painting, music, or literature is

19. Lee with Ellen Burstyn. (From the Herbert Kline/Arnold Eagle film on Lee Strasberg)

20. *The Misfits*—Marilyn's last picture. (Top to bottom) Arthur Miller, Eli Wallach, John Huston, Montgomery Clift, Marilyn, and Clark Gable (Bruno Bernard/Globe Photos, Inc.)

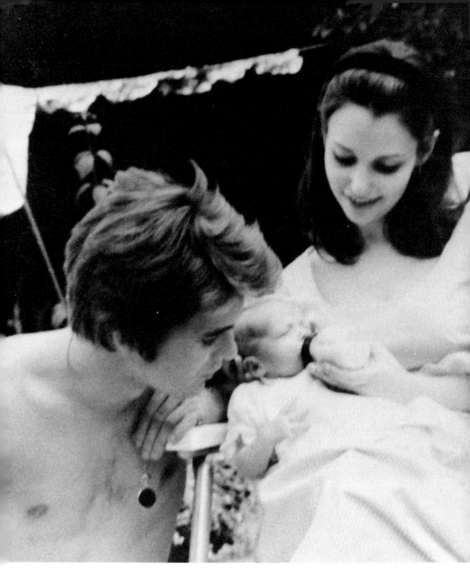

21. Susan with husband Chris Jones and daughter Jennifer. (Courtesy of Carl Schaeffer)

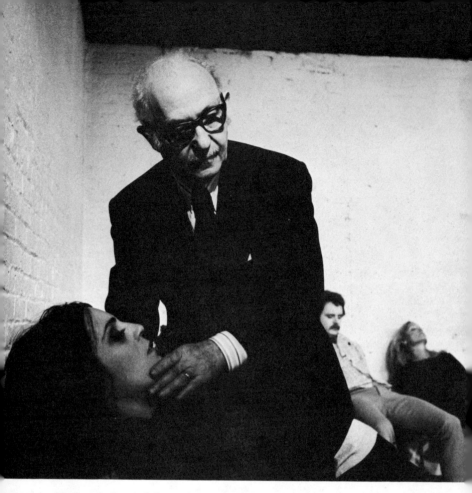

22. Lee in class with his students at the Lee Strasberg Theatre Institute. (Globe Photos, Inc.)

the art of the living person. Lee's own genius was a secondary, almost accidental discovery. His prime interest in the theatre as par excellence the art of people was to discover himself.

People interest him as objects of study. He microscopically surveys mankind's innards as others might butterflies or birds. A decade back two Studio freshmen fell into a scuffle. One hit his head. Lee restrained those who ran to help. "Leave him alone," he commanded, immersing himself in the actor's reaction to this unexpected pain.

Dane Clark was walking San Francisco's streets with Lee when a creep behind them provoked a fight. Dane wheeled around and knocked him flat through a barroom door. Dane went for him again and "Lee, fascinated, stood right alongside me without fear or concern for the son of a bitch who was bleeding and screaming. This student of human behavior was staring at me intently, closely observing one who had been tranquil one moment then in a rage the next. I was huffing and puffing and he said only, 'What made you do that? How did you feel at that moment when you hit him?' He wasn't concerned if I was hurt. I'd nearly busted my hand and another guy's jaw and he only wanted to profit by my behavior."

Accomplishment grows out of singlemindedness and the enormous inner control which must be applied to never let up until you have proven. As though resolved to beat any lack or limitation, Lee held himself like an iron master. With talent he was demanding, as though, If I have been able to overcome and take my own severe discipline then you, too, can take it and do with yourself as I have done and if I whip you and you hurt it's no more than what I've done with myself.

Actors are neurotic. They have to be other people because they can't be themselves. Agrees Shirley Knight, "I've never seen anyone destroyed by him because he isn't the one who caused their harm. But you have to get yourself together. If you have deep psychological problems, then don't study with him because he makes demands on your emotions."

If an actor's neurosis is heavy and interferes with the work he must deal with that elsewhere. But, unlike therapy, Lee doesn't do away with untoward qualities. He channels them. For that reason Viveca Lindfors moved East to be closer to the Studio.

In the late fifties, Viveca Lindfors and Anne Bancroft did Strindberg's *The Stronger*. In the scene the women are competitive and Viveca, who played the weaker, wanted really to be strong. She did not want her character vulnerable. "I've always fought against being weak. My mother was a victim always and here I was again my mother and I had opened this ocean of fear inside myself. Annie was going to her shrink every day, so she worked well. I said, 'Let's have a fistfight in the scene.' This was a stupid, masochistic thing to suggest because she was then in *Miracle Worker* and knew how to fight. Annie turned into a leopard and this leopard jumped on me." They were really fighting. Viveca sank to the floor "and I hated myself for copping out." Viveca tried forming words but couldn't. She broke into sobs. She was destroyed, out of control.

"The result was I started going to the shrink and I'm still going and I'm grateful. You must be healthy to cope with the work. Lee taught me to use my inner life as a tool. He helped me organize my chaos."

Those fed up with the Studio's ids and tics sneer that every time you get a script in your hand you have to put yourself on a couch. You have to see whether whoever you're playing was breast-fed and how often he had intercourse. Right or wrong, many sessions sounded like group therapy with Strasberg the Big Beard.

After actor Andreas Voutsinas completed a scene of having sex Lee inquired, "What did you use there? I saw you were working about something but I don't quite see what."

"I used a sense memory of having had a bath."

"Why? What did that have to do with the scene?"

"I did that because I wanted to get a certain feeling because I have a personal problem and because of this personal problem I could not use the scene just as it was."

"What do you mean personal problem?"

Not a knuckle cracked in the Studio. Not a match scratched to light a cigarette. "A problem. A personal problem. It's personal."

Lee refused to let go. "I don't understand why you couldn't use the scene as it was."

"Okay," shouted Voutsinas. "Okay, I'll tell you. Right after sex

I always feel dirty and awful so as the scene was saying the reverse I had to use a sense memory to make me feel good."

Lee's voice rose. "I don't give a damn about your personal life. I don't want Peeping Tom stories. I don't want to know what your story is."

"But that's the reason why I. . . ."

"If you think I'm here because I'm curious about your personal life get out of here . . . *out* . . . *gettt outttt*. . . ."

Voutsinas moved to calm his teacher. "Please . . . please don't get excited."

Fifty people sat rigid. Lee was suffused. Voutsinas, who insists Lee's anger was such that foam flecks had gathered on his lip, said, "No, I'm not going to leave, so please calm down. You'll get a heart attack. Please . . ."

"The trouble with you," shouted Lee, "is that you're trying to be a director. You're always directing the way a scene should go instead of playing it. I am trying to understand what you were doing up there as an actor not as a person. Why do you assume because it's a personal problem you have immediately to have a substitute."

"Well, because . . ."

Hunched forward in his director's chair with both hands clamped on the armrests, Lee never took his eyes off Voutsinas. "Why couldn't you imagine—you who every time you have sex you feel dirty or whatever—why couldn't you feel that this time, just this one time, just only suddenly this once, it's not like that. With this one woman it's not like that."

"I guess I never thought. . . ."

"Why must you control everything? Why do you want to know everything? This is a living art and you have to go with that. You have to go with *if* I meet someone one day and *is* this that very day? Your problem is you overdo everything. You know too much what the scene is. Stop supervising yourself. Maybe you have highlights which could appear if you didn't sit on them and perform something else that you think should be performed. An individual has to get in touch with himself. Don't demonstrate to me what you think I want."

Says Andreas Voutsinas, "Again Lee knew. The genius is in saying things in such a way that you suddenly discover it as a new truth. He made my failure into a winning point."

Instead of violins or pianos, actors must call upon their own beings to function. To project emotion which isn't really happening is to pretend. To do it for real, to be vulnerable and whatever happens, happens, takes courage. In place of quick gimmicks Lee makes you find things in yourself to use. As Kim Stanley put it once, "He insists we work moment by moment, that we allow ourselves to look and listen, that we trust ourselves not to perform but to let things happen. Then it's cumulative. It works, but it's not easy."

Mike Nichols learned how to direct by sitting in Lee's presence learning how to act. After a dramatic presentation Lee posed an apparently nonsequitur question. "Do you know how to make fruit salad?" "What was that again?" asked the actress, still heaving from her heavy emoting. "Do you know how to make fruit salad?" "Yes, I guess so. Sure . . . why?" "Tell me." The perspiring ingenue couldn't understand where he was headed. "Tell me," he repeated without embroidering, "how you make a fruit salad." "I've been rehearsing this dramatic thing for three weeks. You don't want to discuss my acting?" "I want," said the man, deadly quiet, "to be told how you make fruit salad." "Jeez . . . well, I put together apples, oranges, grapes. . . ." "Do you wash the grapes first?" "Yeah." "Do you peel the apples first?" "Yeah." "Well, tell me all the steps." ". . . er . . . well, I open the refrigerator. I take the apples. I wash them. I dry them. I take a knife and peel them; then I cut them into small slices and cut out the core and the seeds then I take my oranges and. . . ." Lee nodded, "That's right. But you can't get fruit salad unless you do each step and individually cut each piece. You can't take a steamroller and roll over each piece, is that right? You have to do each one by one, is that right?"

"The metaphor stuck with me," mused multiple-award-winning director Mike Nichols twenty-seven years later. "He taught me there's no short cut."

With the impact of Marlon Brando and James Dean, the Studio—and anybody who was somebody referred to it strictly as "the Studio"—came to symbolize a stereotype of the itch-and-scratch, shuffle-and-mumble, naturalistic style. Characterized variously as the Armpit, the Dirty Fingernail, and the Torn Shirt School, its reputation was that you were hissed unless you featured ratty jeans, wrinkled fatigues, and lumberjackets.

Rather than being studied dirty or conformist filthy, the sweatshirts and dungarees came about because "we were all broke, intense, all starting out trying to find ourselves," explains Carroll Baker. "We had to scrounge. Who had clothes?"

The term "Method actor" became pejorative, implying one who was inaudible, slovenly, rude, the colors of Brando's Stanley Kowalski. Ellen Burstyn never mumbled, stumbled or grumbled, and Julie Harris didn't work like Jane Fonda, who came braless even in those days. No two had the same personality. To explain what each received from the Studio except in the most personal terms becomes impossible. There's controversy amid its own practitioners because the Method does not translate into coffee-table conversation. It is that at which one works not that about which one talks. Nonetheless, anybody who sneezed near Jimmy Dean, anybody with a motorcycle and an ability to ape quirky Brando called himself a Method actor. Lee didn't crank out wall-to-wall Brandos. The country did it on its own. The style became cannibalistic. "Anything which is new is misunderstood," sighed the New High Priest whose shabby meeting room with peeling plaster was being immortalized as a shrine and whose hard work was coming up as mystical magic.

The Studio actor was the right person for the right time. He was the anti-hero. He was the truth of American life. Playwright William Inge, himself riding the cusp of contemporary America, said, "The Studio is close to the roots of our time." Ben Gazzara hit as a junkie in Studio member Mike Gazzo's *Hatful of Rain* directed by Studio member Frank Corsaro. Julie Harris hit as a disturbed teen-ager in *A Member of the Wedding* directed by Method patriarch Harold Clurman. James Dean became famous under Kazan's direction in *East of Eden*. He played the unhappy son of a hooker. Carroll Baker became famous under Kazan's direction in *Baby Doll*. She played a childlike woman who sucked her thumb. Marlon Brando became famous under Kazan's direction in *A Streetcar Named Desire*. He was the rebel, the misfit, the slur against universal establishment. This genre characterized by slangy speech and jerky gesture was a social comment, a protest against the time. The public identified. Sad-faced Dean expressed the generation's frustration.

The young mixed-up neurotic was a sociological phenomenon who fit the crazy, mixed-up plays of the day. He was the contemporary juvenile delinquent, the waste product of a drug culture society. He was immortalized into literature by Tennessee Williams. He was directed into this immortality by Elia Kazan. But he was invented by society.

Concentration on the inner self bypassed the secondary characteristics of speech. During a segment from *Room at the Top*, Arthur Laurents complained he couldn't hear. Angrily Lee retorted, "We're not judging vocal problems today." When another shouted, "We don't hear," Lee retorted, "You're not here to be entertained."

Members articulate loudly against the shibboleth of unintelligible grunts, asserting, "We strive for normal sound, a natural tone not any theatrically trained or heightened sense of speaking." Members claim they're casting about, searching for truth in a line. They're trained not to watch words but what's going on inside. They're into themselves. The New York *Times*'s Seymour Peck tells of Brando monitoring still another gloomy Tennessee Williams scene. Brando rose and complained, "I couldn't make out a word those girls said. They mumbled."

Marlon Brando was already a certified genius with Broadway credits before he came to the Studio and consented to be a wax statue melting in the sun and a cash register "tinkling and ringing." June Havoc pictures the early Brando as "whiny, terribly full of himself." Brando questioned Lee. Lee criticized Brando. Brando threw it back. Each detected the weakness in the other. Those who were flies on the wall in those days report a kind of armed truce between the token hotshot and the resident guru. Theirs was a curious gasoline-and-fire chemistry, always in peril of igniting.

They shared characteristics. When Kevin McCarthy cut his hand the first person up was Marlon—not to help—to see. He had to learn from it. What did it look like? Feel like? He gazed deeply into that cut, looking at the exposed little yellow tendon, holding Kevin's bleeding hand himself to perceive the mysteries of life.

Marlon did walkons and gambits with funny collars and props.

As the hilarious Archduke Rudolf in *Reunion in Vienna* he had great style. A pasted-on mustache, full uniform, medals, braid, and, upon removing the boot, a hole in his sock. However, Marlon knew Lee could fire holes into him so he kept out of range. He took a shot at but one lone scene. Often he'd project his negative feelings by lounging in the back or he'd steal the attention by lolling in the doorway kibitzing. His every appearance was a star performance as though to say, "You think you're big, Strasberg baby, well, you ain't seen nothin' yet."

Studio improvisations always pitted opposing forces in conflict. Marlon had tremendous physical strength and was an explosive force. One improv was a concentration camp. Marlon was a "prisoner," Alan Schneider a "guard." Says Schneider, "Marlon did what he was supposed to do but in 'escaping' he damn near killed me. He jumped me and I wasn't about to get my back or neck broken just to keep an actor from pretending to get out of a make-believe place. Had I not stopped it he would have killed me."

In another improv, Eli Wallach was an FBI man searching for dope in Marlon's apartment. "When Marlon barged in he said, 'What the fuck are you doing?' Now, who spoke like that thirty years ago? 'Watch your language,' I said. And he said, 'I'll knock the shit out of you' and began to push. I said, 'Don't push. Now, listen, I'm not kidding.' Marlon lifted me bodily and threw me out. When I charged back in, I lunged at him and he started laughing. Marlon loved to put you on. Then, after all this was over, Lee criticized me for not carrying through my action of finding the dope!"

Lee says, "Marlon could have been the greatest acting talent in the world today but after going to Hollywood he never came back. The routine of Hollywood is hard to break. He hasn't lived up to expectations. He dissipated his talent. He's a great disappointment."

Having begun in a church attic, the floating Studio had relocated to the top floor of the ANTA Theatre where Kazan had an office. James Dean from *East of Eden* was always in and out and around. Dean was a self-absorbed, neurotic personality. His neurosis seeped through everything. Cheryl disliked Dean. "As a human being he was too sick." Those were the days Dean was enthusi-

astic about trees. He had read a book on trees and kept talking
about them as though he'd discovered them.

Slim, light-haired, bespectacled, rumpled Dean was like a
wounded animal. Removed from everything, he'd lapse into excru-
ciating silences. His eyes were off in space. He didn't care if he
spoke or was spoken to. "A sad-faced, introverted oddball," says
Carroll Baker, "Jimmy'd sit alone in a corner by himself even
when we'd all gather together. None of us thought the others
were peculiar because we all were. My hair was in a bun. I was
dreary and desperately trying to be intellectual. Rod Steiger would
always greet you with a French or German or Jewish accent. Rod
was always practicing accents. So Jimmy was no weirder than the
others of us."

In *Waiting on the Beach*, an original scene, Jimmy glanced
up and down the bare stage of the Studio, peered at his watch
then gave the sense of the sand and water. He sniffed the air and
admired the beach. He rechecked his watch then grew progressively more anxious. When his friend didn't show he was completely shattered. It was a staggering performance.

Jimmy Dean had a basic honesty. Says Lee, "Behind everything
he did was thought and commitment. When he pulled a hat
down it wasn't a mannerism. It was a gesture of defiance from
within."

Commitment was in, dilettantes were out. Sundays the tribe
gathered in somebody's house for a pot of spaghetti and to read a
play aloud or imbibe classical music silently. Any girl with
makeup was scorned. "I mean," sniffs Carroll Baker, "we were serious. All that was important was our studying."

Some were too literal. When Eli Wallach was in *Antony and
Cleopatra* his action was to deliver the message, "Antony is married." Lee had hammered home that once your preparatory work
is done you are to complete your action. So carried away was Eli
that he tore into the theatre that night, wriggled into his armor,
quickly buckled on his sword then ran onto the stage. Unfortunately Cleopatra was barely midway through her long speech.
"Oh, Madam . . . Madam . . ." hollered the precipitous messenger. Came a long pause. Eli had axed half of Katharine Cornell's
speech. She glared witheringly until he crept offstage. The next
day he complained, "What the hell is this? I'm all set to do my

action. The action is to deliver a message. I've done all my preparatory work and I'm ready to deliver my message. So, now what?" And Lee said, "Wait for your cue."

The boys and girls were full of feeling and deep into exploring one another. The result was a sensual atmosphere. Member Elaine Aiken says, "You could feel a throb of heterosexuality in the air. None of this casual friendly platonic relationship stuff. Everytime a guy sat next to a girl you just knew they'd end up doing it. There was electricity in the place. You had to know everybody was doing it to everybody."

Steve McQueen exuded a restless bursting-out-of-his-skin animality. McQueen did a scene in bed with the actress who directed him to the Studio and with whom he was involved. It went on seemingly forever. Says Patricia Bosworth, "They were really rolling around and we actually thought they were screwing and everybody wanted to take this girl's place. Steve vibrated enormous sexuality. I just kept staring at him. Finally he came over and said, 'Do you want me to take you out?' I said, 'Yes.' He said, 'OK. I'll take you out.' I hopped on his motorcycle and off we went."

The Sanhedrin welcomed newcomer McQueen coolly. "This one doesn't have it," opined Paula. "Can't understand him. He mumbles," tsk'd Cheryl. Scruffy, rough-hewn, bone-poor McQueen and Peg Feury shared her money. "That's the way we all lived then," says Peg. "We all helped each other." He bounced around in sneakers and hung out at Louie's Bar in Sheridan Square in the Village. A belligerent soul, he'd drink then fight then clean up then head for the Studio. "That was the top of the world for actors. I got a lot out of Lee."

The sessions did their best to live up to the sexual orientation of the members. For instance, you worked on weaknesses. Those who balked at four-letter words selected Elizabethan works and again and again tossed out those words again and again. Then there was the real-life couple taking a shot at J. D. Salinger. She was a nymphomaniac in bed with her husband's best friend. She understood the part perfectly, she burbled, because she'd known the same situation herself. When her actor husband reared up from the sheets, about to self-destruct, she quickly amended it to life with a former mate.

There were nubile young maids forever conquering repressions and inhibitions by disrobing. To one, Strasberg intoned gravely, "You undressed too quickly. You didn't enjoy it, did you?" "No," admitted the red-faced conservative, struggling valiantly to become freer. "Well, it showed. The actor's problem must be faced or it will poison his entire organism of creation. Take your time. Undress fully and carefully." The scene simulated sex and the Olympian comment in front of the whole group was, "It was not complete enough. You are, of course, a sexually frustrated person." "But I've been married," she blurted out not altogether brilliantly. Everybody laughed except the actress who "frankly didn't know what he was talking about."

There was, however, no repression in the area of dialogue except that with Lee it's more a monologue. He can preach any side of any issue in a debate with himself. He knows the number of angels on the head of a pin. The difficulty is he can't just see one. He sees them all. He rarely answers yes or no. He can't commit to so narrow a viewpoint. His serpentine sentences wriggle in, around and through labyrinthine patterns. The born teacher is a born talker.

A story depicting Lee's legendary ability to talk concerns a young man trying to dam this flowing fount. Lee began with: If you walk into a room don't just walk in. Is the room hot . . . are you on a rug because only when the objects are clear can the energy be right since the object creates the measure of the energy. Somehow this segued into Jacques Copeau who ordered his hand to say hello, but it just stayed there and this, he explained, is called the struggle of the actor with his blood which led to the great thespian of olden day, W. Charles Macready, who lamented he could not reach in execution the standard of his conception, thus he was perpetually tortured by his inability to realize his intentions. This triggered thoughts that the body is a live instrument composed of mind and emotions, thought processes and habit patterns which, unlike a musical instrument, contradicts its instructions and whereas Heifetz can hear a wrong note, if we do what's wrong but we think it's right then we can't hear it.

This somehow wound into Sarah Bernhardt, the German Expressionists, how Orson Welles is the most talented individual anyone can think of but that the greatest was Laurette Taylor but that Walter Huston has an authenticity, while Gary Cooper, John

Wayne, and Spencer Tracy who try not to act but to react and respond and be themselves without conscious theories are natural
exponents of the Method. This naturally linked up with America
having as much talent between Fifty-ninth Street and Forty-
second Street, between two subway stops, as they have in all
Europe. The kid, meanwhile, kept trying to insert his two-word
point. At his third tentative, "Excuse me," Lee sharply cut him
off with, "For the sake of argument, shut up!"

The format for an early TV documentary series called for the
actors to do a scene followed by the Artistic Director's analysis.
Lee spoke and spoke and spoke. They ran fifteen minutes over. It
never fazed him. "That was my criticism. That was how I saw it."

His unwillingness to curtail a subject extends beyond the con-
versational. There was the session he searched endlessly for an
item in a reference book. He never resorted to reciting its gist
from memory. Silently he kept a roomful at bay while thumbing
for it. Most respected him for this aberration. They figured he
wouldn't cheat or fake them. Strasberg did not compromise.

The clauses lapse into subordinate clauses, the participles dan-
gle, the thoughts are studded with "etcetera." Omniscience without specifics. Between the qualifiers and the mangled syntax there
are times the medium is beyond the message. He speaks ideas not
words. Sometimes what he says taken literally doesn't make sense
but in talent he sets off sparks. Al Pacino did a scene from
Armstrong's Last Goodbye. He played "a dead guy with a spear in
me. My friend, Penny Allen, did a monologue. It was strictly her
scene. It's not that I had a big death scene. I just lay there dead
—period—with that damn spear sticking in me. Later Lee says to
me, 'You know, you could have helped her.' I didn't know what
the hell he meant but you know something? He was right. I somehow felt he was right and I still don't know what he meant."

Another actor was told the tycoon he's playing was a bulldog.
Literally this meant he had a jutted jaw, bared teeth, and some
wrinkled business around the eyes. What unfolded, however, was
a quality of pleasurably sinking one's teeth into a thing and not
letting go until it is a *fait accompli*. A bulldog Strasberg-style.

Having early decreed that a mechanical continuity was essential, he established an inflexible Tuesday and Friday session from
11 A.M. to 1 P.M. Come snow or hail or influenza, it was unvary-

ing. If illness forced cancellation of his own private classes, from which he earned a living, he always showed for the Studio sessions. So assured was it that international celebrities landing in New York tumbled off the plane into the taxi straight to the Studio. There, at precisely one stroke after eleven, the Artistic Director settled into his faded blue camp chair with the painted LEE in the back surrounded by the symbols of office; tin mug of tea, white metal alarm clock, pencil and file card in his hand plus the other ritual objects—the mike and tape recorder to impress every syllable for posterity. Selected from any playwright, two scenes will have been programmed, each approximately twenty minutes in length. In the glory days the schedule was tight. To do a scene for the Master one had to sign up eight weeks ahead.

Surrounded on three sides by tiers of watchers in a crescent of metal chairs is the space serving as the stage. Scattered battered bits of furniture work as the set. Checking the white card, he announces the scene. House lights, such as they are, are killed. Here is where you flex your muscles . . . go . . . it's yours. You want to try *Hamlet* in a bikini, blindfolded, with a lisp, go . . . try it . . . it's an exercise, a series of scales. Afterward the performer divulges his intentions and problems. Lee's post mortem determines whether he achieved that for which he specifically worked.

One needn't risk performing. One can watch, listen, and sit glued as Pacino did for months. Nor need one follow the pronouncements from on high. One can take or not take Lee's assessment. The Studio isn't a school. Members drop out or return, come or go at will. The door is open on both sides.

Lee's position affords him autonomy. There is no power rivalry. His peers claim he cannot work with equals, let alone superiors. With students he is either God or doctor. For him alone there is safety. He alone can dig up another's insecurities while burying his own. His facility in taking everything out of another receives an assist in his giving nothing of himself. Rendered invulnerable by the armor plate of his personality, this withdrawal is shyness overlaid with protection. He's a perfect fit in a tailor-made setup. He is High Lama and none can get close enough to assay his divinity.

Lee may have felt trapped in an establishment not of his basic concept. He couldn't relish staying put in that first row in that same chair year in, year out, looking with sadness at the Kazans going up while he was going nowhere. Between the dream of what he hoped and the reality of what he had, there existed a wide chasm. Meanwhile the patriarchal image was carefully sustained. He nourished the glory he needed.

CHAPTER EIGHT

The Family

"My father and I never touched or embraced. He never put his hand on me nor did I hug him," said Susan. "He had difficulty responding, so neither of us threw our arms around the other."

"Mother didn't cuddle us either," said Johnny, "nor was she waiting with cookies after school so she wouldn't be called the ideal mother. The only thing is, she was the one I had the most contact with. I could talk to her at least."

"My father never played kid games or anything," said Susan. "There was none of that. He was just there, that's all. He'd read to me, but we never sat and talked. I used to think, 'Oh, boy, what can I say to Pop? What would be a good thing to talk about?'"

Lee's only outside interest was the Giants. He knew every player and every play. "Maybe when I was three I spent one Saturday afternoon with my father. I mean, other than when we went to baseball games when Dane Clark took us," said Johnny. "I didn't have him to myself even then, but it was all right because at least we were sharing something together."

"As a child you get angry because how else can you get atten-

tion?" said Susan. "I provoked arguments just so attention would
be paid, so he'd talk to me. Then he took me behind closed doors
and reasoned with me rather than hollered or gave emotionally. It
was the intellectual point of view."

"My defense was to get angry," said Johnny. "I discovered we
then communicated up to a point, but I had to make him listen
first and I couldn't always. It was hard. I couldn't say, 'Hey, let's
go to the park.' He wasn't that kind. The best he could do was to
share by watching sports. It was always an indirect expression of
love."

It wasn't your average house. The experiences were very
different. When Lee directed *Peer Gynt* the setting was the
Scottish moors. Shocked to learn the moors were papier-mâché,
Johnny, aged nine, couldn't differentiate between what was real
and what was theatre. "Everything was the same at one point. All
unreality."

They lived on the fifth floor of 320 West Seventy-sixth Street.
To the left of the foyer with the dining table was the kitchen,
straight ahead a small hall and two bedrooms, and to the right,
two steps down, the living room. A summer day Lee sat in the living room, separating pages of a new book with a flat-edged fish
knife. Paula announced, "Some people are here to see you" and
ushered in two young men who had no appointment. She then
promptly disappeared. "Yes, what do you want to see me about?"
asked Lee.

Replied one, "We came to kill you."

Lee sensed that if his mind stopped, he'd panic, so with the
extra adrenalin pumping, he kept talking. "Oh, well," he opened
calmly, "if you came to kill me then you must have some sort of
reason. What is it?"

"There's a reason," growled the smaller one. "There's plenty of
reason."

"Well, what's on your mind? Perhaps you can tell me and I can
fix up whatever it is." The voice was even. "What can I do for
you? Could you tell me what it is you have against me?"

"It's your association with the Group Theatre," said the older
one pulling a gun. "You promised our father you'd change the
theatre and make a whole new world and so far you haven't."

"You mentioned your father. Who is he? Do I know him?"

"No, you don't know him."

"But you said he was in the Group."

"He wasn't, but you were, and you swore you'd revolutionize things. You've gone back on your word so, therefore, we have come to kill you."

An enormously thick book in immediate view was *The History of the Theatre*. Unstrung, the older brother seized it and tore it in half. Removing his jacket, he ripped off his shirt with one effortless motion. Lee checked his fears at this abnormal surge of energy and his mind raced for a solution.

Susan arrived from inside and provided an additional threat. Terrified she'd draw attention to herself, Lee ordered her out through clenched teeth. "Get back in your room!"

"But I heard. . . ."

"I don't want you here. Get back in your room!"

At the raised voices Paula rushed onto the scene and instantly zeroed in on the bizarre happening. Johnny was due momentarily from school. With the *chutzpah* Johnny says only Paula had, she reasoned with them. "I understand that you have some business with my husband, but we're worried about our son. I'd better go downstairs and see that he doesn't come up with his friends and disturb us." Unaccountably, they agreed.

The brothers' distorted minds had constructed a weird play wherein the elder of them was Gandhi and Lee the prophet who betrayed him and therefore had to be slain. They explained what was just now unfolding in this apartment was their plot. They had come that afternoon to prove that what they'd written could really happen. "Oh, yes, I understand," agreed Lee, stalling until Paula returned with help.

Now totally naked, the more disturbed one lay on the floor in a severe emotional state. The younger flung himself on the couch against the wall and sobbed. On the steps leading into the sunken living room, with the fish knife behind his back, sat Lee. Fifteen minutes passed before the door burst open and in rushed two uniformed cops with drawn guns. They couldn't quite make out the cast of characters. To them, the nearest one with the weapon looked like the criminal. Brandishing their pistols they barked to Lee, "Drop the knife!"

The police were in the center of the room with drawn guns and handcuffs when in sauntered Johnny. Everyone froze. Accustomed to staged fantasies and far-out types, the offspring of this theatrical family glanced at the motley cast from the foyer then ambled into the bedroom. There was a beat of stunned silence, whereupon the cops hustled the brothers out the door and the drama wound to its climax. Later the father, mystified at his son being that sophisticated as to be totally unimpressed by the danger, asked, "What did you think was going on when you saw this naked man with the gun and the police?"

"I figured it was a rehearsal," yawned Johnny.

At P.S. 9 on Eighty-second Street and West End Avenue, the curlyhaired, apple-cheeked Johnny was president of his class, a privileged class for the gifted child. With all their moves, Susan had attended "a smorgasbord of about ten schools," the last being Professional Children's School, the High School of Music and Art, and the High School for the Performing Arts. Brilliant, with a photographic memory, Susie could devour a book in a half hour and recite the contents of each page.

The artistic subjects, sophisticated conversation, the classical music in the home extended their education in directions beyond the norm. Asked about Passover, little Johnny explained, "It's when Mozart crossed the Red Sea." When junior toughies from a street gang invaded one day, he rubbed his palms together with, "Okay, guys, how about a little Beethoven?" Even as a preschooler he knew it all, if not always correctly. He used to sing the hymn, "Onward Christian soldiers/marching as to war/with the cross-eyed Jesus going on before."

Five-year-old Johnny was taught to pull out Mother's chair in a restaurant and to pay with money she palmed him. When Susan was six, Paula coached her to play hostess. "Take the coats, ask if they want milk in the coffee, and when you finish, curtsy, and say good night." When Susie neglected the last part, she raced back. "I forgot the damn curtsy."

Paula was no more demonstrative than her husband but whereas he left the children alone, she dominated them. She wanted to control them. Paula ran her children's lives. Paula bothered *too* much. She was the reverse of a husband whose modus operandi was such that he couldn't even be coerced into a yes or no. From the perambulator the children learned Daddy's famous

Don't-look-at-me-do-what-you-want-I-don't-make-the-decisions shrug was his answer to most things. It was Sunday. Paula had gone into a bakery. From the doorway Susie piped up, "Daddy, you want bagels or bread?" She then toddled back inside and reported, "Daddy said . . ." and mimed his famous shrug.

Even when sharing a pot of coffee with a woman friend in the kitchen, Paula didn't let down. It was, "I'm a bit worn out" or "Life isn't easy on any level," but seldom did her guard slip. She did, one day, complain to a friend, "Susan is in the room crying. All he has to do is go in and talk with her, but there he sits with his music, doing his own thing, reading his book in the corner." Lee wasn't a father. He never went into a store and bought them a gift. They never went to him with, "Dad, I have a problem." He didn't know how to handle these things. He couldn't be more to them than his father was to him.

"This sort of thing I had difficulty with. I didn't in any way inject myself with Susie and Johnny by showing tenderness or giving them time and affection. They complained of that later. It was a difficult period for me. I was struggling to establish my own identity, to be something and I also had strong needs but . . . they probably needed too."

Nonetheless it was rarefied air in which the Strasberg children lived. Clifford Odets was a godfather to Susan, Franchot Tone was a godfather to Johnny. Six-year-old Susan's first party dress was pink tulle, a gift from Tallulah Bankhead. The recipient repaid Tallulah by crying because it wasn't ruffled. Childhood was spent listening to their father talk for hours but not to them. To anybody, as Susan puts it, from an Isaac Stern to a Zsa Zsa Gabor. Their playtimes were usurped by an Anne Bancroft, a John Garfield. The Sunday brunch differed from other Jewish homes in that those passing the lox and bagels were Kim Novak and Montgomery Clift. At Passover, Burgess Meredith or Joe Bromberg or June Havoc helped serve gefilte fish to Franchot Tone whose Christian ancestry was the most aristocratic and to Rip Torn and Geraldine Page, who enjoyed a game of who could devour the most horseradish.

"It was like we were not their only children," relates Susan. "I was jealous of these others, these 'adoptees' because it seemed so easy for them to ask for things. They had nothing to lose. If I wanted my father's opinion I'd have to gear myself up for two days, while strangers just picked his brains and indulged his time. I thought, WHY? My needs are also strong."

Johnny developed a "So what?" attitude. He related only to those with whom he could make contact. Tormented, lost Montgomery Clift, who had no defense from the hard world around him, would communicate with Lee Strasberg's young son. Johnny thanked his famous friend. "I'm so glad you came over. I've really enjoyed talking with you." Replied Clift shyly, "Well, I liked being with you, too." "I'd really like for you to come over again if you can," began Johnny tentatively. And the quivering flesh that housed Monty Clift stilled long enough to say, "Gee, I'd like it very much . . . do you think I could? Would it be all right?" "Of course it would be all right." "Could you get *them* to invite me again?" he suggested in childlike fashion. Says Johnny, "Monty at least spoke to me. Mostly the important guests would not, so I'd not say anything either. I was very withdrawn. I became a very angry kid."

By accident it happened that at thirteen Susie became an actress. Lee argued that a theatrical career in youth is dangerous, that children are imitative and that their own personalities don't develop because this metamorphosis occurs later. His theory was supported with the eclipse of Margaret O'Brien, Shirley Temple, and Jackie Coogan, who disappeared to resurface years later as a character actor. Few aside from Elizabeth Taylor sustained any degree of contribution.

Jo Van Fleet was doing *Maya* off-Broadway. It was summer—no school. Jo suggested Susan for a part. "You're upsetting your father," parried Paula. "But I want it desperately," urged Susan. "So you'll play a young girl. What will you get from doing this? There's no point in it," pressed Lee. "But I want it," pleaded Susan. "I promise I'll guide her, watch her, protect her. . . ." guaranteed Jo Van Fleet, who then promptly quit. *The Duchess and Smugs*, a live TV show for "Omnibus" with Alistair Cooke hosting, followed. Susan Strasberg, aged fourteen, was on her way.

The brother and sister relationship had been such that at night Susie would lean over to her kid brother's bed and teach him how to spell. It had had a marvelous closeness. The undue attention his actress-sister now received made it hard for Johnny to cope.

For a little schoolboy there could be no victories. He considered this constituted failure on his part. "Things really closed in on me when I was only eleven. Everybody was busy with Susie. The whole family geared up to help her and Susie didn't have time for me anymore. I was so angry that I wouldn't let anything get through. Susie's success made things harder for me and I didn't have the ability to handle it. I'd hide under the bed and bother everybody."

Susan worked at night. Johnny attended school by day. Since they spent no time together, the stressful areas were never resolved. "When Susie grew away from me, I had nobody. I decided I wouldn't need anyone. That decision was my defense to the world. I walled myself in."

He spent summers with Franchot in the hunting lodge Franchot's father built in Canada's western Quebec. They'd smoke and drink. Young Johnny drank heavily. Franchot's children by Jean Wallace, his new wife, Dolores Dorn Heft, and Dolores' mother were there, too, so Franchot wasn't too much help "but at least he was a real person with real feelings and I could make contact."

Johnny's friend, Joey Zelson, born the same day, was having a bar mitzvah. Johnny suddenly wanted one, too. What better way to command center stage for a day? A friend found the lone rabbi who'd perform the services as a special favor, since Johnny hadn't studied. With shaking knees Johnny went to Rabbi Carl Bach at Temple Kahalah Jacob for instruction. Cousin Ruthie wrote each invitation by hand. Aunt Becky personally made a challa. Cousin Cy was called up to read from the Torah. The synagogue was orthodox. The atmosphere was not. Franchot Tone, with the yarmulkah and the *tallith*, the prayer shawl, dominated the front pew. The women sat upstairs. The blond head leaning over the balcony belonged to Carroll Baker. "The whole setting," to quote Johnny, "was something out of Central Casting."

At home during the reception the wrath of God came down on shy Johnny, who was snapping photos with his brand-new camera. The rabbi snatched it from the bar mitzvah boy's hand. "Seems you're not supposed to take photographs of an orthodox rabbi. So how was I supposed to know that?"

Paula, who "had been defecated on by the Group," as one put

it, and lacked even a veneer in early days, had wriggled into a kind of bourgeois decorum. The nobodies who came to her table in Group days had become somebodies, but still they came because they concurred with Elia Kazan that "this Jewish broad had good food." She'd serve a brick of cream cheese with dark bread, or Johnny and she baked apple pies. Once hers burned and he wouldn't let her serve his. When gourmets Alfred Hitchcock, Otto Preminger, Joe Mankiewicz, and Charlie Chaplin visited in California, Paula substituted creativity for caviar. For a few dollars air freight she flew in a whole Nova Scotia salmon from a New York deli. So impressed were the guests that they hesitated to cut it. Paula's mother made *latkes*—potato pancakes—and *kugel*—noodle pudding. To such Jewish delicacies they added New York champagne which someone donated, and Paula Strasberg's reputation was made.

When they didn't have money for necessities they always had luxuries. Foodwise the Strasbergs lived royally as though that horn of plenty was their security. The refrigerator was stacked, crammed, jammed with roasts, grapes out of season, delicacies flown from anywhere, and bottles of champagne. Paula drank champagne. Steadily she threw out quantities of food to make room for new. Their legendary generosity in feeding the world, a throwback to not having it, was overlaid with Paula's Jewish mother syndrome and added to by Lee's shyness, making this an avenue by which he could impersonally extend himself.

A successful salon melds a soupçon from all corners. Paula's open-house ambience was a classic mix between starving artists and big stars. Paula's mother was second-generation American. Her father, a Viennese Jew, came over as a youngster. Paula was American, born on the East Side of New York. "A nice, *gemütlich*, goddamn generous Jewish lady who brought Lee out socially and got people to go to his house," is Kazan's description. "If not for Paula, Lee would probably have sat in a dark, slightly cold room all alone." She was a brilliant hostess. She even said so herself.

Feeding hungry actors became Paula's forte. The peasants provided a backdrop for the celebrities. Important persons and unpersons the world over were commanded, "Come and eat." Her famous New Year's Eve parties for hundreds became *the* gala for

the New York theatrical circle. People will assure you Paula was a
social climber, a celebrity freak. She didn't care who or what, providing you were Somebody. She cared more for glory than for
money. But Paula had a feel. She'd invite Dame So & So and Sir
Such & Such then feed them pot roast out of the pot in the
kitchen. When her confusion was sufficiently organized and her
mix just right, nobody was introduced, nobody separated into mi-
lieus, nobody was cared for specially. She'd beckon to an Olivier.
"Larry, listen to this record Lee's nephew brought." The one was
world famous, the other a poor relation. In Paula's atmosphere
the twain met.

"Tough bitch" . . . "She had balls" . . . are phrases dropped
about Paula. Lee had the talent but she had the drive. A producer
would say, "I have something I'd like to do with you." Lee would
nod. Paula would follow it through. Clifford Odets said, "If not
for her, Lee would be one of the little old scholars who shuffle
around the streets with books under their arms. Lee would be
nothing without Paula."

Susan disagrees her mother was the power behind the throne.
"She walked a few feet *ahead*. She did what *had* to be done."
Paula was an arranger. Paula arranged the social contacts. Paula
arranged the business negotiations. Lee couldn't connect with
people, so Paula made the connections. It was the assumption
that men of ideas cannot cope with the real world of making
phone calls or confirming dates or getting reservations. Burgess
Meredith says, "Lee fumbles like Einstein when it comes to the
complexities of daily life. He lives in a world of eyebrows up and
doesn't care about much else."

Lee takes exception to the premise that Paula made him.
"Starting the Group was my decision. Joining the Studio was my
decision. The New Year's Eve parties became a social event, true,
but those stars came as a result of the fame of the Actors Studio. I
don't take anything away from Paula. She may have been helpful
in some respects but none of that happened as a result of Paula."

Paula set herself as the bridge to Lee. He'd go backstage and
stand there without uttering word one. The outcome was a Paula
who took over. At first she smoothed the rough spots, then she
finished her husband's sentences, then she moved in and did the
talking. "If that woman answered instead of Lee more than twice

in one evening I'd get up and leave," said Burgess. "I mean, this was no mental giant. She never said anything original, only what he told her, but she kept talking."

As Paula extended her areas of takeover, she strengthened her presence. Madam brooked no threats. She stood between Lee and everyone, frantic lest anyone get close to the Godhead except through her. She was scary. To director Frank Perry she was levantine, Machiavellian, sitting in judgment of everyone, suspicious and hostile: "Lee saw my work in his Directors Workshop and invited me to be part of his circle. Staggered that a nobody whom she hadn't picked was to enter the holiest of holies, his hovering wife pervaded that atmosphere. She was omnipresent, offputting, like some evil miasma lurking overhead and you had the feeling she was stultifying to him. Paula was formidable. She scared the shit out of me."

Nonetheless, Paula's fans are legion and stories of her goodness abound. In the starving days of actor Jerry Orbach's wife, Paula bought her dresses although they hardly knew one another. In Group days she made Stella Adler's twelve-year-old, Ellen, a peasant dress with burgundy stitching. She adopted strays. Marty Fried, a cabdriver cum director, was ill. Paula took him in. "I lived with them for a lot of weeks and Paula took care of me. She was my family."

Paula's credo was, "Bring me your poor, your pained and sit them down in my kitchen and I will help all." Not even her strongest detractors can quarrel with her humanity when J. Edward Bromberg died. His widow heard from no one who had shared his political beliefs in the pre-McCarthy past. The only friend to ring Goldie Bromberg's bell, bearing what would appear to be the classic joke—a container of chicken soup—was Paula. Unknown to the world in quiet and in love this flame of goodness burned brightly.

As per one of Hollywood's famous actresses, her nickname was "The Big Wet Tit." She'd help you whether you wanted it or not. Paula was good to the underdog even if she had to find a stone and stick a dog under it. She telephoned an acquaintance asking in a sepulchral voice, "How are you getting on . . . how is your poor son . . . ?" This pitying wail when the person and son were hearty and healthy. The question was posed as though she hoped, the acquaintance had fallen into travail. Perhaps a touch of poverty? Ill fortune? Some unhappiness she could mend? The idea being, you turn to her, she then controls you. In your moment of need you could have her and ever after she would have you.

Given her role of an appendage, this quintessential Earth Mother had a need to be important. If you were beaten, submissive, in need, she was marvelous. If you weren't one to succumb, there could be hostility as though her recognizing you posed a potential danger to her omnipotence. A colleague recalls the original interview. "Paula sat me down, gazed deeply into my eyes, covered my hand with hers and crooned, 'All right, dear, tell me about yourself. What's troubling you?' When I didn't have problems, she lost interest. We remained perennially estranged associates, never friends."

Another who was neither famous enough to impress her nor weak enough to need her, calls her a snob. "She smiled only after she heard I'd graduated Vassar."

Paula Miller Strasberg was colorful. When Ruthie Lippa declined a party because her mother was dying, Paula retorted, "I don't care about your mother dying, darling, I care about you." Paula meant Ruthie was alive and well and that's why she telephoned to invite her in the first place. Her thinking was right. Her delivery was brutal. Incensed, Ruth hung up on her. Later Paula discussed this unmarried sister with Cy Lippa. "Why doesn't Ruth have an affair?" "What the hell kind of a stupid conversation is this to have with me," he exclaimed.

Young director Jack Garfein and his pretty blond girl friend were sitting in the Strasberg living room, which then was in the Belnord Apartments on West Eighty-sixth Street, when Paula announced, "You've been going together a long time. Get married already. We'll give you the wedding." When nobody spoke, she added, "Okay, it's set. I'll take care of the whole thing." Paula choreographed every detail. She booked Isaac Stern to play violin, Susan to be maid of honor, and Arthur Schwartz, Elia Kazan, and Roger Stevens as witnesses. "We had a rabbi who did twenty minutes like it was an audition," Garfein says, "and the action was for Carroll to walk from the front door to the fireplace." They did as they were told and that's how Carroll Baker and Jack Garfein—now divorced—became husband and wife.

At approximately one hundred years of age, Baruch Meier Strassberg was still alert. About one relative Papa shrugged, "*Er's a shtickel* a doctor." "A little piece a doctor? What does that mean?" asked Lee. "He's either a doctor or not a doctor." Papa shook his head side to side. "*Nisht. Er's a shtickel* a doctor." The relative was a chiropractor.

Until the end he took daily walks, but at the end he became forgetful. He'd return to his Brooklyn apartment to discover he'd forgotten to turn off the gas. Sighed Papa, "This is a bad thing. I can't live alone anymore." Paula wanted to take him in, but Paula wasn't kosher. The household didn't speak Yiddish. Susan stroked him and called him *zayda* or grandfather but she had no way to communicate. Baruch Meier himself suggested a home. They found a friendly place operated by one who actually came from a shtetl near Budzanow. Papa was satisfied, and every week Paula sent the check.

Papa Strassberg always rose at six. He didn't complain anything pained him but came the morning he wasn't up to rising at six. At ten the doctor arrived. The diagnosis was, "His heart is good and he'll last as long as his heart will hold, but at his age you can't tell. It could suddenly go out." Papa fell back asleep. At one in the afternoon Lee phoned Arthur to say, "Papa passed away."

Only in later years had Lee begun to get close, to know his father. "Then I learned Papa could quote the entire Talmud. He knew everything from the Bible. Suddenly I developed such respect for him. Only near his death did I appreciate my father."

Paula stoked the familial ashes. Paula brought everyone together and kept Lee in his own family. Taking command of this virgin territory she blew into Arthur's dental office in the Times Building and announced, "You need a new carpet in your waiting room." "Why? It's good enough," reasoned Arthur. Five days later the men from Macy's rang his doorbell with an order to measure for a carpet, courtesy of Mrs. Paula Strasberg.

She surged onto her in-laws with a big, rushing, forceful wave of affection. Once spent, the wave receded. Still, she telephoned, inquired after everyone, dispatched letters, invited the Lippas to baby-sit, kept in touch. She remembered birthdays, sent gifts. Once, a handbag. Again, a silver pin.

But Paula palled. She was erratic, dramatic, larger than life.

Susie confided to a relative, "Mother's wonderful but tough to live with." Overserious Paula had little humor. In place of the light touch were vulnerabilities and sensitivities. Her eruptions were too angry. Given her husband's personality, friends rationalize the bombast. Mrs. Strasberg projected to the second balcony. Still, there was no letting down in public. At worst she'd sigh, "Oh, you know Lee. He's doing his thing," then quickly buttress it with, "but you know how important that thing is."

She despaired his lack of aggression. Chances evaporated because Lee didn't follow through. Paula would tell him, "Call so and so." He'd reply, "I will . . . I will. . . ." Paula would remind him of such and such appointment. "I know . . . I know. . . ." The real frustrations were personal not professional, however. He wouldn't emerge from his withinness. He wouldn't be a husband. He wouldn't give. He wouldn't communicate. He wouldn't react to circumstances. He wouldn't talk.

Paula became the computer and he the program. She was officious. She bustled and hurried him along. "Come, we have to go." She set herself as his filter. What does he think of you? The information sifted through Paula. She set herself as a second Lee. Pronouncements and borrowed profundities tumbled forth. She set herself as his buffer. When Arthur Laurents huffed out of the studio, it was Paula who tried luring him back. She disturbed the ether. She bothered people. She was an achiever who intrigued. Constant machinations prove irritating to one who cherishes peace.

The consummate director, she primed everybody for everything. She created the mystique. In hushed tones she laid the foundation for a visitor. "I'll arrange for you to be with my husband but he's listening to music. Please don't disturb him." Ushered into the sanctum sanctorum, the guest inhaled the Presence during an hour of monastic silence, then tiptoed out, thanking the gracious and benevolent hostess to the Great Man. Paula seemed constitutionally unable not to complicate things. She was intense about the necessity of such and such a situation. She was a fist holding schemes together with human will.

With her imagery she would fabricate amorphous victories if she was staring into failure or defeat. Call it and her eyes grew misty. "I want to make the world better. If I lie it's to make my life more beautiful." In this fantasy world she was the Princess. A Pisces, she was mystical. Psychic. She read cards. She consulted astrologers.

They were not happy in later years. Perhaps the unhappiness surfaced because by then she was an anachronism. She didn't need to push anymore or shape Lee's world. It was done. The need for her was less and the marriage not what it had been. He didn't glance admiringly. He seemed not to take her into consideration. Once home he drew the veil in order to recharge, recuperate.

There remained some underlying, residual tenderness. It wasn't love they shared. Lee did not adore his wife. He trusted her. They were tied closely. Lee petted his dog, never his wife. There was neither intimacy nor human contact. No embrace. No overt gesture. At a table her hand was seen hovering over his but it didn't settle. One could almost see Lee's fingers shrink. He never bought her a present. Someone bought the present to give to him to give to her.

They slept in a regulation double bed. The surrounding coterie would cluck, "How? How'd she get pregnant? . . . Must've been immaculate conception . . . he never *speaks* to her so who tells who they want to get together?" They'd amuse themselves with, "Can't you just see him reading and her saying, 'Come with me for a second' then going inside and 'bothering' him?" Reportedly Paula told a favorite, "Susie and Johnny are *my* children. I had to take it and put it in. He practically had nothing to do with it."

"She always gave the strange impression that if they had any bedtime together it would be talking of things like me or of the rest of their 'children,'" said actress Nancy Berg. "Like 'Isn't it marvelous what Nancy's doing in class' type thing. It didn't seem she was making it up because she told it in such detail. It seemed like their brood was probably all they talked about."

Paula let herself go from sheer frustration. She was starved and to get satisfaction she ate and ate, substituting food for love. Diminutive Paula's legs stayed slim as did her lovely hands but her middle grew thick. "Johnny kicked my stomach out," she was fond of saying. When carrying him she became so heavy it was difficult squeezing through a doorway. When her professional career ended the last barrier to caution was down. It evolved slowly over the years. From a size ten she became gargantuan.

In her slim days she couldn't dress well. Her first cashmere coat she showed off to everybody. Now she couldn't fit anything. She'd compliment large smocks with Bess Eitingon's Lilly Daché hats. From smocks she graduated into ankle-length muumuus and caftans. All black. It isn't that she became physically unattractive. It's that she became a caricature. She added a black shawl. In colder weather a long, thick, woollen black cape and black hat. In this freaky outfit she'd sweep about like a witch. "The Black Spider" they called her.

Her long, red-blond coronet of braids gave way to a bun. She affected oversize tortoiseshell glasses and big jewelry, usually a long, thick gold necklace heavy with trinkets. She wore strong Jungle Gardenia perfume. She masked her rosy skin behind white powder because she fancied a Camille look. Paula loved to play a part even for herself. Her good-looking face which was now hardened still retained the bone structure, so she'd sit there sucking in her cheeks and accentuating the hollows. She became a famed Bohemian. It was as though she had come into her own and reveled in being a character. She wanted not to be in the shadow. Her selection of clothes was a sense of the dramatic. She commanded attention. She was noticed. She alone could do what nobody else would do. Paula Strasberg: a one of a kind.

In the country Becky spied her sister-in-law lumbering toward her in a gigantic caftan which didn't camouflage her girth, a peaked black hat, chalky face and chain with dangling charms and whispered, "Can I hide somewhere? I don't want anyone to know I belong to her."

Finances constituted another area of frustration. Paula never felt the recognition factor was sufficient artistically or financially. She resented the Studio's not paying her husband big money despite the fact that there were no resources and nobody was paid. For his hard and conscientious work, the Artistic Director earned one hundred dollars weekly. The lady of the house accosted Cheryl in usual direct fashion. "Lee needs more money. It isn't enough."

"I know it's too little but there isn't any money. You know there's no tuition, nobody pays, we're not funded. It isn't that I think more is too much for Lee. It's just that I don't know where we're going to get it. It's very sad."

Again it was straight out. "Lee has got to have more money. This man deserves it. He may not have business sense, but he is a genius and it just isn't enough for a man like this."

"I couldn't agree with you more but where are we going to get it from? We just don't have it. Believe me, I *know* this isn't very much money."

Liska March, a handsome housewife with a theatre background who devoted herself to the Studio instead of attending luncheons or playing bridge, served as unpaid administrator. To Paula this was suspect. "Why are you doing what you're doing? Nobody works for nothing." "I have a lot to offer and this atmosphere gives me what I want in exchange for my services even though I'm not getting a salary," is how Liska explained it. This didn't satisfy the stainless-steel lady. When she determined Liska's doctor husband was not wealthy, could flex no muscle and, thus, could serve little purpose in her life, Paula tolerated but never liked Liska March. She came near only to achieve her purpose. "Lee will quit if you don't give him more."

"Look, I'm the treasurer of an empty bank. What can I do? It isn't mine to do. There's a governing board. I only do as I'm told."

The Studio's reputation had increased due to Lee and Lee's reputation had increased because of the Studio. They were mutually interdependent. The Studio enhanced his publicity as a teacher from which the bulk of his modest income came. He gave private lessons at thirty dollars a month. Some students attended free because with young people Paula's feelings turned warm and giving. In space at Malin Studios Lee taught such as Inger Stevens, Patrick O'Neal, George Peppard, Mike Nichols. Lee was the whole staff. If he wasn't well Paula took the session.

Despite minuscule assets, his floor-to-ceiling library was still being supplemented. The impetus to become the self-taught, most knowledgeable person around is not unfamiliar in those with gaps in their education. He'd study anthologies, then order from each published catalogue. The acquisitions were rare and expensive. He knew the disposition of each copy. In the dining room, third section from the right wall, on the fourth shelf from the bottom in the rear, you'll find such and such.

"We can't eat books," sighed Paula. "What you see in this house—the books and records—that's what we have. We have no money." Saturdays he poked in bookstores and record shops. Paula wasn't interested. Neither were the children. He went alone. Even if it was a fifth edition of Beethoven's Sixth he rarely returned home empty-handed.

Lee was without funds but when his sister was in need and her son petitioned for help, he was not found wanting. His check for three hundred dollars arrived at the hospital next day. Ruthie remembers Uncle Lee "shlepping a cheesecake, then taking us all out to dinner." He didn't have it, but he was generous. He says, "People work and work and worry about their future and acquire money then acquire more and they plan and plan that someday they'll do this or that. Well, that someday comes and they're not here for it. I don't think about money. As I have it I spend it. Life taught me never to wait for tomorrow. Maybe there won't be any tomorrows."

Benny Slutzky longed to see Europe but never felt he could spend the money. He eventually spent that money but not in Europe. It was in a quick battle with leukemia. Lee gave the eulogy for his friend.

He lost other of his friends—John Garfield, J. Edward Bromberg, Phil Loeb. It was the period of the House Un-American Activities Committee. "Members of the Group joined the Communist Party in the good faith that it could provide answers to the American social problems and left it when they realized the extent of its international conspiracy," testified Kazan at the hearing.

"Phil Loeb and Garfield, people who got hit the worst, were not real Commies," says Lee. "They weren't anti-Commies. They were young. When they realized they were being used they all left the Party. Garfield died as a result of this whole thing. His heart attack was not because he had a bad heart. He *developed* a bad heart."

Garfield was at Lee's with Dane Clark the night before he died. He had condescended to okay a TV deal. TV in those days was considered low class for movie stars. Garfield was edgy. "I'll go crazy if I don't work. This blacklist has really gotten to me. I can't get a job."

"Don't worry. The TV deal is a good deal," volunteered Dane.

"I always figured if all else fails and worse comes to worse and I can't get another movie then I'll do TV. That's why I finally took this. It's the end for me."

Garfield was called to the phone. The TV deal had been canceled. He came back green. "They told me some guff about the casting director had made a mistake and it was all booked up." He looked ready to crack.

Dane canceled his own flight back to California rather than leave his friend alone. Garfield was in bad shape. Dane assured him they'd keep in touch at the hotel the following day. "Well, that next night came and he went."

Odets' writings and his thinking were well known. Everybody knew from everybody's behavior who was what, but the impression stands that one of the Group, "a pretty good drinker who had been inside the Communist organization," blew the whistle. Odets' testimony cleared Lee. There was still the problem of Paula. For so law-abiding a citizen as Lee Strasberg, it was a heavy burden. Day by day the headlines blared. One by one the names fell. There was no definite word as to when Paula would be called or if she would be called. The world's spotlight was still focused on the HUAC when a woman from the Committee paid a visit to the Strasberg apartment. She wanted them to testify against one particular individual, to say he was a Communist. In fact, he was not. How the Committee came up with his name the Strasbergs couldn't understand.

"The only thing I could possibly presume is that they wanted to get Paula to show a gesture of good faith. In trying to get our cooperation on this other person, there was an implied threat in what this woman said about Paula's involvement. It was a tough time for us. This woman sat in our living room clearly implying how she could be lenient to Paula's situation. She let us know straight out how it was in her power to make it easy for us if we both cooperated and gave her what she wanted to know. We realized things were difficult, but we didn't do what she wanted. The next step was that the FBI came to us. In the final windup Paula wasn't even called."

In testifying, Kazan went out of his way to make the point that Lee was clear, that he was never part of the Party. It was Kazan who named names. The hatred toward Kazan runs so deep that it has not ameliorated over the decades and the bitterness of the Group Theatre's anti-Lee faction was metastasized in these days. They believe Lee backed Kazan's decision to testify because "Lee's weak and fearful and was terrified of being investigated." So, they rationalize, what would "an incomplete person" do but try and align with the government. Spits Morris Carnovsky, "I guess it's a question of personal integrity. What one can do and what one cannot do."

While others took the Fifth Amendment, Kazan, who told me his best friend at the Group was Tony Kraber, named him. Kazan was involved contractually with Twentieth Century–Fox. He responded to the pressures. The strongest being, you want to work . . . you want to do this picture . . . you want to stay in this business . . . Kazan is a pragmatist. Tony Kraber muses bitterly, "We'd go out together and dip into our pockets and pool our money to get enough for dinner. Then he went and sold me out. Would you sell your brother for five hundred thousand dollars?"

Lee says, "Gadge did not check me as to whether he should speak. And I don't know whether or not if I were put in a similar position I would have spoken or not. How do I know what I would do if I were under pressure? I'd like to think I wouldn't have testified, but I might have. I don't know."

CHAPTER NINE

Susan and Johnny

It was 1955. Susan Strasberg's name was elevated above the title in *Diary of Anne Frank*, her Broadway debut. Her second movie, *Picnic*, was released to rave reviews. She decorated the cover of *Life* magazine. Teen-age Susie was running high. She had a secretary. She had a bodyguard. After a man was seen shadowing the house, she had Paula's pet adoptee, Marty Fried, fetching her backstage nightly in his cab in exchange for acting lessons. Flowers came. Presents arrived. Phones rang. Aly Khan sent his chauffeur. Stores brought clothes so she could shop privately.

Paula's sense of theatre kept pace. Susie resembled her except Paula preferred a dramatic look, so Susan's reddish hair was darkened, and Paula shielded her from the sun with picture hats and big umbrellas because she preferred alabaster skin. Paula became hysterical when Susie wanted that hair cut. Susie demonstrated independence by having film hairdresser Sydney Guilaroff lop it off at midnight. When the daughter ran around without makeup, the mother flared, "How dare you go out like that? You are no ordinary person. You are *extra*ordinary." The tensions were apparent. The blowups repeated. The lady was a controlling influence. Even when she underplayed she ate you up. She molded an image with borrowed taste. "Everything I wore she would have the following week," shrugs Nancy Berg. "Paula used me. She'd see me in a cape, then get Susie the identical one."

Paula's fantasies were heavy-handed and inside them Susan was pushed about. Paula fantasized that actors shouldn't be visible offstage, so she prevented Susie from accompanying Lee to Rockaway on weekends. "I don't want her exposed to ordinary people." She'd storm a room filled with friends, announce Susan must have a fitting or a reading or a meeting or whatever and thereby command the commoners and slaves and serfs to vanish while the princess on the hill was served. Opening her daughter's door a crack, she'd whisper to a peeking visitor, "There's the future First Lady of the Theatre. A legend living in her own time. She'll never know what it's like to walk down the street unmolested."

The Strasbergs had moved to Central Park West, a high-ceilinged, twelve-room apartment with two entrances, two wings and booklined walls. Susan's dates would note the titles in Russian, Chinese, German and, thoroughly intimidated, whistle, "Jesus, it's the public library." Terrified of being special, she "always tried to act as though my family was ordinary, just like everybody else."

When Paula forbade Susan's first overnight date to Yale, it was traumatic. "Here I'm earning my own money and I've been seeing him all summer and you're supposedly teaching me freedom and all. You're a hypocrite," screamed Susan. The wailing caromed through the house. Lee acted as though he'd heard nothing. But, as Susan grew in stature, Paula grew in permissiveness.

A child actress found the book, *Love Without Fear* which detailed all the sexual positions. Susie wanted her own copy. Paula bought it personally. "Everybody was very impressed that my mother would buy this for me." The friend and Susan applied themselves to figuring out where you put your legs and how you pleat yourselves into assorted positions. Having mastered that technique, they turned their attentions to rummaging through their mommies' drawers in hot search of a diaphragm.

Susan had her own bedroom, bathroom, sitting room suite within the apartment. She paid the rent on it. She invited dates into it. They spent the evening with no questions asked. Sometimes they smoked pot. Lee walked through in his trance, the living embodiment of see no evil, hear no evil. "I had never gone through adolescence. I was seventeen, successful, earning money and very advanced. If it wasn't okay to bring my boy friends back I'd have left home." Paula had a prepared answer for the conventionalists: "Better she's discriminating with one nice boy than running around with anyone outside just to spite me and coming home with venereal disease. And better in her own room than ending up in the back seat of a car!"

Besides the personal intermingling there was the professional dependence. No physician operates on his own child, yet she was being operated on professionally by her father and her mother. Paula accompanied Susan to Kansas to film *Picnic*. Paula shared the hotel room when Susan did *Stagestruck*. Paula sat in the back during every performance of the out-of-town run of *Anne Frank*. With her own career finished, whatever she might have directed toward herself she redirected toward her daughter. Susan's instruction was Tinkers to Evers to Chance. Lee told Paula. Paula told Susan. "It created tensions because it was what he thought plus what she thought. She tended to speak for him, too, and it was like that telephone game. We'd all have been better if he and I had gone directly." One of his gems concerned *Diary of Anne Frank* costar Joseph Schildkraut, who had a little habit of upstaging his youthful scene stealer. He'd embrace her and, his arm around her mouth, smothered a crucial line. Lee suggested, "Take his hand away from your mouth until you say your line, then put the hand back." Schildkraut never upstaged her again.

Atop the work concern lay the parental concern. Paula involved herself in areas with which her husband was not involved. The young girl had a mother who didn't give affection and was overpowering and a father who didn't give affection and was unattainable. Both lived inside their own dreams and Susan was conflicted with love/hate feelings. Having to measure up was a problem. A costar recalls Lee backstage "giving her hell. He was distressed about her work, said it wasn't one of her better performances." One opening Paula "attacked her, literally screaming at her." It wasn't easy to be Lee Strasberg's actress daughter. Britain's Joan Greenwood repeatedly heard Paula intone, "A Strasberg doesn't do this . . . a Strasberg doesn't do that. . . ."

"What the hell is a Strasberg?" asked Greenwood of director Sidney Lumet.

Susan was frightened most of the time. It was fear she'd fail plus fear she'd shame her father. The theory being, Strasberg can make everybody great but his own. Paula's passion that she be something special was an additional burden. Susan would be the biggest star. Susan would marry an Olivier and nobody less. Paula would make it happen. Paula created pressures.

The porcelain beauty enjoyed a succession of famous leading men. In '57 she did *Time Remembered* with Helen Hayes and Richard Burton, with whom she became involved. The relationship had the papal blessing. In fact, Susan felt "manipulated." Sniffs one who had been close, "Paula was always a star fucker." When it broke up, Susan lapsed into "a deep crisis period. I began to rebel. I knew I had to break away from Mother. Like even who I went to bed with was something she wanted to make her business and either approve or disapprove."

Susan's hostility included her father. Through her tears she'd cry, "I'm in trouble with my life at this moment and I can't go to him because it's useless." Even for answers to theatrical questions she'd cross-talk to friends sitting directly alongside him. She'd drop such as, "I'm going to give you a script to read because they want me to do it for a television show and I'm not sure I should do it." Lee glanced up from his newspaper. "What script? What television show?"

"My father bent over backward to be objective, but who's thrilled with just objectivity? Other parents would be ecstatic that their kids were just on a stage. Mine expected perfection. Their standards were the highest in the industry I'd chosen. And I wanted more than a working relationship. I wanted a father-daughter relationship. I just couldn't handle it."

Susan went to psychiatrists. She had a bad time. She remembers her "cutting the cord" argument with her father. In a rare conversation, Susan waxed political. He retaliated. Suddenly "we were both screaming. He became rabid. He cursed. He actually called me a son of a bitch. And I loved it. We had rounded a point. For the first time we were equals. He had lowered himself to fight dirty and call me names. He was down to my level, arguing on a subject that didn't threaten either of us. Oh, I was so happy."

Susan was half living with someone and to crawl out from under the choking hand, she took another apartment. "There was too much going on, and Mother and I were not close." To choose her own clothes and her own friends, to be free to develop her own being, to find herself, to determine whether it was her own talent or theirs, she accepted an assignment in Italy.

Her father supported the decision. "Paula wouldn't let her go, so I not only encouraged it I almost sent her away. I said, 'Go . . . go . . . go to Rome. You have to go.' She had to leave home. It was a too strong attitude."

Susan lived in Italy almost four years. It was the beginning of a period when the world went through the horrors. People murdered presidents, kids were on drugs, and Johnny was a child of the times. He was ignored in his growing-up days. He sulked in his room. He burrowed deeper within. He grew worse.

Another family would have seen ample signs their child was going awry. Lee's lone indication was in the last year of high school when his son had trouble with his marks. Aware something was not right, the parents went up to the school once. They never considered the possibility of emotional difficulties. They dismissed the seriousness by thinking, he's a teen-ager . . . he's growing up . . . he's having growing pains . . . it's natural. Lee "was completely taken aback by what happened."

Johnny selected the University of Wisconsin because its location was the middle of the country where he knew nobody. He wanted anonymity. "I had to find out who I was. My whole life had been motivated by the need to have a sense of myself. The second week somebody approached me. 'Hey, I know you. You're Susan Strasberg's brother.' Furious, I belted him in the mouth. I thought, 'Here, too? There's no place I can go?'"

Johnny was drinking heavily. Within six months he and college were not compatible. He was enrolled in pre-med but didn't want to be a doctor. He did not want any part of medicine. He cut classes, he wasn't getting along, and the school was about to flunk him out.

Lee did nothing when he arrived on campus. He didn't take Johnny aside. He didn't talk to him. He acted like a bystander. Professor Mosler, a professor Johnny favored, explained there had been moments in the boy's life he thought it might be fine to be a psychiatrist or a neurosurgeon but that it wasn't really his cup and that it was creating an emotional upset. About all Johnny could manage in words was, "The idea of having to do that work drives me batty."

In childhood Johnny had had a fascination with medicine. If someone cut himself Johnny raced for the Band-aid and Mercurochrome. When he gained admittance to the highly rated Bronx High School of Science, the family relaxed into a prideful feeling about their son the future doctor. Medicine freed him from family competition. Johnny couldn't compete with Susan's success, so Paula latched onto this perfect role. Paula, who reached out to the world but couldn't reach her own children, had no oneness with him. In Johnny's presence she would address Susan, "You are going to be a star." To Johnny, whose greatness she didn't sense, it was, "You don't have theatrical talent. You are going to be a doctor." Johnny suffered a breakdown to prove his mother was wrong.

"Paula was a problem for him," admits Lee. "She was too strong." Lee's attitude was, so you don't want to be a doctor, so okay, so what? If you don't want to go to college, it's also okay. I don't care what you do. A month later Johnny quit. "Maybe we should have been more involved with his choices but, anyhow, we told him we were committed to his desire to do and be whatever he wants."

Ambivalent Johnny's many-sided insecurities made him fear the showbiz element, those supra-important powerful celebrities with which his home was surrounded, but he yearned for the theatre. He needed that mask to be able to do and say things he normally couldn't do or say by himself. However, he didn't have enough sense of himself, nor was he healthy enough to ask for help. "Those people I'd known in my house who always looked at me like Little Johnny . . . I'd be damned if I'd beg for a chance. God forbid I should want anything from them."

Paula bent with the prevailing pragmatics. When Johnny washed out, she made noises like, "Oh, it's just so useless for him to go to college with his talent."

Johnny fretted that he didn't want to take advantage of being Lee's son. "You'll never come out equal," sliced Susan. "You already have *all* the disadvantages so why not take some of the advantages?" Johnny couldn't express himself easily. He had a hard time dredging his emotions out of the deepest parts of himself. Still, he steeled himself and bearded his father in the living room on a sunny morning. "Pop, I'd like to study with you." His shocked father had never considered the possibility. The enthusiastic reply was, "If you want to."

Says Lee, "Emotionally I didn't need that he should continue what I was doing or follow my footsteps so, inwardly, this was a time of great concern because I hadn't in any way evaluated his talent. Who knew if he was any good?" To have his son study with him then have to tell him, "Look, I don't think you should do this . . . this isn't the right thing for you" was a development for which he was not prepared. Lee was "quite frightened."

Awaiting his son's first scene, the father "kept no thoughts." He had no idea of what his boy could do on a stage. He could only sit back and wait. "With great relief," he determined there were theatre possibilities.

Studying with his father created a fragile relationship. Johnny found they could talk on theatrical matters. "As long as I asked a question about theatre it was okay with us."

Classes and psychiatry were helping him along until the things happened which were then happening to young people. Johnny was into drugs. He hoped the sensations would make him feel better. He was desperate to experience a little happiness. He needed to prove something but what could he prove? He'd be an actor? His father was. He'd be a director? His father was. He'd be a teacher? His father was. There could be no victories for John Strasberg.

"There was nothing I could do by that time because he had grown up," opines Lee. "It wasn't just the drugs. He'd developed emotional antagonisms which were against the mother as much as the father. See, it's difficult for people like us to have the best rapport with our kids. Often we're away a lot. We're just not the regular nine-to-five parents."

Says Johnny, "All I know is, if a child of mine hooked on drugs I'd say to myself, 'What the hell have you done that your kid is so miserable?'"

CHAPTER TEN

Marilyn

Marilyn Monroe's entrance into the Studio was a front-page item. Cheryl piloted her to the session. When Lee "became aware of the kind of person she was—the kind who had emotional problems"—he suggested they work at home.

She was visibly nervous. At their first meeting she revealed her background. "She told me she was the one summoned if anyone needed a beautiful girl for a convention. Marilyn was a call girl." She could not handle anything approximating formality. Lacking education, able only to speak from her own sensitivities, she did not know how to express herself in the conventional way. She was used and abused by her profession, and Hollywood labeled her "nuts." Hours of discussion revealed, however, her offbeat comments were sound and based on real experiences, only nobody paid attention. In his armored way of speaking, Lee says, "In Hollywood where she lounged around and helped out with this kind of thing, her call-girl background worked against her."

She was having contractual difficulties with Fox. She was having troubles with Joe DiMaggio. Shelley Winters, with whom she'd shared an apartment on Holloway Drive "came to the Actors Studio and told her about it, so she came to New York, too. She wanted to turn her life around." At a New York dinner party she sat across from Cheryl. They discussed the Studio. Marilyn wanted to go.

And so Norma Jean, the little girl from the orphanage, teamed up with Srulke, the little foreigner from the Lower East Side. Marilyn came to class with Estelle Parsons, Bea Arthur, Gene Saks, Albert Salmi, George Peppard. Shy, vulnerable Marilyn signed the attendance sheet like everybody else. She talked little. The feeling she invoked was sympathy. Viveca Lindfors' husband, George Tabori, had written a scene. Eli Wallach and playwright Mike Gazzo complained its meaning was unclear. Hunched forward, her face cupped in both hands, Marilyn listened intently. She raised a hand tentatively, afraid she wouldn't be received, and offered, "Michael thinks that scene wasn't very clear. But life is often not very clear." Above all the intellectual palaver, Marilyn Monroe had just wrapped up her concept of existence.

Occasionally Marilyn arrived alone by taxi. Often she arrived with Lee. Sometimes she'd appear to be drugged. "Get her coffee," Lee would say to the gopher. Shrinking from special attention she'd huddle quietly alone in a corner or the last row trying hard not to be seen. In dark glasses, no makeup, babushka, looking as un-Marilyn as possible, she hid the 37–23–37 inside a dark baggy cardigan, jeans, or black pants.

Fresh and wholesome without false eyelashes or platinum hair showing, she had an Irish face with a turned-up nose. Laughs Shelley, "She'd come out in a shleppy old coat looking like my maid and people would push her aside to get my autograph. She loved it."

A late arrival slipped into a chair alongside "a hayseedy country cousin with freckles" and mumbled an acid aside about the exercise then under way between Gene Saks and Gene Wilder. The hayseed giggled, then tossed her own Judy Holliday style witticism in equally muted tones. The lights went up. The hayseed was Monroe. She attended private classes. She attended Studio sessions. Nestled amid Salome Jens, Julie Newmar, Lilly Lodge, Darren McGavin, and Cliff Robertson, she saw Shelley taking a shot at being Juliet. She watched George Peppard doing a scene nude with a woman in bed. She stared fascinatedly at a bare-breasted

Lady Macbeth, because Rita Gam theorized that in the madness Lady Macbeth might have ripped off her blouse and within the Studio one could venture far out experientially.

She witnessed Anne Bancroft meticulously experimenting with every kind of role. Snipes Shelley, "Bancroft always had a scene ready. Like twice a month she did a scene. It should have been called the goddamn Anne Bancroft Studio in those days." She watched a skinny beanpole in torn sneakers pirouette around with an andiron pretending to be dueling King Richard while stains from his sweating armpits widened. She watched "Lady Anne," a pale blonde with glasses, trip over the galoshes of the front-row spectators and in a Dixie drawl call him "fiend . . . unmannered dawg . . . foul devil. . . ."

She assimilated phrases like "proneness to fall into the pit of being morose," "emotionally riseable," "deepen my understanding of my way to approach myself." Director Frank Corsaro called himself "Marilyn's translator. She didn't know what Lee was talking about half the damn time."

Patrick O'Neal plopped onto the floor to watch a scene of two people making love. They explained the night before they'd worked into the proper mood by doing precisely that—making love. As Lee cremated them, O'Neal peered around and saw the hotshot sexpot of the world sitting cross-legged on the floor next to him. Afterward, Ben Gazzara and Eli Wallach escorted her to the favorite nearby greasy spoon where, at the window, for all the universe to see, sat Marilyn Monroe. Nobody bothered her nor was she considered an outsider. The Studio furnished an umbrella of protection and she was grateful for every kindness.

Eying a lifeless scene from *The Three Sisters* while "dimly talented humans struggled through the murk," Kevin McCarthy wiggled himself around. "Some blonde alongside me sort of materialized. She looked like nothing at first then some vitality flooded into her." She obviously inspired him, because he burst forth daringly. "Jesus God, couldn't they get on with the action without those endless pauses?" Lee ripped into him. "Who cares what you think . . . you need to do this kind of work yourself . . . !" Ohhhh, thought Kevin, the roof is coming down on me. "I didn't dare answer. I didn't dare look at the blonde. I just slunk away."

Eventually he slunk back with guts enough to do a scene. He

selected Anouilh's *Time Remembered*, a romantic play with poetic language about a French prince mourning his lost love. Kevin
thought, I'll do this flowery tearoom thing and Strasberg will
finally understand about me. Lee announced he hadn't known
Kevin possessed such colors. High praise indeed. A come-around
from when he was catching it. "And then this blonde jumped up.
She was so ingenuous. She kissed me and said in a direct, open,
sweet way, 'Oh, it must feel so good to be able to do what you do.
It must feel so good to be you.'"

She was ecstatic at associating with living, breathing, working
thespians. Marilyn had never seen a play. She came nightly to
watch her friend, Eli Wallach, in *Teahouse of the August Moon*.
Eyes round with awe she exclaimed, "Two hours? How do you do
it!" Intermittently this serious actress without the makeup had to
be reassured she was a world-famous beauty. She'd walk along
discussing how she enjoyed writing poetry. Nobody was looking.
Nobody was noticing. Suddenly brakes screeched, eyes popped,
passersby turned, cars ground to a halt, people darted around,
heads shook in disbelief and the world somehow recognized Marilyn Monroe. Nothing had altered visually. She still wore the plain
scarf on her hair. It was just that "I felt like being Marilyn for a
minute." She had simply cranked up the charisma, the come-on,
the light and there it was . . . the magnetism that was Marilyn
Monroe.

The Studio grants visitors the privilege of observer status.
Laurence Olivier observed several sessions. Sir John Gielgud,
Gloria Vanderbilt, Jack Lord, Dina Merrill, Elaine May were ob-
servers. A member requested permission for his friend Rex Har-
rison. Simone Signoret, Alexis Smith, Susan Shiva came several
times. The Royal Shakespeare Company observed the whole time
they were in New York. Marilyn was an observer. Joan Crawford,
who had been nasty about Marilyn and whom Marilyn disliked,
arrived with eyelashes, bracelets, and matching hat to observe.
Marilyn scrunched into the farthest corner to avoid her.

Although the noise about the Studio had been heard before,
Marilyn turned up the decibels. The real fame came in Marilyn's
wake. Primarily the Method was known inside the profession.
Kazan's movies brought it to national attention. But Marilyn

made it international. Marilyn made the Studio a household word.

In 1954 a down payment of eighteen thousand dollars was raised to buy the hundred year old once-upon-a-time Greek Orthodox church at 432 West Forty-fourth Street and the floating Actors Studio officially moved from the Malin Studios on West Forty-sixth to its permanent home. It was a heady time. VIPs flocked to this modest two-story white brick building between Ninth and Tenth Avenues. The heart of the ratholes of Hell's Kitchen became the "in" spot for the chinchilla and caviar set. Grace Kelly, Rock Hudson, Leslie Caron, Eva Gabor, Marge and Gower Champion were grateful for an upended crate or tin chair. It had become a theatrical Elizabeth Arden's: Come in, we make you over. The closely knit group of serious technicians had exploded into a glossy, Jet Set club.

Lee was drawn to anyone with a tic, perhaps because neurotics seem to have heightened sensitivities. He loved highly gifted freaks. He loved that negative-positive level of genius in the crazily desperately talented Kim Stanley and Geraldine Page and Jimmy Dean. Paula admitted her husband was drawn to the very young, the big stars, and the mortally sick. To the young he was a God, to the big stars he was ever the immigrant fan, and to the mortally sick he was a doctor. And the more vulnerable, the more hypersensitive, the weaker they were the more they worshiped because he had operated on them, pained them and, in the ultimate, healed.

Marilyn and Lee were destined for one another. She lacked belief in her own selfhood. He made her feel talented and worthy. He was her teacher and mentor. He was her father/deliverer. He it was to whom she gave her spiritual yearnings. With Lee she felt safe.

Marilyn was under pressure to be beautiful, sexy, talented, intelligent. She was locked in an eternal struggle. And he was taking this famous thing and making it over into an actress. *Pygmalion.* Her work in class was adequate. She caught on to the basics. She wanted to do better things. Even the doubters acknowledged a certain sensitivity.

Marilyn saw Lee anytime she wished. They'd closet themselves to the exclusion of everybody. One house guest dreaded a weekend because he'd run out of things to say, yet Marilyn Moviestar, not exactly a heavyweight intellectually, could brainpick with Lee for two weeks straight. Said Marilyn, who was so fearful of rejection, "When I have problems I like to talk to Lee."

Lee "had a sense of her talent before it developed. She had a wide range but didn't know what to do to expedite it. She'd developed fears and insecurities that were exaggerated by her personal problems. I made Marilyn Monroe an actress even though she was already a star. I worked out her problems for her, too."

Lee was extra gentle. Marilyn was fragile mentally. He didn't criticize. He boosted. Says Julie Newmar, "He loved Marilyn but many actresses felt that same feeling from him. I always felt he favored me, too." In his underwhelming way Lee showed his star adoptee affection. Her wounds were open. When she was depressed he was protective. If not physically then mentally he'd place an arm around her. She felt safety. She confided.

In the absence of a stronger spirit, children, animals, and the helpless who can't compete need that ability to be drawn out. With them Lee was ever kind and loving. "He helped me, too, and I wasn't Marilyn Monroe," comments Nancy Berg. "It was Lee who sent me to a psychiatrist he knew."

Confused, fearful, Marilyn was a lonely heart lost in her stardom. She had no center. Marilyn took to dropping in on the Strasbergs every Sunday. But so did everybody else. Author Rona Jaffe "got in the habit whenever I had nothing to do. One Sunday I had no dates and no place to go. When I came in I saw Bobby Morse and Brenda Vaccaro, and Lee greeted me with, 'Hello, darling.' I burst into tears. Someone was actually glad to see me!"

Marilyn needed friends. She usurped them. She called on the hour. She needed attention so much that when they lived together she'd talk to Shelley while Shelley was in the bathroom. "If you walked out of a room and closed the door behind you like when you went to the john, she'd think you disappeared and she was left alone. She'd open up the door to see if you were still there. She was a little child."

Marilyn had a tough side. She could be mean in a controlled way to anyone trying to reach the Marilyn Monroe part of her. Says onetime sister-in-law Joan Copeland, "She blocked you out

23. Lee and Al Pacino. (Courtesy of Carl Schaeffer)

GF-II-5641-13A

24. Lee in his first movie, *The Godfather, Part II*, for which he won an Oscar nomination. (Paramount Pictures)

25. "The Actors Studio"—Liska March, secretary; Carl Schaeffer, administrator; Estelle Parsons, member. (Courtesy of Carl Schaeffer)

26. At Lee's seventy-fifth birthday party. (Left to right) Carl Schaeffer, Robert De Niro, Lee. (Ken Regan—Camera 5)

27. (Left to right) Cheryl Crawford, Liska March, Lee, Elia Kazan. (Ken Regan—Camera 5)

if she didn't want you around. She just looked right at you without seeing you."

Nobody trespassed on her in the Strasberg house. This incredi-
bly dazzlingly lovely thing of beauty was free and open around
Paula's kitchen. Without family, loose, unattached, she needed
desperately to be loved. The home-cooked meals, the bustle of a
busy kitchen with a Jewish ambience was warming. She'd sit
around the glass-topped table with a Billy Rose or a Jean-Louis
Barrault or whoever else was there and read like everybody else and
slurp chicken soup like everybody else. She washed dishes. "I
know how because I used to be a waitress and in my time
waitresses had to wash dishes." She poked her head into that refrigerator which was really a safe. It was not uncommon to round
the bend in the pantry and have to brush by the world's most famous behind.

Paula's trick was to make you specially comfortable while making it seem no special attention was being paid. Marilyn's favorite
foods were somehow always there. "Marilyn, you like this, don't
you . . . if not, there's something else over here you'll like. . . ."
Paula was ladling chicken soup one mealtime when a prized giblet
fell into the bowl of a young student. Paula scooped it out and
dropped it into the proper bowl.

Friends warn of exercising care when writing of Marilyn because she was someone for whom Lee's feeling is so deep it's beyond logic. She had to have been his childhood dream incarnate,
the embodiment of all his fancied heroines, the epitome of everything a poor Jew from the Lower East Side could imagine. Yet he
it was who was sought by this Goddess. She needed *him*. She
came to *him*.

Her first check to him was for ninety dollars. He has still to
cash it. Nonetheless, ask if the immigrant was thrilled that the
world's sex symbol was at his feet and Lee bridles visibly. His reaction is almost too sharp. "C'mon, darling, that's what America is.
It's made up of immigrants. She was a little scared kid, too. She
also came to what she was from a background foreign to what she
became. It's shaky and scary at the top. Real people don't live in
terms like 'sex symbol' and 'guru.' Marilyn Monroe was a person
with human relationship problems, worries, fears, inadequacies, insecurities. Marilyn Monroe was a dream of a Marilyn Monroe."

Lee is accustomed to slaves who offer anything to get closer to the Master. Some perform chores in hopes of exchanging a word. Some dog the apartment just to be asked to run for a container of milk. About rumors he and Marilyn had an affair, he replies, "Maybe if she had lived and we spent another few years together we might have but she was not my type. My type is more the dark-haired beauty like Jennifer Jones who I admit I had a crush on except I don't think she crushed back. Jennifer is the only other person I ever gave private teaching to in the apartment."

Ask did he love Marilyn he replies, "I don't know what you mean by that but all I can say is that I did like her very much."

Marilyn went for treatment five days a week and eventually found a psychiatrist in the Strasberg building. The anxiety of it all tormented her. The long struggle had been too long. There was too much to forget. Those humbling years, the maligning and denigrating, the success which she lacked stability to handle, had taken their toll. "I'm nervous," she would whisper to Lee. "I don't know what's wrong with me but I'm nervous." As always, he calmed her. "When you're not, give up because nervousness indicates sensitivity."

She worked at perfecting her craft. She was scheduled to do an improvisation. She was to be a kitten. Several scampered about in a store she patronized and the manager allowed her to borrow one. She took him home and studied him night and day for two weeks. She then presented herself to Lee's class as a playful, lazy, stretching, scratching, purring kitten.

The star whose twenty-four films grossed $200 million was painfully shy. It was torture for her to get up in class. Finally she agreed to try a scene. Alan Schneider brought a copy of *The Skin of Our Teeth*, which he'd directed on Broadway. He handed it to her. "Do Sabina. It's a good part for you." Three weeks later he went over to her. "So? What did you think?" She shook her head. "Oh, I don't think so." "Why not?" She had no reason. She was scared.

While rehearsing something for class she had to telephone an actor. Said the star of Twentieth Century–Fox to the unknown on the phone, "Hi, this is Marilyn . . . Oh, you know, Marilyn . . . Marilyn . . . er, Marilyn from class."

The Studio was for the members' use. Anyone wanting to do a

scene signed up. The Studio had no say in what you did or if you did. The time came when Marilyn was willing to try her hand. Lee suggested playing Anna in the first scene in *Anna Christie*. She and Maureen Stapleton rehearsed privately for weeks at Marilyn's place and at Maureen's. The presentation was scheduled, then canceled. Marilyn was terrified. It was finally set for the following Tuesday. There was worry the press would hide inside the night before if they knew, so it was not listed on the bulletin board. Nonetheless, the Studio was jammed. It seemed the entire membership was present.

Selma Leichtling, who worked in the office, took Marilyn aside and gave her a shot of scotch. She was white as a sheet. "Standing on high heels she looked like she'd faint." Many expected her to fall on her face but others sat there rooting for her, praying, "Be good . . . please be good. . . ."

The picture Lee paints of vulnerable Marilyn is "she was engulfed in a mystic-like flame like when you see Jesus at the Last Supper and there's a halo around him. There was this great white light surrounding Marilyn." Those who didn't see this nimbus admit she didn't blow a line, she handled it competently, but that she was too scared to death to have really been good. Filmdom's hottest name, which was then over the marquee in *Some Like It Hot* and whose face decorated every magazine cover, was on trial. She was demonstrating artistic ability to her peers and she was petrified. "She was no more capable of playing Anna Christie than I am," volunteers a male member. "To be honest she wasn't good. In films as a light comedienne she's tremendous. On stage in a dramatic role? Forget it!"

Cheryl rates the performance "quite extraordinary—full of color." She agrees Marilyn was not destined to be a stage actress. "She was paralyzed with fear. It was too rough. She'd have a spasm every time she'd go on."

Maureen tried not to act Marilyn off the stage. She was thus adequate instead of her normally fantastic. Lee knocked himself out to give Miss Monroe favorable criticism, is the way it was described. He portended future greatness for her.

Lee commented afterward, "I wasn't nervous. I knew what she was capable of." Patricia Neal commented afterward, "Watching

Lee and knowing how nervous he was made me realize how much he can accomplish."

When it was over they trooped up to the Strasbergs'. Instead of euphoria, it was a wake. With her tan raincoat still belted, Marilyn slumped in the dining-room chair. Her eyes flooded with tears. "I was terrible."

"Oh no, honey," exclaimed Shelley bending down and locking her in a bear hug. "You were really wonderful at it."

"No, I was terrible. I just know I was terrible. The whole thing was bad. I could feel it."

"That's not true," insisted Shelley. "Everybody told you how terrific you were. You heard it. You heard everybody saying how terrific you were. They even applauded for you."

"The only thing that was great was Maureen," whimpered Marilyn. "Maureen was so great."

"You heard how Lee praised you. You were there. I don't have to tell you. You heard with your own ears."

Paula who was leaning against the doorway spoke up. "Darling, you were good up there on that stage. And you were not just good you were very good. You have taken the beginning steps as an actress and you did us all proud."

Marilyn sat and sobbed.

Shelley looked beseechingly at Paula. "What can we do to help her? She won't believe us."

Paula walked over and stood in front of Marilyn. "Look, Marilyn, Shelley says you were wonderful, I say you were wonderful, you know how great Lee thought your performance was. He said so. Now, if you aren't going to believe our opinions then what can we do? You'll have to work this out with your doctor because you think you're not good and we tell you that you are."

Shelley tried again. "Lee even says that you could be the best actress since Jeanne Eagels and Pauline Lord. He says you're a great star and that you're really turning out to be a great actress." Marilyn wasn't convinced.

There are those who accuse the Strasbergs of having been users. The truth is, each side used the other and Lee and Paula gave as much as they got. There are those who tried to break the Strasberg connection. Scenic designer Boris Aronson was one. "Marilyn would come to our apartment then get up at some hour and announce she had to go meet Lee. I'd say, 'Why are you doing this with him? Stop with this poison you're putting into yourself.' She was an innocent. The ultimate courtesan. How could he try to instill in her that she'd someday be a tremendous actress? She was the greatest at what she was and that's all she was. But he kept leading her on because he loves big names and must have them around."

Marilyn tolerated his put-downs of her adored teacher by treating him as though he meant well but didn't understand. "Boris, you're a nice pleasant old man and I love you for what you are."

Champagne was all she drank and she drank heavily. At night she'd telephone friends. "C'mon, let's go driving. I can't sleep." At 3 A.M. they'd drive to Coney Island or Brooklyn's Sheepshead Bay. Once she was back home, insomnia kept her pacing all night long.

Addicted to pills, Marilyn would query friends, "Don't you ever feel anxious? Don't you have anxiety attacks?" Told, "Of course. We all do," she'd reply softly, "But you're not in my position. When you're on a film you've got to look good in the morning so you've got to get some sleep. I can't sleep. That's why I take pills."

Lee tried to break the habit. She had an apartment on Fifty-seventh Street but she took to sleeping over at the Strasbergs. She couldn't deal with being alone. In the middle of the night she'd be warming milk. "She was emotionally upset. She wanted a family. She wanted to be held. Not to be made love to but just to be supported because when she'd taken the pills they'd somehow react on her so that she would want more. We wouldn't give them to her. That's why she got in the habit of coming over and staying over. I'd hold her a little and she'd go to sleep."

Johnny Strasberg liked Marilyn. She gave him attention. She talked to him. Helpless Marilyn, Montgomery Clift, an exposed raw nerve who literally quivered with insecurity, and Johnny would sit in the living room drinking champagne and eating caviar with their fingers and laughing. Johnny was used to odd types around his house. "It would seem to have Marilyn Monroe eating in your kitchen or visiting with you or sleeping over your house is pretty far-out, but for me it was routine."

One night it wasn't so routine. Marilyn slept in Johnny's room, and he took the couch in the living room. He was sound asleep, but in the middle of the night he sensed something. He opened his eyes. Marilyn stood framed in the doorway wearing a nightgown. "Johnny . . . Johnny . . ." she called.

Now fully awake, Johnny got up immediately. In fact he sat bolt upright in his bed. "Yes, what is it, Marilyn?"

She stuck her head a little farther into the room. "Johnny, I'm sorry to bother you."

"It's . . . it's okay," stammered the terrified young boy.

"I can't sleep," she moaned. "I felt kind of lonely and like I need to talk."

Nineteen-year-old Johnny didn't know if it was sexual. He didn't know whether she wanted to have an affair, but in any case he couldn't handle the situation. Marilyn stepped farther into the room. Slowly she approached his bed and stood there. "I'm really sorry," she repeated, "but I guess I just want somebody to talk to."

She needed human warmth, just an arm around her, but Johnny was too frightened. He held himself together tightly, arms pinned to his sides, his face set and rigid. His tone became cold. Abrupt. He offered only meaningless phrases. "It's all okay . . . everything will be okay."

Lonely and in torment, Marilyn tentatively sat on the edge of his bed. "I'm sorry, but it's just that I don't want to wake your parents."

In the grip of greater terror than Marilyn herself at the moment, Johnny could work his mouth only to say, "Oh, sure . . . sure, Marilyn . . ."

Awash with his own demons, Johnny wasn't healthy enough to be tender or to show feelings. He couldn't say anything as revealing as "I like you." He couldn't express his vulnerability. "I just could not give her what she needed. Even if I had felt excited like Wow-ee! Marilyn Monroe! On my bed in the middle of the night in a nightie! I couldn't show it. If I were dying I couldn't have shown it. And so I didn't show anything.

"I know now she was bitterly unhappy because she sensed she had no way of defending herself. But neither did I. I turned her away without being able to help a bit."

Marilyn's devotion to the Strasbergs caused jealousies. Those on the outside build a case against their teacher. He became inflated as a result of the influx of big stars. His ego, which had been flat, was pumped up. Celebrities sought his approbation. One whose dyspepsia is colored by the fact that she never made it, humphs, "Working actors were shunted into the background while any celebrity who did a scene was rated great. The gymnasium idea was ruined after that. There's no way a struggling nobody can compete with somebody who's flown in with a million-dollar contract."

Declares Rebecca Darke, "When I was going to read for a part, Paula said, 'Darling, you cannot go with the name Selma Grodman' so she renamed me. Then Lee allowed me free teaching after my money ran out, so I'll always be grateful. But the fact is, there developed a change in his vision and attitude. The average student was no longer important for him to bother with because his stature came from the names he was turning out."

His children were also in the background because Marilyn was in the forefront. They were instructed in the care and feeding of the house guest. They felt abused. Only years later, after their analysis, could both children forgive. Susan never saw in Marilyn what her father saw. She didn't resent treating Marilyn as one of the family. She resented treating her better than the family. "Susan thought I overtreated Marilyn and catered too much. I explained the reason was because she was *not* a member of the family." She felt Marilyn was taking her place. It was sibling rivalry. Marilyn was threatening her territory. When Susan moved away, a photo of Marilyn hung in her bathroom.

While Susie was abroad, Marilyn occupied her quarters. Susie resented it. On a visit home from Italy, Susie commandeered her bedroom again. Marilyn and her press agent, Pat Newcomb, watched as she unpacked. Marilyn spied a pale angora short-sleeved sweater. "Oh, I love it," she exclaimed, pouncing on the soft fluffy ball. "I just love it." She shook it and held it up in front of her. "I'd love to have one exactly like it."

"You can't because this one comes from Rome."

"So? You're going back to Rome. You can get another one for yourself. How about giving this one to me?"

Grudgingly she agreed. "Okay. If it fits you can have it. But only if it fits. If it doesn't, I want it back."

"Okay." With a squeal of delight, Marilyn shucked off her blouse and while Susan and Pat Newcomb watched she wriggled into the sweater. "Oh, I'm sure it's going to be just great," came the muffled voice from under the fuzzy wool.

"I don't know, Marilyn," commented Susan, watching her struggling. "I mean, I'm only five-foot-one, and if it fits me it's got to be tight on you." It was skin-tight. Too tight. The truth is, Susan knew in her heart it looked better on Marilyn than it did on her. Nonetheless, standing at the bedside, hands on tiny hips, Susan cracked, "It doesn't fit you. Take it off."

Pirouetting in the mirror, Marilyn said, "It does fit."

"It doesn't."

"But I think *it fits perfectly,*" Marilyn insisted, looking in the mirror this way and that.

"It doesn't fit," snapped Susan. "You said you'd take it off and give it back if it didn't fit. Well, give it back."

Marilyn threw the ball to Pat. "What do you think? Does it fit?"

Unwilling to get in the middle, Pat said, "It looks very pretty, but, I guess, maybe, it is a little snug."

"I said if it fits you then you can have it," repeated Susan sharply.

Marilyn took it off.

During one period Susan adopted the Monroe look and affected backless, cut-to-the-navel Marilyn-style wardrobe. The idea being that now, maybe, Mommy and Daddy will notice me. Marilyn supposedly didn't wear underwear, so Susan went with no bra, no panties. Marilyn was the sex symbol, Susan would be the same.

Parenthetically Marilyn was in awe of Susan because Susan was a big Broadway name. Marilyn and Susan roomed together on a country weekend. Just over five feet and thin and brunette, envious Susan wanted to be five-foot-six and round and blond. The subject surfaced about how each wanted to be the other. Marilyn finally confessed, "If I could be anyone I would want to be you" and Susan sighed, "Well, Marilyn, I would like to look like you" and, as Susan puts it, "And there we sat!"

Marilyn had an insanity about her makeup. Wall-to-wall press could be waiting but if she felt her mask wasn't in place she'd duck into a ladies' room. With the jar of cold cream she carried, she'd wipe all the makeup off and start fresh. There was one of the Strasberg coterie who was rather splendid-looking. When Marilyn spied her, she retreated into a back room to apply more makeup.

If you had an appointment to fetch her, she'd say, "You like how I look?" If the answer came back, "You look terrific," she'd peer in the mirror and mutter, "I don't like the way I look." Ask, "But how can you say that?" she'd call over her shoulder, "Be right back. I forgot something." An hour and a half could go by. Call out, "Hey, you okay in there?" and back would come, "Be right out." She'd emerge looking totally different. She was psychotic about the mask.

Marilyn was punctual only for the opening of *The Diary of Anne Frank*. Susan would never have forgiven her if she'd been late. She wasn't just to be on time, because then the audience would be buzzing over her arrival. She was to be ahead of time. Lee had cautioned her, "Marilyn, darling, this once if you can't be on time, be early."

The Golden Girl was generous. On Johnny's eighteenth birthday she gave him a Ford Thunderbird. She bought Susan a Chagall sketch for her twenty-first. She gave Paula pearls. For Lee she opened book accounts country-wide with standing orders to inform her if anything special arrived. She bought him records, clothes, shoes. She shopped for the McCreedy & Schreiber half-boots he liked. New Year's she'd send a case of champagne.

She contributed ten thousand dollars for Lee to travel to Russia for a Stanislavsky festival. Paula was in a restaurant with Marilyn, Jane Fonda, and Shelley Winters when word came her visa had come through. To make the plane she had to leave right from there, so the group quickly stripped themselves to outfit her. In Jane's fur-lined boots, Shelley's oversize wrap with the skunk lining, and Marilyn's hat, Paula clambered into a cab to take the Soviet Union by storm.

In June '56, Marilyn married Arthur Miller. There was that Sunday the bride invited the Strasbergs to the Millers' Connecticut home for brunch. The family left at nine in the morning. The thought of first grabbing a quickie breakfast was voted down because they didn't wish to offend their hosts by not being hungry. Marty Fried drove, and a mile before the house they passed a bazaar with open picnicking. It whetted the appetite but they didn't stop.

Arriving punctually at eleven, they hello'd. They hugged. They chatted. In her terrycloth housecoat Marilyn appeared to have just wakened. Nobody else was there, not even a maid. Nobody made moves toward the kitchen. Tension floated in the air. It was apparent something was awry.

Miller didn't sip even a glass of water nor offer even a glass of water. He made stilted small talk. An hour and a half went by. Paula interrupted the mechanical conversation to mutter to Marty, "I'm hungry."

Marty pulled Marilyn aside. "Look, I'm starving. If I don't get something to eat I'm going to pee on the floor. I've got to have something to eat."

She panicked. "Come inside." She ran into the kitchen and Marty followed. She pulled open the freezer, put her hands on a frozen steak and stammered nervously, "I'll g-get you s-something to eat right away."

"Hey, try to relax," he said to her. "We all know Arthur doesn't like Lee, but even if Lee doesn't like Arthur he respects him, so relax, willya? Nothing's going to happen. Take it easy."

Marilyn didn't answer. She opened the refrigerator. Nothing was there except a bottle of milk. Back at the freezer she pulled out the frozen steak. "Here," she said.

"This won't work. What else do you have?"

Marilyn began to claw at the trays. She pulled out frozen strawberries, frozen peas. "Marilyn," began Marty softly, "look, we can't do this. It's not just me. Everybody wants to eat; not just me. None of us have anything in our stomachs. We haven't eaten anything."

It was summer. The others were outdoors. Not knowing what else to do they came back out. Marilyn was tight. Arthur just sat. He didn't get up. He made no attempt to help, to go inside, to suggest something or even to try to make his guests comfortable. Susan was out of her mind. Marty grabbed her by the elbow and called to the crowd, "We're taking a ride."

Paula, who wanted to get out of there, raised her voice. "When will you be back?"

"We'll be back in a very little while, don't worry."

They climbed into his cab and headed for the bazaar where by this time little remained except a few spareribs, some fried chicken, and a load of baked potatoes. Marty bought whatever he could, mainly baked potatoes. Back at the house he whispered to Paula, "Go sit in the cab and whatever's there, eat it. Worst comes to worst, just gnaw a baked potato." Paula excused herself and spent the next ten minutes in the back seat.

Susan and Marty had already gorged on cold, spicy spareribs which are so good for breakfast. Stoic Lee ate nothing. It was as though something had transpired before they arrived. As though Miller had said, "I'm not going to feed them . . . make it a visit not a brunch." In any case, Marilyn was panicked throughout.

Lee was good for her. Catching an article critical of her, she'd wail, "Oh, look at that." Lee coolly commented about what kind of person the writer was. He calmed her, made her feel like a person, not a side of beef. He gave her what other males did not: a feeling of worth beyond "her ass-wiggling sexiness."

The attraction in the Strasberg house was Lee. But Paula became the link. Sensing this as a good thing that could rescue her husband from that dusty level into which he might settle, Paula took up Marilyn. She performed the small, intimate tasks. "Need a glass of milk, honey? . . . anything you want me to do for you? . . ."

When Paula worked as Tallulah's secretary and doormat, Tallulah, too, depended on Paula in that same peculiar sense. Paula made herself indispensable. She knew how to do that. She created a need, then filled it. She became Marilyn's alter-ego. She'd ram through whatever Marilyn wanted, then shoulder the blame when it created flak. She instigated little theatrical tricks such as memorizing from "sides" (pages containing only her lines plus the cue rather than a whole script) so the job seemed less ominous.

Marilyn Monroe had an enormous need and Lee could not give up all he had built up. His wife was his surrogate. She borrowed the mantle. Operation Marilyn afforded her status for the first time. Marilyn admired Lee. She drank in Lee. Lee couldn't travel to Hollywood and hold her hand, so Paula inherited the guardianship.

Marilyn did *Bus Stop* in '56. Susan "could actually hear Paula's helping hand. It was pure Paula all the way. I could see my

mother's readings, hear her cadence." Director Josh Logan telephoned Lee for advice in handling his star, and Paula telephoned
nightly from California to relate the problems which he would
then work out.

Marilyn looked forward to her first independent production,
The Prince and the Showgirl. This time things would be different.
She wouldn't be a hired hand with a director who put her down
as did Billy Wilder who, after *Seven Year Itch*, said, "She has
breasts like granite and a brain like Swiss cheese—full of holes."
This time she owned the company that bought the property
which Laurence Olivier had done onstage with Vivien Leigh. She,
in fact, hired Olivier.

"By unfortunate mishandling," as Lee puts it, "her company
also hired Olivier to direct. They gave the whole production over
to his company. It then became *his* company that was producing
it. Marilyn was almost out of it!"

Lee arrived in London. Olivier called. Could he come to the
hotel to see Lee? Alone, at the Dorchester, Lee offered him hints
in dealing with Marilyn. "I explained this was in no sense telling
him what to say or do but just to inform him she was not technically trained so that if he asked for technical things from her it
would throw her and in the second place she wouldn't know how
to do it.

"Lord Olivier didn't take what I had to say well. He took it as
interference. Without replying in kind or anything, you could see
he didn't like it. His hackles went up and he visibly pulled himself
in. It was not too hard to gather that he bristled with this."

Under these conditions things were difficult. Lee did not deal
with him much after that. He concentrated on easing Marilyn because there was considerable tension on the set. She was sick. She
had suffered a miscarriage. Also, particularly disappointing in view
of her expectations, she had no relationship with Olivier. He had
no idea how to handle her or what to do with her. Tempera-
mentally he was not suited to kootchy-koo a Monroe. Convinced
she was disastrous in her role of a semi-hooker because she wasn't
doing what he thought she should be doing "which was to imitate
exactly what Vivien did," Olivier disclaimed responsibility for her
part in the production.

"He never let her find her performance. He just cracked his

whip and expected her to jump. Marilyn's first appearance on the set for her first shot, she had to walk down a stairway and he said to her only, 'Okay . . . all right . . . now be sexy.' She ran off the set. When the movie was released and Marilyn got good notices, Olivier's friends went around saying he had sacrificed himself for her."

The two men fought over Olivier's predilection to using false noses and mustaches for his portrayals. "He always needs to cover himself up. Right away he started putting on things. First the monocle, then the accent. If we had wanted someone else we'd have gotten someone else."

Meanwhile, Olivier conceived an intense hatred for Paula who, reportedly, told the great Laurence Olivier that in her not humble judgment his acting was artificial. The consensus is Paula was a pest. In the genre of Arthur Miller, "she was a *nudzh*." Olivier wanted her booted off the set. Lee concedes, "They didn't want Paula there. It is a fact that they tried to get rid of her. However, she spoke right up. She let them know what's what. Paula wasn't shy. It wasn't easy to get rid of Paula."

Paula had metamorphosed into a certified gura. A harsh lady who employed few shields, if she wanted to say, "I hate you," she'd say it. With herself as the front and with everybody crawling through her to get to Marilyn, she had developed security and confidence. She was emerging into an overpowering entity. She even Silly Putty'ed Marilyn socially. At a gala, the formidable Mrs. Strasberg staged events so Marilyn waited in the limo while she cased the guest list to determine its worthiness. If she decided negatively, the star sat downstairs while Madam hello'd and circulated for a half hour.

Paula was hated on the set. "She really got the shit" is the way it's put. Today, over twenty years later, mention Marilyn Monroe or Paula Strasberg to Olivier and His Lordship shudders.

"The Witch," as they called her, collected the brickbats, never the credits. She alone squeezed a performance out of a woman who was ill, was psychotic, was on pills, was on champagne, suffered skin eczema from nerves, stammered from nerves, was paranoid about growing old and had personal problems with her own husbands and publicized affairs with others'.

Marilyn was a sick girl. Paula was a nursemaid twenty-four

hours a day. She had to shop for Marilyn, who couldn't shop, dress her, coach her, advise her, stay up with her when she couldn't sleep. Paula dragged Marilyn on the set when nobody could. Paula had to control the pills. Paula had to calm her down. It was beyond a full-time job.

Paula was far from home constantly. Her husband was pulling away, developing his own alliances. Her children had pulled away to make their own lives. She fought Marilyn's fears and everybody else's resentments. Paula bore the brunt of it all. She took it from her family, from Marilyn and from the directors, producers, co-stars, and outsiders.

After spending hours and hours alone with Marilyn, Paula stayed up all night with her, then got up at five to deal with the anxieties and responsibilities of delivering her charge on time, when her work as a coach really began. She'd put Marilyn through emotional gymnastics before every take. She'd cough or throw whatever trick necessary to stop a shot she didn't like. When the director went crazy and the star hid in her dressing room, only The Witch was left to deal with the issues. It cannot be said Paula enjoyed her life. Between Marilyn and her own family she was torn apart.

Paula's earnings helped pay for Johnny's psychiatry, the soirées that swirled on in the expensive apartment, the table for the hangers-on every time she and Lee went to Sardi's and for her own developed extravagances. Sable borders were tacked onto the black muumuus; her movable bedstand was cluttered with *objets d'art*; her bed linens were imported from Ireland; she hired a secretary and a maid. When Paula finally laid her hands on money, she spent.

Lee had not yet grown into his major income and he never did see money from the Studio. Marilyn contributed thousands, specifying it was to go to him "but the Studio took it because they said they needed it. So much for all those who say I made money from the Studio." The number one female box office star in the world might have been sleeping in his house but Lee Strasberg was traveling to work on a bus.

During one hectic period there was a fund-raising push for the Studio. Splashy events were organized for theatre and movie premieres. Members delivered tickets on their motorcycles. Ben Gazzara licked envelopes in the office. Brad Dillman sat behind the desk. Steve McQueen answered telephones. Helen Hayes ushered for *The Rose Tattoo*. Kim Novak lent her presence. For *East of Eden* Marilyn manned the phones. She telephoned Spyros Skouras, who was head of Fox while she was his biggest money-maker. "Hello, Mr. Skouras? You don't know me personally, but I work for you." She sold him a table for the benefit supper.

Around the time *The Young Lions* opened, Marilyn was to emcee an evening of scenes for another fund raiser. She was frightened. "What do I do? I don't know what to do. I don't know how to do anything." Considering her presence was sufficient to pack the house, she was assured she had only to stand there and it was enough. Nobody remembers what she ended up saying but everybody remembers it was more than "Good evening" because once those lights came on, Marilyn Monroe came to life.

From what was realized at these benefits, Lee's annual salary was to be readjusted to twenty-five thousand dollars. "The people committed themselves and I was annoyed because I didn't get it." Incorporated as a nonprofit institution and supported by contributions from persons in theatrical and other fields, the Studio trembles on shaky financial ground. Cheryl says the battle of the budget leaves them perennially one minute ahead of the sheriff. Kazan calls the process "chaos."

One year he received fifteen thousand dollars. Another year twenty-one thousand dollars was earmarked for him but Lee says the board decided he should forego this sum because they needed it, so they voted not to pay him. By 1972 he figured they owed him two hundred thousand dollars. "No money I have ever came from the Studio. It came from my own hard work."

Marilyn's last film, *The Misfits*, costarred Clark Gable, Montgomery Clift, Eli Wallach. Arthur Miller did the screenplay. Paula's salary was fifteen thousand dollars, director John Huston's basic premise being: "I've got to get a performance out of this girl, and if she needs the Strasbergs, let her have the Strasbergs." Lee came on location but never stepped onto the set or made his presence felt directly. He stayed in the background. He may have called the plays but Paula carried them.

Before shooting, Paula and Marilyn improvised in terms of the lines. Marilyn uttered them her own way. Paula improvised responses. Utilizing individual phraseology within the context of the scene made Marilyn loose. She'd open up. She'd apprehend the nuances sufficiently to play them in the limitations of Miller's heavy speeches. Lastly, immediately preceding the shot, she did her "preparations"—a throwback to the old "take-a-minute" of the Group.

Following every take she'd check for approval. Paula was positioned behind the camera. If Paula nodded no, she'd demand another retake. Miller's sister, Joan Copeland, also a Studio member, visited the set. Bright-eyed Paula greeted her outside. "You'll adore Marilyn in this. She just shot her sixty-fourth take and it was marvelous." They were readying a scene with Gable, who, it will be remembered, died the day after shooting was completed. Joan stood there two hours. Marilyn went through eighteen takes.

The crew was not partial to her duenna. Marilyn had managed to be a star before she met Paula. Marilyn had moxie. Marilyn was street smart. Marilyn had a natural instinct for whether she was coming on or not. In the words of one who was present, "She knew she was making that camera get a hard-on. She didn't need Paula for that. She didn't need Paula's OK in front of a camera. Paula needed that to keep her control. Paula played on Marilyn's lack of confidence."

Eli and Marilyn wound up not talking. He was impatient . . . and professional. "Like we were doing this scene in the truck and she'd lean down to whisper to Paula. I'd holler, 'What the hell is she saying that you can't learn by yourself? What the hell's she telling you that's so secretive?' Marilyn would whisper, 'You don't understand.'"

Nobody understood. It was an agonizing period. She was wallowing in torment. The marriage was breaking up. When Joan Copeland asked her brother, "Is Marilyn joining us for dinner?" close-mouthed Arthur replied, "No, I don't think so. She's busy shooting tonight." Everyone learned later they'd been split for weeks.

Marilyn was sick constantly. The situation was emotional. Roslyn, her character in *The Misfits*, was getting divorced. Marilyn as Roslyn mouthed bittersweet speeches that choked her. About-to-be-divorced Marilyn had to toy with about-to-be-divorced Roslyn's wedding ring. In the scene where she heads for the divorce, the action called for her simply to cross the street in heavy traffic. Half-way over, she stopped. Cut. "What is it?" called Huston. "I forgot that the ring had a deeper meaning." Marilyn's disordered thinking was clogged with cross-currents. Into an ever-increasing dependency on sleeping tablets, her dosage increased to where she had to battle to rouse herself. An entire company would wait impatiently while Paula walked her around the room.

The Misfits was aptly named. Clark Gable was under a cloud physically. Arthur Miller was undergoing his own personal hell. Monty Clift's "alcoholism, debauchery, homosexuality, insomnia and his own drug addiction made him even sicker than Marilyn" according to biographer Patricia Bosworth. And meanwhile, up in the motel room, Lee and Arthur were quietly at it.

Lee asked to speak to Arthur. Huston wanted to do the picture in closeups. Huston's ideas weren't working out. In Lee's view "the thing wasn't being handled properly.

"Take the morning after she's together with Gable the first time. Huston wanted to shoot this flat out. She's in the kitchen. Gable comes in. He says, 'I'll cook you some breakfast.' And that's it. Straightforward. I felt, 'No.' You have to take this and invent. We worked out an improvisation where she goes to the fields and plucks a flower for him. She kind of touches it to her lips, playfully bites it, sort of munches on it. She carries it back lovingly and sets it on the breakfast tray to be there for him when he comes in.

"Just by showing this visually the scene is lyrically evoked. You see her the morning after in a different way than ever before. He would come in and see he's in touch with a new, different type of woman which, after all, is the heart of the scene. It didn't have to be done our way but ideas were mentioned on how particular scenes could gain a certain degree of life instead of the static quality. But Huston didn't take any. Not one. He wouldn't do anything. The whole thing was therefore disappointing."

Lee warned Arthur, "You have to be careful this movie doesn't turn out to be a respectable movie."

The choice of words startled him. "What does that mean?"

"That means this has to be an exciting, dramatic, moving thing and if not then it will turn out to be respectable and respectable will be the kiss of death."

"I frankly don't see how this can turn out to be bad the way it is."

"It can't be bad, but it does need more of a theatrical quality. I'm not going to tell Huston do this or don't do that. I'm not trying to direct. That's why I'm speaking to you to try to get Huston to understand and do something."

About this time it became apparent that Marilyn and Arthur were finished. "It was by then already a ticklish kind of situation. There was nothing any of us could do about anything."

In January '61 the Millers were divorced. In February, Marilyn was a patient at the Payne Whitney Psychiatric Clinic. She then transferred to Columbia Presbyterian Medical Center. She was seeing ex-husband Joe DiMaggio. She was dating Frank Sinatra. She was drinking.

She agonized about herself. She'd find a ten dollar dress in a bargain store then copy it exactly for four hundred dollars. When Lee flew to Los Angeles, Marilyn fetched him at the airport. At the first red light she turned to him. "Do you mind if we stop off for a minute?"

"No. Where do you want to stop off?"

"At my house. But only for a minute."

"Fine."

Lee waited in the car while Marilyn hustled behind the walls and gate of her small, brand-new Mexican-style hacienda. Moments later, she clambered back and sat there staring at her passenger. She said nothing. Lee waited a few beats, then, "So where would you like to go?"

She shrugged, "I don't care. Anyplace you want to go. Where would you like to go?"

He couldn't figure what was happening. He blinked at her. "What do you mean, where would I like to go? I don't care. Whatever you want. I thought you were planning this."

And there in the car parked at the curb sat the two of them staring at one another in silence. Marilyn didn't say anything. Turned squarely around facing Lee, she finally blurted out, "Well, why don't you say something? I'm wearing a black wig and you don't even *notice* it??"

As Lee tells it today, "I was looking at Marilyn. I saw her face and her eyes. I was listening to her voice. I never even noticed she had put on a disguise. She was upset that I didn't notice the black wig. I saw Marilyn. I didn't notice the wig!"

Back in New York the blonde whom a director sneered "can't act her way out of a bra" and had come to the Studio "because I want respect" used to relax at the little weekend house the Strasbergs rented in Fire Island. She'd walk to the beach alone. Children gathered. She hugged them. "Call me Marilyn, please." One of the clique found a wall medallion printed in Latin, which, translated, read, "Never let the bastards wear you down." She loved it.

Some weekends she sank into her noncommunicating stage. Her face was blank. A mask. Nobody referred to anything. She, Lee, everyone played softball. They batted balls with animal strength to help her get going. Deep in a depressed state, Marilyn was deadly quiet. Lee tried hard to help. He was talkative and up.

He told her his story about overeager teachers. Seems Yiddish star Jacob Ben-Ami, whose *Samson and Delilah* was "the greatest single performance of modern time," decided to try the English theatre. He went to a speech teacher. The outcome was he became overdone. He articulated so strongly and theatrically that "you wondered what the hell he was doing." The result of his English teacher was that Jacob Ben-Ami went back to the Yiddish theatre.

He told her his favorite theatrical critique. Years back Boris Aronson accompanied him to a play. At intermission Lee asked, "Nu, Boris? . . . So, Boris? . . . how do you like it?" The Russian scenic designer responded, "Good. It's very confused." Next intermission Lee inquired again, "So, Boris? . . . Nu? . . ." Yawned Boris, "Now not so good. It's clearing up."

The alive, joking solicitous squire of Fire Island was a foreign being to those who knew only the bronze statue. The first weekend Marilyn dormed with another girl and Marilyn came tearing back into their guest room. "How close are you to coming out?" "About five minutes," estimated the roommate. "Okay, now let's say exactly seven minutes you come out to the porch and turn left. And don't come any sooner than seven minutes."

Marilyn appeared to be having such a good time that the girl didn't ask questions. In seven minutes she did as she was told. "I didn't know what to expect. But I saw Marilyn poised to face me and staring straight into my eyes and directing me to the sight of the Great Guru who was bare-chested, milk-white, in dark boxer trunks, black city socks, suit shoes and a straw hat. Marilyn knew I'd be in shock, because she had gone through it. Seeing her mentor as an anemic-looking Real Person with skinny milky legs, her heart stopped!"

Another couldn't deal with "My Pope" barbecuing hot dogs and speaking everyday mundane words like, "So how much is the toll? . . . do you have enough gas? . . ." This was the same untouchable who "caused me to run right to my shrink when he didn't say hello in an elevator. That set me back months in analysis. I figured he's unseeing and unhearing me because I'm such a terrible actor I'm not even worthy of saying hello to."

A typical Saturday night found the house full of guests sprawled trancelike, imbibing Mozart. Nobody looked at anybody. There was no eyeball contact because there was no conversation. At most you bestirred yourself to scrounge a peanut or a drink. Free-lance movie maker Syeus Mottel remembers "a heavy Marilyn draped on the sofa à la Goya in a bathing suit." Marilyn, who fretted nobody liked her for just plain her and whose apartment featured a white and gilt piano and plaster objects painted gold, thirsted for a certain cultural ambience. There was a pause while Lee changed the record. Trying to fit the intellectual mood of the moment, her voice pierced that hush with, "Anybody like Rachmaninoff?"

Marilyn was drinking more. She was depressed more. She was late. She was sick. She was ragged. Having worked five full days in seven weeks of production, she was removed from *Something's Got to Give* for repeated absences.

Marilyn clung to Lee. "He helps me uncover all the secret sides of myself." Having attempted suicide before, Marilyn had a pact with Lee to discuss her intentions if she ever decided to try again. "When she took pills she would be out of control and forget how many she took. I had extracted a promise from her that if she got in that sort of mood she would call me first. She didn't. On her last night whatever was done was never deliberate. She literally couldn't have known whether she had taken the pills or not."

They had seen one another only shortly before. They had formulated plans for a TV version of Somerset Maugham's "Rain" in which she would play Sadie, the role made famous by Jeanne Eagels. They had agreed she was coming to New York the following weekend to finalize arrangements. Marilyn had said on the phone, "I'll see you next week."

"Marilyn seemed full of plans for work when we talked. People say maybe she couldn't get jobs and as a result of professional experience she did what she did. That wasn't so. She had just written me she wanted to join the Actors Studio. She said she was coming in to finally ask for membership."

Illegitimate, a waif, unwanted as a baby, sexually abused as a child, painfully self-conscious as an adult, "a call girl who somehow made it," in Lee's words, for Marilyn the journey to success proved too much. On August 5, 1962, this bright, ethereal presence flickered out. America's greatest glamour image, who confessed she "was never used to being happy," took enough Nembutal to kill her and died on a dateless Saturday night, all alone. She was thirty-six.

CHAPTER ELEVEN

Actors Studio Theatre

The Studio experienced exciting projects from the fifties to the sixties. David Garfield's *History of the Actors Studio* lists two projects of the early fifties of special significance: *End as a Man* and *A Hatful of Rain*.

Periodically, members pull together on original productions which are privately performed on special evenings. Twenty-four-year-old Jack Garfein developed *End as a Man*, which producers had previously rejected, as one of these workshop projects. With a budget of fifty dollars, the play about a southern military academy was presented to the Studio in May '53. The cast of unknowns—Pat Hingle, Albert Salmi, Ben Gazzara—eventually moved to Broadway. Critics cheered. Calder Willingham, the author, became a name. Garfein, the nobody director, became a property. Gazzara, the star, became a Hollywood "find."

Similarly born at the Studio was Broadway's smash hit, *A Hatful of Rain*. Characterized by a raspy voice, beer belly and reputation for violence, author Michael V. Gazzo, one of the half-dozen students from Lee's director's course at the New School in the forties, "was known to do a little drinkin', so after one year at the

Studio Lee gives me this carpet calldown. 'All you're doin' is hangin' out. You can't just sit around here. You gotta do somethin'.' I was into this hippie jargon and I'd been kibitzin' with friends and ended up with this scene with guys junked up under a fire escape rappin' about death. So I explained I was writin' some original scenes."

A year and a half Gazzo worked on his drama about a wife and her addict husband. Ben Gazzara, Steve McQueen, and student-director Frank Corsaro "who locked onto all the things Lee taught" improvised scenes and found their own values and moods. Lee's teachings. Lee's pupils. Lee's work.

"In '54 it wasn't easy throwin' profanity and we had difficulties findin' a wife. Eva Marie Saint worked in the improvs two weeks, but she got shitscared. She couldn't improvise a letter home to her mother to save her ass. So we went with Garfein's suggestion, his wife, Carroll Baker.

"Lee gave us like four nights to ready it to show it to him, which pissed me, but, still, it was electrifyin'. Everybody was spaced out about it. Even Eva Marie Saint's husband, Jeff Hayden, wanted to option it." With a hand-picked Studio cast including "a very new kid on the block, Anthony Franciosa," *Hatful* opened on Broadway.

Carroll had been replaced by what Mike Gazzo calls, "a big, dizzy-type blonde who was goin' noplace except down the chute" but who plied Lee with endless questions which he answered despite blood vessels popping on his neck. Shelley Winters listened carefully. She assimilated. She worked. Says Gazzo, "This sexpot broad who was plain flat on the balls of her ass when she came to the Studio became a hell of an actress."

The Garfeins had been close to the Strasbergs. One year the Garfeins sent the Strasbergs two Rembrandt etchings. When Shelley won the part, Carroll blamed Lee for not standing up for her. "Today I don't blame him. He could only give what he could give. I made the problem. I tried to make him my parent. I had no right to put him in that position. I idolized him and when he rejected me there was hate on my part. Eventually I had to break away."

As when patients fall in love with analysts, so do Lee's disciples vie to be his favorites. A professional diagnostician, he views them all dispassionately. They get hurt. Sniffs one, "He never treated me unnice but not especially nice, either. About the same as everybody else."

In the weaning process each learns not to swallow Lee's impersonality as a personal rebuff. With Hume Cronyn, Jessica Tandy, Zoe Caldwell, and George Grizzard, Rita Gam played Masha in the multi-million-dollar Minnesota Theatre Company production of *The Three Sisters*. The Strasbergs came like a silent phalanx to see this Tyrone Guthrie production. Rita wanted desperately to hear from Lee. Rita wanted desperately to please Lee. Not one word did he utter. Finally, she couldn't contain herself. "What did you think?" Intoned he, "We must do it at the Actors Studio Theatre."

Immediately following incredible reviews as the new, brilliant star of Kazan's smash film, *Baby Doll*, Carroll Baker was in the coffee shop the Studio patronized. She slipped into a front booth with Anne Jackson. Everybody congratulated her. Carroll wanted to hear from Lee. He started down the aisle for his usual sandwich on rye and tea with lemon. She called out, "What did you think, Lee?"

"I have one criticism." He didn't slide in next to her. He just stood in the aisle.

Carroll said nothing. She waited.

"You could have been freer in your dress. You were always covered up." There was the little catarrhal click he often makes in his throat, then, "Your neckline could have been lower or your hemline shorter. There was a prudishness that I felt."

Carroll replied only, "Oh, I see."

When he left Anne Jackson leaned over to Hollywood's new star who had just dissolved into Strasberg's little child. "You don't believe that, do you?"

"No. I don't agree . . . but it does bother me."

"Then why didn't you speak up? Why didn't you say something to him?"

Carroll shook her head. "I couldn't have done that. I just couldn't have."

Her disaffection grew with the fight between Lee and her husband. Sean O'Casey's *Shadow of a Gunman* was to be staged professionally under the official imprimatur of the Studio. With Jack

Garfein directing it had rehearsed for months, and when it was unveiled for Lee's surgical assessment he pronounced it in need of improvements.

Garfein felt his toilet-training days were over and he swiped at the patriarchal image, shouting that Lee was against *Shadow of a Gunman* because he was against anything bearing the imprimatur of his giant gymnasium because anything might conceivably result in failure so he was therefore fearful of the Studio's doing *anything*.

Paula called Garfein an ingrate. Garfein, who teaches acting in his own school today, says, "For a couple of years they didn't speak to us. We lived in the same building. We'd send our Blanche and Herschel, who were their godchildren, down to their apartment to play, but when we'd all meet in the elevator Paula and Lee would speak to our kids but not to us!"

Carroll's hostilities erupted in statements such as, she was "disillusioned" . . . "The Studio has lost its spirit. It was never the catalyst we hoped it would be. Things never seemed to work out because of the lack of a strong, driving force." Twenty years later, when she came back, "Lee had to know I was hostile but he acted like I'd never been away. I guess that makes it easier for him."

This posture is not unfamiliar. The most illustrative story concerns Marty Fried, who decided he wouldn't talk to Lee anymore. His face was cemented in a proper scowl and he took care to make his silence as deafening as possible. Came the holidays, intermediaries coerced him into going to the apartment. Self-consciously and with a world war raging in his brain about how he'd say so and so if Lee said such and such, he slunk in after years of silence. Lee called, "Marty, pick up those Christmas bulbs and bring them in."

Although Lee Strasberg's jeweler's-eye powers of observation make it arguable as to whether he, in fact, does not notice hostilities, the fact is he doesn't nurture them. He neither entertains real hurts, fancied wrongs, injustices or ingratitudes nor does he assign them a comfortable resting place in his consciousness.

The Studio is a tankful of sharks. Everybody rips everybody. If it doesn't always cut through to Lee, the one ambiguous personal relationship which can pierce the armor is Elia Kazan's. Dichotomous Kazan whom an intimate describes as "having many faces," has a pattern of disaffection. In those fancy fifties, Kazan's underlying hostility surfaced in little ways. Kazan wasn't available for a specially set-up meeting. Kazan was too busy to return a phone call. Kazan would certainly do something about the fund raising if only he had the time. The slices were small. Around '57, resentful of the young Turks talking up Lee, not him, Kazan steamed to Jack Garfein, "Okay, you did it. You're now responsible for it. You'll have to live with it." That's when he made plans to get out. The Studio was Strasberg.

Overlaid with ambivalence, theirs is a love-hate relationship, although neither acknowledges it. The absolute truth can be only an educated guess. A fly on the wall of the Studio says, "One says one thing, one says the other and you get in the middle and they patch it up and you're left on the outside. They've been jealous of one another, yet they've always swung back." Today they're again in bed. The passage of half a century has neutralized their threat to each other.

Kazan was known as being very sexual. One blonde characterized him as "the biggest screwer around."

Relative to his feelings about Kazan, Lee doesn't mind admitting, "I envied him his sex-symbol image. I never had that. I was jealous of the attraction he seemed to have had from women all his life and I don't mind if he knows it." Relative to his emotions about Lee, Kazan bristles, "I'm not jealous. Why would I give a shit what fame he made from the Studio? True, I put him in there, but he helped a lot of people. Anything anybody else says is bullshit and you can't get me to say anything else."

The publicly maintained regard slipped at the turn of the sixties. Richard Schechner in the *Tulane Drama Review* wrote, "When the hatchet is buried it is often in your friend's back" and asked why if there's a United Nations is it too much to ask Kazan and Strasberg to speak to one another.

The problem began with a rival institution that loomed on the horizon in the late fifties. The soon-to-be Lincoln Center for the Performing Arts, encompassing a resident acting school plus its own repertory theatre, invited Elia Kazan to be its director and Michel St. Denis, a French teacher of acting, to head its drama school. The world's foremost acting teacher could scarcely ignore this new force. Lee was eager to be involved in it. The key to the involvement was Kazan. Kazan could block St. Denis plus other pretenders to the throne and pave the way for his old friend. Kazan could make this new theatre an extension of the Studio and bring the Studio in as the resident repertory company. He could. He didn't.

At stake was the Studio and more personally Lee Strasberg. Actor-journalist Gordon Rogoff was the liaison. His euphemistic title was "Administrative Director." His duties were to be a buffer state. Kazan wanted someone who could communicate with Lee and Lee wanted someone who could communicate with Kazan. Neither wanted to communicate with the other.

Rogoff believes Kazan could have done more to persuade Lincoln Center's board of directors to utilize the forces and personality of Lee Strasberg. "Kazan just didn't think Lee was the man to be counted upon to train the company. He didn't think Lee had the stuff anymore, but he'll never admit this."

There were undertones and overtones. Lee belonged at Lincoln Center. Producing a season of theatre works was something he could well do. He felt hopelessness and anger that others were selected as artistic chiefs and held the power while he had to prove himself. Says Rogoff, "He felt why should he have to work his ass off to qualify when the Studio was there and was already *it*. He was quite right."

"Cross Strasberg or leave him. Anyone who is anyone has sooner or later to rebel against him. We all must someday." Kazan formally resigned from the directorship of the Studio. He determined the new wave of his career and rode it. In 1962 Elia Kazan left Lee Strasberg and signed on as co-director of the first Lincoln Center Theatre. That rejection of the talents of the great teacher and his disciples was a bitter disappointment. "The one regret in my life was Lincoln Center. That's what I had come into the Studio for originally. The chance of ever accomplishing it grew slimmer every day."

Kazan's statements were warlike. He cited "disappointment" with the Studio whose "work always stopped at the same point, a preoccupation with the merely psychological." He trumpeted "a different kind of actor" for Lincoln Center. Nonetheless, he approached several Studio actors to join him. Some turned their backs.

Kazan did not long remain with the Center. Marty Fried puts it simply, "He couldn't cut it without Lee." Michael Gazzo is even simpler. "With Lee there would have been a company and a theatre. Without Lee it was three million dollars down the toilet." As usual, Kazan's return to Lee followed a suitable mourning period. Drawls Cheryl dryly, "And they have made up again."

About his buddy's betrayal, Lee says, "I may think Kazan is necessary to an endeavor of mine because I give people appreciation for certain contributions but he does not do similarly. Apparently he does not consider me as being necessary to any endeavor of his, otherwise he would not have gone into that thing without me."

Financially the Studio was tapped out. Professionally it had sustained a blow. Personally its leader had endured rejection. There were mutterings of discontent within the student body. There were probing questions as to its *raison d'être* within the hierarchy. Deeply depressed, Lee admitted to a need for "future direction." Membership was fractionalized on where do they go from here. Five years of unsatisfying negotiations with Lincoln Center had created a hunger. Having tasted the tantalizing fruit of public productions, a brace of progressive souls pushed for a self-producing unit. Out of preparation into performance, came the cry. At the energizing thought that the future was plugged into production—the Group reincarnated with the Studio's reservoir of human resources from actors to directors to playwrights—their collective paralysis received an impulse. From this genesis came the Actors Studio Theatre.

A production board, including Paul Newman, Anne Bancroft, Frank Corsaro, and Edward Albee was established. Roger L. Stevens agreed to be over-all producer. A Ford Foundation subsidy plus a matching quarter of a million from private donations was raised. The first original piece of theatre—June Havoc's autobiographical *Marathon '33*—opened at the ANTA December '63.

At rehearsals June taught Lee the fascinating vaudeville terms he'd never known before such as "the five-minute belly." There's a giggle, a chuckle, a laugh, then the five-minute belly. She demonstrated Jack Oakie's "Triple Skull." There's the take, the double-take, then the triple skull.

"But he didn't understand it," comments June. "If you go

within on comedy you lose the comedic posture. You can't give that inner blocking or go for truth. Natural comics are unique and mustn't be tampered with. But Lee is an innocent. He just does his thing and if that's detrimental it's not his fault. I ended up directing, because to my thinking no one else knew how to handle it and I invited him to advise me so it was *my* fault."

Frank Corsaro, who'd been assigned to direct, lays the finger on Miss Havoc. "That's a strong lady. Lee couldn't control her. Lee said he'd oversee her, but he couldn't. This was the first thing she ever directed."

Notices were mixed. Everyone fixed blame everywhere. Julie Harris was cast or miscast (depending on whom one heeds) as June. The elegant, carpeted, chandelier'd ANTA Theatre was the wrong environment for an extended atmosphere of a tacky dance hall. Script revisions transposed the "special dirty linen of June's Baby Snooks mind into a romanticized version of June's memory of herself."

After *Marathon '33* Paul Newman came up with a comedy by his friend James Costigan. Newman wanted to go back to the theatre, so he, Joanne, and Costigan "got it together and with the addition of a sheepdog we were also the whole cast." The Newmans worked for minimum.

Baby Wants a Kiss was not well received. Newman thought the play "funny but it was probably ahead of its time. The interesting part was to see how you could by sheer pyrotechnics keep people from leaving the theatre. When we first opened people were leaving halfway through the second act. We simply had to overwhelm them with the force of our own logic and magnetism and we had to make them think we saw something in it that they didn't see so that they'd stick it through to see if they saw it, too."

Blues for Mister Charlie followed this off-Broadway divertissement by four days. James Baldwin's social protest came at the crest of the black wave. In this surge of confrontation and revolution, he was originally a savior type, genuinely trying to balance the budget on the blacks and whites. Then there developed a shift in Baldwin and his message escalated to a diatribe against the whites. The Studio could either abandon it or accommodate it.

Rip Torn and Geraldine Page had personally dogged Baldwin until he gave the Studio this angry, extraordinarily revolutionary piece. The price was their guarantee it would be produced exactly as written.

Baldwin's new insertions and rewrites and rethinking weakened the structure. His basic concept that, behind racial tensions are human conflicts which continue apart from the color problem, became diffused. Highly emotional Baldwin was writing pure hate. Needed was an appeal to his artistic side if not his racial or political side. One close to the production who speaks openly only if assured anonymity says, "It was a half-assed production because Lee doesn't have these necessary strengths. He became vague and wouldn't fight. Baldwin needed to cut and Lee wasn't analytical enough. He lacked decisiveness. He was nervous about facing Baldwin."

Rip Torn, Diana Sands, Pat Hingle, and the stellar cast appeared comfortable with the obscenities. Cheryl Crawford was not. Prior to the opening she and Lee faced director Burgess Meredith. "You're going to have to cut out 'mother-fucker,'" ordered Cheryl.

"But that's every other word," protested Burgess.

"We'll get killed by the critics."

"It's not my problem. Talk to the author."

"That word simply has to be deleted."

"So talk to Baldwin."

Talk escalated into confrontation. Baldwin climbed onto a ladder and kept climbing higher and higher. Lee sat at a desk, looking up. In his nervousness he knocked over a glass of water. It was refilled. He knocked it over again.

Burgess turned to Lee. "I think we're making a mistake and that sometime in the future we'll be sorry."

"I hate to make compromises but I always seem to have to make them," sighed Lee.

Baldwin, as panicked as everyone, screamed and yelled but eventually acquiesced. The actors muttered it under their breath but they didn't say it aloud.

"*Blues* didn't go as well as expected," assesses Cheryl, "because Lee's not an organizer. He's not an executive."

In *Strasberg at the Actors Studio*, Robert Hethmon details "this small figure in a black raincoat" hugging the box office and checking audience reaction. Hethmon couldn't reconcile this "haggard . . . gray ghost" with America's envoy to Stanislavsky's centenary. But, then, one who lectures to a thousand rapt faces is not necessarily one to count the house. Position gained as a renowned acting teacher does not automatically vest one with crackerjack organization and executive abilities. The shoveling of blame onto Lee's inadequacies is a familiar exercise.

Lee's dream was a national theatre. The reality was wanting, never doing. A *Hatful of Rain*, a total example of Studio work, was not produced professionally by the Studio. Lee said he wasn't ready. *The Night of the Iguana*, born in the Studio, was similarly sidestepped to Broadway. Lee said we're not ready. *Virginia Woolf*, offered to the Studio, also ended up being produced outside. No, no, no, the time is not yet right. For many the time had been right for years.

What others summarized as fear Lee rationalized as caution. Lee was in his sixties. He was not up and coming as were his itchy disciples. He'd already been there. He'd already lived through the Group and the pitfalls of commercial theatre. Pushing into areas beyond his control could result in failure and he—alias the Actors Studio—would bear the ultimate burden.

He is charged with indecisiveness. Within the security of the womb, never venturing forth nor voluntarily bestirring himself, the feeling was Strasberg would grind on ad infinitum analyzing actors, that the Studio would never be more than it was. A case is made that he was pushed into the Actors Studio Theatre, that the membership began to disintegrate because of inharmonies and nitpicking regarding its future, that some fought him because he wouldn't start this theatre. Explains director Alan Schneider, "Nobody meant to undercut him. We worshiped him. He was Buddha. Christ. Everything. Unfortunately, we discovered he couldn't be more than he could be. We couldn't push him to do things and he wouldn't let us do them without him."

A common plaint is the Studio cannot make a decision without Lee but that Lee cannot make a decision. Example: the Little Theatre on West 44th Street next to Sardi's was for sale for thirty-two thousand dollars but they rented it for eight thousand dollars a week for twenty weeks for Paul Newman's show because, sighs Shelley, "Lee wouldn't commit himself."

Example. The idea was conceived for a road company Studio to travel around demonstrating the Method as a one-night concert or lecture. The college circuit paid well. The actors and the Studio would make money. Spokeswoman Viveca Lindfors met with total ambivalence. Lee "liked it. He didn't like it. He'd think about it. He wouldn't think about it. Approach Lee with a project and he just listens. He says nothing. Eventually comes word from someone that he disapproves. No why or what. Just that he disapproves." The deadline for his answer came and went along with the buyers for the college circuit who reluctantly booked other attractions. "We blew it," says Viveca. Lee won't say no but he won't fight. Whether insecurity or idiosyncrasy, Lee cannot commit to an action that creates upheaval. Appreciate his values or sow the seeds of disappointment.

Burgess Meredith sums up with affectionate wisdom. "In L.A. he had a big domestic argument. He asked me to drive him around. He said nothing. I said nothing. I turned on the music and drove and drove. I could feel all the vibrations of frustration and anger and inability to cope. An hour later he came out of it like an attack of hay fever. He coped with that as he did with everything. He did nothing. He let the stronger force prevail. Lee *can't* cope. His mind doesn't operate like that.

"I've seen Lee throw some of us to the dogs but it didn't anger me. That's the way he is. Some people are able to be tough and some aren't and he just backs up in panic. I love the man and I don't expect anything of him in this other department so I don't get disappointed."

The Actors Studio Theatre had a built-in mechanism of human failure. When the little tendrils nurtured within that hothouse finally shot out, they wouldn't be threatened. Each willfully grew his own way. Each considered he was a star. Each ego cast himself as Richard The Third leaving nobody to carry the spear. Between talented unknowns and famous names, the duel was to the death. One actress "anticipated a blood bath."

Lee didn't tiptoe around big stars in the Group because they weren't then big stars. Now his ensemble was larded with star graduates. This annexation of giant talent that deeds the arts was his proprietary right. But having gathered the rosebuds—what to do with them? Supercelebrities are maneaters. You can't deal with them on an equal level. With a tankful of big stars you're not casting an artistic endeavor—you're juggling a movie studio. The jealousies are malignant.

Inside the savant was the nebbish. Clurman maintains that this immigrant, tenement mind was "deferential, frightened of people in positions of power even in the Group. With scene designers like Max Gorelik who was not high up he'd be rough, and with Robert Edmond Jones, who was tops, he'd be timid."

The *Blues for Mister Charlie* company looked to that patriarchal authority to take a step forward. The step was backward. Baldwin was a star. About *Baby Wants a Kiss*, director Corsaro says, "The play was a piece of *drek* but the mentality was such that if you're a star like Paul Newman and you want to do this then it has to be okay."

The cry is made that Lee went for names. Lee opted for the star system: stars over talent, big names over competent craftsmen. The reality of the commercial theatre is that you need names to sell tickets. Still, Konstantin Stanislavsky and David Merrick make terrible bedfellows and so Lee slid into the blackest period of the Actors Studio.

With everyone wanting its few good female parts, the production of *The Three Sisters* generated animosity. In the slitted eyes of the majority Lee's judgments were wrong. His casting of Kim Stanley antagonized Anne Bancroft. "Annie wanted to play Masha and had agreed to do it. Annie Bancroft is good but hasn't that emotional facility. I'd have gotten it from her but I'd have had to work. Kim gave those values more easily. When it worked out that Kim was suddenly available, Annie became upset. She was hurt. She took it very personally."

Other highly developed workers of good reputation also felt bypassed. They felt their artistic standard was compromised because they weren't big names. "We left the Studio for years," admits Estelle Parsons, "because he selected not the artists but the commercially viable. Who wanted excuses that he needed a certain level of importance to present the work in a certain light? We only knew we were sacrificed."

Lee wanted Brando for Colonel Vershinin. "Brando possesses the evil quality of playing on a weakness. In this face-to-face meeting on the Vershinin thing he showed exactly this to me. He asked about some facet of his acting although not outright because he's smart enough not to touch on anything in the areas where he knows you're strong.

"Whenever I want something I'm weak, so I shied away from certain truths in answering questions about his work. I just kept making those points I wanted to make. Marlon recognized this. He knew I was skirting the issue because I had an issue of my own yet he kept prodding me to give a critique, knowing I wouldn't give it in this case honestly.

" 'Why are you afraid to tell me?' he asked. I wanted to say, 'Because I don't think you're intelligent enough to understand. You'll react like a child and I'm trying to get something from you, therefore I don't tell you.' But I didn't because I still wanted what I wanted and my pressure wasn't lessened because he wouldn't say no right away. He'd say only, 'I'll think about it.' "

Ultimately the role went to Kevin McCarthy. Kevin played Vershinin with geniality according to his comprehension of Chekhov's sparse directives. This did not meld with Kim Stanley's "soap-operatic interpretation. Although Lee never altered my performance, my good humor irritated Kim. She'd snarl at me. Kim emoted as though she were on the cross. Tears streamed from her eyes."

A ticking inside Kim made her an explosive device theatrically. Lee's choice was, admittedly, a time bomb on that stage. Kevin admits Kim's extraordinary talent. He also admits she was occasionally difficult and that these difficulties could have made her ill in the wings. It isn't uncommon for talented people to have nervous stomachs (the green room backstage got its name for that reason). She must have thrown up before coming on stage one particular night because, "When she rushed into my arms with rapturous hunger and this mouth opened . . . whew!!! . . . I had to kiss her with all the fervent passion I could muster. That's when you knew you were earning your ticket as a member of Actors Equity."

Lee was directing. His standards being such that he is constrained under the quickie, fast, frantic production system of the normal four-week rehearsal period which suffices for an efficient if not always a definitive rendering, Lee's work was beyond competent. It was brilliant. Harold Clurman explains it. "No one can say he's not a good director. His work doesn't always turn out as great as others who are his inferior only because he needs ten weeks to do these wonderful jobs but that doesn't diminish the excellence of the kind of work he demands."

In summer stock Lee was to direct a Shakespearean classic with an illustrious cast. The regular rehearsal period was extended, but as time hastened Lee was still unfinished. The bosses had to drag in somebody to quick direct it and get it on. Dane Clark, who was there, calls it this way, "Lee's so effing great and sees so effing much to experiment with that he can't compress it all into a small time. In Europe where they go for six months' rehearsal he'd be another Reinhardt."

Of the benevolent and malevolent rumors surrounding this production of *The Three Sisters*, one is that Lee preferred Susan for the young sister, Irina, but a) Kim wouldn't work with her; b) people resented his casting his daughter; c) Lee felt Susan "was in a mixed-up state personally." Shirley Knight played Irina. Volunteers Shirley, "Lee created a communion with the audience where they wouldn't move, cough, or hardly breathe. Lee's direction was magical."

That from Shirley Knight, whom Lee flayed in rehearsal, says Luther Adler, "so devastatingly that the company made him stop. She screamed, 'Please, I'm a human being . . .' He tortured her until she cried."

It was onstage at the Morosco. A run-through of the third act in the early days of rehearsal. The full company was assembled. One scene with Luther Adler wasn't working. Shirley wasn't getting it together. From the audience Lee yelled, "What is this? Come on, what are you doing?" Lee had been strained. Leery of chopping Kim, of whom you are informed "he was scared shitless," he vented his hostilities on the youngest member. "You didn't do your work," he shouted, rising from his seat and walking onto the set. "If you didn't bother to do your work why did you bother to come here?"

Embarrassed, tears flooding her eyes, the two-time Oscar nominee for *Sweet Bird of Youth* and *Dark at the Top of the Stairs* stood alone stage center, fiddling with the dark, ankle-length skirt rigged by the wardrobe lady to give the feeling of the period. Everyone had backed away, giving her the space. "You mustn't treat me like this," Shirley retorted sharply.

They were face to face. "I am conducting a work session right now and you're giving me sloppy work," he thundered. "I don't intend to accept this poor-quality thing. You call yourself an actress. Well, act. I want better work. And I want you to give it to me now whether you like it or not."

Lee hadn't considered little Shirley's steel backbone. "Stop yelling at me like this," she shouted back. "I'm a person, too. I'm someone, too."

The shocked cast stood to the side, blinking at her. Kim sidled up and whispered, "Don't let him bother you."

"I know how to work. I'm a very good actress." She was still defending herself when Luther stepped in and stopped it.

This was his first directorial assignment in years, and he was under tension. At one point Marty Fried who was stage-managing "had to literally kick him out of the theatre."

It was the first of the two-day technical rehearsals before the preview. The sets were being assembled and crews were synchronizing scene changes, sound cues, and light changes. The show was complicated technically. Four sets, a turntable, fifty lights with multiple cues. One cue had thirty-five parts. The technical script pages were in red and blue. Red for "warn" and blue for "go." Stage manager Fried had earphones on and instruments in front of him with eighteen red buttons and two blue.

Lee had brought in lighting genius Abe Feder. Feder created inkspots around the stage so wherever the character walked she was covered by these tiny spots simulating candlelight. "You had to 'warn' from one to eighteen for these supplemental lights to work properly. Then you had to 'go' each one because as she walked across stage one spot had to go out before the other went on. I was cueing, 'Okay, one . . . one go . . . ready on two . . . kill one . . . two go . . . ready on three. . . .'"

Lee came backstage. Marty was briefing his men. "That scenery has to fly and we need the cue light on this so when you get the go on the sound hit this particular lamp and. . . ."

"Marty," began Lee, "that downstage left light didn't go out correctly. What's the matter? What went wrong?"

"It takes seven–eight run-throughs till the guys get it. Each time they get better or we find out what's wrong and we adjust. It's a bitch, but we're coming along fine. We're on top of it. I'll dry-run it for you."

"When I was stage-managing we used a handkerchief. The electrician watched me and when I dropped the handkerchief he did his thing."

Although he was under pressure, Marty took time out. "On this we have four electricians, not one, plus a sound deck for bird noises, fire alarm noises and those other sounds in the show. These guys work with their feet and their hands plus sticks with boards attached. If I told them I'd drop a handkerchief they'd drop *me!*"

Lee went out front. Marty shifted his earphones then, "Okay, ready on the flies. Warning on fly cue one and two . . . three . . . stage right, you there, John? I'm warning you now for light cue 426 . . . here are the warns on sound, 'a . . . b . . . c . . . .'"

Lee meandered back again. Marty was flicking on red lights which triggered other lights up in the flies. "Listen, what went wrong just now? The cue was out of synch."

"Stage-managing isn't like it used to be when you were doing it forty years ago. You've gotta leave us alone, Lee, to solve these problems."

Lee walked off and stood in the wings. Abe Feder had placed a chair. The spot was marked with indelible yellow paint. Shirley was sitting in the chair but the light missed her. "Goddamn it," shouted Lee, "can't they get the chair right?"

"The chair's on its paint mark," pointed out Marty. "It wasn't moved. It's the lights that have to be reset."

"I don't care whose fault it is. I want it straightened out. Stop everything."

"You can't stop a cue of this magnitude in the middle. It takes an hour to reset. That's an hour wasted in a tough technical rehearsal. We'll complete it then go back over what went wrong."

"*Stop* it," Lee called, running out on stage.

Turntables were turning and everything was going. "Stop hollering stop," called Marty. "The guys'll go insane." He looked over to the confused crew. "Don't stop," he ordered. "Complete the cue."

At the fourth interference Marty raised his voice. "Lee, get the hell out of this goddamn theatre and don't tell us what to do or how to do it. You're just stealing our time and we have a preview coming up and we haven't nearly finished."

Lee went white. Paula stood up and walked from her seat in the darkened theatre toward the footlights.

Marty was perspiring. "Lee, this is not your work. You're in our way. This crew wants to get through this technical with all of us who talk the same technical language. You're a pain in the ass. And if you don't go I'm going to, and you can run this by waving your little white handkerchief."

Lee said not a word. He turned and walked out.

"You shouldn't have done that, Marty," said Paula.

"And if you don't understand this either then you get out, too. When you come back, take notes. Tell him to take notes. That's what they do now. They take notes. Nobody stops in the middle of technicals anymore. We're heavy into unions these days."

Howard Taubman in the New York *Times* raved about this superior 1964 production of Chekhov's *The Three Sisters*. "A masterpiece," he wrote.

Lee didn't speak to Marty for three days.

The offer came to present *Sisters* in London's Aldwych Theatre at the annual World Theatre Season. To represent their country abroad in an international festival which spotlighted outstanding productions and national companies from a Germany or an Israel was considered a golden invitation. Festival organizers called the Studio "a cultural oasis absolutely unique in the annals of world theatre."

In '56 Lee had had tea and canapés with Tony Richardson and John Osborne and the Redgraves and pronounced the English stage, "Stultifying . . . not bad, just outdated . . . it boasts not reality nor conviction but acting." The English, clutching to tradition, were used to the high voice and delicate upper-class style of Mayfair acting. Lee and his famous Actors Studio were singlehandedly changing the English theatre and now the product of this world-famous Studio was coming to London. The critics were waiting.

Geraldine Page, who played the eldest sister, Olga, was pregnant. She couldn't go. "What can I do?" agonized Lee. "Well . . . but . . . so . . . at least I have Kim. Kim Stanley's the most important one in the show."

Kim then announced, "I won't work with Kevin in London."

"I disagree with your thinking. He's right for the production," replied Lee.

"Well, in that case I won't go."

He stared. "What do you mean you won't go? You already promised to go."

"No, I didn't promise to go."

Lee was not about to fight with Kim. "I couldn't say, 'How dare you?' Who am I to command Kim Stanley? If I really was so important that I could command her, then I wouldn't need her."

Lee turned pragmatist. He was in a bind. "Then we'll have to go out and get somebody for that part."

She was prepared. "What about George C. Scott?"

"I don't really see a George C. Scott. He's capable but not quite right for what I want for the part. Scott's good if he's being Scott. He does his thing and that's it. If you want something else I'm not sure you can get it."

"But I think there's a chance of getting George Scott."

Lee acquiesced. "Okay, if there's a chance of getting George Scott, then we'll get him."

Shirley Knight suddenly announced she landed a movie and couldn't go. Paula telephoned. "You *must* go, Shirley. Really, Shirley, you *must* go."

Shirley was upset. "I know I'm selfish. I know I'm letting Lee down, but the director won't let me go to London for those two weeks. He just won't let me out."

"Irina has more to say than anybody. She starts as a baby and grows up in the role. It takes an actress with youthful naïveté and womanly awareness. It's not easy to find somebody else quickly. Please, Shirley. For Lee."

"I know I should place him first and not my career. And I know it's one of the mistakes of my life. I know I should go . . . but . . . there it is. . . ."

Three of the four leads weren't going. This was fatal. Lacking their important stars, it would scarcely represent the Studio's best efforts. A two-week engagement will work providing a superior production remains intact, but not if different chemistry is hastily dropped into it. Well-rehearsed actors cannot quickly be replaced unless a play is totally reworked. National theatres and national

companies work with their own scenery and their same steady
people with whom they've interplayed for years. Like an opera
company, they're prepared. They know exactly what to do. The
Actors Studio Theatre was a pickup company saddled with last-
minute replacements.

It reeked of fiasco. They considered scrubbing it. By then it was
no, too late, the show must go on.

Lee "had to create a whole new production in a few days with
George Scott in Kevin McCarthy's role, Sandy Dennis in Shirley
Knight's role, Nan Martin in Geraldine Page's role, and others
shifted around. The thing literally fell apart." On top of that, Kim
announced she wouldn't fly. Traveling by boat delayed her arrival
and shrunk the already insufficient rehearsal period to eleven days.

In London, rehearsals for this intimate play commenced dead
center in an armory complete with reechoes. "It was a bloody
mess. A godawful disaster," sums up laconic Cheryl. Pleas for a
smaller room cramped them into an area far too tiny. "It's all we
have," declared the authorities.

Since this golden privilege was strictly at Studio expense and
the cost of shipping Chekhovian sets prohibitive, the British supplied the furnishings. The Aldwych has a thirty-five-to-forty-foot
raked stage. A chair must be so constructed as to look level, albeit
it's on a three-foot rake. The antique chairs they supplied which
were perfect for a flat stage tipped way forward. The couch listed
at thirty-five degrees. To screams of, "What's the matter with you
people? Rake the furniture!" came the response, "Sorry about
that, mate. These are antiques. Can't cut 'em."

The scenery arrived late and was slapdash hung together only
the day before the opening. The stagehands hadn't even dry-run
the equipment. The replacements had never played within the old
sets and hadn't even walked through the new ones. And at that
point little could be done about anything.

The actors never stepped onto the stage until opening day. At
rehearsal, which didn't progress through to the last act, George
Scott sported white longjohns with a droopy back flap. It was cold
and his costume was being pressed. Stagehands crept out to gawk
at this romantic type with his drawers hanging out and his trap-
door sagging.

Opening night was actually the first full rehearsal. An actor must slowly accommodate to the feel of any unfamiliar theatre. To give a performance on a slanted stage when you are unused to it and have barely experienced two hours practice time is impossible. It takes days. A week. The incline was so steep anything set down, rolled. Everybody had to walk sideways. Sandy Dennis was to carry water in one scene. It sloshed all over her.

A sixteen-year-old nonprofessional was doing sound. The crew didn't know the show, neither were they trained to Feder's complicated lighting, the wind machine for rippling curtains nor to the best American technical equipment extant. The Studio's stage managers stayed up all night with the girl who adapted the American sound-effects tape to British electricity.

Without time for previews, they had to guess at sound levels. Too loud, you drown out the actors. Too soft, nobody hears the sound effects. Their bird noises, wind effects and fire engine sounds were gauged in an empty theatre. They ironed out the kinks as they went—on opening night!! They winged the multiple cues. Some lights were too bright, others dim, others late. They readjusted while the very show was in progress.

Then what Lee calls "the real difficulty developed. Sandy Dennis insisted on doing her junk. She's a good actress but she was just stupid.

"I cannot describe the atrociousness of her performance. She was an American kid up there, not a Russian young lady of the Chekhovian period. The way she sat and carried herself and walked and gestured was not only bad, it was bad American. And she fought me. It was really terrible. I couldn't tell her in those quick days that she was mannered so I just told her what to do."

"He told me never put my hands above my waist. A girl of that character and period kept her hands down," relates Sandy Dennis. "I always waved my arms and I had no organized way to control my hands from flying around. If I wasn't so new into the Method I could've picked at my finger or played with my ring or reasoned that this is Irina's way and utilized it in her characterization. Instead I did it forcefully and physically. I clasped my hands, hunched my shoulders and stooped over. A reviewer wrote 'Miss Dennis played her role like an ape looking for a banana.'

"As a consequence I got constipation. A doctor gave me suppositories and a prescription, but still I didn't have a bowel movement for two weeks. It was very serious. I was distended. I threw up, which happens if you haven't evacuated anything. Into my dressing room came this Harley Street doctor who ordered me to the hospital for enemas. I was desperately ill.

"It was the direct result of not finding the key to my character. I felt constricted. It wasn't Lee's fault. If what I was doing was only the result, that was MY fault. An actress must find reason, motivation. He figured I had sense enough to do that. Since I hadn't found that organic means I felt tied up. I can truly say Lee Strasberg was the cause of my first major constipation."

This cause of her constipation admits, "The thing was a mess. The show wouldn't come together at all. Sandy I could have killed. So everything had to depend on Kim."

They were booed. The audience yelled, "Yankee go home." People walked out. Half a house was left. The agonizing, laborious opening night ran an hour longer than scheduled "because of Kim," claims Lee. "Kim was way off." The chemistry was such that to accommodate to George Scott she eased down. Others acclimated to Kim's rhythm and a one-minute scene ran six. "She . . . moved . . . like . . . that . . . like she was drugged. I don't know what the hell she was doing. The movements, the speeches, the timing, everything was in halftime. It was completely thrown off.

"In New York she was as near great as you can get. I can only guess that his performance, for Kim, completely destroyed her performance. I don't to this day know what happened because I never spoke to her about it afterward. Kim's not a person you talk to easily. So I just wrote it off. There's nothing anybody can do about the thing."

The scenery kept pace with the actors. One of the birches went down and other of the trees fell about a bit in the background. Sandy had the line, "Oh, what a terrible night" and someone in the orchestra hollered, "It sure has been."

As per script, Barbara Baxley, playing Natasha, slammed the door. The set fell in. Clutching the doorknob behind the scenes, she held up that flat singlehandedly until a stagehand came to the rescue. Calm, low of voice and steely cold, Barbara attacked Lee. "You may feel you can direct. You know more about it than anybody in the world but that does not make you a director." Bar-

bara's memory is that he "turned red, white, purple." She continued in a controlled manner, "Hopefully you will never direct
anything again after this." Barbara Baxley's hostility is such that
she can barely speak of the experience.

The reviews were devastating. The pain was such that Sandy
"had thoughts of suicide in my head." For high-strung Kim this
newest flop was more than she could bear.

In place of phrases like . . . "the failure lay in time" . . .
"there was not time to put together what should have been done"
. . . Lee publicly agreed with the critics. He also blamed his actors. Their "performance fell apart."

George was fuming. Four-letter words spewed out of his mouth,
directed at Lee. Why was Lee defending the critics? With everyone assembled, George told him he was too old . . . and what did
he know about today's methods . . . and he hadn't directed anything in years. . . .

The humiliations mounted. Awash with personal hangups,
"Scott went a little ape," Marty Fried remembers. The second
night of performance he didn't bother to show up at all.

Scott's lost weeknight created a fracas inside Kim's dressing
room. Another actor would have to walk through the role reading
from a manuscript. In the company's view, when the problems
came Lee wasn't there. He disappeared. He went vague. Outside
the dressing room in a little alcove near the staircase a forlorn
creature huddled in his coat. Empowered by some inner mechanism which allows him to function like a mole in a predators' jungle, Lee had overheard the discussion but he wasn't getting into it.
This was not "theatre" to him. This was not what should have
gone down. You don't toss a guru into a melee. You don't ask a
guru to solve crises. A guru only gurus. You come to him only to
learn.

The whole corps de ballet of the Actors Studio Theatre, a bare
couple of years old, went down with *The Three Sisters*. In the blizzard of opinions and blame-throwing and anger, thickened with
everybody hating everybody, Lee, who must bear responsibility as
the final authority, comes in for considerable. He could not cope
with the myriad details. He did not take charge. He just let it happen. He was haphazard.

The actors who crawled away from a terrifying disaster threw mud at his directorial abilities: The Pulitzer Prize winning director's genius lies not in theatrical activity but in teaching . . . Lee's not basically a director. . . . Lee has supposedly admitted, "I'm not so good on business." . . . Lee can't handle the externals, only the internals. Since director Strasberg makes his mixes and creates his chemistry inside the soul, he shies from specific directives. The story goes that in a Group rehearsal, J. Edward Bromberg bet someone Lee could not be pushed into even the kindergarten directive, "Cross left." As the story is told, Bromberg won.

Between the segment that's angry because they weren't chosen and the segment that's angry because they *were*, the Actors Studio Theatre resulted in Shakespearean feuds. Anne Bancroft badmouthed Lee. From Barbara Baxley's nostrils pour steam at the mention of his name. *Blues* made Rip Torn, once very involved, now hostile. His wife, Geraldine Page, is another defector. Never a member of the Studio, George Scott is virulently anti-Studio. Others in the cast of *The Three Sisters* shelved their careers. Kim Stanley retired to the Midwest temporarily to teach at a university.

The fact is, Lee didn't get a fair shake with London. He should never have gone, a major mistake to which he regretfully accedes. "I blame myself for that. I should never have submitted to that pressure that we had to go. I hoped it wouldn't come to so bad an end, but it was already written on the wall from New York. It fell into it in a series of stages."

Voices raise to call Lee "piqued and vengeful" in London. A quiet truth is he will not throw mud back. With all who speak against him, there is no one Lee actively dislikes. Lee won't kick anyone. At most he says, "I will never forget what Kim did to me by dictating to me it would be her way or she wouldn't go to London. I may forgive but I won't forget."

CHAPTER TWELVE

Goodbye

When Susan returned from Rome she met "a very controlling influence who was going to do his number no matter what he had to do or who he laid," says an intimate of those days. Christopher Jones was an acting student. Unruly, undisciplined, charismatic, he was a baby Jimmy Dean. And if he wasn't exactly that yet, he fully intended to get there. Christopher was a talent. It was generally agreed he'd be a star.

Sandy-haired, handsome, he was as slight of build and terribly good to look at as Susan herself and about the same age. Previously drawn to older men, Susan suddenly shucked the father image to pleasure herself with this promising youngster. Christopher was a wild spirit. Sometimes he slept in cars. Christopher enjoyed all sorts of relationships. In his way, however, he was mad for Susan.

Narcissistic Christopher would parade about with nothing on. He was proud of his body, particularly of the size of his penis. He once received a well-known woman author in the kitchen stark naked.

Susan concurs, "Christopher was a rebellion. He was the antithesis of everything. My father liked good music. Christopher liked rock. My father read. Christopher was anti-intellectual. My father was mental, Christopher physical. This was a whole period in my life when I rejected all I'd grown up with."

Deeply possessive and with a genius for manipulation, he tried to control Susan, to move her into what he wanted her to do and be. This sexual power Lee believes he used consciously. "He knew what he was doing because he did it in completely the right psychologically correct way. First he'd get you to give way to small things like Marlon does. They're both a little cruel actually.

"With Christopher I'd try not to get into an argument. He would say something and I would reply only, 'Oh, come on,' because I knew he didn't know what the hell he was talking about. Then he'd say something outrageous that definitely called for rebuttal. I would say only, 'I don't think you know much about it.' He'd repeat it. I'd ignore it. So then, 'Why aren't you saying anything?' He kept it up until you finally *had* to answer. To get you angry and into an argument, that's what he wanted. Then he'd start a whole big thing. Then Susie had to agree with him because she was in his spell. This was a very unusual talent. Chris was strange."

Susan was deeply involved. She loved him. By the end of the summer that they met, they were going together. Susan bought him a car.

It was the craziness that was the attraction. She has a mystical quality and so did he. He played on that. Christopher was different. He was artistic, but his creations were peculiar. He sculpted his own head. He slept with a gun under his pillow. He did little cruelties. At a party, playful Chris threw a knife at a friend. Clearly, Christopher was under some influence. When the plumbing was disconnected in the Fire Island house, which was on stilts, he and Susan "peed under the house."

A famous actress was the first to take up Christopher. Whatever their relationship had been it was sufficient for him to reach into her purse and extract money. This lady's highly sensual find was observing at the Studio when Susan met him.

Chris fell into drugs. Although Susan never went for that much, she took to smoking pot. She segued into dressing as a hippie. She took her own apartment. Christopher moved in. In their five

28. Anna and Lee with his granddaughter Jennifer and his two sons David and Adam. (Irv Steinberg/Globe Photos, Inc.)

29. Lee and the author in a session at the Actors Studio. (Photo by Syeus Mottel)

30. The author and subject. (Photo by Syeus Mottel)

31. (Left to right) Anna and Lee Strasberg, owner of Peng's Chinese Restaurant, Joey Adams, and author.

rooms, furnished with some of her pieces from Italy, they staged noisy fights. Beyond rebellion, it was as though Susan were shouting, "Hey, everybody, I want some attention paid to me."

Susan didn't "trip out too much—maybe once or twice. She held pretty much together, but he was flaky," says a friend. "Like you'd think he was out of the house, then suddenly you'd find him scrooched down behind the couch spying. Christopher was into stuff far beyond the normal pot trip. She tolerated his being el freako because she was locked in emotionally. She responded very much to his sexuality."

Susan's moral de-escalation was the progression of basic psychological procedure. Destructive spirits as clever as Christopher make you give on little things to which you do not take exception. Presently you slide to something else you ordinarily wouldn't do. After a while you surrender your will.

Susan knew better. A bell went off in the back of her head and she knew this was not right. They broke up and Susan traipsed off to Central Park to decide her fate. She was searching for four-leaf clovers. Christopher came after her and found two. "I thought, 'That's impossible. He must have *bought* them. How could anybody find *two* four-leaf clovers?' It was like karma. Christopher was a force. He carried me further and further."

Susan had been a star in Europe. After three and a half triumphant years abroad she had returned to do *Lady of the Camelias,* her second play after *Anne Frank.* Of this disaster she says, "They were writing the script in the bathroom two hours before we opened." She was terrible. The production was worse.

The whole family at this point was in analysis. Even Lee. Paula had gone first. Paula's emotional difficulties had started with her relationship with the children. For that reason Lee had accompanied his wife when she went for treatment. "The doctor wanted the two of us so we could both say whatever we felt about the problems." Her experiences with Marilyn, however, were affecting her seriously. Sustaining those repeated body blows created a severe mental strain. She was in a kind of transference relationship called *folie à deux* in which one person takes on the illnesses and insanities of the other.

"Paula would wake up screaming. The nightmares went back to God knows what else, because it was some recurring dream about someone who died. She'd yell, 'Mama . . . Mama . . .' I don't know what it was. A lot of things were taking place inside her. It was a difficult time."

More difficulties surfaced as Lee pulled away. An estrangement was growing between them. "Paula changed mightily in the second half of our marriage."

And Lee changed. He became important. Women chased him. And Paula was always watching to see he wasn't fooling around. But, in fact, he was. With Paula constantly away he began to make an effort to go out. This bothered her. "She was possessive to a greater extent than I thought even reasonable."

Lee was not responsible for the phenomena of beautiful, nubile maids sniffing after him. They threw themselves at him. He did nothing. Propinquity to the source of the magnetism—goes the thinking—precludes the need for development. A young girl wants to be a star. There's a hollowness in her artistic being. She lacks technique. Every time she's on stage she's in panic. She comes to the Studio, sees a little man pinpoint her problem and it's as though someone cleaved her open and poured in liquid light and gold. The attraction of the moth to the flame.

One who lived through it ties it up in a scarlet ribbon. "Look, he had Marilyn, even if not in the biblical sense, and every starlet wants to be the next Marilyn Monroe. For that they'll kiss his pecker in Macy's window."

There was the night Paula telephoned Liska March at 2 A.M. Liska's doctor husband kept early office hours. Liska quickly grabbed the phone and stuck it under the covers. Shouted Paula, "Tell me where is Lee. WHERE IS HE???" Liska told her never do this again, never call late at night again. "I mean, what was I going to say? The girls were all crazy about Lee."

One, particularly overt, had gotten it into her head to have an affair with Lee Strasberg and she set about it.

Lee had invited her to join Jane Fonda, Johnny and others at his table at a dinner party. When the party broke up she stood alone so, ever gentlemanly, he said, "I'll take you home." At her place she suggested, "Come in for a minute."

"Quite honestly I didn't want to. She was a lesbian and in any case I didn't have that feeling about her. But I figured, 'what can it harm?' Sure enough she came out all naked and everything. So therefore I slept with her. But it was the only time. What pleased me is the flattering thing she said. It was satisfying to her and her experiences with men started after that. I have an idea I was her first because what she said quite simply was, 'Finally . . . finally . . . a prick in my cunt.' But I had no continuing relationship with her whatsoever. That was our whole 'romance.'"

He admits a deep attraction to one lady. Had the situation been different, he thinks he would have pursued her. The lady was married, but she remains one of the few for whom he ever made an effort. He bought her a wristwatch and his "behavior when she was around was decidedly different than when I was with Paula alone." Still, his wife never fathomed the depth of his feelings for this beauty who always dressed in the image of an Easter basket, in lavender and lace.

With black hair off the face, a perfect forehead, white skin, rounded figure, she had a freshness and innocence, and from full lips came sayings that were both naïve and wise. However, he says, she was just a little "off." This wanting to protect her was precisely what drew him. Her emotional needs appealed. "Somehow I go for people with psychological problems, but it was more than my liking her very very much. She's the only one I ever had the least inclination toward in my years with Paula."

In these latter years strain appeared in place of rapport. At certain moments one felt he couldn't tolerate his wife. He seemed almost embarrassed by his zircon in the rough. She was not a book person. She was not a music person. Lee's intellect was geared to someone of wider culture and as the chasm widened so did the impoverishment in the relationship. He was tired of Paula.

Paula had been running fast to become something and she felt all marriages go through this sort of thing. Anyway, what would she have been on her own but a teacher of acting in a lesser atmosphere? Paula jealously guarded her position as Lee Strasberg's wife.

"We had sort of made peace," sighs Lee, who might secretly have been scared to face life without her. "We had already weathered the crises and . . . well . . . to some extent we settled it. I'd gone through whatever it is I'd gone through and had accepted that I would end out my life with Paula and that's the way it was going to be.

"To divorce I would have to have somebody to divorce for. It would have to be more a reason than that I just didn't want to live with her anymore. And so we had come to a calm sea. You get to a certain age and you just look to live out the rest of your days."

The breaches were several ways at various times. Theirs was a competitive family life, each in the theatre but each in his own world. Each interconnected but each a little disoriented. Paula and Lee bored with one another, Susan in a rebellion, and Johnny at war with the world.

Hooked on drugs, Johnny and Christopher were friends. Susan confesses, "They were very close, particularly when Johnny took a header."

Money was touch and go, but Johnny only tapped his parents once. "A junkie pal needed a hundred dollars. He put his guitar up and I cosigned." Johnny was pestered for the hundred. He was scared. Lee sent the hundred. Marty Fried responded to one SOS with a few. Ruth Lippa managed to get Johnny's number to inquire if he needed clothes. She wouldn't send money for fear he'd buy drugs. "He was appreciative but he didn't see me."

For a time he adopted his middle name and carted his laundry to a place under the name of Johnny Carl. "It sounded like a rock 'n' roll singer and it was my fantasy name. Then I thought, hell, it doesn't solve anything and sooner or later everybody will know who I am and eventually I'll be introduced as, 'Here he is, Johnny Carl who really is John Strasberg.'"

No single cause triggered Johnny's crisis, but he cites several as disturbing influences. His godfather, Franchot Tone, died. "He smoked a lot and drank heavily but I never figured he was going to go. It hit me hard." Another was his "resentment" at Marilyn giving him a car when he was a teen-ager. Looking back, it rubbed him wrong. He felt he didn't deserve it.

Another was the career decision. When he auditioned at the Studio he "was scared. Oh, so scared. I was filled with fear. Downstairs beforehand, I was lying flat in a basically frozen state, so anxious, so petrified. I couldn't function."

Johnny went off to the Coast. He was set to do his first job in the movies "when everything went blooey."

Meanwhile, sensible, together Susan knew enough to wrench

herself out of what she was in. Having been reared with values, having seen neurotics and alcoholics, having worked with Franchot, who was in such bad shape that he fell during rehearsals, Susan knew "it was time to go back and collect my blessings."

Her mother had been devastated at the marriage to Christopher. A newcomer actor was not exactly the son-in-law of Paula's dreams. Paula was possibly even a little scared of offputting Christopher. Why is Susan doing this? she'd ask. But Paula had heightened sensitivities, Paula could see beyond. Paula was aware. She and Susan maintained a relationship of ambivalent emotions. Love with hostility. She knew Susan was running away.

Christopher landed a TV series. He made a few movies. Publicly Paula made such noises as "It's natural Susan should be attracted to someone wildly exciting and untamed and not run of the mill. Could I ask her to marry a simple man? Did I?"

Christopher was on the threshold of success when he became no longer employable. When Christopher got heavily sucked into drugs, Susan went into Reichian therapy and called her father. This was to be the final break. Immediately his daughter asked for help in severing the sick relationship for good, Lee stepped in full. The two men had a quarrel in a theatre. "She doesn't want you anymore. Leave her alone," said Lee coldly. "And leave us all alone. You're interfering with rehearsal."

Christopher brushed past him onto the stage. "Where's my wife?"

"I'm telling you to get out of here and I'm warning you that if you come around again I'll kill you. Do you hear me? Stay away or I'll kill you."

They were nose to nose on the stage. Christopher swung on his heel and rapped out, "Where is she? I came for my wife and I'm not leaving until I get her. Now you go find her for me."

Tensed, his face set, Lee walked right up to him. "Look, don't give me this kind of stuff. You know me. I'm not wild. I'm not you. But if you keep this up and you don't leave her alone I'm going to kill you or. . . ."

"Yeah? You and who else?" sneered Christopher, his small fists doubled up.

". . . or I'm going to have you killed," finished Lee with an icy calm. "Don't think that you can come here and put on your act.

I'm not afraid of you. The truth is, the more you're going to carry on the less I'm going to be afraid because that's the way I react. So get out. Get the hell out of here. . . ."

Johnny sided with Christopher. It created a barrier between brother and sister. While the sister was climbing free of this destructive influence, it was at work on the brother. Johnny's dive into hell was partially the result.

Twice Paula had been hospitalized. Twice she had a biopsy. Even after her breast was removed she told close friend Peg Feury it was a miscarriage. Some heard from the doctor that her back was gone. They thought she was having massages for it. Upon release from the hospital, she asked Lee to bring a black silk dress from home, a black straw hat and her black Gucci purse styled like a narrow shopping bag. She had been hospitalized for weeks but she wanted to leave dressed to the eyes. Paula played to the balcony.

If Paula cared, there was nobody she could not make her friend. And if she cared enough to make you her friend she would shape happiness for you. Shelley Winters was doing *Cages* Off Broadway. "Lee worked with me before the opening. Paula wasn't well and it was awfully cold in the theatre, but Paula stayed right there with us all night long."

The complexion was still rosy but the lovely waist-length hair had thinned and the coiled chignon hung loosely, helter-skelter about her face. A thin chain replaced the clunky necklace but her great spirit still flamed. She received actress Jacqueline Bertrand on the couch in the living room. "I gave my favorite cookbook to someone, I gave something else to somebody else. You I'm going to give aggression."

Her pretty disciple looked questioningly, wondering why "that marvelous woman" was giving things away. "You I'm going to teach how to be aggressive," she repeated.

"Oh, Paula," demurred Jackie softly, "you know I was brought up in French Canadian convents. That's hard for me."

Paula ignored the interruption. "You just need to learn your values and develop trust in yourself. Tell yourself, 'I'm better than anyone else. I'm greater and stronger than anyone else.'"

"But agents and casting directors and the people in the business are hard. They look right through you. It's frightening."

"Walk into a room and know that everyone there is as frightened as you are, if not more so. All you need is a fuck-you-all attitude."

"But why are you telling . . . ?"

Paula leaned forward. "Remember, you've got to have balls in life."

Paula's condition plunged downward. She was bedridden. She and Lee no longer shared the same room. There were occasional visitors. Dr. Louis Finger attended her. Ruthie Lippa brought her favorite homemade blueberry muffins. Paula's sister from California. A few friends.

Viola, the secretary, telephoned actress Elaine Aiken. "Mrs. Strasberg wants to see you."

The apartment was dark and quiet and sad. Paula refused to go to the hospital. Lee never left except for class. Intermittently he shuffled in to ask did she want something. The performance was low-key. His first wife had had a mastectomy. His sister had had a mastectomy. He could not stay plugged into the misery. He clicked off. He was not there. Almost, he sat back watching to see what life dealt.

Elaine slipped into the back bedroom and sat down, waiting to hear what Paula wanted. Nothing consequential was forthcoming, so Elaine sparked a little nonsense small talk. "You look terrific with that huge weight loss."

Paula nodded. "I'll be competing for parts again now that I'm as thin as when I was a young girl."

It was a short visit. "Come back. The day after tomorrow. Come back."

Two days later Paula told the good-looking divorcée hovering at her bedside, "I don't really feel that good, so I'll stay here. You go in and have dinner with Lee."

Elaine did as she was told. She sat at the table. The maid served. Nobody spoke. Elaine ate quickly and excused herself.

Monday Paula told her to come back Tuesday. Tuesday night Christopher Jones was on TV. Elaine and Lee ate dinner in front of a portable set in the dining room.

"Lee, can I walk the dog?" asked Elaine. Anything just to get away.

"Oh, yes, sure. Be right back."

Elaine doesn't quite know how but in retrospect she thinks, somehow, Paula had been trying to control things even at that point. She'd known she was going and somehow decided that of all the available ladies around Elaine was the best of the lot. "I'm sure it was something like that, although before those final Command Performances I never got the feeling Paula liked me."

Lee's dog, Cherie, and their orange Persian, Sweetie Pie, sat in the stillness mutely, staring at Paula. "Get them out of here," she ordered Delos Smith, the family friend who lived with Lee. "Get them out of here."

"They were spooking her," says Delos.

Paula looked so poorly that Delos suggested they notify the children. Lee blinked and said nothing. Both were on the Coast. Delos wrote them to come home. Business manager David Cogan telephoned them to come home. Paula was under heavy medication when they arrived.

Doctors had forbidden Susan to take her month-and-a-half-old baby on the plane. Jennifer had come into the world March 14, 1966, with two holes in her heart. Susan's marriage was foundering. Her baby was suffering a serious heart condition. Her brother was having his terrors. And her mother was dying. "This was painful time for us all. I wanted Mama to see her grandchild. She had that last burst of energy that the dying sometimes have. She was conscious and saw us both."

Johnny was shattered. He hadn't known she was that ill. "Nobody ever said. I'd dealt with her complaining about not feeling well for so many years that it just hadn't registered anymore. To me . . . well . . . that was my mother . . . I never expected what I saw."

His mother didn't recognize him. The eyes were sightless. The face masklike. The skin "just hanging there. I sat next to her and I was thinking just as hard as I could, 'It's all right . . . I'm here . . . you can sleep now. . . .'"

The ambulance sped Paula Miller Strasberg to Beth Israel Hospital. It was the last day of April, windy and biting cold. She was fifty-five.

BOOK FOUR

"ANNA"

CHAPTER ONE

Resurrection

Paula's final matinee, at 2:45 at Riverside Memorial Chapel, would have pleased her. It was Standing Room Only. Among the hundreds were Stella Adler, Anne Bancroft, Arthur Penn, Brooks Atkinson, Jose Quintero, Senator Jacob Javits, Harold Clurman, Maureen Stapleton, Kim Stanley, Julie Newmar, Kevin McCarthy. Sidney Kingsley and Cheryl Crawford spoke. Playwright William Gibson was scheduled to speak but was too overcome. In black and fresh from her second Oscar, Shelley Winters wound up her eulogy with, "And where do you go on New Year's Eve now?"

An endless cortege of cars braved the blizzard to the cemetery. Ashen Susan in dark glasses and mantilla clung to her visibly shaken father. Lee threw down the first handful of dirt. He took out his handkerchief. He wept.

Back at the house he appeared in control. To expressions of sympathy he simply nodded. At the collation afterward, with the groaning table of smoked salmon and ham, it was as though Paula were still around, in another room, helping with this newest party.

Says Shelley, "I just felt Paula was looking on somewhere saying, 'All these celebrities and no photographers!'"

Johnny climbed into a car and screamed all the way back to Los Angeles. When he hit California it was a steady tailspin. A month later Lee's realities developed priorities.

The phone call came at five in the morning. Johnny had OD'd on LSD. He'd gone through a window and lost considerable blood. Hospital authorities doubted he'd make it. The last rites had been administered.

Johnny had tried a lot of things. A sniff of this, a shot of that, everything, but mainly amphetamines. Pals cautioned, don't take amphetamines then drink and take coffee or you'll die. "Oh, yeah? So I took the stuff and polished off alcohol and a cup of coffee to find out how far I could go before I killed myself."

He hung around wrong places with wrong people. Everyone was sick. He was sick. "I'd walk into a pad where everybody's eyes were too glazed to focus. They were all with, 'Hey, like, man, this is it!' This is what?! 'Oh, hey, like, man, we're feelin' so good.' They didn't give a damn for anything. So I figured they're right because I didn't want to give a damn for anything either.

"I remember a living room with a bunch all stoned out of their heads and one chick who was in bed acting like she was four years old. Every guy in turn made it with her. I just sat there. I didn't move all night."

Johnny holed up alone playing the guitar. The night he went through the window there was no conscious thought of self-destruction. At that point he just had to get out of the room. His first thought was to call someone but he didn't feel there was anybody to call. And it was from deep despair that he thought, Well, I've just gotta get out . . . I've gotta get out. . . .

"I was in a hotel room on the second floor. The walls appeared solid, but thanks to the drugs the window looked like water. When I threw myself at it I wasn't aware I was hitting a window. It seemed soft. I bounced off the supposedly unbreakable glass. I began kicking my way through it. I kept going until I got through. Then I hit the screen outside the window and I was at that screen for a while. I really tore up my legs."

Lee flew out alone. By the time he arrived, Johnny was conscious. He recognized his father. "I'm okay . . . I don't need any help."

Susan had her own problems and wanted no part of her brother. Lee was not in shape financially. Paula's illness had drained him. The whole period was dramatic and traumatic.

Lee spent a bare few days on the Coast. "Even when I was right there, Johnny's reaction was to Christopher not to me. Their relationship was more than just drugs. It was a whole thing. Christopher came to the hospital and Johnny wanted him there." It was a terrible disappointment to have such a son. Lee did whatever he could and flew back to an empty New York.

Johnny denies Christopher was his downfall, the theory being that nobody gets you on drugs if you don't want to go. "He was a miserable, sick person but I was hanging around this sort of thing even before him. I was looking for happiness." With the world still too painful to bear, Johnny slipped back into the subculture. The drug trip lasted two years.

Christopher would manipulate Johnny into telephoning New York late at night to get a rise out of the old man. Christopher would listen on the extension. One night they did get a rise out of the old man. Wearily, he told them, "I'm just trying to be nice to you but don't think I feel guilty. I'm not even interested in you anymore. I'm sick of your baloney. You want to do something . . . go . . . do it. . . . You're grown up enough. Do whatever you want. I don't give a damn about you anymore." They stopped calling.

In the long run John Strasberg was too bright to succumb. One five in the morning he pulled himself out. He was alone. He talked to himself. "This is stupid. What are you doing? You want to end up like that addict who thinks she's four years old? Get out!" And he got out. He stopped cold. "I survived because I come from good stock."

Back in New York a layer of dust began to form over everything even though Lee had help. Listening alone to Beethoven's *Fidelio*, he looked like a dowdy old man. One evening Shelley found him in the dark. "What are you doing sitting in the dark?"

"I don't know how to turn the lights on."

His brother, Arthur, invited him. Friends kept in touch. Luise Rainer "was amazed at how he did not speak of Paula at all." The married Jacqueline Bertrand accompanied him to the country. The unmarried Nancy Berg accompanied him to theatre.

He invited people to his small Fire Island house and got for them and did for them. He barbecued steaks. He made coffee. After one stifling day a friend prepared to sleep on the couch. "You'll need a blanket." "Oh no, I'm quite warm," demurred the friend. "But it gets cold at night." "No, no, no, I'm fine." It was so cold that the young man couldn't sleep for shivering. His teeth chattered. In the middle of the night the host tiptoed in with a blanket, threw it over his guest who was feigning sleep and tiptoed out quickly. He shared information on books he'd read, records he'd heard. He never articulated in terms of saying, I'm hurting or I'm lonely. He communicated by sharing.

Paula had maintained if anything happened to her he'd find somebody in six months to continue doing the same things for him that she did. Lee concurred. He told Harold Clurman's ex-wife, Juleen Compton, "I'll marry again. I have to be part of a family unit." "I wish it were that simple to find someone," murmured Juleen. "I can't find someone to fit my life." "That's because you have to love somebody," he replied softly. "I only have to be loved, to have someone love me. That's very different."

He changed after Paula's death. Paula had kept him separated, inaccessible. Forced out of his shell, forced to make contact with others, he turned out to be such a quick study that people labeled him a swinger.

One Thursday, which is when he often had his favorite Chinese or Italian food or maybe a movie, the voice on the phone said, "Elaine Aiken, please."

"Yes. This is she."

"Elaine, this is Lee. Lee Strasberg."

Elaine knew the voice. Quickly she babbled, "Yes . . . yes, Lee . . . what is it . . . ?" Almost as though to say, "What's the matter . . . what's wrong?" He had never called before.

Pause. "What are you doing?"

"What?"

"What are you doing?"

"What am I doing?" Not comprehending this was a prelude to a date, she began to tell him—as one would right after completing a scene in the Studio—what she was doing. "I'm dyeing sheets. See, I have this maid, Eva Newton. She's a big black lady about seventy who's been with me for years. Well, she's helping me tint my sheets. I wanted a particular blue and couldn't find the exact color so I bought white ones and right now I'm brewing the dye and actually Eva was just dipping them when the phone rang."

Patiently he listened through. Finally he said, "Do you go out for dinner?"

Unable to fathom what this had to do with her sheets, Elaine nonetheless replied, "Oh, of course, yes." Then, "Oh, yes . . . yes . . . yes, of course."

There was that little catarrhal click in the throat he sometimes makes. "Oh, well, would you like to go out for dinner?"

"Sure. With whom?"

Awkward pause. "With me, my dear, of course. Who else?"

Stunned, Elaine had never expected it. He never made a phone call. He never extended himself. He never instituted a social action.

Like any suitor he came by to pick her up and they taxied down to a little place in the Village. Elaine had selected "a noisy Italian joint away from his regular Sardi's people." They laughed. They had fun. Over the spaghetti, Elaine confided, "You know, Lee, I've never seen you like this. Very few people have seen you like this."

He appeared surprised. "What do you mean?"

"Well, you're not always friendly. It's as though you don't like people."

"I like people," he replied softly. "It was Paula who thought I didn't."

"Well, tomorrow morning in the session, when I come in, I don't know whether you'll even answer my good morning or not. Most times you just give a grunt."

His eyebrows raised. "I do?"

"Lots of times I don't even bother to say good morning and others don't either because nobody knows if you're going to answer."

Lee was talky, charming, and the conversation was apart from work. She maneuvered it into light things, newsy things, chatty, not personal.

His telephone calls followed a pattern. "Hello, Elaine? Elaine Aiken? This is Lee. Lee Strasberg."

To keep it lively and interesting and to keep the evening rolling, she suggested Radio City on their second date.

Over three months they dated a few times. He'd come to her Park Avenue apartment, settle happily in the most comfortable chair in the living room and wait for her with the TV on. A gracious, generous date, it was champagne or the best restaurants. Afterward he'd drop her at her door with a kiss on the cheek. "He knew all the civilities."

His most personal gift to her was a book inscribed, "To Elaine with fond memories and best wishes." She made him a rice pudding. That was it.

Beautiful women have blessed Lee. At each stage there seems always one to care for him. In his newfound bachelorhood an assortment came into the picture strongly. He always appreciated a pretty girl. In the early days classmates sensed Inger Stevens charmed him but it was only in these years that he openly reacted.

In the beginning he was lost but came the transformation. Alone and "lonely," he was forced to develop social graces. "I had nobody anymore to open doors for me. After Paula, I had no buffer. There was only me to make the approach so bit by bit I learned. I developed friendships with women. I went out with them. And I did it all on my own."

They helped a little. In fact, some did the whole thing. Said one, "It was like the bus driver—just sit back and leave the driving to us."

A beautiful black singer and dancer played the part of the Master's mistress for a season. En route to Paris from a Guadeloupian tour, she passed through to catch some acting classes. Marpessa Dawn, who had starred in *Black Orpheus*, became an observer at the Studio in February '67.

With her "hangup for men who did something for humanity like Jung or Einstein, all the love, admiration and respect came tumbling out for Lee who's on that level." Plunking herself behind his reserved seat and unaware one was to be more reverential, she slung her things across the back of it. "And I made the first move."

They went to the ballet. She cried at its magnificence. Although she had nothing to wipe her eyes and nose on but her gown, he didn't seem to mind. They watched her film. He loved the atmosphere of the all-black cast.

In April she left for Paris. He wrote her a lonely sort of letter saying people imagined he didn't want a rapport with them and he didn't know how much of that he was personally responsible for and how much came from the other side. Outgoing Marpessa was unaware he was supposedly reticent or unresponsive "or a difficult case since he responded to me right away." Other letters were exchanged and when she returned they became "very friendly."

"Marpessa did go after me, yes, but I definitely gave her the impression I was interested. I made it clear even in writing that I would welcome her return, which I would usually never do. I must say I did encourage it. I liked Marpessa very much."

Thirty-three-year-old Marpessa left her girl friend's Riverside Drive apartment and moved in. "This was the first time we were together. We made contact right away. When he opened the door he embraced me as though the affair had already been going on. It wasn't the embrace of someone who was afraid of entering into something.

"I didn't have bags with me. That first night I had come just for the night. We fixed snacks in the kitchen and there were long moments of calm and not speaking. He kissed me and since I don't have any fear of anybody I wasn't afraid of him or afraid to suggest making love. I was the aggressor, but, then, I'm always open in relationships and he was comfortable with me. It wasn't a passionate flame. We weren't head over heels. To me it was like holy.

"Lee has terrific muscle tone. His calves and biceps were like a young person. Not flabby at all. I was surprised because he doesn't get that much exercise outside a little walking.

"He was a gentle lover. Maybe like everybody else, I wanted something from him, too. Maybe I wanted his aura. It took place in my brain first so the orgasm was almost already taken care of but I found it fulfilling physically. The others I've had with the great passion didn't seem like passion anymore. By comparison they were like frantic. With them it's sex to relax. With him, it's relax then sex.

"Our lovemaking was neither a long all-night session nor the wham-bam-thank-you-ma'am thing. It was gentle and nice."

They did simple things. They watched Westerns on TV. They shopped in the supermarket. "He had this kind maid who didn't mind serving another black. Some quit if they have to serve another black." They saw his friends. They visited Arthur Penn's Stockbridge house and treasured the silvery May sun shining through the birches onto the verandah.

With Marpessa's giant mane of hair which she made even wilder by crimping it in curlers, she featured ethnic clothes. Indonesian batik sarongs, American Indian beaded headbands with braids, African voodoo outfits. She took guitar lessons. She'd improvise dances for her audience of one to the record, "Missa Criolla" wearing something filmy and flowing over her naked body.

"I don't wear nighties or bra and panties but I didn't float around nude because some behavior I wouldn't execute in front of Lee. He's shy and I wanted to respect his space. Ironic that he as a teacher teaches people to open themselves up and has never really done it himself."

He gave her a pair of dangling earrings. He supported her. She studied free in his private classes for about fifteen hundred dollars' worth. He gave her six hundred dollars cash. "I'm the perpetual broke lady. To feed my five kids, I sold a piano."

The inevitable ending came when she went back to France and he to the Coast. To this day Marpessa Dawn wonders "if maybe I was one of the few who taught him to open himself up. I don't know, of course, but I wonder. . . ."

"Marpessa filled an important part of my life because at that time I couldn't make an approach. I found it much too difficult and I'm grateful she did it for me."

Lee enjoys the feminine presence. For the first time in sixty-six years he could sit back and relish beautiful women fussing over him. There were a number of them, all in their way equally significant. Those beautiful women who did that fussing concur their fuss-ee was not the instigator. Lee was passive. The ladies were aggressive. He did not risk rejection.

One woman made a particular effort at a time "I definitely could not make it and needed it and wanted it and would have appreciated almost anybody who made the connection." Predictable Lee had his rounds. Up by eight. Stroke the Persian, who had come to him as a neurotic but whom he had healed, feed the dogs, read the papers, leave by ten-thirty. His sessions all begin at eleven. To his Studio sessions he'd taxi to Ninth Avenue and Forty-fourth Street then walk the half block west to get a little air. The days he taught class he'd lunch at a place on the corner. He was partial to their thick hot chocolate.

She'd see him there. Shelley Winters, who claims to have missed her chance because of being too polite and respectful, cautioned everyone to leave him alone but, Lee says, "I didn't want that. I was very lonely with no way of instigating any aggressive activity. Not even aggressive—just any activity."

Snappy, thin, beautiful, small but firm bosom, she taught him the social mores. She taught him about mixed drinks. He drank whiskey sours with her. She educated him to dining elegantly.

"This whole function she played was for me a very important one. If she hadn't come into my life I don't know what would have happened." She was gay, fun, different from what he'd had. She encouraged small talk and laughing and giggling and attitudes he'd had no need for over the years. "Since she was not a person I was settled with there was, therefore, a need to make a new connection so, naturally, you talk about a lot of new things you wouldn't otherwise talk about. So this was a time of great discovery for me. She completely threw me out of the environment I was in."

Paula's loyalists color this lady driving, hard. A tough cooky. The loyalists did not favor her becoming Heiress Apparent. They cited as reasons that she already had a beau.

When she drank she talked of marriage, but she didn't really want it. Lee was not averse, but he didn't pursue it and was relieved to be free of it when her entanglements became apparent. This was a lady who was spinning several wheels.

"I had to look for somebody else, because I couldn't just sit around anymore. She was upset with that. She wanted to continue and saw no reason why she shouldn't. She obviously liked me in her way. I was a value. I gave her something other than what she had. It's just that I either have professional relationships or love relationships or marriage relationships. I don't have other kinds of relationships.

"I wouldn't sleep with someone just to sleep with someone. I would not have been with her if I hadn't liked her. There are too many people in the environment for that. People I went with are people I responded to.

"But there was no point in continuing the way she wanted it— with him and with me. Having her involved with another man wasn't what I wanted. Either we had something or we didn't. It wasn't clear what she wanted. She was a very complicated person."

CHAPTER TWO

Anna

Lee made it apparent that if you wanted him and wanted to share his life, he was interested. Joan Crawford figured the role suited her. Following an evening at Jennifer Jones's, she sent the following note: "At dinner last night at Jennifer's you were very sweet and I meant what I said when I asked you to marry me. I think we'd make a wonderful couple."

Tired of hopping from liaison to liaison, Lee had had the high life. "I wanted to stay with someone I would later marry. I needed to belong to someone."

He was off to the Coast. "Look up a girl there who was active in John Lindsay's mayoralty campaign in New York," recommended Liska. "She has good contacts with Lindsay and she might prove useful in helping the Studio. Her name's Anna Mizrahi."

Her family were Sephardic Jews from Palestine. Anna Mizrahi's grandfather had been a Mukhtar of Jerusalem. Her father fought in the underground and escaped from the British assisted by Ben-Zvi, later President of Israel. Anna's mother followed to Aruba, where the child of the reunion was born.

The family settled in Venezuela. Anna attended the Sisters of Cluny, a British convent in Trinidad. Advanced creatively, her essays and compositions were read to the seniors. She directed a play when only a youngster. Part Venezuelan, part British, born Jewish, educated by Irish nuns and speaking English, Spanish, French, and Hebrew, she fitted no mold. Her parents opposed her theatrical bent and transported her to Israel. Flashing an independent streak, she fled to Rome.

Her father's wealth came from land. One of five sisters and accustomed to luxuries and new gowns every week, beautiful Anna bypassed offers of marriage. "I was too filled with myself. I traveled. I had clothes. I had money. Every time we went to somebody's wedding, my mother nudged me. 'He asked you first, you know.'"

In '59, when she was in New York with her family, a friend asked her to pass out leaflets for Kennedy. Mrs. Mizrahi couldn't see this treasure standing on a street corner distributing literature. A fine South American lady was readied for marriage, not work. Anna was always chaperoned. Dates were told, she brings her mother or she can't go. The friend escorted them to Rockefeller Plaza's skating rink where, flanking a uniformed admiral, stood two nice-looking young men named Bob and Jack. Jack winked at Anna. Cracked the friend, "NOW will you work for him?"

Anna distributed leaflets. Then Chet Huntley telephoned. "Listen, you may not know who I am but . . ." and asked how about working for Lindsay.

Daddy's UN friends created a job in their cultural office. On her first day they said, "Call Mrs. Roosevelt. See how she wants the Casals benefit handled." Casals? Mrs. Roosevelt?? Call where???!

When the Mizrahis returned to Venezuela, Anna succumbed to the growing process that affects the young and stayed to try her hand at show business. She quickly lost the umbrella of protection. "The theatre didn't give a damn about me."

New York *Post* columnist Martin Burden reminisces that, "She'd come to our house for food. She was stone busted broke. One night this beauty with the lovely figure and lovely accent cried because everything was going wrong."

A friend told her how to conserve pennies. "Don't pay Con Ed. They mail notices but you can always tell when they're getting serious." Three months later she owed twelve dollars and the lights in her Fifty-eighth Street apartment went off. Panicky Anna knew somebody who knew somebody. Turns out Con Ed hadn't disconnected her electricity. Her fuse had blown.

Ill prepared for the subplots of New York, Anna fell for schemes. She was told the way to get into a show was to pay people off. She succumbed to every hard-luck story going. Her father didn't want her being an actress but he didn't want her starving either, so he sent money. Anna's pride was such that she'd refuse it. "I don't need anything. I'm dieting."

Anna became involved with the Washington Square Players on Thirteenth Street. She enrolled in Sanford Meisner's Neighborhood Playhouse "where Sandy talked against Lee Strasberg and his 'Method junk.'" She landed a movie opposite Richard Conte. She was getting featured roles on TV. Her career was flowering.

Meanwhile, Lee's attraction toward neurotics seemed to be waning. A really healthy woman wants more than to hang onto words and worship. A really healthy woman wants you to do your part and she'll do hers. Lee was moving toward that. "With Anna it was sort of love at first sight."

An observer at the Studio in California, Anna was told to read Stanislavsky. "I couldn't get through the bloody book. I was no devotee. I didn't go for the whole Method thing and I had no intention of being caught in the Strasberg mystique. I only wanted to perfect my craft."

With her tiny waist, full bosom, and thick, long chestnut hair, Anna was independent, involved with herself, and pleased with herself. In what she calls "the worst audition on record," she assisted playwright Gabriel Walsh in his tryout as an actor. It was the picnic scene from *The Goddess*. Clutching roses her lone line was, "Marry me . . . marry me. . . ." Anna sat with her back to the judges and her shapely legs propped up.

Gabriel Walsh went blank. In any case he paused for the whole five minutes allotted. Impatiently she flung the roses at him with, "Okay, if you don't want to marry me" and stalked off. Lee's total comment? "That's the greatest pair of legs I ever saw!"

At a gathering later she stood in a corner. Conversation with "a nice, kindly gentleman" veered toward psychic phenomena. He asserted he couldn't believe in what he couldn't prove. She had recently visited Chaplin's renowned eighty-year-old psychic who predicted she would live partly in California and partly in New York. She'd also just had a reading from a New York psychic who experimented with parapsychology in universities and who predicted she'd meet a man she had already met but had not yet really met.

Shortly thereafter she was at Jack Garfein's pool. Sitting with Carroll Baker's mother, Virginia, Anna watched Barbara Bain, Debbie Reynolds, and other beauties lionizing "the nice, kindly gentleman." She clicked into the whole picture quickly and just as quickly clicked off, thinking what a shallow experience must be a life comprised of sycophants.

Lee disengaged himself to address her. "Want to talk about psychic phenomena?"

Humphed uppity Anna, "No, not particularly."

Lee wanted to continue a dialogue, but everyone was starting for the Daisy. "Uggghh," she thought, "if he suggests that discotheque I won't be able to stand it."

"Would you like to go for an ice cream soda?" he suggested.

Grins the fiery lady, "And then I loved him. When he asked me to go for ice cream, I loved him."

He did the courting and the wooing. He flew to Paris for a seminar. He wrote her. He phoned her. He cautioned her to pay no attention to things said about him. "Don't let anybody change your idea of me." From New York he wrote her. He phoned her. Their telephone bills mounted. On the biweekly call to her mother Anna repeated Lee's understatement, "I hope you like books because I like books." Mama remembered Anna's childhood prediction. The little girl had spent so much on books that Mama had cracked down and the ten-year-old had pouted, "Someday I'll have the world's biggest, most perfect library and a man to enjoy it with me."

They crisscrossed the continent. He to California to see her. She to New York to see him. The romance was barely months old, but he didn't care to continue so light a relationship. If she wanted to get married, fine. If not, he'd look for somebody else. "I was already in love with Anna. Mentally I had cast her for the part."

She was physically attractive and had a good Jewish family background. She possessed the social attributes he admired. She was a career girl. She'd walk into casting offices and Hollywood people knew her. She traveled in good society. Even her contacts with Lindsay were a consideration "but after I saw her I didn't give a damn about her contacts. It was a whole package. She had good energy. She was right for the part.

"This wasn't someone to sleep with. This was different. She wasn't old, but she was not a young girl either. She was a woman who had lots of opportunities including a guy who put a private plane at her disposal. But, strangely, I felt that she wanted to stay by herself."

Skittish Anna didn't choose to get serious. Strasberg was everything she cherished, but she didn't want to lose her freedom or way of living. "I had my own minks and Bentleys before I ever met him, so I said, 'Look, don't count on me. I'm just passing through.' But he staged the scenery well. He lived at the Bel Air Hotel where there was always a wedding taking place complete with iced swans."

She flew East to consider his proposal, "Either marry me or forget it." On board Lee had her read, *The Fervent Years*, Harold Clurman's history of the Group. When she landed, she moved into Lee's apartment. "That's nothing unusual. His place is a hotel. It's Kennedy Airport. So, true, okay, I was staying there with him but so was everybody else!"

Although she's in the neighborhood of thirty years younger than Lee, she will not discuss her age. He shrugs, "Who cares how old she is? She can't be as old as I am." She admits, however, "My male chauvinist daddy was so glad I was finally getting married. My mother had been frightened her old maid daughter would be left behind totally. My mother was Paula's age, but she didn't say Lee was too old. She was happy he was a nice Jewish boy."

Anna's sister lived a block from Sanford Meisner's Neighborhood Playhouse. Leaving her sister's apartment, the future bride was on the street hailing a taxi when Sandy Meisner spied her. Dragging her inside, he introduced her to his class. "Meet one of my most talented students, who's doing so well. What brings you to New York?" Tongue-tied Anna, mindful of his acid comments about Strasberg, "couldn't announce I was marrying Lee and was going over to get him even then. I mean, I had suddenly become Sandy's star pupil!"

Anna wanted nobody to know they were getting married. Lindsay kept City Hall open specially and their license was issued after the reporters left at four o'clock. "When something is meaningful you keep it quiet."

In the presence of the bride's mother and sisters and the groom's daughter, brother, and sister-in-law, they were married Sunday, January 7, 1968, at Temple Emanuel. When the rabbi asked, "Do you take this girl to love honor and cherish as your chattel . . . ?", the bride in her white lace exclaimed, " 'Chattel'?! I wanted to walk out but I saw my mother's face." Lee thanked the rabbi with, "You passed the audition."

On their wedding night the newlyweds—she in a wedding sari given by her mother—attended the Rubinstein concert. Says Anna Mizrahi Strasberg, "We went alone so we'd have something to remember all by ourselves and of ourselves."

The following morning the brand-new chatelaine poked sleepily out of the bedroom in her robe and smacked into six Japanese from the Kabuki. They were touring the apartment. "Oh, prease to excuse," they bowed. She ventured into the dining room and found TV cameras and lights and cameramen staring at her. The groom was filming an interview. She ran back, slammed the door, and stayed put the rest of the day. "Nothing prepares you for this sort of life."

CHAPTER THREE

Reverberations

With the congratulations came the shock waves . . . Who is she? . . . They only know one another since the summer?! . . . She must think it's a good deal to be Mrs. Strasberg . . . It'll last an hour, mark my words . . .

To the supposes . . . suppose she doesn't stay? . . . suppose the marriage doesn't turn out? . . . the groom responded, "Suppose you go in WITHOUT doubt and worry, does that guarantee it'll last? You can have big expectations with one show and it flops. You can figure another's a big nothing and it's a smash. The Theatre Guild couldn't get investors for *Oklahoma!* and it turned out to be their biggest hit. How can a thing work out if you don't try? Okay, so it won't work out. So what? So I tried."

It was uphill for the bride. There was considerable how-the-hell-did-she-ever-manage-to-get-him-to-marry-her kind of talk. There were people determined to get rid of her. There were calls at three in the morning from those who thought they owned Lee. She was in the way. Anna the usurper.

Amid such remarks as, "Let's face it, she was never anything much on her own," Anna overheard two women discussing her work in a Studio production. "She's good in it." Sniffed the other, "I find that hard to believe." Said the first, "Well, I can't stand her either, but as hard as it is for me to tell you this, the truth is she's honestly very good."

Being resented by so many was all so new. The first year she cried constantly. "It was madness. People just shoved me out of the way to talk to him."

When Anna entered a meeting in progress in the living room, the undisciplined, talented, temperamental Shelley Winters attacked her with, "We're having a meeting!" Anna responded in kind. Then Shelley accused her of monitoring incoming phone calls so she couldn't talk to Lee. An impartial voice rose to restore order and was shouted down. "Be quiet. All of you," thundered Lee. An uneasy calm settled and he ripped Shelley. "This is our home. My wife is entitled to come into her own living room. If you don't accept that then have your meeting someplace else."

Larger-than-life Shelley deflated and went down and down. Next day she called Lee. She called the others. She called Anna. She blamed everybody. Shelley adores Lee. She adored Paula. She wasn't accustomed to having to adore Anna. "She didn't like me," admits Anna. "She complained my black stockings were too sexy. I thought, 'Oh, dear God, I can't live inside other people's dreams and fantasies.'"

The new Mrs. Strasberg maintained a low profile. "I was really in shock at the beginning. Traumatized. At a party I'd sit frozen with a smile, praying, 'Please, God, just let one human being walk up to me quietly and give me his name.'"

She let the dozens go by and worked to know one person at a time. Not knowing who hated who and who liked who, her standards were simple. Each was judged on his dealings with her. She dealt only with the present.

She had come at a bad time for Susan. Susan had a blue baby. Her marriage had crumbled. She had pulled away from her father. Susan was an empty vessel. No role could ever prove more dramatic than the one she played in life. But Susan was no complainer. She never spoke of the love she didn't get.

The two women were not close. To circumvent the sensitivities, realistic Anna put herself in Susan's place. She felt the greatest courtesy to her stepchildren was to stay out of their past. The past was not prologue. She told Susan to help herself to whatever she wished. "Take what you want, because I have what I want. I have your father." Susan took her mother's set of porcelain with the violets on it.

In New York Susan stayed with a friend a few blocks away. If it was distressing for a father he didn't show it. He went over there to see her.

It took awhile for Susan to come to terms with Anna. Anna is warm, "an out front lady" from a close family who touches and hugs and yells and loves. The younger woman accords all honor to her stepmother for the healing. It is she who brought them together. It is she who brought the daughter back to the father. "I liked Anna better than some of the others, but I was suspicious. When I saw she obviously loved my father, we began hitting it off. She's responsible for bringing Lee and me closer."

Johnny also selected mementoes, some of which he subsequently lost, and he, too, "returned to some extent but there's more work there that has to be done yet," comments his father in a typically guarded statement. "It's a continuation of his past difficulties. He hasn't found himself completely."

Johnny had met Anna at a bookshop. Both circled one another shyly. "I'm happy they're happy and that's all there is to it. I didn't know when they were married. I wasn't invited. We're a funny family. Nobody remembers birthdays or anything. I'm the only one who remembers. After awhile there's only so much you can do when nobody cares. . . ."

February 26, 1968, Elaine Aiken threw a belated wedding party for two hundred. Happiness and joy reigned. When the groom paused, momentarily holding the cake knife aloft, the hostess teased, "To cut a wedding cake, Lee, you don't need motivation."

Midway through the festivities one of Lee's ex-ladies, from whom he'd been told to "back off," showed up uninvited. Taking the bride aside, Elaine whispered, "Don't worry. No way will this bitch walk off with Lee nor will anything come of it. Just let her knock herself out maneuvering. At some point she'll stop."

The determined scene stealer phoned at all hours of the night. She badgered him into a meeting for old times' sake, then "put on a whole act as if she wanted the old relationship back. I had no intention of cheating with her or anybody else. She made a real effort."

Anna finally confronted her one day. "Look, I am Mrs. Lee Strasberg. I am not a bad dream. I am not going to go away. Now, you either measure up or take off."

Nor was she the only female to try and steal the spotlight. At Studio sessions, another who had enjoyed Lee's favors deliberately tried to move back in. Tongues clucked noisily. Lee burned quietly. Years back a newspaper, confusing Susan with someone else, printed an incorrect story about her breaking up Laurence Olivier's marriage. It was then Lee propounded his rule for handling malice. Do nothing. If there's truth behind it, ignore it because there's truth behind it. If there's no truth behind it, ignore it because there's no truth behind it. And that's what he did. Nothing.

Meanwhile, his wife was doing something. She was cleaning house. She early determined she could not tolerate a public marriage. Cabalistic Mama Mizrahi had given her daughter charms and amulets as a child. Anna believed this life had been predicted and that she was "destined for a different kind of marriage than my friends." Anna set out to change Mecca into home.

The household operated with a staff of seven: chauffeur, cook, maid, secretary, and assistants. Paula's longtime secretary functioned as majordomo. Everything was relegated to her charge. She supervised the food. She checked the bills. The custom was a month's vacation with pay. Anna changed that to two weeks. The custom was to order lunch by telephone for the dozen or more who might be around. Anna changed that to shopping in the supermarket then preparing in the kitchen. The custom was nobody okayed prices so the bills were exorbitant. The master had never been interested in money and the madam had always been preoccupied. Well, the new mistress was different. Gradually conditions became cramped and the lady of the house replaced the seven with one maid.

The labyrinthine apartment with the large rooms and high ceilings and groaning shelves and endless piles of books and stacks of records dominating everything and nearly obscuring the picture postcard view of Central Park plus the myriad *objets du théâtre* such as a cigarette case guaranteed to have belonged to Stanislavsky and a ringlet of Duse's hair hermetically sealed and the loveseat used by Eli Wallach and Maureen Stapleton in *The Rose Tattoo* and a glassed-in handwritten personal letter of Edward Gordon Craig plus the corridors of paintings, photos, playbills, curiosities, and memorabilia was like setting foot into Dickens' *Old Curiosity Shop*. "I'm sure Stras loves me," cracks Anna. "He cleaned out five closets of things for me."

Frankly uneasy, Lee was prepared to move. "I'd been in this one apartment a long, long time. I didn't think it neurotic if Anna wanted to leave here. For her sake I thought we should."

Anna didn't want to move. She did, however, want to change the look. She kept chandeliers but replaced furniture. Sober pieces were reupholstered in reds. The wall-to-wall carpeting was removed and an area rug installed. Anna imported favorite pieces from her old apartment. She added Victorian lace throws and hand-embroidered pillows which are so typical of her. She sanded walls and doors and floors. Wherever it appeared lifeless before "it now bounces," smiles her husband.

"The whole spirit has changed. Anna has so much life and vigor and spunk and determination that around her everything changes. Even me."

CHAPTER FOUR

Adam and David

When Lee addressed a seminar she went along. When Lee taught classes at Carnegie Hall she went along. They lunched daily at the Russian Tea Room. "I enjoyed being with him," says Mrs. Strasberg. "On top of everything I liked him."

Lee finds difficulty understanding why she married him. It bothers him. "To give up her life for me? This I didn't expect. It may sound naïve and maybe I have no sense of myself, but why I would be attractive to her, this still puzzles me.

"Anna and I and the love we have for each other is a miracle. It's hard for me to understand that she would love me so much. I loved my first wife so she sometimes worries that I don't love her as much as she loves me. I can't say that it's all wiped out, all my other years and lives and wives and family. I can't say she's the only one I ever loved. But I love her so much that when anything happens to her I tremble."

There were the usual smart remarks about his age and his sex life. "He's still talking about the future. What future? He's up against the future right now."

Lee fed on the idea that he had a reprieve. "Instead of being the end there was still additional time. A new lease on life. A completely unexpected third life. Beyond that, who had any sense of anything else?" That fate dealt him another chance was stunning to him. Anna wasn't interested in children. He guaranteed he wasn't marrying her for that. They were each assuring the other that neither had intentions of a family when Anna became pregnant.

The excited daddy monitored the labor pains. When the intervals between contractions shortened, he dialed the doctor. "In the last few minutes the time between dropped suddenly from fifteen minutes to four minutes."

"It looks like it's happening," diagnosed the doctor. "Can you bring her right in?"

"Well, I've had a car and driver in front of the house on a relay system around the clock so I'm all set. I'll bring her right over." As he was concluding the conversation the other phone rang. Anna grabbed it.

"This is Los Angeles, California, calling Mrs. Lee Strasberg," said an operator.

"Yes, this is she," she gasped.

The crisp voice of a female movie star crackled on the line. "Mrs. Strasberg, you and I don't know one another personally, but I'm taking the liberty because I would like to observe at the Actors Studio."

"Anna's forehead glistened with sweat. "You'll have to forgive me, but I'm right at this moment on my way to the hospital so I. . . ."

". . . I'd like you to ask Lee to call the Studio, tell them that . . ."

"I beg your pardon," Anna cut in, "but I'm actually in labor right now and I'm having a terrible time, so I'll have to hang up."

"One minute," crackled the voice sharply.

"You don't understand," repeated Anna, clutching the receiver with both hands. "I'm having a baby right now. Could you call me in a few days after I give birth?"

"But this won't take long. I only need a moment. I'm calling from California. I only. . . ."

"Look, I'm sorry. I can't speak to you. I'm having labor pains and I have no time. . . ."

The voice rose, "Does that mean you're not going to cooperate? You're not going to help me?"

"She's on her way to the hospital. Get off the phone," hollered Lee, slamming the receiver down.

Downstairs a taxi was letting somebody out. Lee maneuvered his wife into it, completely forgetting the waiting limousine. "Mount Sinai. And fast!"

The driver was so nervous he lost his way. "Hey, lady, you're not going to give birth in my car, are you?"

"No . . . no . . . don't . . . worry . . . about . . . it. . . ." managed Anna.

Anna's son was still being cleaned and had yet to be handed to her when the delivery nurse beamed, "You know something? I'm not really a nurse. I mean, I am a nurse but what I want really to be is an actress. I went to the School of Performing Arts with Susan. I really would love to get into the Actors Studio."

Anna closed her eyes to allow the sensation of what she'd been through to wash over her in a private moment. When she opened them the nurse/actress was reciting her list of credits.

The father spread the gospel late that night by telephone. A woman neighbor who always bade Lee, "Hello, how are you, nice day isn't it?" called Anna the morning their son was brought home. "I said to your husband just now, 'I hear you have a beautiful baby boy' and he said to me, 'You saw him?' This is the first time in seventeen years he ever spoke to me!"

The baby was named for the first man, Adam, and given a hyphenated Lee. Only Shelley, who adored Adlai Stevenson, could make Adam-Lee more diminutive. She shrank it to Adlee. His middle name was his grandfather's, Baruch, meaning "Blessed One." While he was still in the cradle godmother Shelley Winters hung over the side, singing him the entire score of a new musical.

With this child Lee was the experienced one. He was first to take Adam, first to carry him. The night Daddy burped him as he was wetting his diapers and crying, this father said to his barely two-week-old infant, "Adam-Lee, would you like to hear the story of the history of the theatre?" Retrospectively Lee grins. "I must have done a good job of it because along about when I got to the part about D. W. Griffith, he stopped crying."

The marvel of his infant son raised a painful memory. In the late forties Paula aborted a child. They were poor. They had just moved into a small apartment and there was no room. Learning she was pregnant, Paula panicked. She became hysterical. "When she asked me in fright, 'what are we going to do?' I also thought, 'Yes, what are we going to do?' when there really was no problem about what to do. We could have managed and put it in the living room like anybody else. You can adjust. The thing is, we were unprepared for it and Paula's hysteria, which had no logic, transmitted itself to me. Abortions were difficult to come by then. She went somewhere in Jersey. It cost around seven hundred dollars, the same to abort as to give birth, so we really could have had it.

"It's emotional for me when I think about it. I always felt sorry about that. It was all so unnecessary. That's why I always felt in some funny way that Adam was the boy I would have had earlier."

January 30, 1971, Number Two Son was born. Lee named him David or "Beloved." His middle name was Isaac for "God's granting him a son in his old age."

Lee guarded against the trap whereby one day his wife would resent the children and want back what she'd put into them. He minded the babies and diapered the babies. He didn't want her ever to complain she'd missed opportunities because of him. So eager was he for her to pursue her own life that she agreed to do a play.

To Anna's horror, her billing on the marquee read, "Lee Strasberg's wife." "How much are the tickets?" he asked. "What's the difference?" she wailed. "How much are the tickets?" "Ten dollars." "I don't believe in free passes on anybody's reputation. I do believe that the audience has a right when they're paying ten dollars to see Lee Strasberg's wife at eight-thirty. However, if they're still saying this at a quarter to nine, then you're in trouble." She did the show.

Lee fondled his babies. He cuddled them. "With Susan and Johnny I couldn't do that physical thing." He played games with Adam and David. He showed affection and warmth. He gave them his patience, time, and attention.

Devouring these gifts of his golden years, he clenches his fist into a knot and knocks wood. "The thing with Anna is as close to a miracle as you can get. This new life. This new love. This new family. Someone once asked me if I ever experienced a miracle. I said this new life with my wife, Anna, this is a miracle."

CHAPTER FIVE

Institute

In these years Lee came into his own. The seminars started September '67. Director Alain Resnais and actress Delphine Seyrig suggested he demonstrate the Method in Paris. The sixty-dollar series at the Théâtre National Populaire lasted sixty hours over several days. It was conducted in English with literal translations as well as actors to demonstrate. The 350 students included Jean-Louis Barrault, François Truffaut, members of the Comédie Française and chorines from the Moulin Rouge.

Since he had sparked the Hall of Education Program at the New York World's Fair in '65, lectured on "Styles of Acting" at New York's Museum of Modern Art and on "Roots of the Method" at the New School for Social Research and spoken on theatre at Harvard, Brown, Brandeis, Yale, Northwestern, Wisconsin, and UCLA, it was a normal progression. Anna's idea was for him to travel. She pushed for it.

To his seminar at the Festival of Two Worlds in Spoleto, Italy, and his four-week course in Vienna sponsored by the United States Embassy, he added sessions with overflow attendance in Germany and Brazil. In Buenos Aires a journalist rhapsodized,

"He held sway over an audience of 500 Argentine actors like some high priest in a temple."

Lee was ready for the marketplace, but he lacked the business acumen to mine the potential. His income was measured. His livelihood came from teaching and such earnings were limited by the number of students he could physically handle. He owed money to the doctor who attended Paula. He had borrowed to bury her.

This, despite a name that was magic within the profession. When he visited Montreal, Bill Greaves, who taught acting in Canada, says, "Everybody fawned over him like a fucking Dalai Lama."

The time had come for a series of Lee Strasberg dramatic schools that would be so complete they would even include rehearsal rooms. Heretofore, to perfect a scene, his poorest student had to part with two dollars an hour for a rehearsal room. Says ex-student David Gideon, "The cheapest was, naturally, the raunchiest. Like one awful place in the West Forties that was mirrored on three sides was the perfect rendezvous for a rat and a cockroach. If we had a barefoot scene the filthy floor felt icky like when you go wading and there's slime and ooze underneath. It was the pits."

Lee wouldn't package the Method à la frozen food. He intended to ensure the personal approach by supervising, conducting seminars, and utilizing instructors he had trained. Negotiations commenced with people in Hollywood willing to invest $275,000 to franchise him. The outcome was that "those first few years after our marriage were probably the worst I've ever gone through."

Through attorney Carl Schaeffer, a backer of *The Three Sisters*, Lee met a moneyman whose other enterprises would be enhanced by a theatrical involvement and who proposed subsidizing the venture himself. For 20 per cent he would put up $500,000. Lee halted the Hollywood negotiations.

The moneyman introduced a third element, an international financier whose machinations were known to cause headlines and headaches. The financier changed the deal. He foresaw a big public offering. He'd float stock. He estimated Lee's share at three million dollars. Meanwhile nothing happened.

Finally, $125,000 was invested but the ambitious undertaking of schools on both coasts was geared to a projected flow of $500,000. Lacking supplemental investment to support the standard, the project couldn't develop. It was set up too big. Intermediaries informed Lee that since they weren't earning money he couldn't have a salary and for the additional capital, they'd take 50 per cent.

He says bitterly, "I should have known. When you need money these are the deals made. People warned me, but I said, 'I'm not going in with *them*. They're going in with *me*.' I wasn't prepared for such tactics. Their shenanigans were terrible."

He couldn't file bankruptcy, lest the operation be bought out from under him. He couldn't progress because they had prepared a summons and complaint and litigation was pending. Lee would not accede to their businesswise ideas for a profitable venture. They who operated on a profit-and-loss basis anticipated no return with one who refused paying students for lack of potential. Antagonisms raged on both sides.

Lee took the schools over himself. He ran the entire operation alone and for almost ten months took no salary, funneling back whatever money he would have taken. "I built the thing. Nobody knew, but it was a bitch. Equity built up the third year, but still, not enough. Those were bad years for me. I couldn't move. I couldn't do anything. Those first three years with the school, that was a bitch. On top of it those guys insulted me. This I'll never forget."

Lee was heavily in debt. He'd paid cash for the New York building. He owed $25,000 to the bank. "Things were not good. People think Anna fell into something big, that she married me for my money. What money! All this happened in the beginning of my marriage. Those tough years I won't forget for a long time."

To befriend Lee, Carl Schaeffer bought out the other side for $75,000 "although it wasn't worth five cents except for good will." Lee had in mind giving Schaeffer 25 per cent, but didn't argue at his new partner's idea of 49 per cent. "We'd be fighting about 49 per cent of nothing, so I went ahead."

Today his East and West Coast institutes number approximately 1,500 hopefuls. Tuition is divided into twelve-week registration periods payable in advance. There exists a special fee structure for Lee's personal classes, which he teaches Monday,

Tuesday, and Wednesday and for which he earns over $100,000. Fifty per cent of the money he personally brings in is left in the Lee Strasberg Theatre Institute. "We're now in a good position. It's a million-dollar concern."

In the early sixties there was a girl who couldn't get into the Studio. "Pushy" and "not so talented" was the feeling. Her only fan was Eli Wallach who had her sing at a party one night. Today Barbra Streisand and others in glamour-conscious Hollywood form Lee's golden circle. They've paid a thousand dollars an hour for Lee's golden teaching.

Lee personally teaches in New York October through April and the other six months in Los Angeles. The business has grown into the largest dramatic school in the United States. Daytime and evening classes, full and part-time programs are continuous. Students register any time. The systematic teaching is discontinuous only in that students disappear when they land work. Since working professionals cannot attend all day, Lee evolved the unit idea whereby each progresses at his individual level within his unit with an instructor who at times has been Kim Stanley, Lee Grant, Shirley Knight, or any Strasberg disciple.

He works tieless for comfort and, in class, he never moves, never blinks, never goes to the bathroom. His concentration is total. Opaque, fascinating, exasperating, Strasberg is an awesome teacher. "Bewilderingly complicated," explains Paul Newman. "His perception is stunning." He watches critically, stonily, not a flick of an eyelash disturbs the facial impassivity. Neither impatience, reaction, nor pleasure peep through that stony façade until he's ready. "As close to actors as a psychoanalyst and as distant as a God," opines Sidney Kingsley.

Referred to as Dr. Mabuse, a character who existed in a state of catatonia, Lee deliberately masks any show of emotion. "I try not even to wiggle my foot if an actor doesn't have it. Nobody can tell what I'm thinking and I don't ever say what I don't want to say. Actors look carefully for outward signs of what I think or for the slightest hint they're doing something wrong. I never show anything that could throw them into a tailspin."

Some he terrifies before they reach the classroom. As a teenager, Joanna Miles was interviewed in his apartment, which was crowded with road-company Brandos and Deans. The Master didn't have his interviewees read *Hamlet*. That they could do. He had them put on a coat that wasn't there. That, he determined, they couldn't do. Lee's rule was if you wanted to be an actor, he heard you out, but if you wanted to be a star he saw you out. Nervous Joanna carried her theatrical photos plus a volume of Shakespeare. When the little man answered the door, the young girl said politely, "I'm here to see Mr. Strasberg." "I am Mr. Strasberg and you're late."

She was the last interviewee. Everybody had left. She and Lee were alone. He told her to call his secretary which she determined meant acceptance. Joanna quickly snatched up her coat and grabbed the doorhandle to let herself out. The knob she grabbed was to the closet. "I was so nervous that I just stayed in that dark closet once I walked in. I didn't know what else to do. I saw the toes of his shoes at the little space at the bottom. He waited on the outside, facing the door and I, suffocating, barely breathing, waited inside.

"We stood on opposite sides of this doorway staring at each other's invisible eyes for several minutes. See, this was his kindness. He hadn't wanted to humiliate me by letting me out. Finally the footsteps pattered away and I ran. I'll always be grateful he allowed me the grace to sneak out unseen."

Today's students are interviewed daily at the Institute by teachers trained by Strasberg. Anna oversees much of it. If there is no potential, they're not accepted back the second year.

Files overflow with applications. Raymond St. Jacques, John Garfield's daughter, Julie, Gabe Dell, K. C. Townsend, Sugar Ray Robinson's wife, Edna, Lynn Redgrave's husband, John Clark, when he was a child actor. Shepperd Strudwick wrote in support of CBS-TV's soap opera queen Eileen Fulton. Jo Ann Pflug wrote from Miami "I am definitely a novice on acting." Adrienne Barbeau's handwritten lower-case letter in green ink states, "i have studied briefly with stella adler (an unfortunate experience) . . . i feel you are the teacher who can aid me in the exploration and discovery of my dramatic talent."

Elliott Gould's listing for 1964 says, "Admitted to class immediately." Virginia Gilmore's letter one week after admittance says, "I do not feel that this class would prove beneficial to me. It is with great regret that I come to this conclusion because for many years I have been stimulated and inspired by your discussions at the Studio. I have paid for the full three months. If a refund is possible I should be most grateful." The notation on the letter states: "Mr. Strasberg's check for full amount refunded."

There are letters from Franco Zefirelli and Dustin Hoffman "who would annoy me in class half the time. I had no way of knowing what he'd do. Sometimes he was obstreperous. Sometimes he showed me great assiduousness. He says we had terrible fights. This I don't remember." There are letters addressed to Strassburg, Strausberg, Strasbourg, letters from foreigners containing photos and résumés for consideration from Israel, Brazil, Thailand, Venezuela, Argentina, Uruguay, Switzerland, Canada, Mexico. There's even one from Mount Kisco in 1977 from Gian-Carlo Menotti, complaining, "I've been waiting five years. If your time is so valuable I'll waste my time no more. My time is valuable, too."

Students range from the top black model Beverly Johnson to porno queen Linda Lovelace, who arrived in a chauffeured Rolls, to Carroll Baker's daughter, Blanche, to at least one topless dancer who wanted to "improve my assets."

Lee has investigated the work of Grotowski, Meyerhold, and the Living Theatre. He knows Artaud and Brecht. He "appreciates" the Japanese theatre. The Peking State Opera, the official Chinese theatre whose actors possess such skill that they simulate a rocking boat when only a bare stage exists, he pronounces "thrilling." All reinforce the belief in his own technique. The Method is a composite of the processes gifted actors have employed for centuries to conquer varying problems. Stanislavsky recognized these techniques. Strasberg refined them.

To execute a Beethoven sonata, a tyro must first study the simplest scales. Strasberg's theory is that the actor's primary task is also to master his instrument. With the pianist it is the piano. With the actor it is himself. Fundamental training commences with work on oneself, the exercise of one's concentration, will, and sensory responses.

It took years to develop the Song and Dance, the Private Moment, the Inner Monologue and other exercises which form the basis of the work. An average Monday morning class numbers about thirty-five, mainly youthful. Incidental music plays. "Have you done pain?" he asks the kid with the sandwich in his back pocket. "No." "What about over-all sensation?" "No, just sunshine." "How is it?" "Okay." "Have you done shower or bath yet?" "No." "Do shower."

Reports someone named Richard, "I'm having trouble with personal objects. My concentration is in and out." "Okay, never mind personal objects. Take sharp taste with a running monologue."

Several who are attempting his relaxation exercises are going, "Aaaaahhhhh." "Too many of you are making noises. Don't make the sound unless you move the muscle attitudes. Sound by itself is meaningless." The relaxers are sprawled in folding chairs, letting it all go to the hope of falling asleep. To one, "Put the head back." To another, "Stuart, don't assume a posture that doesn't deal with the tensions that exist." A tall boy in jeans stamps his feet while slumped in the chair. Nobody cares. He lifts a student's arm, lets it drop to tell if the owner's faking. He discovers tension. "What do you mean you can't let the muscle go? Whose muscle is it? You don't have to be tense just because you're worried. It's enough that you're worried."

Another burps loudly. Over the burper, "Physical tension interrupts the flow of mental thought. Before you can learn concentration you must learn relaxation."

A blonde with braids crawls like a monkey, smacking her hands in front of her. A long-haired beauty lies on the floor laughing to herself with nobody paying attention. A jiggly, braless bosom does pain in a corner. "Relax the chin," he calls to the jiggly, braless bosom. A heavy-set boy in a plaid shirt stands with legs spread apart, shaving with a nonexistent razor and crying. "Watch that Atlas stance," calls the Master to the shaver.

A bearded thirty-year-old tries a dance. "What do you mean you can't dance? Suppose the play calls for you to do a hot, jazzy dance while you have pain. So you can't keep the pain when you do a dance? I told you the other day that you didn't move enough with the pain. That's why I asked you to dance and move your body, to teach you how not to lose the pain. You can't seem to do two things at once. But you have to onstage."

Three others walk self-consciously around and around an area.

He orders them to remember the last ten movies they saw. They begin concentrating. The difference in their walk is startling.

To another camping on the floor on a blanket, singing to himself, "What are you doing?"

"A private moment," whispers the fellow, never breaking his doleful withinness.

The classroom is a zoo. "Good . . . that's good . . . when it's exactly like a zoo it's good." To the private moment, "Where are you?"

"Outdoors."

"Where outdoors?"

"On the ground." He moves his feet. "Barefoot. Warm sand."

Others see nothing odd about this. He's getting in touch with himself, gaining experience with creating realities he hopes to harness in future roles.

To one seemingly in a trance doing an emotional memory, he admonishes, "Describe only what you have sensorily experienced. What you see, hear, touch, taste, smell. You see something, smell something, hear a voice, remember the feel of a touch, get a taste in your mouth. You experience kinetically, which means bodily sensations. Parts of you are getting warm or feeling cold. Never tell us the story. Teachers who've heard of our work and then try to do it, say to tell them the story. No. We're not interested in prying. The more it remains your secret the better it will work."

Her first time in class, Ellen Burstyn watched a woman of about sixty rubbing an imaginary ice cube between her thighs and crying, a young fellow lifting his face up and grunting, and a girl in bra and panties singing to herself. "This was manic behavior. What did I know about a private moment or releasing your emotions while doing an over-all sensation like sunshine? I thought this was a nuthouse. They were all nodding in agreement as the Master told a guy hopping around being a chicken how great his progress was.

"Lee insisted I give it six months or it would do me no good and I'd be confused. I was ready to leave after the first session. What the hell has a guy pecking on the floor like a chicken got to do with acting?"

Estelle Parsons, several times a Tony nominee, Obie nominee, Oscar nominee and Oscar winner for *Bonnie and Clyde*, insists,

"Lee's genius enabled me to develop. All his crappy, creepy primal exercises are necessary. Being a chicken makes you aware of what you're capable of. That's what his whole method is geared to."

Many remember his coffee-cup exercise. One says, "Lee spent twenty minutes on why I didn't have the physical feeling of that goddamn cup. Twenty minutes on an invisible cup!" Dane Clark told him, "I can pick up a cup fifteen different ways. I don't need that shit!" Many relate an experience tacked onto Julie Harris. Told she didn't do it well, she bristled, "If I wanted to do a cup I could have done the best fucking cup in the world!"

Ellen Burstyn also remembers the now famous coffee cup. "I was intense about everything. I *really* touched that cup with fifty times the energy required to do it. Lee teaches you to allow it to flower, allow it to happen. Don't *do* every inch. I didn't allow anything. I was controlling the cup, my impulses, the emotion, everything. That's why my work wasn't artistic. It was always pre-planned with the brain. Oh, I know what I'll do. I'll pick up the cup on this line then I'll turn and smile on that one. I was mechanical.

"After six weeks I went onstage to do my cup with my usual head-on frantic determination. He said, 'Ellen, do you ride horses?' I knew this was a loaded question, coming from somewhere, so I said, 'I used to.' 'Did you ride well?' 'When I rode I rode well. I haven't ridden in a long time.' Long pause. I continued creating my cup, getting more and more tense.

"Then he said, 'Well, you don't have to ride that cup.'

"And, WOW! it was my whole character pierced. He'd plunged right to the heart of how I did everything. Genius. Genius!! He's like radar. Without knowing what's churning inside you, he goes exactly to the image that hits you.

"The next two weeks I was shattered. In tears. That little exchange landed on me like a Zen Master's thwack across the back with a stick. It was a terrific shock. I understood profoundly. It developed a kind of conscious awareness of my behavior. I knew what armor to give up, but since my whole life was worked out with this armor I wasn't sure I could go onstage without it. It's like holding a bird firmly but not so that you crush it. I'd been crushing a lot of birds.

"It's a question of vulnerability. He insists upon your shedding all your masks and going onstage totally exposed. I thought to be a good actress meant to pretend better but it meant to stop pretending and, with craftsmanship, to expose your soul. Up to that point I was adorable, cute, sparkly, full of personality and I said my lines real bright. But I was safe. There wasn't a real human being there. Just a series of cute mannerisms which would never have won me my Academy Award."

CHAPTER SIX

Studio

The Studio has come upon hard times. The atmosphere is not the same as in those old days when there existed a mix between the somebodies and the nobodies and "Bud" Brando and Tony Quinn and Dorothy McGuire shared the Paramount coffee shop on West Forty-sixth with the kids making the rounds.

The gods are gone. Even the Albees, the Inges, and the heavy playwrights are gone. There are assorted reasons. When they're going good they don't need it anymore. They get what they want and they go away.

They've heard it all. It's the same problems and the same solutions. They've heard whatever Lee's saying over and over. Complains one, "He endlessly overdoes those explanations until you can't hear them anymore. In '59 I heard A . . . B . . . C . . . D. In '79 it's still A . . . B . . . C . . . D."

If the basics are always being taught, it's that the Studio is organized for new people. New faces drive out the old. The reaction parallels that provoked by a new kid on the block. Jealousy. Competition. A feeling of displacement. New hearts are eager to risk themselves. The discussion stagnates at that level and major leaguers won't sit while Lee coaches the minors. If private rooms existed for special people to work in privacy, they might be willing to extend their horizons but no one collecting a million a picture will let anyone see that his abilities need sharpening. He won't risk a reputation that could affect his earning capacity.

And there are individual complaints. "Lee never got to page two. He always stayed on page one. Always reality, never theatricality." Patrick O'Neal.

"Diminishing returns set in because criticism became too inbred. It was based too much on what we knew of each other." Tom Ewell, back in the fifties.

Estelle Parsons explains why the Studio changed. "The best actors are no longer in New York. They're now in Los Angeles. Period."

Although the economic climate compelled members to gravitate where the jobs were, Lee was not supportive of a California branch of Actors Studio. Stars on the West Coast were similarly apathetic toward their support of the East Coast operation because, they theorized, we're way out here and he's way back there.

The idea of Actors Studio West began to take root. An early meeting was in Carroll Baker's house. Carroll, Jack Garfein, Susan Strasberg, Shelley Winters, Joanne Woodward, and Paul Newman started things without Lee. They started it over a store. Then they found a place on El Centro. The landlady inquired, "Now, what's this here thing for?"

"For actors," replied Paul Newman. "We're going to use it for actors."

"I don't rent to no actors." She peered at him suspiciously. "You gotta pay in advance."

As Paul Newman produced his personal check, she muttered, "How do I know I can take this?"

The most famous blue eyes in America focused on her. "Trust me, lady. Trust me."

Subsequently, the Department of Parks turned over the million-dollar estate of the old time Western hero, William S. Hart, which had been deeded to the City of Los Angeles a decade earlier. In 1965 this two-story, gray-shingled mansion became the West Coast branch of Actors Studio with Garfein as administrator and Carroll Baker's mother, Virginia, as secretary.

Carl Schaeffer, the financial fairy godfather who became treasurer and national administrator, sent a check for one thousand dollars to open the account for Actors Studio West, and Lee arrived at the Beverly Hills Hotel. For the historic occasion a couple of hundred VIPs were invited—Paul Newman, Joanne Woodward, Shelley Winters, Cloris Leachman, Walter Matthau, Franchot Tone, and on and on. The gala cocktail-buffet was given by member Dennis Weaver.

As one of the Studio execs remembers it, "Dennis had an elaborate home in an elegant section of town and we had a tremendous turnout. Everybody who was important was there that night. When Lee got up to make his speech, Dennis took me into the pantry.

"He had little notations on a piece of paper. The hors d'oeuvres for the party cost so much and this was the bill for what he laid out for the booze. The whole tab was only like a couple of hundred and while all the celebrities were still in his house he wanted the money. I had to pay him right then. I was so nonplussed that I wrote out the goddamn check."

Spending would appear foreign to these artists. They suffer from insecurity. They'll give willingly of their time but rarely of their money. Shelley says, "To my knowledge Anne Bancroft is not exactly a large contributor to the Studio." At the annual benefits, Estelle Parsons is one of the few to buy a table. It's even difficult to sell them individual seats. Mildred Dunnock buys her single hundred-dollar ticket. A lady on the administration side calls them "pains in the behind. You want them to come because they dress up the function, so you invite them to *your* tables. They all expect to come free."

Years back appeals dispatched to eighty affluent members elicited seven responses. Paul Newman, Eli Wallach, Marty Balsam, Shelley Winters, and Tony Franciosa sent checks immediately. When the office genteelly followed up on pledges, no real money was forthcoming. The Studio doesn't want its heavyweights staying away for fear they'll be tapped every time they show. The Studio, therefore, does not pressure.

The rising stars don't volunteer either, because they're saddled with debts from years of not making it. When they get lucky they owe for the time they borrowed when they didn't work.

Shelley favors taxing members in proportion to their income. Lee won't consider it. Remembering when he didn't have it, he even resists ten dollars monthly dues although it would net five thousand dollars.

Through the State Department and other avenues, the Studio has been host to distinguished theatrical representatives from Argentina, Australia, Belgium, Brazil, Burma, Canada, Ceylon, Chile, Colombia, Costa Rica, England, France, India, Israel, Iran, Ireland, Italy, Japan, Korea, Mexico, Nigeria, the Netherlands, the Philippines, Poland, Portugal, Spain, Sweden, Thailand, Trinidad, Turkey, the U.S.S.R., and Vietnam who, on behalf of their national theatres, have come to observe the technique. Members of the Studio have been nominees or winners of over four hundred theatrical awards. The Moscow Art Theatre had six stars. The Group had fewer. The Studio has dozens. For all its power, the place operates like a candy store.

Its multimillion-dollar talents worry how to keep the place open. Lee hasn't been paid in years. The West Forty-fourth Street building costs minimally $75,000 a year to run, even though its operations are reduced to essentials—a room, a teacher, and actors. Its opulence is such that members voluntarily sweep it out, clean it up and repaint. When the ceiling collapses, the decor is enhanced by buckets. Entry is via the basement door and a major expenditure is new locks. The Studio is broken into frequently. It is not in the chic-est neighborhood.

It features a wall pay phone, posters of the famous and near famous, His 'n' Hers toilets, a message wall in the reception room, an office which is repeatedly robbed of the air conditioner, typewriter, stamp machine, and adding machine; a pot of coffee, paper cups, and a narrow stair leading up to the main, horseshoe-shaped hall with its high-raftered ceiling and peeling blue and white walls. There seems little to steal but whatever there is they keep stealing it. The insurance is high.

The building is manned ten to five, five days a week. To save expenses the secretary enjoys a forced summer-long hiatus. Come July and August they grab someone to sit at the desk eleven-to-three for, maybe, $75 a week just to keep the place open. The maintenance man cum stage manager, who is usually an actor, works a certain amount of hours a week and sees that lights and props are in order. Despite nighttime sessions, they cannot keep the maintenance man evenings. The third staff person is the cleaning woman from six to nine weekday mornings. The payroll with a few extra gophers comes to $25,000 annually.

Winter heating, before fuel prices rose, ran three hundred dollars a month. Getting judges for the bimonthly preliminary auditions, getting moderators for the sessions Lee is absent, getting people to sign up for scenes nowadays, the telephone can run to $200 a month.

Some additional expenses on a year's list were:

postage meter	205.04	
Xerox	780.09	
accountant	1375.00	
petty cash	1902.50	(milk, sugar, coffee, toilet paper, soap, napkins)
stationery	345.00	
watercooler	108.00	
poster frames	66.75	
coffeecups	112.35	
messenger	114.05	(when Lee wants something in a hurry)
hardware	504.61	
garbage	505.89	
mimeo	305.20	
exterminator	87.50	(mice and cockroaches are visitors)
coffee	280.42	
Con Edison	3889.64	
lumber	113.45	
insurance	3198.00	
supplies	293.56	
tapes	226.26	
fire extinguisher	39.25	
miscellaneous	266.20	(paper towels, light bulbs, etc.)
storage	180.00	
taxis	9.95	
plumbers	170.00	
postage	29.39	
tape recorder	207.00	(they stole the old one)
typewriters	604.00	(same reason)
fans	400.00	
legal fees	856.40	

newsletter   174.45
new locks   246.96
gift   15.50
Lee's new chair   37.00
typing   120.00 (for a fundraiser who had been hired)
loan to Studio West 1000.00
repairs   5571.00
party   73.75 (for end of season. jugs of wine @
                              $10 plus leftover pretzels and potato
                              chips sold to the Studio for the
                              shindig.)
truck   49.00 (to pick up donated desks)
curtains   19.35 (members made them for the upstairs
                              windows)
T-shirts   306.00 (Stencilled "Actors Studio" which
                              were sold to members.)
Players Guide   28.00 (to learn who was working where)
Xmas bonuses   290.37
percolator   49.00
architect   1800.00 (designs for enlarging the 40×60
                              building, but it never got done.)
costume cleaning   15.50
music   25.00 (for showcase)
photos   15.00 (for showcase)
production   1368.31 (for producing the showcase, "The
                              Alamo")

This was against the income which was, in part:

Contributions   36,835.00
T-shirt income   76.00
Insurance   452.00 (reimbursement for theft)
showcase income   3712.55 (from "The Alamo")

Total income for the year was $41,786.99.

Producing showcases yearly costs $10,000 with expenses to the bone. The budget for one lists: "set"—$119 and "publicity"—$4.50!

Showcases are often original productions. The Playwrights Unit, formed in 1956, included Albee, Inge, Odets, Saroyan, Baldwin, Robert Anderson, Israel Horowitz, Jack Gelber, Arthur Kopit, Jacques Levy (who created *Oh! Calcutta!* there), Norman

Mailer, Eleanor Perry, Paul Zindel, John Crosby. At meetings 5 to
7 P.M. Mondays, scenes were read from works-in-progress and
moderators commented. In 1960 the Directors Unit formed with
Arthur Penn, Daniel Mann, Jerome Robbins, Frank Corsaro, Joseph Anthony, Alan Schneider, and Martin Ritt. The roomful of
writers proved as exciting as a drawerful of left-hand gloves, so
in 1974 the Playwrights and Directors paired into one unit.

In a two-week experimental program, the playwright presents a
play, the director chooses a cast, the actors discuss, the author
rewrites, the group re-evaluates, everyone rereads aloud, and the
end is a possible showcase.

Tennessee Williams' *Night of the Iguana* and *Camino Real*
were developed in the house. *End as a Man, A Hatful of Rain,
The Best Little Whorehouse in Texas, The Zoo Story,* and Paul
Zindel's *Ladies of the Alamo* and *The Effect of Gamma Rays on
Man-in-the-Moon Marigolds* were born in the Studio. Zindel
agreed they deserved a percentage, but nobody enforced it, so nobody received it. Liska March envisioned a 3 per cent royalty and
started to prepare legal forms "but, somehow, we never got our act
together." Since they never followed through on legalities, nobody
followed through on royalties.

Modest grants have come from a few foundations. Incorporated
under the Supreme Court of New York State as a nonprofit,
educational, cultural institution, the Studio offers tax benefits on
donations. Important contributions cannot be dangled as pass-
ports to the Studio. Strasberg exacts a high price. A father offered
twenty-five thousand dollars to push his daughter's acceptance. "If
she has talent she'll get in for free. If not there's nothing we can
do."

Periodically, society names accept the fund-raising chair-
manship. They learn it doesn't buy connections. They learn the
place is not glamorous anymore. "It's *shlumpy*," exclaimed one
wealthy, glittering lady who intimated the Studio doesn't give
anybody anything and once was enough. The only other reason is
reflected glory—To invite their friends to a glossy benefit, to parade their gowns and jewels, to run around in hopes they'll shake
hands with a Dustin Hoffman who doesn't need it, doesn't care
and mightn't get up from his table if, in fact, he showed up at all.

While directing kept Kazan busy and producing kept Cheryl

busy, only Lee kept the Studio together. Today board member Shelley Winters claims, "Lee has withdrawn somewhat from the operation. It's new people now who care about the Studio." Now he shows up only one session a week, Friday. There's no hope of his marshaling this into more than it is, yet you can't go over him or around him. A pillar of the organization who is "tired of him" asserts "nobody else can ever mean a goddamn thing while he's around because it's like a court around an emperor. Disagree with him and you've got trouble."

When someone assumed charge of showcases because Lee hadn't time, Lee didn't approve the choices. The result was cross-purposes and no one in control. When someone first took Papa Bear's seat and moderated, the cold Lee had was as nothing compared to the chill that ensued. Nuances. Undertones.

While Lee is alive, nobody else will wield power. A unique operation, the Actors Studio really needs a board capable of helping financially without infringing artistically. No administrator can make policy because Lee makes policy. Lee's the artistic head. Lee's the president. Nobody crosses Lee, at least not eyeball-to-eyeball. One around since early days sighs, "They'll just wait until he's gone; then everybody will pounce."

The Studio will not outgrow its hard times unless there are changes. Lee is not prepared to prep a favorite son to take over. There are small moves around him, but all with his approval. For instance, he personally selects each moderator who substitutes in his absence. Arthur Penn, Estelle Parsons, Anne Jackson, Eli Wallach, Frank Corsaro, Shelley Winters, Ellen Burstyn bear the seal of approval. Elia Kazan is another superb moderator. Unlike Lee, Kazan locks the door and doesn't allow drifters in and out for coffee, phone calls, appointments, or trips to the john.

Like Ellen Burstyn, Estelle Parsons is a moderator one day and a student the next. A season ago she was conquering her qualms about Shakespeare. Friday she was a moderator evaluating a fellow member's work and Tuesday moderator Frank Corsaro was evaluating her work. Estelle was doing Lady Macbeth's sleepwalking speech. In her total absorption she let the candle she carried catch a sleeve, set fire to herself, and singed her hair. While Estelle carried straight on with the scene, members raced to put out the flames. Strasberg's training forbids stepping out of character no matter what because "Suppose it happens on stage? Then what are you going to do?"

He encourages experimentation. One actress slashed at her clothes. She hacked her dress from top to bottom. Everybody was horrified he'd let her use scissors up and down her body, but this is one ringmaster who wouldn't interfere if his animals strangled themselves.

Over the years Lee has tried to infuse the Studio with inspiration. Once he thought they could produce a movie of Thomas Mann's *The Magic Mountain*, starring their brightest names. Sidney Kingsley argued the discovery of penicillin rendered its subject matter, tuberculosis, passé, therefore the book was not a viable project. True to his modus operandi, Lee didn't push.

Again there was a move through Ellen Burstyn to connect the Studio with the Paramount lot. With Paramount's sound stage and equipment plus directors and producers masterminding open workshops, stage-trained members could become film-oriented. Here unions proved the obstacle. Technicians wouldn't permit the set or equipment or stage to be used so this idea, too, fell by the wayside.

In '75 federal money was pumped into the arts with little to show for it in the theatre. Lee submitted to the National Endowment for the Arts that the Studio form a national theatre with guaranteed ongoing federal support. They would even dispatch companies to areas of America that couldn't afford it. The NEA turned it down. Disappointed, Lee commented, "America goes out of its way to help foreign groups but isn't concerned with its own cultural richness."

There was a time Anna was for his giving up the Studio. She believed it was taking him for granted. Having found the building for the Lee Strasberg Theatre Institute in New York and recognizing the Institute as their future, she resented anyone thinking that all her husband did was work for that Studio. Occasionally civilians would come up and ask, "What else does he do?" Anna hated it.

CHAPTER SEVEN

"The Godfather"

His students complained there was no time to "take a minute" in films. James Dean couldn't adjust to Hollywood's emphasis on externals. "What angles are best for your profile and how you stand to appear taller and what path to use for walking from here to there and all that stuff. That's all they're interested in." Paul Newman talked about "this ridiculous profession. You're getting hit with this and adjusted with that. All departments are interested in their areas of responsibility. There's the powder-puff man, the makeup lady, the hair person, the costume person, the marker guy, the cue girl. How do we act while all this is going on?"

Lee would reply, "Acting is acting. The ridiculous things that go on are part of it also. Close your head out. The medium does not affect the art of acting."

Put in Shelley, "Everybody tugs and pulls at you. Then somebody announces, 'You're all set now . . . action. . . .' You then have to act to a camera. But how do we do all our stuff in front of that machinery?"

"I'm not interested in all that about the machinery. Learn about acting first, then do whatever you have to do."

"But," argued Marty Balsam, "the actor only gets the last minute. Others always get all the time they need. The light guy says, 'I think we should have a little more flood . . . wait . . . whoaaaa . . . wronggggg. . . .' The camera guy wobbles then adjusts. I mean, it's tough."

They talked of technical things like hitting chalk marks that dot the floor for positioning. Lee bristled when his students gave him, "It's all very well what you say, but that's because you don't understand the difficulties of moviemaking." They could say it because he had never appeared in front of a camera nor experienced its confusion. It rankled.

Francis Ford Coppola was set to go with the second part of the Corleone saga, *Godfather II*. The multimillion-dollar sequel was starring Al Pacino picking up as the new Don where he'd left off in the original film. Al thought the role of a Miami crime czar, a Jewish mob figure called Hyman Roth, was perfect for Lee. "I always recognized the actor in Lee. And when I have an idea I move on it."

Al went to a party at Lee's. He ducked around surreptitiously and "sort of shuffled in" carrying the script. He felt strange because the first person he saw was Elia Kazan, whom he knew Coppola wanted for the part. Pathologically shy Pacino, who wouldn't string seven words together in a large gathering, hid behind a hat and dark glasses with the manila envelope under his arm. "In my brilliant disguise I thought I looked like a messenger."

Not one to rush up to Lee, bang him on the back, and shout what's what across a crowded room, he pretended to amble in his teacher's direction. "Oh, hi, Lee," greeted Pacino.

"Oh, Al," replied Lee.

"Lee, would you mind if we just stepped off to the side for a minute? I'd like a word with you."

Hugging a relatively free corner of the wall, embarrassed Al pushed the unmarked envelope into his hand. "Do me a favor, read this for me, okay?"

In contrast to Pacino's behavior, Lee was quite open. "What's in the script? What sort of a script?"

Readjusting the dark glasses and shifting his feet, Pacino mumbled, "Just please read it, okay? It's the *Godfather II* and there's a great part for you in this movie."

"Well, I'll try to get to it. I'm a little busy right now but. . . ."

". . . yeah, well, okay, Lee, then I'll just leave it here for you, okay?"

"All right. I'll look into it."

"Yeah. Okay."

"Quite frankly," began Lee now holding the manila envelope under his own arm, "I've been offered such things before but I've never really been interested."

"Yes, I know, Lee, but I just thought this would be right for you, y'know what I mean? So when you get a chance, you look at it."

People were pulling at them both, so the conversation ended. "All right, why not," replied Lee.

"There's a really great part for you, and if you like it, then we'll talk about it," threw out Al, and disappeared. Typical Pacino. Cool. No push.

A month went by and Al never brought it up. Lee never brought it up. One day Al rang and, after discussing several things, asked casually, "Did you like the script?"

"Yes."

"Are you interested in it?"

"I might be interested. I think the part might have to be rewritten because the part is not there."

"I think you'd be great in it, Lee. I really do."

"Well, as you know, I get scripts all the time. Sometimes I read the thing, sometimes I don't. People are always bringing me scripts either for them to be interested in or for me. I mean, Ruth Gordon wanted me to do an original play because she wanted me to act with her but. . . ."

"Yeah, I know, Lee. But it's a great part for you. You'd be great in it. It's just great for you."

"I've had many offers through the years and I've never turned anything right down. I'm always open to offers. I'm frankly mainly interested just as part of my own investigation into my technique to see how it works in films."

Al didn't push Coppola nor denigrate those Coppola was testing for the part. He moved carefully. "I had to be cagey, because

Francis usually acts opposite to what I say." Al said only that he thought Lee Strasberg should be "considered."

Lee had to fly to L.A. for a Studio benefit. He had to leave early in the morning, and Faye Dunaway needed his ear the night before. It was a very rushed period and he arrived bone-weary. The speeches and interminable proceedings made the evening endless. Two in the morning, New York time, he was still sitting on the dais. When it came his turn to speak he rose heavily from his chair. This weariness strangely paralleled a facet of what was built into the character of the syndicate boss, Hyman Roth.

Al had quietly piloted Coppola to the benefit. They'd sneaked in and were tucked away in the back of the room. It was Francis Ford Coppola's first exposure to Lee Strasberg. Coppola watched him carefully. His manner of speaking plus his heaviness was sufficient for a speculative look to light Coppola's eyes. To Pacino the character was pure vintage Strasberg. Knowing it was a long-shot last choice, that Coppola had set somebody else, Al suggested his old teacher was right to play this part.

"I guess so," shrugged the producer-director. "It's a little unusual . . . I don't know . . . maybe. . . ."

Time was short. *Godfather* was already shooting and they were nearing the section of the picture where Lee's role was to be filled. Still, Coppola and Lee had yet to meet face to face. Fearful somebody would be signed before he brought them together, Pacino engineered an "accidental" meeting so Francis wouldn't feel threatened and Lee wouldn't be on guard. If Lee sensed he was being assessed or Coppola believed he was being manipulated, both would balk.

Came the machinations. In league with Anna, Al began his conspiracy. A party was scheduled for the last day's shooting of *The Day of the Locust*. On the adjacent lot the *Godfather* crew was tossing a Christmas do. They had to get Lee there. The day of the parties Anna announced, "I'm in the mood to drop into the Paramount shindig tonight that John Schlesinger's tossing for the windup of *Locust*."

Her husband peered at her. "Why all of a sudden do you want to go to a party? You never want to go to parties."

"I don't know. I guess I'm just in the mood." Anna put all her Method training into her role. "I hear it's going to be a great bash." Knowing how to handle her husband, she threw away the next line, "But, listen, you don't have to go. You can stay home."

"Why should you go alone? I'll also go."

"Okay," called Anna, busily opening closets and shutting doors and grabbing shoes.

"But maybe we don't know anybody there."

"Oh, we'll know somebody," she hurried on.

"Well, I don't really care about the whole idea, but if you want to go, I'll go."

"Okay, so then it's set. We'll go."

A quickie stopover at the Schlesinger gala and then . . . somehow . . . the idea surfaced to drop in on the *Godfather* party. Anna did the groundwork. "At least you'll know Al and Bobby De Niro over there."

"Okay. I don't mind so much if I know some people because then it's nice and I know I'll have a good time."

Robert De Niro saw them first and whispered to Anna, "Is he going to do the part?"

"I don't know. Nobody knows. He doesn't even know."

Al came over. "Hi, Lee."

Actress Sally Kirkland was primed to point Coppola in Lee's direction and chatter to him gaily, "Hey, look who's here. . . ."

Anna spied the food table and muttered to nobody, "Hey, Mexican food—I'm hungry," and quickly made herself scarce.

In a melange of choreography, Coppola's sister came over. "I used to study with you." Coppola's father came over. "I used to be a flutist with Toscanini." Lee was unaware he was being watched by Francis and that Al and Bobby were buzzing and that Sally and Anna were charged up. Having heard nothing further from anybody relative to this film, Lee had deemed the possibility dead and was just enjoying himself.

"They're all talking," commented Al, "only Lee's not talking to Francis." Minutes later he issued a second communiqué. "Francis and Lee are talking."

The first week of January came the offer. They were already filming in Santo Domingo and were ready for him to start within a week. They offered ten thousand dollars. "Forget it," said Lee.

"What should I counteroffer?" asked the friend acting as his agent.

"With nothing. Don't counter with anything. Look, this is nonsense. I don't play games and I don't bargain. If this is their offer, they're not serious. They shouldn't even begin with ten thousand dollars."

"I don't get it," retorted the stunned agent. "Why are you acting so strong?"

"Because I didn't go after this thing in the first place and so if I don't get it I don't care in the second place so it isn't hard for me to be that strong."

"You could blow the whole thing."

"This thing I'm doing, if I'm doing it, only for my own pleasure. For my own experimentation and investigation. It's not too important a part. It's a small part. Not too many people will even notice it. I tell you the truth I'm not even sure it's worthwhile doing considering all the various offers I've turned down in the past. I mean, I'm not an actor. Acting isn't my career."

"But this is a terrific thing. It's a three-hour picture."

"But I'm on camera maybe seven-eight-nine minutes. It's not that big a deal. But, still, if they want me they should offer something reasonable."

Strasberg not only knew how to act, he knew how to negotiate. They finally came up with an offer he couldn't refuse—sixty thousand dollars. With the per diems and added benefits, it came close to eighty thousand dollars. It was a Friday. Could he leave for Santo Domingo on Saturday? No, but he could leave on Sunday.

His friend Carl Schaeffer advised against it. "By putting yourself on the line you've got a lot to lose." Lee, however, thought if it didn't work, nobody would notice. He anticipated little response. He was going to put into practice what he'd been preaching for half a century. For him it was little more than a pleasant change.

"I hadn't considered there was so much to lose or I wouldn't have had the nerve to do it. Also if I'd had an acting career on the line I would have tensed up thinking of the repercussions. As it was I had no inkling this would become a big thing, so it didn't transfer itself to me in nervousness. If they'd challenged me like, I dare you to do it . . . go ahead and prove yourself . . . then I wouldn't have done it. Challenge I back off from. You want it?

Okay. It's all yours. Take it. Fighting, challenge, that's not my thing."

Strasberg's first movie, at seventy-three was a big one. Approaching his eighth decade he was to make his screen debut in an epic. He had the tools but had not personally used these tools as an actor in forty years. Some things didn't work. "I didn't always have ready what I needed. I had to try on the spur of the moment to see what golden key would work. Acting tired or sick or happy, that I knew I could do. But when it came to the emotional things, I didn't know, frankly, what would get me going. I wasn't certain which one I should use so I would have different things in case one didn't go."

For Strasberg's disciples his utilization of his technique with a degree of competence would be an affirmation of themselves. The cast had worked with other Method actors before. Now they were going to work with The Method Himself. Everybody was waiting. He'd been teaching and preaching for years. Now they'd see if he could do it. Those who can't do, teach, that's what they always said.

Al was aware of the incredible pressure. Worried that when it's heavy into shooting there isn't sufficient consideration of the actor, he suggested that before they shoot they sit down with whoever was part of the shot "so we get some sense of the reality of the scene, so we all know why we're here."

Coppola was very shrewd. Lee's first scene was, chronologically, his last scene—his assassination scene at the airport—but it was the first he was to shoot, because it had no dialogue. This overcame his uneasiness about working with words and allowed opportunity to adjust to a camera crew and the atmosphere of the set. This brand-new actor who hadn't memorized lines in forty years had fretted, "Can I remember lines? I can lecture for hours, but can I remember lines . . . ??"

On the stage an actor is in sight constantly. The eye of the beholder is tantamount to shooting with multiple cameras and viewing with multiple screens. In the movies moments are missed when the camera is looking elsewhere. It is the cutting and directing that fashions a masterpiece out of a mediocre performance or mutilates a great one. In movies the behind-the-scenes personnel don't care whether you get time to "take a minute" or not. They grin, "Beautiful" if the actor hits his mark and doesn't blow a word. That one must make a commitment to an emotion to something that happened out of sequence to what he's working on affects them not at all. Today it's Scene "R." Tomorrow it's Scene "B." This cinematic habit of working out of sequence always took Lee "a few minutes to prepare."

Ad nauseam the teacher had allowed as how it was the actor's problem to supply the continuity. Now he had all the problems he'd made light of with students. "One Take Strasberg," as he was known, muttered God was punishing him by giving him every misery known to film actors. It was as though God was saying: Let's let him know what they're talking about. Let's let him experience the heavy emotional breakdown scene right away at eight in the morning the first day of shooting. Let's make him do a middle moment—just the small high point—out of a continuous larger running scene. "They want you to have an emotion at its peak," he crabbed. "Nothing even leading up to it."

"You always told the students it was 'no problem,'" yawned Anna.

"But they want just the very peak itself. No leadup."

"It's 'nothing special' you always told them."

In one scene the thirty-three-year-old pupil, Pacino, directed a gem of dialogue to his seventy-three-year-old teacher: "You're a great man, Mr. Roth. There's much I can learn from you." There were "vibrations" underfoot, but neither spoke about it at the time.

Although the pupil consciously tried to be his teacher's protector, Lee insists it was he who was protective of Al. In his view Al was not treated properly. Al lacked the perquisites of stardom. He was not accorded sufficient deference. "He hadn't learned to be a star yet, so I tried to force certain things so that he would get them. If we were sitting outdoors after a scene and it was cold and you could see he was shivering, I'd say, 'Where's your coat?' 'Oh, yeah,' he'd say. 'I'll go get it.' But nineteen people were there waiting to get it for him. I'd have to say, 'Wait, why are *you* going for the coat? Have you nobody to do this for you? Let *them* get it for you.' He'd say, 'Yeah, that's a good idea.' Then I'd have to say to one of the hangers-on, 'Why don't you get him a coat?'

"Also I wouldn't talk to him once he had that makeup on. He

would stay in character. I could drop it once in a while between takes, but Al couldn't. He takes his characters to heart."

The part was based on the septuagenarian Meyer Lansky. Although Lee did no research on the real-life Lansky, he changed perceptibly into the character. It was progressive. By the third week he acquired strange characteristics. He became secretive. If Anna asked, "Where are you shooting tonight?" he'd weigh why she wanted to know. He wouldn't part with the information as though he were, in fact, a crime czar unused to speaking openly.

As he burrowed deeper into the characterization, he pushed her to go to the Casino. After several nights she balked. "I don't want to go to the Casino in the hotel again."

"Why?"

"I don't really know how to gamble and I don't even like it. I don't want to go anymore."

"Go back downstairs there again. Go and enjoy yourself."

"But I don't want to. I'm tired. I want to go to sleep."

He kept wanting to be by himself. A line of dialogue to his onscreen wife was, "Here, go take some money and play bingo or the slot machines or whatever." The same thoughts were taking place in his offscreen consciousness.

One night a crowd surrounded Anna, who had stacks of chips in front of her. She played the day she and Lee met, their wedding date, her children's birthdays, and she kept winning. Pacino wandered in and saw her surrounded by money. "They're letting you win."

"The hell they are," she exclaimed. "I'm really winning."

"How much you winning?"

"I don't know. A couple of dollars. Maybe five bucks or something."

He stood there long enough to see she didn't know what she was doing and also that she was winning about five hundred. "Come with me. I'll show you how to play."

He spread money all over a fresh table. "I've got to play quick before they recognize me and then I can't play at all." He covered the whole table with money. He lost it all. Anna left him flat. "Why should I listen to you? I'm winning. You're losing. I should play like you?"

When the subject of billing came up, Coppola asked Lee how he wanted it. Lee shrugged, "I don't care. I don't want any billing."

"What? C'mon, Lee. Everybody gets some kind of billing."

"I don't care about it."

"C'mon, what is this? You must want to know how your name is going to be listed."

"I tell you what," replied Lee. "You do what you want."

"It's important to have billing," shrilled Lee's agent.

"Not important in my case," he said.

Accustomed to every ham spelling out precisely what size, color and type of lettering he wanted, Coppola gave his new find a special gift. Lee Strasberg was individually positioned as the last name you saw.

There were to be no pictures, no interviews. Immediately Strasberg was signed, everybody wanted a statement. One reporter flew across the country but the set was closed. After the picture ended the incredible spate of publicity began. "It was a big surprise to me when it happened."

Lee had not watched the rushes for fear he'd find himself subconsciously directing. He didn't want to interfere with the concept he had created. Apprehensive about whether what he did actually came off, when he finally saw the movie he was excited. "My first thought was that I didn't look like me but that I looked like my brother Arthur." At the screening Elia Kazan exclaimed, "Jesus, what a great job he did in my part!"

Theatre buffs dissolved into movie fans. He was recognized on the street, not just in Sardi's. Groupies collected his autograph. People congratulated him. He loved it. Like a pouter pigeon, he preened. "How does it feel to be a star?" asked Liska. He talked *with* his students not *to* them. Lee Strasberg the actor now kibitzed across the booths at his favorite coffee shop. He stood up and, something never previously done, demonstrated actions in the Studio. Acting out a tenet was indicative of a sense of freedom. He could actually act out his examples because, after all, he, too, was an actor, wasn't he? Now it was different. Now everything was different. He was one of them. Glowingly, he explained how he had prepared for the part.

He likened it to when he had had an offer to play a German

general. He mentally *thought* like a German general. He determined to *be* a German general wherever he was. "People would think something's wrong with me but then I knew it was working." He *felt* like a German general. He wore gloves even indoors. Then he wore only one glove, as though he'd been wounded.

He explained to his class an actor must not fear doing something the director hasn't specifically requested, but, in fact, the actor's own activity must be stimulated. As a scientist explores every possibility before reaching his conclusions, so must they try to see the definite series of steps they can take. Even in looks.

His Hyman Roth he played without glasses. It gave his eyes a tired look. An associate of Meyer Lansky's insisted Lee's portrayal was such that he actually looked like Lansky. When the human being takes one step, he told the students, it leads to other steps. "If I tell you to relax, you are not simply relaxing but you are feeling more deeply, thinking more clearly, your voice changes. The human being is a marvelous instrument because the parts are so interrelated. You can get to the other step only by making the first step."

In his favorite after-session haunt, Joe Allen's, one could see he wanted to mingle with the actors. He wanted to talk about the film and rap about creativity. He expanded on how Rembrandt worked weeks just for the feeling of a bracelet on a moving arm and Da Vinci made endless sketches of little things such as a child's foot. They weren't at arm's length anymore. They were all equals. They were all actors.

Lee's performance won rave notices. He won acclaim from the New York Film Critics Circle. He won an Oscar nomination. In an epic crammed with stellar performances, his Hyman Roth was perfect. "I admit what I did was good. I don't have so much false modesty that I say I wasn't good. I was."

When Paramount telephoned with news he'd been nominated as Best Supporting Actor, Lee was so underplayed that his studied reaction was, "For what?" In the grip of his enormous control, he wouldn't get his hopes up. Certainly he cared if he won, but more important was that he was nominated. An Oscar is always won on the basis of one big scene, he theorized. Something comes over and the audience catches that magic or that special moment. Another factor is sympathy as when it went to John Wayne in compensation for years of not getting it. But he had only a little part. Where was he in this?

By a coincidence, all the godfathers in the *Godfather* films were Studio alumni: Marlon, Pacino, De Niro, and Strasberg. By some other irony, his competition for the Academy Award was his own student, Robert De Niro, for his performance in the very same film. When Fred Astaire's name was entered, Lee fretted Astaire might draw the sympathy vote "even though he didn't deserve the award. I knew I'd never get it over Bobby. I knew Bobby should win. Bobby's performance was a more complete and better thought-out role than mine. I was only afraid Astaire would get it."

A little boy in the weeks leading to the Big Night, he hoped somebody would mention it so he could be very humble. Positive he wouldn't win, at first he wouldn't attend the ceremonies. Then, convinced Bobby would win, he would attend the ceremonies. Finally he not only attended but wore a tuxedo and wangled extra seats for Susie and Burgess Meredith.

Did Lee ever thank Pacino? Both indicate it was so apparent and mutually understood that he never had to. When Pacino enters a room Lee lights up. He'll put his arm on Al. Al will touch his shoulder. The warmth between these withdrawn people, apparent although never verbalized, is stunning to see. Nobody can say for sure whether Al moves in and embraces Lee or Lee moves in and embraces Al. They seem to reach out for one another. With Al, Lee appears almost unafraid to show his love.

"Thanks wasn't applicable," said Pacino. "I don't do anyone favors. He was right for the part. The fact that he did it was great. The fact that he was even greater than anybody could have been was the greatest."

Finally
Reflections

Cassandra Crossing with Sophia Loren followed. The TV movie *The Last Tenant*, with Tony Lo Bianco, followed. In '78 *Boardwalk* costarring Ruth Gordon, filmed in Brooklyn. Its shooting schedule was throughout hot summer months. It was physically tiring. Lee fractured a rib.

Until then, Lee Strasberg had viewed his tomorrows, if ever he ruminated on them, through the lens of indestructibility. He never mentioned death. Lawyer Carl Schaeffer began one conversation with, "If, God forbid, you died . . ." It never registered. "He didn't absorb it," marvels Carl. "You could see it didn't touch him. He just brushed it off."

Says one wryly, "Lee figured he was an institution. Twenty-five years ago the Studio started taping every session. Recording for the future is for larger audiences than the roomful sitting around. It's guaranteeing your presence will go on and you'll be bigger in perpetuity. He feels his name—therefore he—will live forever."

That he has ego is not an uncomplimentary acknowledgment. Ego provides motivation. It provides insulation against mortality's brooding thoughts of finiteness. If, in fact, he has an affinity for the eternal now, its effect is salutary. His sons jump about him and he enjoys the frolicking. His wife lands on his lap and he relishes the playing. He drops something on the floor and he energetically retrieves it. It isn't that he refuses to bow to age. It's that it doesn't touch him. The man's mind is so perpetually involved that he is perpetually youthful.

He doesn't wallow in retrospection or introspection. He doesn't look backward or inward. He doesn't agonize. "I don't think that way. And I don't complain. Whatever I did I was forced into by the situation or it was the outcome of something which couldn't be controlled."

Neither does he indulge in dreading the future. "For me, facing whatever may happen ahead, there are many things I still want to do. The future is always one of further possibilities. It's an infinite world. I only look forward."

Ask what he wants on his tombstone and it's, "That stuff is for others to think about, not the person himself. I didn't live for public acclaim so I think everything will be on a personal, individualistic human level rather than any ostentatious level."

Although his Studio tapes are secure in Wisconsin's Center for Theatre Research, no similar provisions are made for his personal effects. "Anna will arrange all that. I haven't clarified any of this in my mind."

Lee hadn't come to terms with the subject. The lack of specifics is because he hadn't thought it through. After he fractured his rib, a metamorphosis set in. He was visibly scared. He couldn't breathe for two days and hard realities pushed to the surface. Involuntarily one reflects on the facts. He begins getting his house in order. "I have thought about what will happen when I'm not here, but not as an age thing except that additional element creates a more concrete awareness than before. When you're in a situation that has to be dealt with, responsibilities must be faced up to." Lee reviewed his will. He made provisions for Anna and their children.

The man who reuses dental floss has known financial ease only lately. The Los Angeles house is mortgaged. With fans paying fortunes in auction for a star's panties, his Monroe memorabilia might bring money as would his library, but the only real equity is the Institute. Its New York building escalated in value and the enterprise is estimated at three quarters of a million as a going business. Operation Fractured Rib spawned the idea to buy Carl Schaeffer's 49 per cent interest in the Institute. Anna bought the shares, and today Anna Strasberg is Lee Strasberg's legal business partner.

"Anna services Lee," says Burgess Meredith. She mothers him. In her efforts to see he isn't driven beyond his powers of reserve, she displaced half of New York on a recent New Year's Eve. Anna took Lee to Palm Springs for Christmas before beginning his fourth movie, Columbia's *And Justice for All*, with Al Pacino. I telephoned one afternoon. He was sleeping. "He's just *too* tired," explained Anna. "I don't even want to think," he offered.

When he speaks of Anna, he glows. Anna had brought a white coat of Marilyn Monroe's to Maximilian, the furrier, asking if they would clean whatever it was. They informed her this whatever-it-was was the world's finest, most expensive Russian ermine. "Oh, yes?" she laughed. "I didn't know." Had that happened to her husband he "would have gone through the floor. I couldn't take that so lightly. I should have *known* it was ermine. For me that would have been embarrassing!"

But with Anna he can make mistakes without worrying because "she'll correct them. She straightens everything out for me." Men tend to marry the same woman over and over. He nods amiably when one mentions his wives share certain similarities. "Yes. Anna's the same as Paula in that she's forceful. She runs the house, establishes the rules, and so on. Even Nora was that kind of powerful individual. She had the same qualities."

Carroll Baker says, "Anna's doing the identical things Paula did . . . running interference for Lee." Shelley Winters agrees, "I close my eyes and I hear Paula. All I can say is Lee must do something that creates it."

In the old days a hairdresser summoned by the Mistress cut the Master's hair at home. In these days a hairdresser summoned by the Mistress cuts the Master's hair at home. Only the cast of characters has changed. The refrigerator is still jammed. The house is still busy. In Kazan's words, "Lee's got another wife to do the same things for him his last wife did." From another's mouth: "There must be a master script somewhere because each of his women has been a Paula."

The difference is in the personality of Anna. Anna pulls him out of his deep silences, whereas another lady could not. Anna makes a homey atmosphere whereas Paula could not. Anna can make him laugh. Anna can have a boy-girl relationship. She's loving. She gives him what he needs. The children are happy. The home is happy.

With typical boldness Anna anchored the shadows in perspective. "I think of Paula as a mother-in-law. She was an incredible being. Paula had him in the formative years. I come in and . . . listen . . . it's the best of times. I get the icing."

Sometimes, when the simplicities have been stripped thin, it's a bit much. "Quiet is the one thing I don't have. When I get uptight and have the need to find 'me' again I run off for a few days.

"I changed, of course. I couldn't help it. I was nicer before. I feel badly about that but I try to do the best I can. Let's face it, there's a lot of pain in living with a genius."

Anna has pride in her achievements. She works for UNESCO. Her name is high on committees devoted to the underprivileged. Anna labors for Israel, for actors, for children, for Mexicans. Yearly she stages *The Masque of St. George and the Dragon* complete with medieval mummery, audience participation, a dragon, a giant with paint cans lashed to his shoes and a king whose spear is a length of pipe. This Elizabethan Christmas pageant for children troops to hospitals and institutions. With actors getting jobs or kids getting sick, one cast of eighteen withstood seventeen changes. It's not easy.

Anna is a hugger and toucher. Anna fusses over Adam and David. Anna insisted on taking the boys abroad with them and the man who couldn't be touched, who flinched at the onset of intimacy, is today an involved parent. "I permit myself to be much more emphatic in my handling of the children now. But that's not only with them. This behavior is part of a general influence that happened to me since Anna. Even the physical contact is different with the children now. It's equal with me as it is with her."

Sitting in his living room as this biography was nearing completion, the biographee found himself staring at his youngest. With a start he drank in David's youth and smallness and "it was a shock to realize that's the way I must have looked." Suddenly he saw himself in seven and a half year old David. He was that age when he came to this new country. "It was a strange sensation."

He viewed the bud from inside the blossom with such intensity that David reacted. "Why are you staring at me? Why you looking at me like that? Is something wrong?" His father remained transfixed. David turned. He walked away. He looked back. His father was still locked on him.

David's face is more Anna's. Adam's curly hair is more Lee's. David barrels in gung ho. Adam is careful. David eats anything. Adam has diet preferences. Adam is more reminiscent of his father, yet Lee hadn't experienced this flashback when Adam was that age. "I'm sorry because then I could have gotten a sense of myself."

In a rare millisecond of reflection, he wishes only that he'd treated his older children differently. If they came to him he listened but, admittedly, made no effort to find out about them. "I was removed and they suffered very much, as I learned later. I can't say I also suffered from it but it was something that I permitted. What they say about me in that area is justified."

The stream of consciousness spilled into other areas. "I could never be aggressive with someone who was fighting another way. In any opposition between two I back off even in a lot of other things, because who knows in advance that the other guy's way won't work? Who guarantees results? When Paula became aggressive and took over the family strongly, it's not maybe what should have happened, but she was willing to fight, so I figured, let it be. Whatever happens, happens.

"Therefore my one regret is that I wasn't more perceptive in my youth. It would have changed events in my relationship with Susan and Johnny."

The Strasberg walls enclose an anthology of short stories. Paula with her problems, Marilyn with her pills, Johnny with his drugs, Susan with her guys, now Lee with his new family. The little boy snuggled under the pookh on the pekalik on the bake oven today enjoys hand-embroidered Porthault linen, four hundred dollars for the set—bottom sheet, top sheet, pillow case. The struggling teacher who attended a seder at his brother's three-room Brooklyn apartment, then slept over with his family, now heads America's oldest theatre organization whose members win 25 per cent

of the industry's awards and to any seder in his own two-thou-
sand-dollar-a-month apartment come senators and mayors. The
man who never learned to drive gets presented with a neon
blue and chrome, block-long limo with velvet upholstery at the
same price as his simple black Oldsmobile, which the dealer pronounced too conservative for "the Godfather." Hyman Roth
might ride around in it, but Lee Strasberg wouldn't set foot in it.
It went back.

Yet as we sit and discuss his biography he says softly, "I don't
see this as much of a story. There's no excitement in me. I'm not
colorful. Mine's an ordinary sort of life."

In summarizing his span on earth, Lee's ending thoughts were
what he would have liked to accomplish but didn't. "I was never
able to bring to fruition a national theatre. Now, whether that's
still possible for what's left of my future, I don't know. If I had
been at Lincoln Center, if we had been the producing, organizing
unit at Lincoln Center, things would have happened differently
. . . but . . . who knows. . . ."

He has watched the theatre change. With a cost of two million
dollars to produce a musical, there's more technical facility but less
financial mobility. A play hits or flops. Fewer excellent vehicles are
tried. There no longer exists the same passion about theatregoing
or even about theatre people. In the forties, Lee presented Lee
Shubert with a play. Shubert's playreader pronounced it lousy.
"You want to direct this?" growled Shubert. "Yes." "So count me
in for half." Lee, whose favorite actors include Duse, Chaliapin,
and another pair who won't brighten today's TV screens, Sylvano
Grasso and Mei Lan-Fong, sums up, "That respect for talent is
what made those old-timers really great theatre people."

Today Srulke Israel Strassberg is more active than ever. He does
a couple of movies annually. He makes up whatever personal
classes are canceled by his movie schedule. Students even shuttle
with him between coasts. Somehow he'd like to present on TV
Odets' last play, *The Flowering Peach*, about Noah and the Ark.
"The Studio has facilities, directors, and the kind of writers that
gave commercial television its original stature."

And to disseminate his knowledge to a wider public ("I can tell
in an audition's first moment if the person has it and I've never
had to revise an opinion"), he's writing four books. The first is on

acting. "One small part turned out to be over two hundred pages. The editor is cutting it." The second deals with directing. "Harold Clurman's book told us some of his plays were hits but others were flops. That's no good unless you extract general principles." The third is a picture book. "Sort of a theatre of my lifetime." The fourth is a history of the art.

"I don't have hobbies. What I do is also my hobby plus my abiding interest for now and whatever future I might have." Eyes off in the distance, the man who is phasing out his seventh decade muses, "This is my life. If I wasn't in the theatre today, what the hell would I go for?"

In an era where conversations about him begin with, "Let's face it, he won't be around forever. . . ." he remains controversial to the last curtain. The gratuitous remarks are reminiscent of Marlon Brando immortalizing all actors as "neurotic . . . self-indulgent . . . narcissistic . . . bums" with a need for "attention." From one Studio intimate: "Lee and his 'new' wife have no more ties than the newest alliances that are formed." Another actor sinks another shaft of sarcasm: "Lee makes a universal connection with big talent. He sees it as his extension. The newies still sticking around him are Pacino and Burstyn. He drops them in every conversation."

And in the last hurrah the writers are taking bites. Uta Hagen's work on acting condemns his tenets. "She has no idea what the hell she's talking about. To blame the exercises because she failed at them is ridiculous." Even a friend, Josh Logan, chipped away in his latest biography. An "anti" article by the Group's Phoebe Brand "startled" Lee. "She has the nerve to write she didn't want to do what I wanted her to do, then says I was 'difficult.' She stupidly thought she knew better than I. I worked my ass off with Phoebe plus I had to shield her from the feeling that she's bad. They all think they're marvelous. Well, they aren't so marvelous. I made them marvelous."

About the Studio's impressive roster, the late Noel Coward yawned, "Doesn't prove a damn thing. A lot of great actors came out of burlesque. Does that mean we should support burlesque?" The controversy still swirls abroad. Sir Michael Redgrave is for, Lord Laurence Olivier ("a great actor who has done hardly any great acting") against.

The older Stanislavsky grew the more he eschewed any conclu-
sive solution to anything. Strasberg himself sighs, "Half the people don't know what the hell the work is all about." Possibly no
one assimilates it totally. The Method hasn't actual A, B, C, D
step-by-step procedures, and even its most famous practitioners
suffer the Guru's hand. Shelley Winters is "a classic case of someone who never attained the discipline of the Method, only the
stimulus. That's why there's so much hysteria in her performances. She's not in control." Pacino, he told me, worries him because "it's not right that he carries an identity with him long after
a role is over. It isn't healthy. Al has not absorbed all the steps in
the system."

The Group and the Studio are marked by visceral feelings for
and against this or that method, this or that exercise, this or that
actor, this or that compromise. A 1978 journal of an Actors Studio
benefit sums it up with, "But in both, these tensions have been
part of a family quarrel, part of the intimate relationship of people struggling to make a dream come true."

While a faction burns and churns and turns on the Method,
the Group, the Studio and the Guru himself, more believe there's
insufficient recognition for the American Theatre's Teacher
Emeritus. A feeling grows that he should be a monument
enshrined, that every drama department of every college in this
nation should create endowments in his name, that he should be
accorded his own national theatre with the best technicians and
equipment and given six months to do whatever production he
wants to do and that anyplace else in the world Lee Strasberg
would be a state owned, state supported project.

Voices rise in agreement with *Hatful of Rain* playwright Michael V. Gazzo that "like the Poles honored Madame Curie for
radium our government should do something about Lee. This
man is a national treasure."

INDEX

386 *Index*

Noskin, Louis, 70
Novak, Kim, 229, 273

Oakie, Jack, 287–88
O'Brien, Margaret, 230
O'Casey, Sean, *Shadow of a Gunman*, 283–84
O'Connor, Carroll, 25
Odets, Clifford, 11, 18, 114, 129, 130–31, 139–40, 141, 145, 150, 151, 159, 172, 183, 188, 192, 207, 229, 233, 242, 360
  Awake and Sing, 154, 160, 181
  Big Knife, The, 196
  Flowering Peach, The, 29, 382
  as playwright, 152–53, 154, 168
Oklahoma!, 333
Olivier, Laurence, 23, 207, 233, 248, 256, 270–71, 336, 383
O'Neal, Patrick, 8, 205, 206–7, 240, 255, 356
O'Neill, Eugene, 75, 114, 136
  Anna Christie, 261
  Iceman Cometh, The, 205
  Mourning Becomes Electra, 205
Orbach, Jerry, 234
Osborne, John, 297
Ouspenskaya, Maria, 79–80, 81
Overgaard, Andy, 172

Pacino, Al, 1, 4, 8–9, 13, 205, 221, 366–67, 372–73, 376, 379, 383, 384
Page, Geraldine, 4, 205, 206, 208, 229, 257, 288, 297, 303
Pankin, Jacob, 57

Paramount Pictures, 363, 375
Parrington, Vernon, 142
Parsons, Estelle, 8, 22–23, 210, 254, 292, 353, 356, 357, 362–63
Patten, Dorothy, 114, 129, 136, 146, 150–51
Peck, Seymour, 216
Peking State Opera, 350
Penn, Arthur, 317, 324, 361, 362
Peppard, George, 240, 254
Peretz, I. L., 55, 70
Perry, Eleanor, 361
Perry, Frank, 234
Persoff, Nehemiah, 202
Pflug, Jo Ann, 349
Picnic (film), 245, 247
Piscator, Erwin, 195
Playwrights Theatre, 182
Pola Zion (Workers of Zion), 49
Polus (Greek actor), 81
Preminger, Otto, 232
Prince and the Showgirl, The, 270
Processional, 84
Progressive Dramatic Club, 53–54, 55
  See also Jewish Art Theatre
Provincetown Playhouse, 75, 142
Pulitzer Prize, 163, 164, 179

Quinn, Anthony, 355
Quintero, Jose, 317

Rainer, Luise, 18, 187–88, 319
Ratner, Herbert, 125, 129
Ravel, Maurice, 141
Ray, Elizabeth, 3
Redgrave, Lynn, 14, 349, 383
Redgrave, Michael, 3, 297

Index

Smith, Alexis, 256
Smith, Art, 125, 128, 151, 158
Smith, Delos, 314
Some Like It Hot, 261
Something's Got to Give, 278
Soraya (former Empress of
     Iran), 3
Sosenko, Anna, 28
Stagestruck, 247
Stallone, Sylvester, 3–4
Stander, Lionel, 14, 97
Stanislavsky, Konstantin, 2, 7,
     24, 25, 30, 76, 80, 81, 90,
     103, 113, 116, 117, 121,
     123, 147, 155, 167–68,
     172, 178–80, 199, 267,
     290, 292, 336–37, 350,
     384
  improvisations and exercises,
     80, 81, 90, 103
  My Life in Art, 16
  See also Moscow Art Theatre
Stanley, Kim, 1–2, 214, 257,
     292, 293, 294, 295,
     297–98, 299, 301, 302,
     317, 348
Stapleton, Maureen, 23, 202,
     203, 261, 262, 317, 337
Steiger, Rod, 25, 218
Steinbeck, John
  East of Eden, 215, 217
  Of Mice and Men, 203
Steiner, Ralph, 142
Stern, Isaac, 229, 235
Stevens, Inger, 240
Stevens, Roger L., 235, 287
Stoddard, Eunice, 114, 115–17,
     125, 128, 130–31, 148,
     161, 174
Strand, Paul, 142
Strasberg, Adam-Lee (son), 16,
     340–43, 378, 380, 381
Strasberg, Anna Mizrahi (wife),

12, 13, 14, 16, 23, 24, 30,
     327–43, 345, 349, 363,
     368–69, 372, 373, 378,
     383
  acting career, 328, 329,
     331–32, 333–34
  as mother, 380
  personality, 380
  similarity to Paula, 379
Strasberg, David Isaac (son),
     16, 342–43, 378, 380–81
Strasberg, John(ny) (son), 26,
     186, 188, 191–92, 225,
     226, 228, 230–31, 238,
     249–51, 263–64, 267, 272,
     310, 312, 314, 318–19,
     335, 342, 380, 381
Strasberg, Lee (Israel)
  Academy Award, 375–76
  as actor, 24–25, 54–55,
     68–70, 82, 83–86, 89–90,
     97–98
  affective memory theory, 122
  appearance, 2, 3, 12, 13, 24,
     29, 57, 128, 131, 175, 278,
     289–90
  childhood of, 9, 35–51,
     53–57
  as coach, 7–8, 9, 14, 19, 22,
     27, 28–29, 202–8, 209,
     210, 212–14, 216, 220–22,
     247, 255, 257, 259,
     270–71, 275, 278–79,
     362–63, 365–66
  as director, 73, 89–90, 101,
     112–13, 123–24, 126–27,
     128, 132, 133, 135–36,
     141, 147–48, 159, 160–63,
     164, 171–72, 182, 184,
     196–97, 282–84, 286–87,
     292–303, 362–63
  education of, 19, 44–46,
     57–59, 77–82